LUXURY
RAILWAY TRAVEL

To a household of girls; my wife Kay, daughters Cara, Lovetta, Lanni and the family poodle Millie for having the forbearance to put up with the many hours this writing adventure has involved.

LUXURY
RAILWAY TRAVEL
A Social and Business History

MARTYN PRING

PEN & SWORD
TRANSPORT

AN IMPRINT OF PEN & SWORD BOOKS LTD.
YORKSHIRE · PHILADELPHIA

First published in Great Britain in 2019 by
PEN AND SWORD TRANSPORT
An imprint of
Pen & Sword Books Ltd
Yorkshire - Philadelphia

ISBN 978 1 52671 324 7

Typeset in 10.5/13.5 pt Palatino
Typeset by Aura Technology and Software Services, India
Printed and bound in India by Replika Press Pvt. Ltd.

Pen & Sword Books Ltd incorporates the Imprints of Pen & Sword Books Archaeology,
Atlas, Aviation, Battleground, Discovery, Family History, History, Maritime, Military,
Naval, Politics, Railways, Select, Transport, True Crime, Fiction, Frontline Books, Leo
Cooper, Praetorian Press, Seaforth Publishing, Wharncliffe and White Owl.

For a complete list of Pen & Sword titles please contact

PEN & SWORD BOOKS LIMITED
47 Church Street, Barnsley, South Yorkshire, S70 2AS, England
E-mail: enquiries@pen-and-sword.co.uk
Website: www.pen-and-sword.co.uk

Or
PEN AND SWORD BOOKS
1950 Lawrence Rd, Havertown, PA 19083, USA
E-mail: Uspen-and-sword@casematepublishers.com
Website: www.penandswordbooks.com

Contents

Acknowledgements

How did this project emerge? Books possess the unique ability to provide inspiration behind many television, film and screen formats. This book, however, started its journey the other way around as part of two simple concept ideas for television based around the themes of a 'History of Luxury' and 'Trains, Boats and Planes: The Story of Glamorous Travel'. Whilst these projects have yet to translate to the small screen, I must express my sincere thanks to a small band of individuals from different disciplines who helped in the initial curation process, namely Paul Atterbury, Andrew Martin and Ann Harrison, amongst others, in trying to bridge that leap. The barriers to entry for intelligent documentary making are immense and as popular history presenter Dan Snow observed 'mainstream broadcasters operate a commissioning system where one or two people decide what they think you want to watch.' Notwithstanding, a considerable amount of material was created in order to understand the luxury constructions of our transport pasts. Colin Divall, railway history professor, suggested the scope of these ideas were three PhDs in one! A combined text would scarcely do justice, resulting in only a cursory investigation merely scratching the surface. A more bite-sized approach was clearly evident eventually morphing into this initial exploration of luxury rail travel.

Although a railway (and transport) enthusiast from a young age, this book would not have come about without the contribution of those who are far more expert than I in their respective specialist knowledge. In order to obtain a firm grasp of the dimensions involved, a distillation of ideas was required, and I gratefully acknowledge the contributions of those who have taken the time to write in days gone by imparting their professional and invaluable expertise. In this country we are so blessed with individuals who possess such a rich and special penchant for railway, social and travel histories. This book recognises not only a contribution from the academic literature but also a much wider wealth of railway and social material. Combined, this should entice readers into a serious and intelligent conversation surrounding the many dimensions explored, coupled to a framework of understanding how modern luxury travel industries have evolved over the past century and a half. In short, a snap-shot of previous eras and a throwback to a sepia-tinted past that have indelibly left their imprint on modern scheduled and tourist-based railway operations.

Given the nature of this book it was necessary to call on many different foundations. I am particularly grateful to the following who took the time to read a first draft providing priceless comment, insight and encouragement including Professor Alan Fyall, Rosen Collage of Hospitality Management, University of Central Florida; Professor Colin Divall, Railway Studies Institute, University of York; Christian Wolmar and Mark Smith, The Man in Seat Sixty-One who operates at the front-end of the rail travel business. In addition, Dr David Turner, Railway Studies Institute, University of York; Dr Hiroki Shin, Birkbeck, University of London; and my daughter, Cara Pring, School of Management, University of Bath who have taken time to advise on specific elements. Just as important has been the contribution of rail industry observers and the people who run these modern, splendid trains, namely: Tim Littler, Golden Eagle; Gordon Rushton at the 5-BEL Trust; and Ryan Flaherty at Caledonian Sleeper. In addition, my sincere thanks go to all at Pen & Sword and my commissioning editor, John Scott-Morgan who had the inspiration to recognise a gap in such titles. As ever, all of the behind the scenes help and effort provided by PR, media and support teams from various organisations including Emma Wylde and Mia Jones, Belmond; Julia Spence and Natasha Baker, Golden Eagle; Charles Carr, Serco; Nick Hanlon, Weber Shandwick; and Elizabeth Bundy and Aoife O'Connor at the British Newspaper Archive and findmypast.com.

In bringing together the visual contents of this book, I should like to thank a range of people who have given their time to supply specialist images especially that of Dr Richard Furness whose work documenting British railway posters is of historical importance. In addition, Greg Norden, Travelling Art Gallery; Peter Waller, Online Transport Archive; Jessica Talmage and Tom Gillmor at Mary Evans Picture Library; Miho Oguri at the Japan National Tourism Organisation; the personal collections of James S. Baldwin and John Scott-Morgan; Eric Bottomley for permission to use his Russian P36 locomotive artwork and painting; and Jasmine Rodgers at the NRM Pictorial Collection/Science & Society Library.

And finally, whilst every effort has been taken to record and interpret events correctly, I am sure there might be errors and omissions for which I take full responsibility. I would be delighted to hear from readers of any comments and suggestions that may be incorporated for a future edition. Please contact via info@martynpring.co.uk

Martyn Pring
Dorset
September 2019

Introduction

Many words are used to conjure up luxury train images and ideas surrounding civilised and convivial ways to travel by rail. Over the past century and a half of development, the luxury train concept has progressed from one where it was incorporated within scheduled passenger services and on-demand ocean boat trains, to a position now where it is regarded as a distinct subset of the luxury travel sector. It also bestrides an enthusiast and general rail tour holiday market, where upscale itineraries and services are packaged by specialist operators. Whatever individual requirements, rail travellers nowadays are presented with glamorous and luxury rail tourism options dovetailing with short-break and longer-stay holidays the world over. Routinely, travel firms slot the flexibility of air travel (and cruise itineraries) with luxury trains, providing guests with an ever-increasing array of route and destination experiences in familiar but also exotic destinations, radiating excitement factors and taking in some of the most extreme and stern of weather conditions found on the planet. Simply watching the Arctic winter glide by from the comfort of a domed observation car is one of life's great adventures.

It might be appropriate, at this stage, to borrow from the aviation sector to describe luxury train travel since short-haul and long-haul definitions help to identify scope and nature. In Britain, the short-distance luxury train market is dominated by a small number of specialist companies operating day excursion trains such as the *Northern Belle* and the *Belmond British Pullman*. Some companies may charter certified mainline steam operation locomotives that leave a profound imprint in the popular imagination including iconic engines such as the restored *Flying Scotsman* or new-build *Tornado* - the current standard-bearers of a bygone age on steam romance theme trips or short rail tours. Other businesses put steam haulage at the heart of their operations by owning or having special arrangements with locomotive owners, providing trips with a variety of carriage seating arrangements but invariably including a luxury element defined as premier or Pullman dining styles and offering fine-dining options and highly distinctive travel experiences all linked to specific themes, events and destinations.

For older generations of customers who pine for something that is not there anymore, they provide an easily accessible escape mechanism. These trains do not provide sleeping accommodation but return guests to the location they commenced their journeys or alternatively to the next leg of a rail tour. Yet the short-distance classification is ambiguous, since luxury trains like the *Belmond Royal Scotsman* and the *Belmond Grand Hibernian* Irish operation provide sleeping carriages for upscale short break itineraries lasting several days. In addition, short-distance may also be rather problematic since some luxury trains such as the *Belmond Venice Simplon-Orient Express (VSOE)* and the *Golden Eagle Danube Express*, also straddle more than one European country, reflecting journeys of comparatively short durations. As Britain was the cradle of the railway revolution, it is hardly surprising to find a network of world-class heritage lines where journeys for a couple of hours allow consumers to step back in time sampling varying degrees of travel and dining indulgencies which for the most part are likely to be steam hauled. Such opportunities should not be underestimated since these representations fuel desires to experience longer journeys providing a steady stream of potential luxury train customers, as an industry based on yesteryear's world of travel with its impeccable levels of service and etiquette has moved from niche to mainstream operations.

On the other side of the coin is the long-distance luxury train travel market. In terms of product, it is completely different, providing not only unique combinations of fine-dining, sleeping accommodation (in a number of grades) and visitor experiences, but running across big distances with journeys lasting many days and involving thousands of miles of travel. These may be variously described as hotels on wheels, hotel trains, land cruises, rail cruises and cruise trains but a key aspect is that they all form part of a vista of the broader panoply of luxury branded goods and services. Providing a stage to aspire to, they engage with and simply indulge in the many and varied guises of luxury. The luxury train, very simply, is part of an ongoing process where luxury travel concepts are constantly redefined and are part of a continuing trend where consumers are prepared to trade up and are willing to pay for unique luxury travel experiences. Regions such as Australia's outback, the Canadian Rockies or the Russian Steppes are some of the world's destinations on offer; for guests they are simply breath-taking indulgences where luxury trains have now moved to performance brand arenas, shaping the way customers feel.

So, what constitutes luxury? The *Oxford Dictionary* defines the word as an habitual use of, choice or costly products – food, dress, furniture – but also enjoyable, desirable or even indispensable. Words, meanings and their interpretations change as language evolves over time. Other words become synonymous; 'posh', for instance, is forever associated with a more comfortable form of sea passage to India and the Far East but origins date from the end of Edwardian era defining a close association to the smart, stylish and luxurious lives enjoyed by the upper-classes, a period that would have such a noteworthy impact on luxury train development. Yet travel and the seeking out of luxury crafted goods have been with us since the dawn of European civilisation. The Silk Road that extended from Europe's citadels through the Middle East, Asia Minor to ancient China was one of the world's first trading routes where the exchange of rare and unusual goods – silk, tea and spices westwards, wools, gold and silver in an easterly direction – was central to the purpose of early travellers. In today's world, the mercantile dimensions have changed to one where it is now replaced by businesses creating a mix of travel exploration and tourism experiences. The ages afford us with many examples of exotic goods conveyed by traders ranging from Chinese earthenware to luxury Persian carpets gifted to the Athenians. Since the early Egyptians, history is littered with stories of rare and specialised gifts made exclusively for and presented to royalty and nobility. Non-essential items such as luxury furniture, books and printed material took hold in the eighteenth century. The French, a hundred years later, constructed mechanisms to preserve and vigorously protect their fine food and drink industries; the first examples of modern luxury crafted goods such as perfume, handbags, stockings and haute couture. In modern times, this is big industry as global legal firms preserve the intellectual assets of luxury branded firms representing powerful combinations of forces.

Luxury has always been an exclusive club with access largely determined by connection, power and financial means. Thorsten Veblen in the late 1890s expressed the term 'conspicuous consumption' describing luxury as a minority privilege and only available to a few in his theory of the leisure class. Luxury products have always been tracked by wealth where money is no object, with individuals willing to spend, but increasingly the notion of luxury is seen as a fluid concept prone to cultural influence, change, consumer commodification and, increasingly these days, wrapped around celebrity notions, symbols and endorsement. Professor Robert H. Frank in *Luxury Fever, Money and Happiness in an Era of Excess,* published by Princeton University Press in 1999, suggested that we were 'in the midst of another luxury fever', that in the decade or so since has been a dominant feature of the retail, travel and hospitality sectors; the latter demonstrating remarkable growth with long waiting lists at many fashionable restaurants. Luxury has different interpretations and meanings fuelled by an almost insatiable worldwide consumer demand for products and services fitting the mould, but such aspirations may be 'different in different social circles.'

The British, for instance, may be considered slightly less ostentatious in their presentation of wealth, whereas new prosperous overseas citizens loudly demonstrate indulgences in London's exclusive 'alpha territory' neighbourhoods as the super wealthy start to move away from the more populous ranks of the mobile, professional middle-classes. But the all-encompassing need of demonstrating life's success has spawned a rapid expansion of the luxury goods market in recent times and across many sectors including clothing, timepieces, jewellery, homes and personal transport where the world of the highly visible super-car is a sub-set in its own right. Super-cars have become brazen shows of wealth and social commentaries on vehicle drivers who are largely successful and wealthy individuals who have 'made it'. Dr Ian Yeoman and Professor Una McMahon-Beattie describe the modern luxury goods phenomenon as a blurred genre that is no longer the preserve of the elite.[1]

Price and exclusivity have never completely disappeared but what constitutes luxury nowadays is less clear, as society continues to shape and define boundaries. Uché Okonkwo-Pézard, writing in the *Journal of Brand Management* in 2009, suggests that luxury is neither a product, object, service concept or lifestyle but an enveloping identity, philosophy and culture that permeates business and society. Luxury travel is not an object but a precious journey and immersive experience; for individuals it is a process that has personal authenticity that consumers wish to treasure as they are prized, rare and invested with emotional value. Professors Michel Chevalier and Gérald Mazzalovo go further in *Luxury Brand*

Management (John Wiley and Sons, 2008), concluding that special luxury products are not consumed but are iconic objects, 'that are exceptional events, charged with emotional and social content.' Arguably, indulgence travel brands such as Belmond are shared constructs, that is 'open source objects' co-created by the firm and the consumer. Together, they generate highly valuable luxury travel experiences consumed by their storytellers.

Of course, there will be parts of the travel experience that may be touched, such as physical surroundings, culinary and gourmet participation, the hospitality venues, shopping and destinations themselves, but they form part of a broad, rich tapestry of personal memories and engagement experienced individually or collectively with fellow like-minded travellers. Luxury travel brands are constructed with complex dimensions where an absence or under-performing element of the product's mix can alter customer experience perceptions. As Chevalier and Mazzalovo go on to observe, there is no single, conclusive meaning to luxury brand definition but often a deep-rooted and authentic legacy is evident, based on the craftsmanship of family business founding fathers integral to a luxury brand's identity. In the modern world, all of this has to be carefully cultivated, ensuring prestige and aura continues to differentiate and set luxury brands apart from competitors. The sum of the whole creates commanding histories translating into luxury brand tales, yet currently in our rapid technological revolution, fostering and communicating a heritage inheritance is increasingly challenging. In an era of global social networks, brand meaning, image and equity can easily be eroded.[2]

Digital platforms create the potential for instant consumer engagement in the forms of followers, likes and friends; thus, luxury brands must work hard in a frenzied world to maintain distinctive character, image and genuine legacy. Luxury brands are storytellers which consumers strive to be part of, operating at an intersection where both business and enjoyment meet. Luxury may be entwined across different business sectors such as hotel, private accommodation and resort sector operations as well as with individual and collective transport modes, providing the means for people to move to special places often delivering unique, unfiltered customer experiences in their own right. Within luxury tourism, it is not possible to acquire and keep product that has physical context, but for buyers of these services they must deliver rarity and emotional value to be consumed and experienced with distinctive narratives in very specific and special environments and settings. These narratives can take the form of a dynamic circular system of ongoing processes, whose actions cause a series of reactions generating a fundamental basis of luxury brand meaning. Therefore, luxury travel brand meaning is not only consumed, but simultaneously re-elaborated and created conveying people to characteristic destinations. The transport mode and, in the context of this title, luxury rail travel, assumes the shroud of a special place itself immersed with authentic (possibly re-engineered) and historical connections associated with the great named trains of the world.

During the past twenty years, the luxury tourism industry has evolved rapidly, answering the needs of a mature segment of international travellers but also changing lifestyles of a new and younger customer bringing complications as the notion of luxury travel becomes well-worn; a stock readily bandied about but where one individual's interpretation is likely to be very different to another person's description. Yet, from the new millennium, tourism industries worldwide, aided by new digital communication technologies, have exhibited consistent growth; their impact and scale permeating virtually every society on earth. One of its most interesting aspects is how the industry in most of the globe's major tourism markets has reacted as quality thresholds progressively transformed tourism services, particularly in the context of accommodation, hospitality and service standards. Very simply, tourism, aided by the integrated efforts of both a smart private sector and national, regional and local destination organisations, has moved upscale, impacting on traditional notions of what constitutes luxury travel and tourism. This presents an industry conundrum, since nowadays sunny luxury holidays are part of a bespoke landscape and within the means of increasing numbers of people, as worldwide consumer affluence brings new customers. It does not matter from where they emanate. Fifteen years ago, it seems inconceivable there were correct predictions of the growth of some 250 million new middle-class consumers holding passports from motorized and populous Chinese, Indian and Far Eastern economies. It is no longer about where customers spring from, either mature source markets or new emergent middle-class communities. Increasingly, markets are growing as family units invest in education, instilling in children life-long interests in culture, geography and history, creating a thirst for adventure and informative travel experiences. For others, an upbringing steeped in relative privilege brings a norm of luxury and frequent travel. But this all represents significant challenges for the future of the luxury travel industry and its response to new global travellers. Putting it simply, luxury travel is now a main-stream tourism phenomenon.

Whilst this book is largely drawn from a British context, developments that have taken place on the continent and elsewhere in the world have clearly left their mark as operators created new wares. And it is appropriate to comment perhaps that nothing is entirely new – a recurring theme in this title. In 1927, the provision of sophisticated and luxurious first-class services was paramount for the Big Four railway companies recognising passenger needs as central to their business agendas. Throughout the following decade, railway technology continued to progress and in terms of product, the design of seats ensuring passenger comfort was key to the London, Midland and Scottish Railway (LMS), whilst the London and North Eastern Railway (LNER) introduced continuous innovative ideas and promotion, particularly the use of advertising poster media, to attract first-class passengers. The inter-war years was an era where the traditional first-class setting was displaced by an emergent upper middle-class knocking on the door which only a generation before was beyond their access and means.

Whilst growth was more orderly in days past, today's marketplace is far more unpredictable. Travel providers now have to respond in different ways to opportunities as travel experience indulgence involving new destinations, hotels, islands and resorts is within the grasp of increasing numbers of middle-class consumers. In short, the concept of 'luxurification' has become commonplace and diffused through a 'luxurification of society' process.[3] Such approaches predictably dovetail with other leisure industries, providing the opportunity to participate in or watch certain luxury and upscale recreation activities. The marketing profession describes the event industry in different ways, but the most discernible aspect is new found wealth allows consumers, not necessarily rich but possessing healthy savings or disposable incomes, to pander to and desire interests that matter to them most. Effectively, luxury has developed into 'affordable constructs' particularly in travel and tourism markets where it is possible to indulge in genuine five star hospitality environments, enjoy first-class service whilst accessing a wide range of facilities and things to do that are not only different but distinctive travel experiences. In addition, there are customers

LMS **PASSENGER EXPRESS**
THE SYMBOL OF COMFORTABLE TRAVEL
NORMAN WILKINSON, R.I.

LMS employed considerable emphasis on carriage development with the construction of low waisted and large window vestibule coaches. Passenger comfort, particularly for longer distance travel, was an important priority as this poster from around 1935 demonstrates. Norman Wilkinson's 'Symbol of Comfortable Travel' work underpins LMS's express train image and a theme continued by British Railways up until the 1960s. (NRM Pictorial Collection/Science & Society Library)

who have not reached financial maturity but wish to dip into luxury styles, pursuits and unique customer experiences as and when the opportunity presents itself.

Luxury competition prizes, for instance, are powerful inducements. Consumers may be prepared to put up with much to tap into luxury indulgences such as travelling by difficult means, long queues, leaving home in the middle of the night for an early morning departure or even being subjected to cramped conditions on budget airline aircraft – all perfect examples described by Professor Alan Fyall as the 'tourism schizophrenia' phenomenon. At the other end of the spectrum, elites require insulation, a world where travel to private based luxury destinations is discrete, privileged and only available to those with necessary connections, power and wealth to secure such access. The financial component delivers exclusivity as simply not everyone is able to reach it. Davos, an upmarket Swiss Alpine destination (which until the late 1870s was regarded as a primitive Swiss enclave), is home to the world's most glamorous schmoozefest – a no-go world in mid-January of exclusive networks and advantaged class backgrounds accessed only by private invitation. In many ways, the luxury proposition presents an industry conundrum since its composition is multi-faceted with many different entry points, as everyone, it seems, desires their little piece of personal involvement.

Coupled to luxury tourism are notions of adventure, expedition, exploration and nostalgia which increasingly form an important part of the destination vista. Luxury train travel in the past ten years has moved into the long-distance mode where journeys now routinely cover continental landmasses, providing guests the opportunity to discover and unearth exotic new destinations. The exotic is nothing new; from the 1860s middle-class Britons were always tempted to try their hands at exciting recreational pursuits. European trains (and connecting steamers) transported Victorian tourists to Norway's natural heritage and to Switzerland's mountains where an Alpine sports industry was born.

The presence of increased numbers of British visitors in Switzerland's mountains prompted the beginnings 'of a new chapter in Swiss social and economic history' leveraging exquisite natural resource with a fast developing upscale tourist industry.[4] The draw of unusual destinations may be inescapable but more important is the need to travel with a degree of panache and with appropriate levels of personal service and attention accompanying the experience. This defines markets by people, who they were and what they did. Today it is more about customer types, household incomes, where people live and their lifestyles. The late Professor Harold Perkin ventures substance: 'One of the functions of the

(Victorian) railway was to separate out the classes according to taste and ability to pay, in holiday habits and resorts as in their urban and suburban homes.'[5]

Railway companies on both sides of the English Channel and, indeed, evolving travel packagers (who worked hand in glove with railway operators, shipping lines and hoteliers) were progressively and skilfully adept at latching on to new technologies to develop tourism and travel services in order to make life easier, more enjoyable and to unearth new customer experiences. And there were corresponding commercial undertones driven by increasing numbers of upscale consumers receptive to new ideas. Witness Thomas Cook dabbling with motoring holidays in the late Edwardian period and the Great Western Railway's (GWR) acquisition of two motor-buses rather than extending the Helston to Lizard branch line. The Lizard charabanc, not considered at the time to offer any form of competition to the railway industry, featured prominently in Great Western's Cornish Riviera promotion. Similarly, in Scotland, the Great North of Scotland Railway (GNSR) pioneered these new transport arrangements.

In the second decade of the twenty-first century we now have the benefit of the best part of a 150 years of increasingly sophisticated travel packaging. Consumers now want to encounter something different, requiring travel experiences to deliver simplicity, connection and self-discovery. For the highly privileged, conspicuous wealth is no longer the key driver as material consumption fatigue kicks in, substituted by a hunger for new experiences. Luxury tourism is a scarce commodity product that responds to trends and competitive pressures whilst providing opportunities for customers to engage with individual interpretations of what they hold precious in life. Yet luxury travel too is one of the few industries that operates within the juxtaposition of modernity but at the same time has the innate capability of packaging customers in a rich cultural heritage of authentic settings, providing meanings to encapsulate dreams, imagination and engagement with an aura of a bygone, slower, luxury travel age.

The world of the luxury dining train delivers today's travellers with access to new but also familiar destinations; an allure that is quite heady. Few railway texts have considered the complicated relationship between railways, the operational companies and leisure and tourism sectors. Where investigation has taken place, it has tended to concentrate on the lines and routes that link holiday regions as well as the extensive use of railway marketing materials to promote city, town, country and seaside resort destinations. Even from an academic perspective, there has been a dearth of serious examination, something railway historian Dr Hiroki Shin, writing in *Business History* (vol 56/2) in 2014, considers anomalous, given 'railways possibly made the most extensive contribution to tourism promotion up to World War II, the lively field of tourism studies still has a poor understanding of how, and how extensively, the railway companies promoted travel.' Glamorous trains and luxury rail travel is inextricably bound up with tourism although in the case of Britain, with most Pullman services radiating from the capital, there was always an element of the business market connected to their operations. So much so that by the late 1950s, the vermilion and cream liveried Trans Europ Expresses (TEE) together with the new Nanking Blue British Pullmans, both using diesel-powered end cars with fixed carriage formations, were for the first-time unashamedly targeting the business community. Charles Fryer rather eloquently observed:

> 'The "de luxe" atmosphere was not that of the domestic parlour but of the boardroom. Gone were the period-style moveable chairs, the polished brass work, the pink-shaded table lamps and glass-topped tables, which made such pleasant surrounds for an intimate tête-à-tête between friends but were not particularly relevant to the business decision.'[6]

Scheduled luxury rail travel was, therefore, adapted for a new breed of first-class business traveller which progressively was seen as a market segment in its own right where product specifications were specifically designed to meet the needs of the late twentieth century executive seeking to maximise his or her time away from the office in the most productive manner possible. This continues to be the direction most railway operators have taken in their quest to provide services with extra comfort and speed to mount serious competition to short-haul air travel as the no-frills sector continues to dominate, vacuuming out the last vestiges of any flying enjoyment. The expectation of any degree of magnetism attached to short-haul flying belongs to a much earlier era, when boarding an aircraft had not been stripped of every last shred of pleasure.

This book is not just a precis of the activities of well-known luxury trains of the past (and present) with well-publicized services oozing glamour, romance and sophistication but also seeks to examine the dimensions and influences that brought these activities into existence. Ever since the Midland Railway's introduction of sleeper and day parlour Pullman cars in the mid-1870s ushered in a new era of luxurious rail travel, the British Pullman Company and Wagon-Lits in Europe have become synonyms of better ways to travel long-distances. George Nagelmackers 'was the real father of the Orient-Express, quickly coming to dominate the luxury train market with his beautiful carriages, which were used in a network of international expresses steaming across Europe.'[7] Luxury rail travel has undoubtedly evolved over the past century and a half with many different organisations now running tourism-related services the world over. It is, perhaps, a demonstration that Pullman and Wagon-Lits services so regularly spring to mind but it must be remembered in the last quarter of the nineteenth century, Britain's pre-grouping railway companies began to construct bespoke luxury train services pitched directly towards wealthy customers. Large numbers of passengers were ferried between London, the Lake District and Scotland, to Devon and Cornwall and to the south coast's top resorts of Bournemouth and Brighton. Two special named trains were written into railway lore; the *Orient Express* and the *Flying Scotsman*. The former created the blueprint for European luxury train travel, whilst the latter laid down the gauntlet for dazzling and atmospheric non-stop train travel in Britain in the inter-war years.

This book is primarily through a British lens emphasising the main routes to Scotland, the West Country and to the south coast where premier train services ran forming a blueprint for regular luxury train travel and the other connected hospitality and tourism services that quickly followed. In the *Flying Scotsman's* case – both locomotive and train service – so much has been written by others with abundant rich material drawn from a variety of historical sources as to render it almost impossible to add anything new of substance. The named train, though, acted as a catalyst supplemented by other glamorous and luxury trains on the famous east coast route provided by both the Pullman Company and the LNER railway company. Progress was always at the forefront as the 1935 *Silver Jubilee* offered passengers an entirely new prestige service creating the high point of interwar interest in luxury train travel. Informed observers may consider there have been omissions regarding the selection of past celebrated luxury trains.

The *Calais-Mediterranée Express, Côte d'Azur Rapide* and the *Rome Express* from the French Belle Époque; pre-grouping GWR and London and South Western Railway (LSWR) *Ocean Specials* together with London and North Western Railway's (LNWR) Euston to Liverpool Riverside *American Specials* service; the Anglo-French connecting trains of the inter-war period featuring the *Blue Train/Le Train Bleu, Golden Arrow/Flèche d'Or, Côte d'Azur Pullman Express* and *Night Ferry/Ferry Boat de Nuit*; the Harwich Parkeston Quay and Hook of Holland expresses featuring the *Hook Continental*, the *Berlin London Express, Rheingold* and *Edelweiss* amongst others; the era of the superliner trains from Great Western, Southern and LMS and in the post-war days British Railways Southern Region *Ocean Special Pullmans* have all been included in a separate volume on the luxury boat train.

Whilst this title should be seen as a distinct sub-set of luxury tourism, it is important to recognise luxury rail travel is far from routine, with a storyline that makes it such a fascinating subject. Over the past forty years, many vintage trains – locomotives and carriages – have been resurrected for both main line and preserved heritage railway operation in some form or another by a growing band of enthusiasts, specialist organisations and entrepreneurs. Such developments similarly opened new opportunities the world over for carefully constructed craft-based luxury tourism products putting luxury train travel at the centre of operations. This in turn has led to agenda changing tour operator businesses who market these luxury tourism products. Brand new, slow and luxurious trains utilising the latest rail-based technologies have been built around the world, serving gastronomic feasts fashioned and prepared by Michelin chefs reflecting local and regional foods from where trains run.

Luxury rail travel is conducted in beautiful surroundings, with good food and company, where dress, style, the way one conducts oneself, conforming to prescribed conventions but all neatly packaged together with new forms and presentation of yesteryear heritage transport. Without similar-minded people with comparable economic, social and cultural capital, there is no magic as people simply breathe life into inanimate objects. They are birds of a feather flocking together, transforming the social space of train travel. Luxury dining trains such as the restored *Belmond British Pullman* and the *VSOE* curate the many memorable tourism-based experiences consumers long for. Likewise, they are the perfect opportunity for them to realize important milestone celebrations in life as luxury travel brands occupy the same landscape as other luxury goods. Arguably, people act as double agents, simultaneously consuming and producing meaning operating in a sensory world with an association that fosters real fantasy, emotion and engagement.

Luxury travel is about policing the borders of social distinction; in the prestigious events industry, appearance and arriving in style are absolutely essential prerequisites. Inappropriate dress codes and behaviour may be subtle examples of Bourdieu habitus and exclusion but such distinguishing features are mechanisms prohibiting access to particular days in the social calendar. Historical transport forms may be perceived as conspicuous features of upper-class leisure but turning up at Royal Ascot, Henley or Wimbledon in a beautifully restored vintage car, charabanc or motor coach undoubtedly sets a different tone. Heritage conveyance represents both an individual and collective experience that may be deeply personal but the use of yesteryear transport in the mix is just as important as the privileged set that has the means to arrive by private helicopter. When James Sherwood launched the restored *VSOE* and *British Pullman* in 1982, he had clear ideas of his intended market, comprising the 'wealthier middle classes'. Writing in June 1985, he reflected:

> 'My perception was that the affluent tourist wanted the adventure of taking the historic *Orient Express* from London and Paris to Venice and to travel on the *British Pullman* rake on excursions to race meetings and historic houses. The success of this perception can be measured by the long waiting lists for places on our trains and the good return on our investment which is now being achieved.'

Historian Lawrence James in *The Middle Class: A History* (Little Brown, 2006) takes a similar view arguing, 'Today's 'heritage' industry in all manifestations is a response to middle class-demand. There is still something within the psyche of a wide segment of the middle-class which finds reassurance in being surrounded by objects of the past, whether original or not.' In his memoir, James Sherwood, almost thirty years later, recounted his aspirations for the project. 'I also had a very clear idea of the image I wanted for the whole venture. The train and the trip had to suggest an experience of special quality, unusual, exclusive and luxurious, evocative of a time when travel was glamorous and service was perfect.' It could be argued that Sherwood and his company's brave innovations together with Johan Vos's enterprising South African initiatives at Rovos Rail, literally reinvented luxury train travel. The magnitude of these developments were not fully appreciated at the time but they set the pace for global expansion of a new industry. Across the world, pioneering new entrants took an embryonic travel sector in different directions as inventive brand concepts took on new forms wherever rails ran on land. The expansion of Sherwood's rebranded Belmond operation bears testimony to the direction of the luxury tourism revolution.

Timelines selected in this book are understandably influenced by major world events. War had profound impacts on railway operations across several continents, as most forms of luxury passenger transport were curtailed. Luxury carriages were relegated to goods or storage yards off the beaten track. Significant economic, technological, business and social changes were at play with a dominant middle-class whose aspirations were the key subscribers to modern tourism and travel service agendas shaping the glamorous travel industry story. At the end of the Victorian age there was a gradual widening in the numbers of people employed in middle-class occupations and with it came many improvements in the quality of rail (and sea) passage.

Railways were instrumental in delivering middle-class leisure activities especially outdoor pursuits. Chimneys belching smoke created poor air quality making city life difficult, leading to a peak in interest in more rural based leisure pastimes such as camping, cycling, fishing, hiking and more sedate relaxations such as golfing and pleasure-boating.

These activities developed significantly at the inter-section of the Victorian and Edwardian age as a health gaze was based on the restorative and recreational properties associated with the natural environment and destination landscapes. Railway companies took these ideas in their stride, latching on to place making themes; The Great Central Railway (GCR) promoted a *Seaside, Farmhouse, and Country Lodgings and Hotel List*, a booklet that served as a means for the company to differentiate its offer from other pre-grouping railway competitors. The GCR went on to develop this theme using display advertising in the shape of a palm of a hand promoting itself as the 'line of health' with 'bank holiday excursions to coast and country health resorts in the

Midlands, Yorkshire, Lancashire' and to the Chilterns from London Marylebone. These advertisements were run in publications such as *The Illustrated London News.* Likewise, the Anglo-Scottish carriers viewed Scotland and the Highlands and Islands for its wider passenger potential, ferrying a hotchpotch of middle-class tourists drawn to the great outdoors such as campers, canoeists, cavers, climbers, cyclists, pioneer map-makers and even budding scientists. Societal change in terms of greater numbers of people with enhanced income, status and wealth, together with increased volumes of domestic and international tourists, were the real drivers in the growth of better ways to travel leading to a British, European and American first-class market that held sway for the best part of seventy years until the mid-twentieth century's assault of modern civil aviation.

This book explores a range of social dimensions associated with luxury rail travel. Social history study is a relatively new phenomenon but one where historical investigation and reflection helps determine our understanding of the world and how it developed, particularly in the relationships and hierarchies of the stratification of social division and its impact on the world. Social class structures determined by income and wealth had an inordinate influence on the way one travelled. Once, it provided a neat encapsulation of people, typologies and how consumers behaved and travelled but present day social class is a far more multifaceted affair, where marketing practitioners have to consider the many varied components and complexities of modern society. Nowadays, in the highly organised travel world, there will always be trend-setters. Media growth across many new technological platforms has been aided by an explosion in celebrity endorsement and focus has altered the travel landscape to personal forms of transport that are only shared by invitation or through places of work. Nowhere is this more evident than in the world of trans-national sports ownership, where luxury travel modes are clearly seen. For those involved, they become part of the workplace ethic and travel luxuries are considered the norm for transportation to the world's sporting arenas. Across Britain and Europe's elite football clubs, the infrastructure to support a sporting/celebrity industry is immense, as players and their support staffs are routinely marshalled from private planes onto limousine style coaches and straight off to palatial hotels in preparation for match-day fixtures. But again, they are perfect examples of the nothing is new concept. Football and other spectator sports owed much to the railways in the late Victorian era.

Transport writer Christian Wolmar in *Fire and Steam* (Atlantic Books, 2007) sums up the position admirably: 'Without (the railways) the players and, crucially, the paying fans would not have been able to travel to watch their teams play.' As long ago as 1907, a former Pullman car used by the Great Northern Railway (GNR) as a morning breakfast and afternoon tea car was placed at the disposal of Newcastle United Football Club on a frequent basis for travelling to away matches. Life is never quite so simple now.

By the turn of the twentieth century, the main railway companies and small band of specialist operators responded to the challenges of change. No longer was it a case of pandering to the whims of a narrow band of upscale customers as a rapid expansion of western society middle-classes broadened the market for better ways to travel by rail. The Pullman Company in America, the British Pullman Company, Wagon-Lits, MITROPA and others in Europe became totemic symbols of civilised luxury rail travel. But even here, there was a hierarchical structure to travelling as some carriages of the same class were for lesser gentry whilst others, such as Pullman's mid-twentieth century *Rosemary* and *Rosamund* cars, were conferred with royal patronage. The Pullman car *Audrey*, according to railway author Michael Williams (*The Train Now Departed*, Penguin, 2015), 'had another, more British, claim to fame, having reputedly been the Queen Mother's favourite dining carriage'.

This story covers a relatively brief period in history but one that oversaw immense societal change; this is ongoing and change remains a constant as technological progress dictates an evolutionary treadmill where, periodically, a combination of factors coalesce bringing fresh opportunities for railway companies and travel operators to create new products and services, packaging and marketing unique travel experiences. It is not just about rejuvenating the old; travelling in style can be found in brand new forms of transport such as luxury slow trains and small, intimate, boutique cruise ships borrowing from past traditions where new tapestries are woven into the travel product body fabric. Such innovations in the past catered for the needs of a discriminating market and continue to do so currently, as new forms of commodification present across travel markets. In previous years, Britain's imperial tentacles stretched around the globe; by the end of the Edwardian era, there were few places on earth where thousands of miles of steel rails and wooden sleepers did not leave their global footprint. The wealthy travelled majestically over long-distances whether in Canada, Argentina or closer to home. Attendants in starched uniforms on today's luxury dining trains provide not just a foot in the past but a living link to a type of vanished travel experience which is the anthesis of the modern dictates of everyday transport. Elegance has always been an important tool to wrap around better ways to travel as firms, such as the highly profitable Thomas Cook organisation which dominated the late Victorian and Edwardian travel scene, enlisted greater emphasis on experiences.

And so too is food and drink, since it is part and parcel and inextricably linked to so many aspects of luxury travel; the quality, sourcing, styles and culinary presentation of gourmet foods is pivotal to the total travel experience. In the twenty-first century many consumers now regard themselves as foodies, a term first coined in the 1980s but now deeply lodged in public consciousness. Our food culture is a modern revolution with an infusion of the many influences currently taking place in Britain and other former colony-owning nations. In addition, the notion of food remains high on consumer agendas largely in response to the single-minded and large multi-national corporate organisations in former years dictating culinary agendas with industrialised foods with no discernible source or personality. Historically, this was not the case in a nation of individual shopkeepers; it was not only a matter of taste and nutrition that determined what and how we eat in this country, it was also heavily inclined by social class divide rather than regional geographies as was the case of many European countries.

Nowadays, though, food, culinary and wine tourism is fast becoming a key discriminator in upscale destinations' marketing armoury, where it is used as a means of differentiation, a mechanism to achieve competitive advantage and as a hook to attract visitors. There are, of course, always new food trends but many aspects of culinary exhibition are not entirely new. Food served on Wagon-Lits' expresses crisscrossing Europe in the late nineteenth century was not just a gastronomic extravagance but a move designed by the leading chefs of their time to demonstrate the breadth of their culinary skills through a reflection of the local dishes of the regions trains travelled through; in effect they were the original food on the move taste-makers.

On the inaugural running of the *Rome Express* in November 1897, one seasoned continental rail traveller was amazed at the quality of the fare provided at lunch shortly after boarding the train in France and shared his thoughts with *Railway Magazine*. He declared:

> 'Simple and wholesome. The peas had been brought from Brindisi, ex Corfou, by the home-coming *Peninsular Express*, which had arrived in Calais the day before. The pears at dessert were the finest I have ever eaten, and the grapes were Chasselas – the real thing.'

The story was not just about sourcing of quality foods en route but a deliberate attempt by company management to personify food cultures, delivering to new audiences, particularly to American travellers, an appealing and highly distinctive journey experience enticing them to return time and time again. Trains operating across Europe provided the means to bring home overseas flavours to an increasingly discriminating customer, thus establishing a renowned gastronomic tradition. Similar dimensions still apply. The *Napa Valley Wine Train* in California is a heritage line train using exquisitely restored Pullman vintage dining and lounge rail cars dating from 1915, providing tourists with gourmet dining experiences using locally sourced produce, together with other food and drink itineraries amongst the historic wineries found along the valley route. Inextricably linked to food and drink provision is the railway hotel, though lamentably few now survive to offer truly luxury international standards with five star ratings incorporating the kind of gastronomic, flair eateries now demanded by today's sophisticated traveller, who arrive at their venues in the main by private car, taxi or even occasionally in major cities by public transport.

The delights of 150 years of elegant rail travel can now be unravelled creating for the reader a fascinating journey of cultural discovery, exploration and experience whether your interests are in railway, social or travel histories.

CHAPTER 1

1860-1900: Victorian Expansion – The Emergence of Luxury Travel

From the late seventeenth century, it was fashionable for British and continental elites to visit Europe's cultural centres. A personal pilgrimage known as a 'Grand Tour' of Europe would be conducted taking months or even years depending on one's resources and family connections. It was a foundation stone and rite of passage for the young. Its influence was pervasive, providing the basis for the modern tourism phenomenon. Until the 1800s, travelling for pleasure or non-work reasons was restricted to a narrow band of wealthy upper-class men. Few people made lengthy journeys but the visitation of crucial sites of European civilisation was a keystone of privilege, mobility, individual needs for cultivation and education, expanding social horizons and marking one's place in society. By the end of the eighteenth century, the word 'tourist' had entered the English and French languages, just as 'tourism' entered the official lexicon with an 1811 entry in the *Oxford English Dictionary*. At the same time the term 'tourifying' and the acquisition of objects from around the world was coined by hardened travellers such as Byron and William Bankes. Britain's glorious landscapes – the Scottish Highlands, the Lake District – were painted and filled with tourists for the first time.

Whilst tourism was not a creation of the railways, before their arrival, long-distance travel could only be accomplished by walking, by horse and carriage and on water by rowing or by sailing vessels. Non-mechanised transport modes would be replaced by steam-based technologies but, even now, walking for pleasure and the horse still form important leisure pursuits. As a primary transport mode, the horse and carriage would ultimately be jettisoned to another age, but it did not disappear totally and without a fight even on journeys involving several hundreds of miles. In its fight to survive railway intrusion, the horse-drawn coach held an advantage. Public stage vehicles made point to point journeys from town centre inns, which for many passengers were conveniently located whereas new railway stations were largely located out of town. The mid-century represented the final stand-off between the railways and the horse-drawn carriage era as a long-distance method of transport. Still, it was a well-connected and established industry with specialist manufacturers producing coaches for the transit of mail, the public and for rich private owners, providing the means to convey them at will. Private carriages were renowned for their comfort with well-cushioned seats and seat-backs. Elegant in appearance, built with quality finishes they provided a luxury product for the wealthy, delivering a means of travel and private social space. Horse-drawn carriages were a centuries-old tradition with many influential supporters such as Charles Dickens.

Mark Twain, a seasoned traveller across America, took the view stage-coaching was 'infinitely more delightful than railroading' and lost no time in sharing his view with his readers in *The Innocents Abroad* in 1869. Yet the transition from the horse-drawn coach to the train was not entirely smooth and without problems especially for the privileged. Town centre inns – good or bad – were staging posts, a focus of activity and places of enjoyment but the railway stations in the early days tended to be desolate spots until adequate waiting rooms and hospitality arrangements were developed by emerging operators. This all took time, providing the horse-drawn carriage with an extended life until the emergence of private and public motors cars at the turn of the twentieth century. The horse-drawn carriage as a form of long-distance transport eventually succumbed to railway expansion as the new industry had significantly lower operating costs and scale, providing travellers with the benefits of speedier and more comfortable means of transit.

But before the arrival of regular rail passenger services, a new industrial world had a say in developments and in shaping passenger transport. The mining of coal, tin and other extractive industries used in the production of iron and steel and other metal products gave rise to rapid industrialisation; a process that had begun in the second half of the eighteenth century. Aside from coastal maritime transport, the railways played their part as they gradually supplanted canal traffic as the means to move large quantities of raw materials used in manufacturing processes. This could be undertaken as railways were speedier than horse-drawn or steam-powered barge.

New industries attracted people from the countryside who were required to work in commercial enterprises, leading to a swift expansion of towns and city settlements that were once villages. Industrial development would take place on land owned by the aristocracy, providing valuable windfalls for mineral extraction, the selling of rights and for commercial and urban housing development. Professor David Cannadine, writing in 1990 in his book *Decline and Fall of the British Aristocracy* (YUP) takes the view that:

'the British gentry and grandees were, collectively speaking, the wealthiest of the European territorial élites. In part, this was because they came to the most profitable terms with the Industrial Revolution. Britain was after all, the first nation to industrialize, the patricians themselves owned so much of the land surface, and they were more advantageously placed to exploit the minerals beneath than many continental owners. As a result, there were also more very wealthy grandees.'

Similarly, Professor Harold Perkin in *The Rise of Professional Society* (Routledge, 1989) took the view that by the second-half of Victoria's reign, there was a succession of 'landed business men' who were prime movers in the development of railways firmly establishing themselves as part of a new industrial plutocracy of rich and powerful figures. Many landowners, unsurprisingly, were fleet-footed in extorting as much as possible from railway companies for their land rights, although in time, many were to realize the commercial and travel access benefits of having railways close at hand. Thus, railways were embedded in the so-called mid-Victorian economic boom delivering unprecedented prosperity.

Whilst aristocracy benefited from industrialisation, they were likewise joined by the ascendancy of the new commercial and industrial upper middle-classes; they were the revolution engineers and creators of Victorian wealth. Naturally, they wanted better residential places to live and to travel so by the mid-1800s, many resorts near London were connected by the railway and thereby, according to Perkin, 'subtly graduated in the social hierarchy of middle-class values'. Rapid urban expansion ensured station locations were eventually absorbed within the central confines of towns and cities which by mid-Victorian times had grown tremendously.

In later years, these stations connected to the new spoke-like suburban railways surrounding London and other large urban centres in the Midlands and the north, allowing the wealthy middle-class to decamp en masse. As Perkin commented, this provided the perfect environment for 'the well-to-do middle class to live miles from their work in the fresh air of the country or at the seaside, and for an increasing number of lower middle-class clerks and even well-paid artisans to live on the fringes of the built-up areas'. The suburban railways, and in later times the tram and omnibus, became the means of separating residential neighbourhoods by social grouping. This in turn speeded up the flight of the wealthier classes to the new suburbs, places described as 'compact self-contained villages within walking distance of the station'. This process was not only restricted to London and the south east, since Birmingham and Chester had their own high-class suburban neighbourhoods by mid-century.

London as the Empire's financial and commercial heart, fuelled a growth in high-class outer suburbs made up of loosely settled communities. The notion of long-distance commuting had been introduced. These were made up of a relatively small group of rich upper middle-class and an increasing number of middle-class workers who made their living in the City, typically with incomes of between £1,000 and £5,000 per year. They had both the time and the money to afford first-class season tickets. The idea of the 'city-flyer' is nothing new but whilst they are not an endangered species, their commuter first-class carriage may be.

In July 2017, the British government unveiled consultation plans to scrap segregated first-class compartments on crowded commuter trains in a move to ease rush-hour passenger congestion pressures. In Victorian Britain, there was quite naturally a desire to travel amongst elite society that comprised moneyed aristocracy and the new upper middle-classes who had acquired the habits and tastes of the upper-classes, seeing themselves as increasingly mobile, driven by travel stories of exploration from Britain's expanding empire interests. The ability to travel at leisure was fuelled by growth in the power and wealth of the better-off middle-classes. As historian Lawrence James notes, the middle-classes by late Victorian times 'had gradually supplanted the old aristocracy of pedigrees and acres, but they desperately wanted to absorb its finer qualities and, by doing so, justify their ascendancy'. Travel was considered one of the better things of life, and for this group apart, the ability to see more of the country and the wider world became a key aspiration in order to demonstrate arrival. This did not always go down well with aristocracy since the arrival of the motor car in the early years of the twentieth century ensured country homes were more accessible, threatening one of the landed elite's 'most cherished institutions' of country isolation and an ordered life.

The car, according to David Cannadine, gave rise to the 'quintessentially plutocratic custom' of the weekend house party. A combination of express trains and station pick up by motor car ensured that many country estates easily accessed from London became fashionable for the weekend invitation. With such access, quite naturally, the middle-classes wanted places in the sun. If the English coastal destinations of Kent and Sussex were insufficient, then sun drenched Mediterranean hot spots provided ideal locations, all suitably aided by new continental railway networks with their safer, secure and faster means of admittance to the Azur coast. What once took days could be accommodated in hours in later Victorian years. And with it, the English colonisation of the French and Italian Riviera had begun in earnest.

The developments taking place in Britain were only achieved by the railway networks continuing roll out, as promoters by the second third of the nineteenth century saw unrivalled opportunities. Such was the clamour amongst the public to obtain an investment in the future, a temporary stall to railway development was to follow as the bubble burst but, by the early 1850s, a period of consolidation began, as a new age of Victorian empire-building activity saw the emergence of Britain's industrial classes take central stage. Factories and warehouses and other commercial activity sprang up alongside railways. With lineside development came a new breed of entrepreneur and manager with the necessary skills to run embryonic enterprises. This gave rise to the business traveller, as journeys could be made the length and breadth of the country in support of visiting other commercial establishments. Railway companies eventually saw opportunities as business and leisure travellers all demanded better services. People with means began to travel more widely than ever before. The almost universal use of standardised 'railway time' made planning journeys far easier for both business travellers and for the leisured classes.

Whilst railways might have displaced long-distance horse-drawn transport, the horse continued to play a key role in the lives of the privileged as railway companies tried to encourage society's upper echelons by running trains with special wagons where individual horse-drawn carriages were attached. It must also be remembered that by mid-Victorian times it was quite common to find members of the aristocracy appearing on the boards of railway companies, particularly when they were close to where railways traversed country estates. Such influence gave way to specialist private carriages (and private station halts, in time) but the movement of horse by rail was one of the last remnants of privileged Victorian travel before the private motor car took central stage. In Britain, horse boxes would be added to passenger trains as profitable side lines to goods and freight. David Wragg in *The Race to the North* (Pen and Sword, 2013) informs us that on the Anglo-Scottish routes 'there was even an overnight express for horses and (private) carriages so that these would be waiting for their owners when they arrived'. Moving horses around during the First World War, together with the rapid expansion of the horse racing industry in the twentieth century, created horse box wagons, a phenomenon to last well in to the nationalised railway era.

By mid-Victorian times, the benefits of industrialisation could be seen with an increasing level of leisure time afforded to a large proportion of the working population. A six-day working week for many left Sunday free. The opportunities to explore further afield flourished as railway mania progressively gripped Britain. From the 1840s onwards, the country was on the move in a way that had never been seen before. An increasingly mobile public prompted railway companies to move beyond their original purposes as transporters of industrial freight and cargo by identifying people with a keen desire to travel. Excursion traffic became an accepted railway activity, representing a good source of income for the companies involved as they consolidated and expanded their networks. A standardised track width (with the Great Western's seven feet and a quarter inch broad gauge and Ireland's imposed five feet three inch gauge as exceptions) enabled passengers to travel long-distances without changing trains. For the first time, railways provided Britain's ordinary masses with access to daily outings and short excursions.

Society was beginning to change as for first time all social classes were able to experience unfamiliar vistas, cultures and surroundings far from home. Many of these trips were to seaside locations but not always so. Attractive market towns were often in close proximity to large urban conurbations and easily accessible by rail. Responding to customer demand, railway companies were adept at putting on trains for a variety of specific events. In 1836, the Bodmin & Wadebridge Railway achieved a degree of notoriety by running a day out excursion for a public execution. There may have been some confusion in date recording but Dr Susan Major reports 'In April 1840 an excursion ran from Wadebridge in Cornwall, with three trains carrying 1,100 people, to see the public execution of the Lightfoot brothers at Bodmin Gaol'.[1] Despite the ghoulish nature, this was perhaps a precursor to the modern events-based industry so readily at play nowadays. In addition, there was the emergence of excursion agents, enterprising individuals who worked with railway operators to organise and promote planned railway trips. Many of their services were targeted at ordinary working people with an unpretentious aim of transporting large numbers of customers on day trips.

Trips involving an overnight stay or longer were simply beyond the means of many of the working classes. Whilst the adoption of sophisticated marketing practice was perhaps the best part of a century away, social class segmentation could be clearly seen in the 1840s. Major notes the embracing of market segregation techniques at an early stage of development by the railway companies as 'the working classes went on "trips", the middle classes went on "excursions" and the upper classes went on "tours"'. At the top end of the spectrum, excursion agent entrepreneurs positioned their businesses accordingly. Whilst Thomas Cook over time has received plaudits for single-handedly developing the excursion business, this is not exactly the case as they were just one of several specialist agents operating at the time.

Cook's began life as a business running short excursions for temperance campaigners but 'his long-term strategy lay in the direction of tourism rather than excursions.'[2] Temperance societies were good customers for the nascent Cook organisation. He was not only able to lever strong relationships with colleagues in the temperance movement but also with key railway company contacts to create packages for middle-class customers of longer duration. As Major reflects:

'Cook's role in the invention of excursions is significant, but it is as one of the first creators of "tours" as a rounded experience and combined tickets, rather than cheap trips, pioneering, for example, annual tours from South Wales through Birmingham to the north of England and to Edinburgh.'

Thomas Cook and another agent, Joseph Crisp, focused their attentions on middle-class tourists with longer and more expensive tours using first and second-class ticketing arrangements. By 1845, Liverpool-based Crisp was already offering continental excursions, reflecting fast-changing travel pattern demands as European railway networks expanded.

Public clamour for greater comfort and more elegant surroundings surfaced especially as quality hotels were springing up around railway termini. However, at first, railway companies had an arm's length relationship with their running, so the better facilities found at an end of a railway journey was yet to be transferred to the railway carriage. But the first appearances of class distinction could be seen in coach design, construction and in standards of overnight accommodation. Railway companies took notice, responding to the needs of travellers who were no longer prepared to put up with standards previous generations endured with stage-coach travel. Yet this did not occur overnight as during the mid-part of the century, passengers were treated little better than as a basic commodity.

Railway development in Britain and Europe brought travellers improved carriage standards. Higher society was on the move, requiring more opulent and spacious modes of transport but despite gradual improvements in carriage size, this did not expand significantly until the 1870s with the introduction of bogie stock. Cramped compartments were a feature of the day. To some extent, improvements were driven by steamship technology and growth of the Atlantic Ferry where on-board amenities and services improved significantly during this period. Railways opened up the continent of Europe and the rest of the world in a way that travellers and indeed society, had not witnessed before. Railways, in terms of the facilities they offered customers, lagged behind the steamship lines and naturally there came demands and expectations from those who could afford such luxuries, for better ways to travel by rail. This ultimately manifested itself in more appropriate and new standards of coaching stock which included furnished carriages, glazed windows, complete coverings, lighting by oil lamps and, in time, a more comfortable ride.

The role of the old order of European royal families and the creation of specialist royal trains to transport monarchs across Britain and the continent had a significant impact in the provision of luxury rail travel, since they established a seal of approval for more appropriate, civilised and rapid methods of transport. Royal trains were effectively at the forefront of developing travelling comfort and convenience ultimately benefiting all travellers by the end of the 1900s, be they first, second or third-class passengers as the pace of railway progress outpaced an elderly monarch's travelling requirements. As Hamilton Ellis quizzically noted in *The Royal Trains* (Routledge, 1975), 'By the 1890s, British royal trains had become decidedly old-fashioned compared with ordinary expresses running up and down the country'. Yet all this was in the future. In a July 1957 *Tatler and Bystander* feature, Sydney Carter described the beginnings of luxury train travel by 'pointing out that in this sphere it was royalty who served as the daring innovators for their subjects in the latest form of transport'.

In 1842, a young Queen Victoria was encouraged and persuaded by an open-minded Prince Albert to use a new-fangled and giddy form of transport innovation – the railway. The Prince Consort had been favourably impressed by railway developments and the speed with which journeys could be conducted. Whilst the Queen, in time, would become an inveterate railway traveller, she was nonetheless content to travel on the slow line for the rest of her life. Six years later, on 28 September 1848 and as a result of bad sea weather, at short notice a railway journey was organised returning the Queen and the Royal Party from Montrose to London Euston.

Queen Victoria travelled in a first-class carriage but because of her nervousness of the new means of transport, progress was slow, involving over-night stays at Perth and Crewe. Importantly, this journey marked the beginning for the normality of long-distance travel in Britain and beyond. These were highly symbolic endorsements, as royal courts and their entourage would likewise travel by train. The development of royal trains, although expensive exercises for railway companies, were exemplary marketing and promotional tools, ultimately leading to increased patronage by those who could afford to see the world. These trains became the original image setters for luxury rail travel and their use and what Victoria and her party consumed in the royal dining car attracted considerable press attention. Over the next fifty years, Britain and Europe's emerging railway networks allowed the Queen to travel extensively.

Depending on the journey's length and whether stops were required, in later years luncheon, afternoon tea and dinner might be prepared for the travelling party by accompanying chefs.

David Duff in his book, *Victoria Travels* (Muller, 1970) records that on the continent, Victoria used:

> 'her own luxury railway coaches, the speed of her train being limited to 35 m.p.h. by day and 25 by night. Stops were made to enable her to dress and undress and so that the engine driver could have his dinner. When those who travelled with her were overtaken by the demands of nature, they had to telegraph to a station ahead, where a halt was made. If they were of sufficient seniority a red carpet was laid from their compartment to the relevant convenience.'

Slow transit over continental metals did provide a spectacle though. In Britain, the GNR provided a new level of luxury to be sampled by Victoria with a special royal train made up of eight carriages in August 1851. Three of the carriages had been built especially for the season's trip north to Balmoral, accommodating the Queen and the Prince Consort; the Prince of Wales and his brother and sisters as well as a separate saloon vehicle. The LNWR would not be outdone in the royal train stakes. In August 1853, the Queen and Prince Albert with their two eldest boys travelled to Holyhead by train to the awaiting royal yacht for onward transit to the Great Exhibition of Dublin. By the 1880s, sleeping cars had been added to royal trains on both the east and west coast routes. On 6 June 1889, the Queen and her party departed for Balmoral aboard LNWR's special royal train consisting of fourteen carriages. The coaches were 'fitted with electrical communication and all the most modern improvements'.

In 1897, the GWR unveiled its Diamond Royal Jubilee Train; it cost a shade under £40,000 but given that the Great Western had always been the Royal route 'the Company was resolved to turn out a train which should be in all respects worthy of the memorable occasion to which it is to be devoted,' as *Railway Magazine* reported that July. When Edward VII ascended the throne in 1901, the GWR royal train with its electrically lit vehicles was used for several long journeys after more than a few alterations were suggested by Queen Alexandra. Although predating the futurist movements of Italian Filippo Tommaso Marinetti and others, with their appreciation for swiftness and modernity, the king was a keen admirer of speed. A GWR royal train achieved the then fastest recorded speed for a royal train in March 1902. Kingston, though, records this event to have occurred the following year. But competition was near at hand as other railway companies introduced new state of the art royal trains to complement the *Victoria and Albert* and the smaller *Alexandra* royal yachts. Together with the new king's interest in the motor car, a variety of the latest forms of mechanised transport provided the means for the pleasure-seeking King to amuse himself amongst society's many fashionable pleasure domes. The London, Brighton & South Coast Railway (LBSCR) had built a special new royal train for the King in 1897 when he was still Prince of Wales, noting Edward's passion for horse racing, the railway being rather fortunate in having courses at Epsom, Goodwood and Lewes within its territory.

In some quarters, Edward might have been considered little more than a highly privileged wastrel but his indulgences acted as a magnet for luxury goods and service providers. Despite his love of better things in life, Edward was popular with his subjects. Mr Frank Smith, a crack LBSCR engine driver used to working royal trains, recounted a story of his working life to reporters from the *Lincolnshire Echo* in December 1934 on commemoration of he and his wife's Christmas Day golden wedding anniversary.

> 'Once I was fireman on the train which took King Edward to Goodwood. I was oiling the engine when we got there, and I heard a man on the platform say. "That's a nice engine you've got there." Without looking round, I said, "Yes, she's a beauty, isn't she?" Then I turned and saw it was King Edward. I apologised, and the King laughed heartily.'

In December 1902, the LNWR, anxious to preserve its status as the 'Premier' line, handed over a Christmas gift of special importance with two intricately designed and luxuriously appointed twelve-wheeled saloon carriages decked out with interior designs and furnishings akin to a yacht and even benefiting from the inclusion of electric cigar lighters. The builders, LNWR's celebrated Wolverton works, according to Jenkinson (*The History of British Railway Carriages 1900-53*, Pendragon Partnership, 1996) 'built more elaborate twelve-wheelers than anywhere else in Britain'.

Two world wars displaced numerous former European royal train carriages. Many were lost as former states around the world dispensed with their monarchs. Some individual royal cars found their way into railway museums, whilst others from the early part of the 1900s were assigned to new duties such as the imperial train of

Kaiser Wilhelm used for the *Berlin-London Express* in the early 1920s. George Behrend (*History of Trains de Luxe*, Transport Publishing Company, 1977) captures the sentiment rather eloquently:

> 'When it came to royal trains, no elegance, grandeur, comfort, advanced engineering, safety or magnificence possible in the design and manufacture of railway carriages was spared in creating prestigious vehicles worthy of crowned heads who were to travel in them.'

But there was always a special allure associated with royal trains and where they travelled. Apart from dedicated royal trains provided by the railway companies themselves, transporting royals cemented the reputations of both the Wagon-Lits and the British Pullman Company organisations. Royal patronage from such as King Leopold II of Belgium (a key benefactor in Wagon-Lits' early development) and two successive Princes of Wales helped transform the Azur coast into an aristocratic and upper-class playground. For Wagon-Lits – or the International Sleeping Car Company as it was known in its early years – the relationship with Europe's royal and imperial households went far deeper. The company was a carriage builder par excellence, constructing royal carriages including those for the Emperor of Russia and the French President.

The influence of the royal train in modern times has found its way into the province of the luxury dining train where many inspirations are seen. The *Golden Eagle Trans-Siberian Express* has its footprints in Russia's Tsarist past whilst the *Majestic Imperator – train de luxe* launched in Vienna in 1998 is a complete reconstruction of the Habsburg imperial and royal court railway train using the chassis platforms of period wagons. The *Majestic Imperator* now plies routes across countries of the former Austro-Hungarian and German empires.

Travel segregation by social class was a feature of railway travel which by the early 1860s adopted a three-class division. For the aristocracy, the attachment of private individual railway carriages and in time private railway stations introduced a further dimension to social segregation. Dr Piers Brendon, writing in 1991 (*Thomas Cook: 150 Years of Popular Tourism*, Secker and Warburg) notes the Duke of Portland 'had a special railway carriage built to accommodate his own barouche' – a four-wheeled carriage with a collapsible half-hood. Notwithstanding, these private arrangements gradually waned due to the practical difficulties of inclusion on regular timetabled train services. The GNR, nevertheless, was still building family saloons in the early twentieth century; no. 807, completed in 1912, still survives in operation. The ferrying of wealthy families between their London homes, country estates and Season events around the country was still de rigueur in the years before the Great War. In August 1904, *The Bystander* reported that the LNWR entered the top end of the market with a luxurious 57ft private railway car in a move the company saw as breaking the monopoly of the American millionaire.

The Tatler ran a feature on private railway stations in October 1903, describing the country's only female-owned station at Dovenby near Cockermouth and also the Duke of Sutherland's extensive amenities at Dunrobin on the Highland Railway's Wick and Thurso line. The station, the publication ran, was:

> 'surrounded by extremely characteristic Scottish scenery and can rank as one of the prettiest railway stations in Scotland. The waiting-room, booking office, and other rooms are all comprised in a charming picturesque building which is built of the best Scots fir and pine, and the little station has all the usual accompaniments and facilities of its larger compeers. There is one line of rails only, and trains are only stopped at Dunrobin when required to either set down or take up members of the ducal household or guests. During the shooting season whilst the duke and duchess stay at the castle the station is kept comparatively busy as they entertain largely.'

Whilst the station housed the Duke's own private carriage and locomotive, he was characteristically generous, having financed the line extension himself, ultimately writing off the £300,000 capital expenditure some years after the line had been completed.

In the United States, the private carriage lasted much longer. They were offered by Pullman and other companies for rent and also owned by wealthy individuals who had the means to acquire their own private cars. America's luxury train sections were known as varnish trains and for the rich and famous and the business elite they were the ultimate status symbols – much in the same way as private jets and yachts nowadays. Private carriages lasted beyond the Second World War, as the running of private vehicles on trains was easier to achieve given the vast land expanses enjoyed

BRITISH ENTERPRISE IN RAILWAY TRAVELLING :
THE SALON DE LUXE

For years past the luxurious private railway car has been the monopoly of the American millionaire. British enterprise (persistently said by a certain excited faction to be dead or at least moribund) has now altered all this, and the magnificent car seen in our illustrations has been constructed by the London and North Western Railway Company for the use of private parties at the low minimum cost of ten 1st-Class fares. It is 57 feet in length, divided into separate compartments, and is beautifully upholstered and fitted with all modern conveniences. It is so constructed that for a day journey the two centre compartments can be formed into one very commodious "Salon," 17 feet in length and 8 feet in width, but if required for a night journey, a bed can be placed in each of the four compartments

One of the Bedrooms of the Salon de Luxe

The Commodious Day Compartments

Exterior view of the L. & N. W. R. new car for private parties, which commences a new era in railway travelling

The Bystander kept an eye on its prosperous readership with editorial content based on new LNWR vehicles designed to take private parties to key events in Edwardian England's social calendar. In August 1905, these carriages acquired the title of the 'American Grouse Train', known for carrying wealthy parties streaming off liners that had docked in Liverpool bound for Scotland. Such developments undoubtedly were in response to US railroad and private varnish cars and the sophisticated, open plan facilities afforded to first-class passengers on LNWR and LSWR luxurious American boat trains en-route to awaiting ocean liners. (Illustrated London News Ltd/Mary Evans)

by US railroads; rail traffic congestion just did not exist in the same way as in Britain.

Pullman was even offering customers car upgrades in the 1950s. In November 1869, as a result of federal government policy of settling north America's vast interiors, the eastern and western halves of the United States were joined commercially by a trans-continental railroad. Ideas surrounding 'travelling for pleasure' were taken up in Union Pacific's promotional literature advertising the great ceremonial event in Omaha of 10 May 1869, linking the Atlantic and Pacific coasts. A through service to San Francisco in less than four days with 'luxurious cars and eating houses' together with 'Pullman's palace sleeping cars' ensured luxury travel was firmly on the map.[3] George Pullman's initiatives were set to become synonymous with America's Gilded Age.

On this side of the Atlantic, the first-class railway carriage proved to be a great social leveller, forcing wealthy elites to share space with fellow passengers from the new industrial plutocracy whom they might have previously chosen to avoid. First-class railway travel was set to become a Victorian status symbol, yet, despite American progress, the experience in Britain and the continent of Europe in the mid-1800s was far from enjoyable as relatively long periods of carriage confinement and enforced companionship with unknown people had to be endured.

When the dedicated Anglo-Scottish *Special Scotch Express* London to Edinburgh passenger service commenced in 1862, its primary purpose was to provide more comfortable ways to travel longer distances, with new locomotives hauling a standard railway carriage design. Despite advances, four and six-wheeled railway coaches were standard fare, with a basic design more in keeping with the days of the stage coach, forcing passengers to endure relatively cramped conditions especially as comfort levels had not made significant strides forward. Yet despite inherent problems, one of the key advantages railways had, proving to be the death knell for long-distance travel by stage coach, was the ability to manage passenger luggage. For the first time, carefully labelled luggage could be left at stations in advance of travelling, put on to trains by the guard who would ensure the luggage arrived safely at its destination for onward collection or delivery by the railway company. And in Victorian times, first-class passengers might have travelled with considerable amounts of luggage. Depending on social status, this could involve a complete entourage of domestic staff and luggage to accompany the wealthy classes.

A theme of this book is to explore what luxury means to different generations. The standard conventions of the past are remarkably different now. Creating more comfortable ways to travel and the experiences they provided, whether by rail or by sea, required significant leaps in Victorian engineering and technology. Coupled to this was an eventual willingness by both railway companies and shipping lines to invest in and commission new locomotives, carriages and ships, all driven by customer demands requiring greater comfort and sophistication.

The first real examples of luxury trains built to British specifications appeared in the second half of the 1800s but progress in rail development did not exist in a vacuum, requiring advances on both land and in sea travel. The enormous technological strides that brought about huge progress in the size and scale of passenger liners, the improvements in the standards of accommodation and facilities found on them and mirrored by improvements in culinary excellence and service borrowed from a fast-developing hotel sector, were reflected in luxury train travel culture. Trains carried first, second and third-class passengers to and from ports to board steamers making cross-channel and short sea crossings, as well as large ocean-going ships transporting goods and increasing numbers of passengers as Britain's imperial interests expanded on four continents.

By the mid-1800s, railway companies had gradually adopted a process of gentrifying their services, grudgingly acknowledging that premier fare paying passengers offered profitable revenue streams. Although the Atlantic Trade was driven by emigrant traffic, the numbers of prosperous passengers crossing the pond in either direction increased substantially, especially with numbers of wealthy American tourists venturing to Europe after the end of the Civil War. The Prince of Wales endeared himself to American society, having spent most of 1860 in America and Canada where he was described as 'a riotous success' with praise flowing back across the ocean. From the 1880s, the sound of the American accent became progressively familiar. The likes of tycoon W.W. Astor and other American magnates who formed a smart-set of self-made plutocrats could be found in Bertie's notoriously wide circle of social acquaintances and all valuing the connections to be found in Britain. Financiers such as Sir Ernest Cassel and Sir Thomas Lipton of shopkeeper fame became firm members of the future king's royal entourage representing a confluence point in time where wealth, power and social elites merged.

Thus, David Cannadine reminds us, a 'carefully integrated and functionally significant social system began to break down. In London high-society, the aristocratic monopoly was broken, as the new super-rich stormed the citadels of social exclusiveness and flaunted their parvenu wealth with opulent and irresistible vulgarity.' Wealth creation established a nouveaux riche grouping primarily consisting of industrialists and traders who bought country houses, landed estates and, in Scotland particularly, shooting estates. This in turn created a veritable country sports industry, transforming large tracts of upland area as the newly rich queued up in their thousands anxious to participate in a stylish holiday pastime. In time, Victorian railway companies would go out of their way to tap in to this new money-spinning market.

Wealth creation was occurring on both sides of the Atlantic as increasing numbers of prosperous Americans were travelling to Britain and Europe in ever increasing numbers. Harvard educated Oliver Wendell Holmes whose fount of knowledge took him in many directions as a physician, university academic, poet, travel writer and all round polymath noted in 1887:

> 'Our tourists, who are constantly going forward and back between England and America, lose all sense of the special distinctions between the two countries which do not bear on personal convenience. Happy are those who go with unworn, unsatiated sensibilities from the New World to the Old; as happy, it may be, those who come from the Old World to the New, but of that I cannot form a judgement.'

Class membership on either side of the Atlantic was powered by a heady mixture of academia, culture and politics. Wendell Holmes' *One Hundred Days in Europe* bore testament to this fusion; his daily dealings were in the choicest of British and New World company, including fellow countryman Henry James. In the last quarter of the 1800s, the United States was a generator of huge wealth, altering the tourist landscape and demanding better and more comfortable forms of transport. Wealth in time warranted sufficient grounds for many Americans to gain access to London society's upper echelons but many were unaware of the intricacies of circumnavigating the supreme

British institution of snobbery. Excess, luxuriance and snobbery would reach a pinnacle in the Edwardian era but by late Victorian times, wealth became the criterion for admittance and was no longer determined by just land and titles, the traditional patrician barometer.

Harold Perkin concluded that 'for the first time in history, non-landed incomes and wealth had begun to overtake land alone as the main source of economic power.' Given these remarkable changes, it is hardly surprising shipping lines, port authorities, railway companies and travel agents would work hand in glove to create a raft of tourism-related services to attract and retain free-spending first-class passengers in what was set to become a highly competitive market place.

But it was not all plain sailing for the railway revolution. In Britain, with so many providers, the efficiency and quality of rail services varied enormously, with journeys often slow, frustrating many tourist experiences. Wendell Holmes suffered first-hand experience of such matters following an annoying trip south to Oxford from Scotland affecting evening plans. 'We were too late, in consequence of the bad arrangement of the trains, and had to dine by ourselves, as the whole party had gone out to dinner, to which we should have accompanied them had we not been delayed.'

Railways were an intrinsic component of Victorian big business. Messrs Mitchell, Chambers and Crafts in a University of Warwick research paper in 2009 suggest the railway sector amounted to approximately one quarter of all the securities quoted on the London Stock Exchange by the early 1870s. Not only was Britain the workshop to the world, it provided a range of ancillary services such as banking, insurance and other financial services that made capitalism and the Empire tick. With a growing colonial base, Britain's merchant marine provided the means to carry finished goods around the globe and with it transporting a new breed of administrators from the best schools together with a new generation of civil engineers who possessed the intellectual and technical knowledge to build the imperial infrastructure

Big business brought about new management structures to supervise these organisations. As Perkin noted, British companies needed 'managers, engineers, accountants, and lawyers, besides an army of clerks and skilled and unskilled workers' resulting in the 'professionalization of industry' and the 'enormous growth of the salaried middle class which is important a feature of modern society.' Britain's railways possessed new managerial functions in abundance. Railway writer Simon Bradley describes the railways as gradually establishing a 'new class of professional manager' where 'membership was drawn overwhelmingly by promotion or recruitment from among their own staff.'[4] Railway managers contributed much to the solidification of a new professional middle-class strata. By late Victorian times, it was not uncommon for senior managers, particularly from engineering and design spheres, to move from one railway company to another, bringing transferrable skills and new ways of doing things. The railway companies attracted the brightest of minds. The LSWR, for instance, guaranteed £100 per annum for railway student fees at the London School of Economics. Railways offered secure and rewarding career prospects for managerial functions and by the Big Four era, the consolidated railway businesses took the development of talent, training and progression of a professional and managerial class system very seriously. There were those who would not always agree. The railway manager might have been held in great esteem, yet in March 1904, *The Bystander* magazine noted the sufferings of the travelling man as a sign of the times. Their feature correspondent said he had 'a natural respect for railway managers. They represent, as it seems to me, more than any other class of men, that innate conservatism, statuesque impenetrability to ideas, deliberate inability to regard the wants of their customers, which we are accustomed to consider in this country the signs and symbols of the business man. The railway manager is, in fact, the business man - *par excellence*, in excelsis, and, in plain English, through and through. That is why railway travelling in England is so exceedingly uncomfortable.'

Despite these quirks, in the years leading to the Great War managing Britain's disparate railway transport system was to become highly professionalised, forming part of a broader meritocratic industrial world where, as Perkins says, the 'increasing centralization of the British economy, both commerce and manufacturing,' was to be found 'in managerial corporations based in London.' Railway companies with their head-offices based around their London termini, offered prospective careers to educated middle-class young men with the added enticement of the all-important concessionary travel facility. Whilst the railway companies plunged headlong into the development of tourism services and the travel literature market, the reflections and word of mouth tales of their travelling managers was an inspirational source for the growth of promotional material.

Railways may not have invented tourism but their activities had a profound impact on its development, especially on coastal and remote communities where, by mid-Victorian times, the numbers of resorts flourished as a visit to the coast or the countryside moved from an exclusive upper-class recreation activity into a national institution for the ever-expanding ranks of a new bourgeoise keen to match the aristocracy's desires by partaking of the air and waters of a seaside or rural holiday break. It was not just the conveyance of well-to-do passengers but the railway's initial focus on freight activities that allowed in time the fast transit of fresh foods, providing a stimulus for the development of quality hotel accommodation pivotal to the expansion of tourism in the new British destinations of Cornwall, Scotland and the Lake District, although as Wordsworth observed, the consideration of extending the railway to Grasmere was an intrusion.

The journey time on the west coast line from London to Glasgow might have taken more than thirteen hours in the early 1850s; only marginally shorter was the time it would take to reach the English Lakes. Yet railway developments opened the region to tourists, aided by early examples of travel guides such as Sylvan's Pictorial Handbooks. Their Cumbria and the English Lakes publication produced in 1847, grabbed Victorian interest as walking and touring became serious past-times. The newly arrived railway was a regional stimulus increasing the west coast line's popularity; with progressive developments in railway infrastructure, the journey time to the English Lakes was reduced to around nine hours by the turn of the twentieth century. By the 1860s, long-distance railway travel had spread throughout Europe, connecting most of the continent's capital cities. Speed of access and transit transformed the market place, particularly for the articulate and well-off classes keen to engage with Paris and Vienna's centres of culture. Railway companies in Britain and on the continent played pivotal roles in developing destinations, transforming many small locations into thriving tourism places. European maps showed new railway routes representing hitherto unrivalled travel opportunities for the leisured classes.

Railway expansion in Britain opened up new destinations, providing travellers with a bewildering choice of resorts shaping the holiday habits of successive generations. Bournemouth and Brighton grew into towns whilst in the Lake District and the Scottish Highlands, small communities would become key visitor economies by the late 1880s, not only basking in a comfortable resident community but also attracting a similarly affluent tourist customer. Whilst these new upscale destinations had more in keeping with more genteel watering places and spas, they would in time accommodate a mixture of middle, lower-middle and working-class tourists but these destination images were by and large far removed from the Lancashire and Yorkshire coastal seaside holiday resorts that, courtesy of the railways, had developed close to the key industrial centres. By mid-century, the rise of literacy aided social mobility and smoothed the way for middle-class expansion. The Thomas Cook organisation by the 1860s was selling advertising space in their gazette to hoteliers catering for, at the time, a relatively small and privileged market but this was to grow significantly with the expansion of prosperous, professional and well-educated middle-class travellers. Most of Cook's customers were regarded as being serious-minded. This was not restricted just to Britain as the Swiss Alps, the Riviera and Europe's cultural capitals became the places to visit all brought together by adventurous upscale tour operators and railway businesses criss-crossing the continent. In reviewing J.A.R. Pimlott's book, *The Englishman's Holiday,* (Faber and Faber 1947), the *Spectator* magazine's Janet Adam Smith noted that:

> 'Railways, steamboats and nineteenth-century industrial prosperity turned many of the preserves of the rich in to the playgrounds of the many; the smart and wealthy fled from Brighton and Margate to Switzerland, to the Riviera, to Norwegian fjords, to the West Indies - with the pursuing mob of organised tourists barely more than a stage behind.'

Not only did railway companies transport prosperous passengers throughout a multitude of competing routes, they quite naturally involved themselves with places to stay, building some of the finest hotel accommodation of the day. Railways, therefore, held a key role in the commercialisation of leisure patterns during the last quarter of the Victorian age.

European railway companies benefited immensely from relatively calm times; the continent to a large extent remained free of significant conflict for the best part of sixty years, facilitating a steady expansion of tourism and travel services. The good old days of the traditional Grand Tour might have been over, but a new era of railway expresses would take hold, opening up Europe to a new form of holiday travel. The French *Belle Époque* prompted a rapid development of the country's railway system. By the second half of the 1800s, Britain's increased numbers of leisured classes loved to travel; France benefited enormously as Britain's close neighbour.

Modern-minded Victorians had thrown off the shackles of isolationism imposed by the Napoleonic wars as the new railway transport systems across Europe provided the opportunity for unrestricted exploration, ably supported by the nimble and sprightly numbers of railway company-owned steamers and in time a growth in railway-owned tourist accommodation. They had their paws on many commercial activities in the future but in the initial stages, they were slow to retain their best clients' patronage, particularly as industrialisation brought about a need for a new kind of holiday. The railways provided the means for the middle-classes initially to escape their home and working environments and eventually for large numbers of the working-class as well. Perkin describes the process thus; 'Together, industrialism and the railways were to begin that redistribution of leisure which has become much more far-reaching in its equalitarianism than the redistribution of wealth or income.'

Over a twenty-five-year period of the mid-Victorian era, large tracts of Britain were given over to railway construction. Three separate mainline railway routes between England and Scotland were built, opening up the central belt of the country as an industrial heartland and also as a tourist destination. The scale of these massive endeavours are still with us, now linking the main Scottish cities of Glasgow and Edinburgh with long-distance trains to and from London. Two principal routes were constructed along east and west corridors. The east route referred to as the East Coast Main Line (ECML) and the west route as the West Coast Main Line (WCML). A third, lesser-used line which ran up the centre of the country was completed by the third quarter of the 1800s. Currently, much of the fascination associated with travelling on these routes regrettably has gone as high-speed, electric and, sometimes heavily congested trains run regularly between the cities on the hour.

Whilst the glamour may have disappeared, fast access was never far from the pre-grouping company managements' thinking in the later years of Victoria's reign. David Wragg reminds us, 'With three groups of companies competing for the valuable Anglo-Scottish passenger traffic, it was inevitable that sooner or later speed would become an important element.' Yet speedier train development on

Anglo-Scottish routes was generally hampered until improvements in signalling methods and adequate braking systems on steam locomotives and carriages were brought in – all necessary for safe operation at higher speeds. Continuous vacuum braking on east coast trains was introduced in 1881, providing an opportunity for railway showmanship and the 'Races to the North' speed war contests. Although not creating immediate extra travelling traffic, by the late 1890s the initiatives had generated both tangible gains in schedules and increased public awareness. This, combined with the railway companies' newly found general promotion of tourism, would ensure that Scotland was portrayed as a country of romance and picturesque beauty so that it became a much in vogue destination as tartan themed tours attracted a steady stream of wealthy visitors from Britain, the Americas and the continent of Europe. Scottish historian Eric Simpson observed in his 2017 book *Hail Caledonia: The Lure of the Highlands and Islands* (Amberley, 2017) that 'Queen Victoria's annual pilgrimages to the Highlands were a potent factor in turning the Highlands into a playground for the rich.' Her passion for Scotland's natural heritage and a traditional form of upscale leisure relaxation based on the region's fishing, shooting and walking resources in time created a sporting estates industry which was a timely stimulus for the country's emergent national tourism business. Ultimately, by the end of Victoria's long reign, Scotland was firmly entrenched on the tourism map as Holyrood Palace in Edinburgh and her Balmoral summer residence together with the surrounding Deeside region became the focus of tourist interest in royalty.

But in 1860, better ways to travel had still to arrive in Britain and Europe. Comfortable railway travel was still in its infancy as railway carriages, even for first-class passengers, were rather crude and uncomfortable. David Wragg noted that 'enlightened self-interest that would have improved facilities to enhance the appeal of railway travel was sadly lacking'. Carriages were hardly spacious; it would take the next couple of decades before the average coach length slowly increased. Even travelling on the *Special Scotch Express* was a pretty grim experience for first-class passengers. Carriages might have had glass windows and seat cushions, but they were dimly lit, had no heating, possessed no corridor connections and no lavatories.

It was one of those strange paradoxes of Victorian life that four separate forms of illumination – candles, oil lit lamps, gas lamps and electric lighting – would sit comfortably alongside each other as railway carriage lighting technologies for the next thirty years. The exteriors of the first-class Pullman carriages were lit by bronze kerosene lamps, but gas represented a clean technology, becoming a standard for railway carriage lighting in later Victorian times before eventually being replaced by improvements in electric lighting. Carriage heating was a problem for passengers especially travelling in winter. Wooden railway carriages let in the cold as they aged. Steam heating took time to catch on, so the renting or the owning of a foot-warmer or the railway rug, initially a first-class privilege only, was a phenomenon lasting well into the turn of the new century.

The British position mirrored Europe at the time. French train travel, even first-class, was not totally endorsed by American visitors. Mark Twain's reflections on the tedium of a long train trip through France was only made bearable 'because all the scenes and experiences were new and strange'. Whilst comfortable, Twain was less than impressed with French railway carriages;

'The cars are built in compartments that hold eight persons each. Each compartment is partially subdivided, and so there are two tolerably distinct parties of four in it. Each face the other four. The seats and backs are thickly padded and cushioned and are very comfortable; you can smoke, if you wish; there are no bothersome peddlers; you are saved the infliction of a multitude of disagreeable fellow-passengers. So far, so well. But then the conductor locks you in when the train starts; there is no water to drink, in the car; there is no heating apparatus for night travel; if a drunken rowdy should get in, you could not remove a matter of twenty seats from him, or enter another car; but above all, if you are worn out and must sleep, you must sit up and do it in naps, with cramped legs and in a torturing misery that leaves you withered and lifeless the next day - for behold they have not that culmination of all charity and human kindness, a sleeping car, in all France. I prefer the American system. It has no so many grievous "discrepancies".'

By the early 1870s, events were to change in Britain courtesy of the Midland Railway, under the expert guidance of their long-term general manager, James Allport, who had spent a year in the United States observing the operation of American railroads at close quarters. In addition, he had studied the business model of George Pullman, whose company was responsible for transferring the best elements of hotels to rails with unrivalled food quality and impeccable service delivery. The Midland thus practically invented British luxury train travel by introducing Pullman carriages, polished to gleaming perfection, on many of their north-bound services. Allport's Midland progresses together with the introduction of bogie carriages helped create new standards, making the experience of railway travel pleasant and providing the basis for a modern industry to evolve.

In a review of his life some ninety years later and conducted in the mire of Beeching's swamp, Allport was recalled by the *Birmingham Post* in 1963 as a 'Doughty Champion of Rail Development' displaying 'Great Astuteness and Forcefulness'. In March 1872, the company startled the railway world by laying the foundations of a predominantly two class railway system – first and third-class – and the beginnings of a marketing strategy in which customer perception viewed the company as a progressive and superior railway operation. Two years later, on 7 October 1874, the Midland once again threw a spanner into the works by announcing its intention to reduce first-class fares which would take effect from New Year's Day 1875.

The ramifications of these actions reverberated in every railway board-room across the country especially at Euston and King's Cross headquarters. The Midland came under intense pressure, especially from LNWR and GNR, not to reduce fares but the company stood firm. As Pimlott drolly noted, 'This was no leap in the dark but a well-considered change of policy, based on the realization that the three-class system was uneconomical and that larger returns were to be derived from stimulating than discouraging third-class travel.' Whilst the Midland Railway was a relative latecomer to developing its network, its actions were profound. By the mid-decade, the company had not only completed its London to Manchester and Birmingham to Bristol links but similarly its longer tortuous route through the centre of the country to the north of England and Scotland via Settle and Carlisle. The company's Scottish route admitted third-class passengers, greatly assisting revenue streams, whilst the east coast companies perpetuated a first-class service only operation until 1887, based on rigid four and six-wheeler carriage stock seldom fully utilised. In addition, the Midland's first-class fares were the cheapest on offer between London and Scotland. Such initiatives helped to increase overall travelling public mobility. By the end of the Victorian era, Pimlott observed, 'Britain, always famous for its express services, also stood out for the excellence though not the cheapness of the facilities which were provided for third-class passengers.' Not everyone amongst the new middle-classes could afford to travel first-class, especially when families were involved. A country rector wrote in October 1883 to the *Standard* in response to a 'Pastures New' editorial. He wrote:

> 'It hits the right nail on the head, for it not only indicates a new and delightful form of taking holiday rest for many a well-to-do family wearied with gaieties of the London season, but what is far more important, it suggests the best, and in some the only, holiday for the families of a largely increasing class – the poor gentry and the less wealthy traders. How many thousands there are of struggling clergy, doctors, and other professional men, who, when the holiday season begins, are at their wit's end what to do. The faces of the six or eight children show to plainly the need of fresh air;'

Aware that its intended northern routes could not compete on speed as they were longer and slower, the Midland in 1874 pioneered the notion of comfortable and plush travel and a new deluxe variation based on American styled luxury Pullman mainline trains. Three convertible sleeping cars based on Pullman's US 1865 dual purpose patent where beds could be rearranged with day-time seating together with other carriages were flat packed, shipped and assembled at Derby by the Midland Railway. This brought a hitherto unknown level of passenger comfort as well as the first examples of coach heating with hot-water pipes located beneath the carriage floor on its services from London to the north of England. Based on the American travelling model, the fold down bed sectioned off by curtains took some getting used to by less adventurous Victorian passengers.

Such developments engendered considerable columns of press reporting, including the idea of paying Pullman a supplement fee for travelling on their vehicles. US travellers on the other hand were used to quality dining and sleeping accommodation on long trans-continental journeys. Britain was an obvious target for Pullman as British railway companies became increasingly aware of passenger demands for similar facilities on longer-distance runs. Pullman's efforts eventually bore fruit but not before other mainline British railway companies responded, developing their own luxury coaches with quality facilities such as superior seating, on-board catering, fine-dining restaurants, sleeping accommodation and at the end of the journey; the railway hotel. And coupled to this was the notion of the 'Pullman Idea' whereby luxury travel was defined above the ordinary first-class specification at the time.

So British land-based luxury travel may be charted from 1874 with Midland's introduction of US designed Pullman carriages whose livery and décor was clearly identifiable. Two years later, its Pullman drawing-room cars would be included on the third Scottish route between St. Pancras and Scotland with expresses connecting via the North British Railway (NBR) Waverley route to Edinburgh and Glasgow by the Glasgow & South Western Railway (GSWR) line. Business was brisk, especially in early August for the start of 'The Glorious Twelfth' shooting season when newly-rich tourist traffic would reach its peak, especially to the Scottish Highlands made fashionable by royal and landed gentry patronage.

Whilst improved facilities were noticeable, the practicable problems of 'convenience' still had to be addressed. On-board toilets before 1880 were in little evidence, although the use of chamber pots was included with most sleeping cars on long-distance trains from the mid-1870s. By 1882, lavatories were installed on some GNR expresses but the clear majority of carriages at the time were of the non-bogie and non-corridor type rendering practical problems for the installation of lavatories on what was predominantly either four or six-wheeled short length stock. But the gradual introduction of longer bogie carriages provided the necessary space to incorporate lavatories, although technology had to catch up as Victorian engineers grappled with the issues of developing a design for flushing water closets to efficiently remove bodily waste and the removal of dangerous sewer gases. Prior to this, various entrepreneurs came up with a variety of means for both men and women to employ when the necessity to relieve oneself became paramount. As the railway network expanded, so too did the numbers of passengers. Such convenience contraptions were almost respectable and readily available through department-store and mail order newspaper advertising. The initial carriage lavatories were rather crude affairs and certainly not available universally as first-class passengers were the only benefiting travellers. Notwithstanding, by the mid-1880s, providing carriage lavatories, with or without corridor access was a common feature of express train travel.

The problems of fresh water supplies and personal hygiene correspondingly inhibited the development of specialist facilities for cooking and the serving of food on board trains; the first recording of railway food produced in carriage galleys came in the late 1870s. Progress in science had established the connection between unsanitary conditions, disease and the eating of food but by the mid-1880s many of the problems associated with the cooking of food for greater numbers of people had been overcome. In 1878, the GNR trialled the first dining car formations on its London to Doncaster route. The birth of proper British railway dining occurred on 1 November 1879, when an imported Pullman dining car was launched on GNR's London to Leeds service. The Pullman car *Prince of Wales* came with a fully functional kitchen located at one end of the carriage where meat, fish, puddings and pre-prepared food was cooked over an open fire. The idea was a success and progressively, dining or restaurant cars were routinely introduced on long-distance routes for first-class passengers removing the necessity of stopping at appointed stations (despite their often-grand settings) for meal breaks where the quality of food and staff engagement could never be guaranteed. Bradley summarised the position:

> 'These surroundings often belied the brusque exchanges that occurred in railway refreshment rooms, especially those of the Swindon type that depended for custom on brief passenger stops. The flurries at Swindon were far from unique. Passengers on the London & Birmingham Railway were likewise allowed just ten minutes at its midway stop at Wolverton in Buckinghamshire, and periods of five to ten minutes are described as the general rule in *The Railway Traveller's Handy Book*.'

Even on the new prestigious *Special Scotch Express* service, passengers were presented with a half-hour lunch stop at York. On other Anglo-Scottish stops such as Normanton and Preston, stops could be even shorter. On the west coast route, passengers on the morning and afternoon services were given just twenty minutes for a meal break and expected to consume a full three-course meal served in the station's dining rooms.

Despite this state of affairs, Mark Twain on his 1867 European tour found the French experience of the railway refreshment stop to take food and drink much to his taste. He concluded:

> 'But the happiest regulation in French railway government, is - thirty minutes to dinner! No five-minute boltings of flabby rolls, muddy coffee, questionable eggs, gutta-percha beef, and pies whose conception and execution are a dark and bloody mystery to all save the cook that created them! No; we sat calmly down - it was in old Dijon, which is so easy to spell and so impossible to pronounce, except when you civilize it and call it Demijohn - and poured out rich Burgundian wines and munched calmly through a long table d'hote bill of fare, snail-patties, delicious fruits and all, then paid the trifle it cost and stepped happily aboard the train again, without once cursing the railroad company. A rare experience, and one to be treasured forever.'

Twain would have to wait until September 1872 for his first British boat train encounter (in time, boat trains provided some of the most prestigious of services) travelling to London after docking in Liverpool. It is said he took the journey in great humour finding fellow passengers reading his book *The Innocents Abroad.* Twain does not record his experiences of the London bound train but a refreshment stop – and the necessity to have relieved himself – is likely to have occurred.

The taking of food onto trains in Britain to provide sustenance on long and even comparatively short journeys is a feature of railway travel that has never left us – witness our present coffee retail culture for instance. Food parcels or baskets were first provided by enterprising suppliers such as caterers Spiers and Pond in 1871 but like station food, the quality of fare they and other providers offered was open to question. Over time, driven by customer exasperation, the quality of food baskets did improve but by the turn of the twentieth century, the basket trade was on the decline due to better quality fare offered by railway companies in their own restaurant and buffet cars. Whilst no longer a feature of modern western life, the concept of the food basket is not entirely lost within Russia's great expanses. Christian Wolmar reports in his blog that it is still a feature of travelling on the Trans-Siberian – one of the great rail enthusiast bucket lists of our time – where delicious bread and cheese can be bought at well-advertised station stops.

The first sleeping cars in Britain were also trialled on both the ECML and WCML routes but they were initially comparatively primitive non-bogie types. In 1873, the NBR introduced the first form of specialist carriage on-board sleeping arrangements whilst in the same year, a couple of LNWR west coast sleepers made an appearance. They were six-wheeled affairs built with two compartments with just one bed in each and two separate seats split in the middle of the coach by a water closet and lavatory which could be accessed from both compartments.

In 1874, the Midland Railway went one step further by offering a Pullman bogie sleeper on its then unfinished Anglo-Scottish route finishing at Bradford. The ECML consortium incorporated sleeping car trains from the late 1870s, experimenting with less lavish Pullman sleeping cars but these proved to be unpopular and were transferred to the Highland Railway in 1885, where they were used on Scottish night trains for many years. Small four and six wheeled stock stifled coach development until larger bogie coaches became commonplace. Sleeping and restaurant cars were thus slow to evolve, as the comparatively small space and layout of short wheeled based carriages meant they were not profitable revenue streams for railways, rendering them only attractive on the longer ECML and WCML routes. In 1878 and 1881, two types of early bogie sleeping cars appeared with separate compartments containing berths with lavatory access by side corridors. Whilst Pullman carved out its distinctive niche in the US and Canada, its style of sleeping cars based on a saloon layout with curtains to provide a level of privacy to each berth never caught on in Britain. As railway writer Brian Haresnape observed in 1987 in his *Pullman: Travelling in Style*:

> 'These required passengers to undress whilst on the bed - a complicated manoeuvre for Victorian ladies complete with bustled skirt and tight corsets! The British public, at least those of the wealthier class who could afford to pay for the privacy of a bed on the train, took even more kindly to the idea of having separate compartments to sleep in, linked by a side-corridor.'

Despite a promising start with the Midland, progress for the Pullman Company was slow but by the end of the Victorian period, the organisation had managed to create strong business relationships with a limited number of middle-distance route pre-grouping railway companies. *The Railway Magazine* of September 1897 felt that the Midland Railway 'was the pioneer in what may be called the luxury of travel' laying down ground rules which other companies duly copied resulting in a position by the end of the 1800s where 'drawing room, sleeping, and dining and refreshment cars have become almost general in the English express services.' The Midland knew it could never provide the fastest routes to the north of England and Scotland but acknowledged developing a competitive positioning based on superior comfort and service providing passengers with the most relaxed of travelling experiences would serve it interests well.

The tail end of the Victorian era saw significant advances in rail travel, especially in the areas of locomotive development, providing speedier services especially on the Anglo-Scottish routes. Railway companies paid far greater attention to their customers leading to noteworthy

Clerestory carriage stock still dominated prestige Anglo-Scottish expresses but by 1898, the east coast route was powered by the first 4-4-2 locomotives. GNR's No 990 entered service in May of that year with fellow locomotive classmates providing a service and lasting well into the mid-1930s. (John Scott-Morgan Collection)

improvements to passenger travel experiences. The *Illustrated Sporting and Dramatic News* in June 1901 chimed the right notes:

> 'The development of modes of travel is a most interesting subject, and when we remember that coaching had a short life only, and that the railway is not much more than sixty years old, the facilities we now have for getting about are truly wonderful. Railway travelling has been brought to a pitch of comfort and perfection which could not have been dreamed of half a century ago by the most imaginative person.'

Whilst passenger ships had developed separate social spaces determined by class, it was different on British railway trains where multiple compartment coaches were the norm. Some express trains would include exclusive first-class sections whilst other services might include a mix of first and third-class compartments in the same carriage but with an increasing level of freedom to move around the train was reached by vestibule connections. Social spaces were open to all and not restricted by gender as on Atlantic Ferry steamships.

Notable developments in British railway coach design across all carriage classes took place, resulting in plusher stock incorporating lavatories, electric lighting and heating in sharp contrast to the rather basic facilities passengers had to endure in previous years. The last quarter of the Victorian era was a period of innovation as railway companies trialled new niche-market ideas, establishing a true luxury product specification and placing it firmly on the passenger agenda by mirroring similar developments that were taking place on ocean liners. First-class carriage design moved progressively from the wealthy drawing room décor characterised by stuffy and sumptuous upholstery to a more simplistic style emphasising comfort. Part of this trend was a rejection of Pullman's open plan cars and the progressive adoption of gangway and corridor connected compartment coaches. As railway writer R.W. Kidner observed of the period, 'The British loved their cramped compartment carriages; the openness of a Pullman took time to get used to'.[5] Adrian Ross, writing in *The Tatler* in 1905, made the pronouncement:

> 'The compartment system grew up in England from the unsociable disposition of the Englishman, or rather his readiness to be sociable merely in a small circle of friends and relations.

This longing for privacy, selfish as it may be and ungracious as it often appears, is not to be condemned without reserve. The isolation of the Englishman, his self-reliance and self-dependence in the past, have helped to make the Empire great and generally disliked. The mental conception of the Briton formed by continental Europe was that of a traveller swathed in a rug, with a travelling cap drawn down over his brows, and his bags, gun cases, wraps, and general property disposed on all the seats of the compartment. He would show his ticket when desired by a duly-accredited official; his passport was in order, his purse well filled, and he would even condescend to move one or two minor packages to accommodate another passenger, Still, he resented intrusion as an injury and an insult, and took refuge behind the massive sheet of *The Times* in a glacial silence. The first-class compartment was built, if not designed, for such a man, and if he had nothing amiable, he had much that was at once respectable and formidable.'

But in the early years of the twentieth century Ross detected a slacking of the old-school reserve noting:

'But we have changed all that, or most of it. The corridor carriage and the Pullman car, the growing hugeness of the ocean steamer, have helped to melt the lonely iceberg of British exclusiveness. The disappearance of the second class is another striking feature of the times.'

Yet it was the first-class compartment environment that provided ample opportunity for passengers to declare their status in life and having luggage that had many travel labels attached to it was one such statement. Edwardian traveller and essayist Max Beerbohm once wrote, 'Travelling in a compartment, with my hat-box beside me, I enjoyed the silent interest which my labels aroused in fellow-passengers.' Classic one-upmanship perhaps but the idea of the compartment hung around for a long time. The South West Trains franchise was still providing part first-class compartment carriages for the benefit of regular commuters on their Waterloo to Weymouth service until the early Noughties. Railway companies were keen to ensure their premium coaches looked the part, reflecting the thoroughly modern businesses they were. The inclusion of what now would be described as a company logo incorporating intricate heraldry designs featuring the towns and cities within their territorial routes became common features.

Larger corridor coaches allowed passengers the freedom to move around the train, meeting passenger demands for easier lavatory access which was totally restricted by older non-corridor stock. The old system of long-distance trains halting for refreshment stops generally hindered the train lavatory development. With regular planned stops at fixed intervals, railway companies saw little need to introduce such facilities to carriages when passengers could relieve themselves at stations. But this approach was outdated and by the 1890s, the technology employed in water closets had been refined. Thomas Crapper patented his valve-and-siphon design in 1891, enabling railway companies to start building water storage tanks in carriages. Thus, lavatory facilities became a more common feature available to all passengers, although cleanliness was questionable as well as the proverbial problems of limited water supplies running out.

Electric coach lighting technology had been available since the early 1870s but its adoption, like gas lighting, by railway companies had been slow. Electric lighting was pioneered by the LBSCR in their 1881 Pullman cars, yet its uptake was sporadic, hindered by the poor quality of light they provided. It was the best part of twenty-five years or so before it became firmly established in coach design. Not until new technologies arrived in 1894, with dynamos attached to bogey wheels charging batteries supplying electricity for carriage lighting, did the pace of inclusion improve but with so many pre-grouping railway companies involved in sourcing and building their own carriages, adoption was not rapid. Competition excelled; by the end of the Edwardian era, there were many companies designing electric lighting for railway coaches. Similarly, advancements in gas lighting technology did not change the carriage experience overnight. It was not until the 1890s that carriage gas lighting became the dominant technology, replacing lighting from oil lamps. In time the quality of electric lighting improved significantly with its usage across all classes of railway carriage. Gas lighting, like oil lighting, in railway coaches was eventually consigned to history but gas technology hung around for some time as even in the early 1900s, lighting technology benefited from the latest industrial development. The last gas-lit coach, though, was not withdrawn from Southern lines until 1938, whilst Haresnape reports that a few gas-lit carriages were still running in British Railways days.

Likewise, the use of clerestory coaches by railway companies, where the roof was raised in the centre of the carriage to provide additional natural light through small windows, progressively waned as they were replaced by elliptical shaped roofs and larger windows. Effective carriage lighting within individual carriage compartments provided the social space for railway companies to expand their advertising activity. In time the promotional platforms of station waiting rooms, concourses and bridges were recognised as revenue earners.

Progressive advancements in carriage technology enabled railway coaches to become mobile hotels on wheels providing refreshments and dining, together with better sleeping arrangements. There was a cost to carriage improvement, together with an increase in the weight of trains that did not necessarily increase the numbers of passengers being carried. Higher fares could be charged for first-class carriages, but the Victorian era likewise saw significant competition between different operators, often linking the same cities. Early Victorian laissez-faire attitudes to early railway development inevitably led to duplication of routes and a position described by Mitchell, Chambers and Crafts as 'everyone agrees with (P.J.) Cain that there was "'waste and inefficiency' on the British railway system" but when, how much, and how far it was management's fault has been obscure.'

Given the disconnected nature of the railway network, it is reasonable to suggest such piecemeal investment inhibited the climate for developing luxury travel products, leading inevitably to parochialism amongst individual railway companies and the absence of a more coordinated approach to planning passenger travel services. Advances in carriage development paved the way to new, more efficient and powerful locomotives but capital investment was required to finance locomotive technologies. Railway company managements were under no illusion that such investments were essential to create new and efficient generations of engines necessary to haul heavy passenger trains.

Not only were trains getting heavier, they were getting longer as more passengers wished to travel. Improvements in carriage design came about, mirroring the advances in ship building technology where first-class customers were offered a superior quality of passage. From 1876, on the longer Anglo-Scottish routes,

HOTELS ON WHEELS.

I.—BY THE MIDLAND RAILWAY.

The late lamented General Wade, despite his admirable efforts in the far north, immortalised in unforgettable doggerel, did not make Scotland

INTERIOR OF A FIRST-CLASS DINING-CARRIAGE, SHOWING PORTION OF SALOON WITH SMOKING-ROOM, ETC.

accessible with such ease as the modern traveller demands. The railroad put Macadam in the shade, and for forty or fifty years we have been content to rush northwards in express trains, on which the greatest advance has been made in the matter of speed. Yet speed has its limits in satisfying the travelling public. It seems a very remarkable thing that, with all our progress on the railways, half a century should have been allowed to elapse before journeys lasting from ten to twelve hours should have to be undertaken under the conditions that have been allowed to prevail. One need not be a sybarite to think it hardly good enough to make such journeys in the narrow compartment of a carriage which stops only a few minutes at distant stations, and which affords room for six or seven people aside, unable, at the worst, to do more than sit bolt upright, and at the best to stretch oneself on the uncomfortable ledge afforded by the cushioned seat. Everything comes to the man who can wait, and to such of us who have been permitted to wait until this year of grace the old order has given place to a revolution in third-class travelling, which consists in being able to pass the journey with as much comfort as if we were passing the day in a first-class hotel.

The Midland Railway Company has started well on the race, as it has invariably done in every new development of railway business. It was the Midland Company that led the way in recognising the importance of the third-class passenger by allowing him to travel by all trains, and by giving him a dining-car it has again shown its belief in

the third-class client. The new afternoon Scotch service, running between London and Glasgow, is undertaken in a corridor-train, built on the principle long familiar to Americans, and hitherto sorely missed by the ubiquitous Yankee who cares to visit the old country. Take two 60 ft. long carriages, one first class and the other third class. Both are 8 ft. wide, 6 ft. high at the doorway, and furnished with a clerestory roof 8 ft. 6 in. high, with lights and ventilators on each side, while they are mounted on two six-wheel bogies with steel under-frames, oak body frames, and panelling of Honduras mahogany. Connect the two carriages with a flexible gangway, and you have the main principle of the corridor-train. Let us make a journey from end to end.

In the third-class carriage abstract all the ordinary partitions except two, and you get three compartments of varying size. That farthest from the flexible gangway forms a smoking-room, seated for thirteen persons. It leads into a much larger compartment, which is the dining-saloon proper, accommodating thirty persons. In both these compartments the seats are placed transversely nearest the windows and divided by a passage, on one side of which there is room for two passengers and on the other for one. Between every two seats, and occupying the place of the door in the ordinary carriage, a small table is placed, hinged to the vehicle on one side and supported by a leg on the other, the whole being removable at will.

Passing from the dining-saloon, you enter a tiny compartment, fitted up as a pantry, with cupboards for glass, table linen, provisions, and wine, and it also has a boiler, hot-plate for keeping dishes warm, a grill for chops and steaks, and a refrigerator. It leads out to the narrow flexible gangway, and that, again, into a compact and fully equipped kitchen, in which stands a large cooking range and boiler, heated by compressed oil gas, another refrigerator, and a carving table. This is the domain of the *chef*, who is able to turn out a dinner for sixty persons.

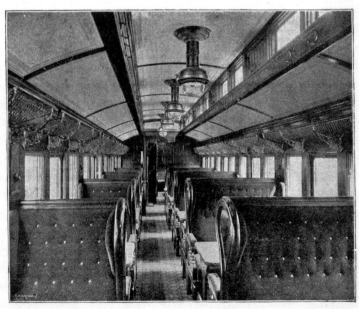

THE THIRD-CLASS INTERIOR.

Still proceeding towards the first-class carriage, you pass through a pantry very similar to that in the third, except that it has a sink for washing up, then to the dining-saloon, and, last of all, to the smoking compartment. The main difference between the two classes is that the first has only one seat on each side of the gangway, and is upholstered with crimson morocco, while the third is upholstered with crimson plush rep.. When it is stated that each carriage has two separate lavatories, a luggage compartment, electric bells to ring up the waiters, and hot-water pipes, it will be seen that the new corridor-trains are practically hotels on wheels.

We start from London at half-past one in the afternoon, paying the same fare as by ordinary train, all food, of course, being extra. During the next hour, as we whirl past the Welsh Harp, "which lies 'Endon way," St. Albans (the ancient Verulam), Bedford, and Kettering, we may

A THIRD-CLASS DINING-CAR.

lunch luxuriously, first class for half-a-crown, third class for two shillings, or à la carte at buffet prices, as per daily bill of fare. Teas (from sixpence) are served from half-past four until six, during which time Nottingham, Sheffield, and many other towns are left behind.

On leaving Hellifield, at which we may shed some of our fellow-travellers for Manchester, Liverpool, and the district, dinner is served— first class, three shillings and sixpence, and third class half-a-crown, or à la carte, as at luncheon. The service is excellent, as well it may be under the direction of so experienced a hand as Mr. W. Towle, manager of the Midland hotels. The scenery after this part of the line is specially lovely, while darkness hides the hideousness of that part of the journey where the train rushes through a forest of chimneys.

After dinner, one, perhaps, has retired to the smoking-room for a pipe and an evening newspaper, not a whit wearied by the journey. Then, in the darkness, between ten and eleven, myriads of lights are flashed past in quick succession, and the train slackens speed. "Do we sleep, do we dream, or are visions about?" for here we glide into St. Enoch Station, Glasgow, before we know exactly where we are. The journey is done by a quarter to eleven, and we feel as if it were but an hour since we left St. Pancras in the full glare of daylight. We may feel puzzled—like Mr. William Nye at this sudden transportation from the Thames to the Clyde, but we share none of his doubts about civilisation. Here, at least, it is *not* a failure.

Next week the dining-car service of the London and North-Western Railway will be dealt with.

The 1890s saw significant strides in express train carriage development with improved comfort and passenger facilities ensuring longer rail journeys could be enjoyed rather than endured. *The Sketch* editorial highlighted closer working relationships between railway operators and new-style popular weekly publications providing the significant numbers of affluent readers the railway companies wished to attract. (Illustrated London News Ltd/Mary Evans)

the Midland Railway adopted similar approaches to the White Star shipping line's ocean steamer operations by making their carriages more luxurious than their competitors, based on inclusive first and improved third-class passenger designations. Such initiatives and the running of crack express trains to Scotland essentially made Midland its name.

On 20 October 1883, the Midland Railway announced that they were purchasing their Pullman drawing room cars running on the mainline from London. The cars were to come into the railway's possession on 1 November as the Midland gave instructions to conductors to leave the service of the Pullman Company. *The Globe* reported on the acquisition: 'A scheme is under consideration, whereby these cars will be used as first-class carriages without any extra charge'. The crux of the matter was to maximise passenger revenues as all first-class passengers would travel on the Pullman cars, leaving the company free to remove its existing first-class carriages which were run half empty. The public did not have to wait long for Midland's Board of Directors to sanction the proposal and in the process upping the ante in their commercial frays with LNWR (the Euston based company had recently introduced twin saloon carriages) by running its Pullman day cars on rail journeys between St. Pancras, Manchester, Liverpool, Glasgow and Edinburgh but priced as ordinary first-class fares. The *London Standard* considered the move to be radical 'with the other great companies running north' contributing to the bold business decision. As the *London Standard* commented, the decision 'will be welcome news to many travellers' whilst concluding:

> 'As a step in advance, it is almost as revolutionary as the abolition of the old second-class carriages, which was decreed by this company some years ago, and may be regarded as a gradual approximation of the English railway system to that in vogue on the other side of the Atlantic.'

The move was equally applauded by the regional newspapers found on Midland's routes. The *Liverpool Mercury* described the company's initiative thus:

> 'The thousands of travellers who yearly patronise the Midland Railway system owe a deep debt of gratitude to the directors, who, from time to time, have been the pioneers in schemes of comfort and improvements in their working system which have gone far to make railway locomotion pleasant and even luxurious.'

In 1888, Midland's contracts with the Pullman Company ended with the company buying the other existing Pullman luxury coaching stock with its unique décor and distinctive use of materials. These carriages ran on their Anglo-Scottish services for some time thereafter. The GSWR which ran the Glasgow portion of the Midland route from Carlisle advertised day and night Pullman provision to services between London and Glasgow in 1881. However, the Midland Railway, like other railway managements, started to look at their own resources by developing in-house solutions, making its Anglo-Scottish services even more relaxed.

These initiatives proved highly successful, providing customers with real value for money as the Clayton designed stock offered a degree of comfort not seen elsewhere in the country. In time, Midland and GSWR would develop their own quality joint stock carriages for the Glasgow route which would last until after grouping days. Some companies like the GWR were slower to react to the opportunities of luxury travel services; the first restaurant cars did not appear on Great Western metals until 1890 and on the company's routes to Cornwall until 1899 but once the nettle had been grasped, they were quick to adapt as modern pioneers of sophisticated tourism travel. New stock in the mid-1890s was well received. A *St. James's Gazette* correspondent wrote, 'The new corridor coaches on the Great Western Railway are now warmed in a rational manner and constitute the most luxurious travelling to be had for the money in the world.' By the turn of the century, longer bogie restaurant cars became the norm on most long-distance routes. Despite undoubted British advances, America was still ahead of the game as in 1883, Pullman had introduced buffet cars to provide light meals and snacks in carriages when a dining car was closed. Similarly, built-in buffet areas began to appear in parlour cars on other railroads. As the distances covered by US railroads was considerably longer, these types of refreshment facilities were designed as complementary services and never intended to replace the dining car.

By the 1890s, Britain's railway companies developed a form of home-grown sleeping carriage possessing little in common with American and continental formats. These sleeping cars were first-class-only services, built to a specification and layout including small compartments known as berths running off one side of a corridor running the entire length of the carriage with standard corridor connections between the coaches. This allowed passengers to move around the train at ease, enjoying dining and lounge area services provided by railway operators before retiring.

The east coast consortium, together with the GWR, introduced these new styles of sleeping cars with traverse sleeping compartments. In other words, passengers slept perpendicular or crosswise to the direction of train travel, this layout innovation remaining the norm ever since. Sleeping cars were targeted at affluent travellers, especially business customers making the best use of time by travelling at night. When looking at luxury rail travel, it is important to consider the totality of marketing as a business concept and how it applied to Britain's pre-grouping railway companies. Whilst concepts such as margins and perishability were yet to enter management speak, ideas surrounding the modern marketing process had gained much ground within commercial life by the end of the nineteenth century. In terms of railway development discussed thus far, much has centred around the physical components or the commodity nature of the railway operation, routes, locomotives, carriages and the strong corpus of railway companies providing competitive services to outdo their rivals often over rails that were effectively duplicated. These elements relate to the core railway product and its basic passenger travel qualities of speed, safety, comfort and convenience.

Yet the railway product is more complex, composed of outer layers comprising bundles of ancillary services making up a complete product incorporating ticket sales, waiting facilities, on-board provision and end of journey services. Within this bundle, a travelling class specification or quality threshold exists whereby a superior service defined by enhancements to seat comfort, more leg room and space, improved surroundings, reduced numbers of fellow travellers and access to additional train services is provided, based on the passenger/customers' ability to pay. Across this it could be argued that a third dimension to the product exists, based on hospitality whereby catering and accommodation services may be included in the ticket price or purchased separately at the point of sale. These components historically made travelling by rail, rather than other transport modes, more amenable and less stressful. Such arrangements are now commonplace across all forms of transport.

The GNR's 1851 royal coaches laid down an initial format of greater sophistication with the creation of great splendour approved for royal transit. Three coaches of a similar design base were built by the company, with the Queen's saloon carriage the most luxurious. Writer David Duff says:

'The mouldings were of gilt, the doors bore the royal arms, and over each was a gilt crown. At one end was a couch, and at the other a withdrawing-room, with full length mirror and washstand etc. While the carriage of the Queen was lined with "the richest white brocaded Indian silk", the other two had to be content with "plain drab brocaded Indian silk". All windows were counter-balanced with weights, allowing finger-tip control.'

Despite advances for monarchs, rail travel in Britain and Europe by 1860 was still boring, slow and uncomfortable. Mark Twain crossing France was underwhelmed by the railway experience:

> 'We are not infatuated with these French railway cars, though. We took first class passage, not because we wished to attract attention by doing a thing which is uncommon in Europe, but because we could make our journey quicker by so doing. It is hard to make railroading pleasant, in any country. It is too tedious.'

Progressive engineering and technological achievements would eventually impact, making rail travel across Britain and the continent considerably easier, safer and more enjoyable during the last third of Victoria's reign. In the 1880s, signalling systems in Britain were improved by the introduction of a system of tokens or tablets connected by electrical circuits for sections of track controlled by a signal. A new token to enter a new track section could only be issued once the previous token for the track already passed on was surrendered. Such infrastructure improvements would lead to more frequent and quicker train services.

Railways presented a mirror picture of Victorian Britain's progress that had largely come about driven by societal changes to the game of wealth, power and access. For the first-time by the mid-1870s, wealth was not entirely bounded by land-based incomes. Harold Perkin captures the mood faultlessly:

> 'Although there had always been rising men and women, royal favourites and mistresses, successful politicians and public servants, generals, judges, bankers and merchants – provided always that they bought the necessary ticket of entry, a landed estate – and, of course, heiresses of any variety of wealth, it was only in the late Victorian age that wealth alone rather than land and titles became the chief claim to membership of "society".'

Such momentous changes meant that society was on the move in a way not seen before. By the late 1800s in many quarters of British aristocracy, the leisure class was making way for the pleasure class. As Cannadine observed, 'In London and the shires, social life became more frantic and free-floating. Staying at home seemed less enjoyable than going abroad.' Britain's railway companies were now ideally placed to transport first-class passengers in a manner to which they were accustomed. Hardly surprising, therefore, that railway company management should decide to invest in significant enhancements to the treatment of their best-supporting travelling passengers as the aristocracy, always relatively small in numbers, yielded place to the increasing middle-class populace.

Railway companies started to survey new opportunities, especially when presented with the conundrum of what passengers may do at the end of the journey. Travelling for business or leisure meant there were considerable numbers who did not return to their home at night. The railway hotel in its many forms began to appear after the 1850s and was something most railway companies, either directly or indirectly, would become involved with. Railway companies were the great collaborators of their age. All cities needed a supply of suitable high-quality hotels to meet the needs of domestic travellers as well as continental visitors. But hotels, initially, were a business the railway companies were reluctant to enter on their own volition.

Growth in tourism travel fuelled the development of the grand hotel with British and European railway companies building some of the best. North America saw similar high-quality hotel development too. Known as terminus hotels, they were constructed at the end of lines or near important cities along routes they served. The first in Britain appeared as two separate establishments at the entrance to Euston station in 1839 considered not only as novel but impressive and built on an American style of operation. New purpose-built hotels were railway showcases, imposing buildings designed by some of the era's leading architects. Revenues generated by the railways allowed the companies to finance their building. By 1854, the GNR had built a hotel at King's Cross whilst at Paddington (still a suburban village at the time), the Great Western had built another impressive hotel. London railway hotels were trustworthy institutions acquiring good reputations. As Professor Jack Simmons commented, 'In the [eighteen] sixties and seventies they helped to initiate a change in the social life of London. Dining in public was scarcely thought of by respectable persons in the early Victorian age.'

Yet there was a limit to the railway company's perception of the value of hotel operations as they considered their primary focus was carrying passengers. Simmons takes the view that '…the railways had never gone into the hotel business as an investment; they were concerned with it only as a feeder of traffic to themselves.' Nevertheless, by the late Victorian period, changes were afoot as the value of hospitality arrangements was increasingly recognised by Britain's railways. In Scotland, there was much invention with the smaller railway companies not subscribing to established industry views. They turned their attentions to targeting prosperous tourists by building a string of new resort hotels. In 1899, the GNSR opened the magnificent Cruden Bay Hotel in open countryside connected by a tramway whilst the Highland Railway opened the Highland Hotel at Strathpeffer in July 1911 – a spa town with a claim to have 'the most efficacious waters in Europe'. The new railway hotel was promoted with 'every comfort and convenience' ideally situated for 'the Baths, the Wells, the Gardens, and the Golf Course'.

New developments of this type paved the way for upscale tourist accommodation in relatively remote locations but accessed by railways. Taking on-board London's fusion of hospitality and dining ideas, the Scottish companies evolved new hospitality concepts with the creation of 'leisure resort hotels' as, for some English visitors, Scotland was still perceived as a holiday abroad. Railway line extensions allowed the construction of new-build hotels close to the sea and to first-class golf courses whilst targeting a customer base seeking first-class or even deluxe accommodation. Recognising the importance of tourist traffic, the Midland's west coast partner, the GSWR, constructed the first railway hotel for golfers at Turnberry in 1906, whilst earlier, the Highland Railway had built a large hotel at Dornoch overlooking a golf course. The concept of luxury grand hotels providing gracious new ways of living were at the heart of railway-accessed golf resorts, which in turn would become upscale tourist hotspots.

By 1914, there were very few major British cities without a railway hotel, whilst others had more than one. Often, they could get away with premium pricing; the rack rate for the best rooms at Midland's Victorian-Gothic style St. Pancras Grand – in architectural terms considered to be more cathedral than hotel – when the first-stage of construction opened in 1873 were some of the most expensive in town. Whilst ocean liners were the floating palaces of their day, railway hotels were the land-based equivalent. 'They boasted 200-300 rooms,' observed food historian Jeri Quinzio which 'included guestrooms, restaurants, meeting rooms, bars, and ballrooms along with modern features as indoor

The GOLF COURSES on the
WEST COAST OF SCOTLAND are
most conveniently reached by the

MIDLAND &
GLASGOW & SOUTH WESTERN
RAILWAYS

APPLY FOR PARTICULARS TO THE
MIDLAND RAILWAY Co., DERBY

The potential of golf as a leisure pursuit had been noted by railway companies since late Victorian times. Building new courses, combining sophisticated layout planning together with atmospheric hotel accommodation designed to attract wealthy tourists, particularly free-spending Americans, quickly moved up railway company agendas. Golf was to become a constituent and valuable element of Scotland's tourism mix cementing strong US/Scottish ties. Ayrshire's Atlantic coast was home to two of the country's finest championship golf courses at Troon and Turnberry, something the GSWR lost no time in exploiting building a new station at Troon in 1892. The company, though, had a much closer relationship with Turnberry, (Lord Ailsa, the club's first president, was the local land owner and a member of the GSWR board) producing a world-famous golf course and luxury hotel ahead of its time all connected by railway. The first course opened in 1902 and a second a decade later. In Edwardian times the company presided over a golf boom in north Ayrshire; these two 1910 posters demonstrate the considerable efforts the GSWR made with its Midland Railway partner to securing prosperous visitors.

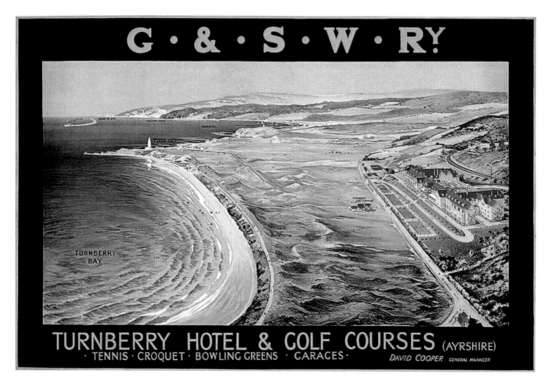

plumbing and elevators.' They contained socio-inclusive spaces where ladies felt at home in public dining rooms. In many cultured establishments at the end of the 1800s, women were actively welcomed. These places were perceived to be sufficiently respectable for females to dine alone or with other lady friends. Within a year of opening its new Manchester hotel, the Midland Railway was using its dining car menus to promote 'The Ladies Concerts' held mid-afternoon twice a week. The value of the female pound was clearly recognized. Jeri Quinzio, reflecting in her 2014 book *Food on the Rails* (Lanham, Rowman and Littlefield, 2014) on hotel dining, says, 'Dining at the hotels was not only seemly, it was fashionable; it was an opportunity to dress for dinner in a style befitting the opulent surroundings'. Britain's Victorian railway businesses rolled out their construction programmes across the country so that each main city was likely to have a grand railway hotel.

This was also mirrored in Europe with similar grand hotels constructed in Belgium (home to the George Nagelmackers empire), France, Germany and Italy and by the end of the nineteenth century regularly popping up in most key European cities linked to the railway network. Grand hotels were built in key US cities such as Chicago (Pullman's home turf) and New York but American hotels by and large were not built by railway companies but by thrusting entrepreneurs aided with a plentiful supply of new money. Canadian railways were involved with the construction of hotels, turning virgin wilderness into sophisticated destination resorts like the Banff Springs Hotel and Chateau Frontenac in Quebec. Whilst these developments were highly visible by the end of the Victorian period, the identification of wealthier hotel patronage was on railway company agendas.

The Furness Railway was credited with developing the first 'country hotel' aimed at tourists in Cumbria in 1847. Dr David Turner comments on LSWR, who in 1866 leased the Southampton Imperial Hotel. In doing so the LSWR's directors stated, 'a first class hotel will be obtained which will be conducive to the comfort of the passengers to and from Southampton, as well as advantage to this company.'

Apart from leisure hotels, the Scottish railway companies were also innovative in developing their own large and prestigious hotels in Edinburgh and Glasgow, the Caledonian Railway's Edinburgh establishment noted for its impressive frontage. Railway companies increasingly documented the value of their grand hotels and indeed the spread of hotels across their routes. This was recognised in their general marketing. The Midland Railway, for instance, undertook hotel promotion largely independent of its other railway divisions but as a proportion of total advertising in 1891 and 1892, company hotels accounted for some ten and a half per cent of its advertising expenditure.

From the 1870s onwards, railway hotels formed part of broader promotional stance adopted by the railway companies. This included the development of large numbers of so-called 'tourist programmes', which were small booklets containing timetables, maps and short descriptions of tourist attractions. Such examples of marketing collateral are described by Shin as 'new media'. For the first time, this type of integrated approach ensured that railway companies could appeal to the personal tastes of their potential customers, which were becoming increasingly diverse and particularly so amongst wealthier clientele. The Midland Railway's Gothic-style Grand London Hotel, according to railway writer Roy Williams, was 'one of the finest in the world, run by the former manager of the Victoria Hotel in Venice, equipped with every luxury, even to a telephone system for listening to live concert performances'.

The GSWR added to Glasgow's hotel estate by building the St. Enoch Hotel, the largest in Scotland when constructed at its main terminus. From the 1890s, LNWR used its hotels for promotional material by circulating information to Liverpool bound passengers on Cunard and White Star liners forming part of a comprehensive bundle of travel related services for all classes. Indeed, Thomas Cook's New York managers, surfing the back of enormous numbers of American tourists recorded, 'Thanks to the "fairy tale" quality of accommodation on board ocean liners, smart clients were now willing to cross the Atlantic second class'.

Stephen Crane, an American short-story teller, also encouraged American thriftiness describing third-class accommodation on the *Scotch Express* as 'almost as comfortable as the first-class, and attract a kind of people that are not usually seen traveling third-class in Europe. Many people sacrifice their habit, in the matter of this train, to the fine conditions of the lower fare.' Crossing the Atlantic had never been easier as cashing of traveller's cheques and the issuing of railway tickets on-board ship before docking became routine operations. The practicalities of taking foreign currency for travel purposes had been formalised with the American Express

Company's invention of the traveller's cheque in 1891 and their speedy acceptance by British and European banks as well as by railway companies and grand hotels for payment of services. For overseas visitors to Britain, the administrative task of obtaining sterling was facilitated by the establishment of correspondent bank relationships. Although the number of high street deposit banks reduced from 121 in 1875 to twenty-eight by 1914, branch visits of the same bank around the country was straightforward.

The experience of much improved first-class service caught the public imagination, but it was not entirely smooth sailing as trials and tribulations could ensue. In the winter of 1883, the *Edinburgh Evening News* reported on the 'adventures' of one such passenger travelling on one of the Midland's open style veranda Pullman cars:

'I was one of two passengers, a few days ago in a Pullman car from Liverpool to London. As we approached the beautiful part of Derbyshire through which the Midland Railway runs, I left the car by the end door to get the view from the open platform. I passed through this door by simply turning the handle. The day was cold and the wind rough, the hills covered with snow, and I, therefore, soon turned to re-enter the comfortable carriage, but found the door which opened so readily to let me out was fastened with a spring lock, and declined me readmission. Though startled, I did not at first realize the situation, expecting the train to stop at a station, or the conductor of the car to discover me; but neither happening I resorted to the very few means of escape I had, without success. I tried to attract the attention of the conductor and my fellow passenger, but there were three closed doors between us. I tried to pick the lock; but it was hopeless. I tried to break the window: it defied me. I tried to reach the communicating chord; it was a yard over my head; and I remained in this plight for more than an hour, while the train travelled 40 miles or so of alternate tunnels, cuttings, banks and bridges, over the roughest part of this or any other railway in the kingdom, on a bitterly cold and stormy day. I have escaped with a severe cold so far; but to many such a misadventure would mean a long illness or even death. My name is at the service of the manager: but it is better to warn the travelling public than to complain to railway officials; hence this letter.'

The introduction of the corridor arrangement offering passengers comfort, convenience and movement between luxury carriages was a few years off though.

For the wealthy, the second half of the Victorian age was an era of culinary showmanship. Much in evidence was the portrayal and the ostentatious presentation of food, particularly French cuisine

The small Highland town of Strathpeffer by late Victorian times was a popular spa resort founded on medicinal springs discovered a hundred years earlier. This July 1909 *Tatler* Scotland for holidays advertising and editorial feature was typical of early municipal initiatives to promote tourism with newly developed facilities designed to attract upscale visitors. A branch railway linked to the Kyle of Lochalsh line brought many affluent tourists keen to avail themselves of the town's water properties and the medical treatments afforded. Before the Great War, visitor interest was at its height as the Highland Railway ran a new direct train between Aviemore and the rural resort. Known as the *Strathpeffer Spa*, the named train avoided an Inverness stop bringing customers directly to its new hotel. In this Highland Railway poster, the chic spa town was described as 'The Fountain of Health in the Highlands of Scotland'. These promotional initiatives made the resort a favourite and fashionable location. In the 1920s the LMS described the resort as 'Sweet Strathpeffer Spa' yet within a decade its rustic charm according to one leading travel writer at the time, had given way to 'big hotels, modern houses, and shops far from countrified.' (Illustrated London News Ltd/Mary Evans, NRM Pictorial Collection/Science & Society Library)

STRATHPEFFER SPA FOR HEALTH AND PLEASURE.

PERHAPS no part of the Highlands is better known than Strathpeffer Spa, its magnificent situation, healthful climate, and varied scenery of mountain, loch, and fir in conjunction with the unique excellence of its waters having all been factors in the creation of its reputation. There can be obtained the Plombières treatment, the Nauheim, the Schwalbach, the Douche, the Peat, the Strathpeffer Baths, also massage and other medical treatments which have such a beneficial effect on the system.

Over a century ago the leading medical authorities were eulogistic regarding the peculiar properties of the sulphur and other springs, but it was not until 1867 that their merits were universally acknowledged. To-day Strathpeffer Spa, which is under expert medical supervision, is second

STRATHPEFFER SPA—THE PUMP HOUSE

respect Strathpeffer waters are in a class by themselves.

Opposite the bath establishment are the Pavilion Gardens, which are very

is a spacious concert hall where concerts and other entertainments are given.

Railway facilities from London are by the west coast route controlled by the L. and N.-W.R. and the other companies associated with them, who have arranged a daily service from Euston, or by the east coast route from King's Cross (G.N.R.). The Highland Railway, with which both routes are associated from Perth northwards, have exerted all their powers to make Strathpeffer Spa a most accessible spot from any part of the United Kingdom. Special tourist fares are in operation.

Doctors can assure their patients that the maximum of travelling comfort has been arranged, and luxurious through sleeping and restaurant carriages leave London for Strathpeffer every evening

THE STRATHPEFFER ORCHESTRA IN THE RUSTIC BANDSTAND IN THE GARDENS

STRATHPEFFER SPA—A PEEP OF THE GARDENS FROM THE BANDSTAND

to none for its treatments for gout, rheumatism, asthma, and similar ailments. There are four sulphur springs which are well known for their richness in sulphur compounds and relative poverty in sodium salts, especially sodium chloride. In this

prettily laid out with long winding walks and shady corners, where the Strathpeffer orchestra plays. A new pump room has been erected in the gardens, a rustic pergola extending along one side, which gives shelter in wet weather. In the Pavilion

in the week except Saturday, and can be joined at the principal provincial centres. Passengers by other than the through trains change at Inverness, which is connected with Strathpeffer by a branch line.

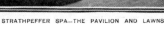

STRATHPEFFER SPA—THE PAVILION AND LAWNS

STRATHPEFFER SPA—THE CONCERT ROOM

with culinary interpretations of rich meats, fish and desserts. The gastronomic influence of French chefs was pervasive. Whilst it was not possible for every household of substance to employ continental chefs, their influences were unescapable. What was happening in the best Victorian homes was transferred to hotels, restaurants, railways and ships.

Domestically, the kitchen was a hive of activity with an array of chefs, cooks and servants providing meals for families up to three times per day. Dinner was the culinary focal point with up to twenty or more dishes prepared for important occasions and eaten normally later in the day. A tradition of afternoon tea evolved, warding off the pangs of hunger before the evening meal which for many households would not begin before eight o'clock. The dining room was the centrepiece and a symbol of standing of wealthy Victorians. Homes were ornate, with fine furniture, cutlery and china to impress guests. The conventions and settings of wealthy homes, the dining room, the drawing room and the smoking room were in turn transferred to a new quality-inspired hospitality industry in late Victorian times. And with these new-found hospitality facilities a luxury travel industry emerged.

Aside from some noted exceptions, British railway companies at the turn of the century tended to make on-board train dining experiences of a type most passengers were familiar with. The course they took was of a general direction towards an industry perception of what customers would encounter in their own homes. As railway writer Chris de Winter Hebron comments, 'The object was to make the travellers feel something like their own drawing-room, and to feed them accordingly.'[6] The Nagelmackers Wagon-Lits European offer on the other hand was 'to provide outright luxury for a restricted clientele' with none of the so-called 'boiled cod' fall backs that might be found on some British dining car operations.

The rationale for the British position was to provide a moderate level of comfort together with 'cuisine and service standards typical of the period rather than outstanding' as the numbers of passengers travelling was increasing. The end of the 1800s saw three railway companies in particular stand out, promoting up-scale food related images; the Midland Railway; LBSCR; and the GWR. Culinary provision would become central features of their respective offers but on Anglo-Scottish services, the Midland, as ever, was the exception to the rule.

Author Roy Williams noted, 'In the affluent, leisure years of the mature Midland, food was used to good effect as a most potent inducement to entice passengers away from the Euston or King's Cross rivals'. The same was expected of international boat trains, where customers expected a superior service but likewise for Pullman on its South Eastern and Chatham Railway (SECR) and LBSCR continental bound routes, regular passengers and first-class commuters required a train-de-luxe offering five days per week. In the years before the Great War, the idea of railway companies (a period when many of them were at their most profitable) seeking to constantly add to the comfort and accommodation of their patrons was a process that would become commonplace.

CHAPTER 2

1901-1920: Edwardian Elegance and Gathering Clouds

The death of Queen Victoria in 1901 heralded an Edwardian era marking a period of elegance that lasted beyond Edward VII's death in 1910 until the Great War outbreak. It is difficult to imagine a short period accounting for anything of real significance, but the years represented immense changes. Edwardian society was likened to period railway carriages where with clear first, second and third-class partitions everyone knew their rank. Similar to America's Gilded Age and Europe's Belle Époque, the Edwardian period was a retrospective label used to define a time delivering many memorable moments of significance, before the sudden realisation that much in life was to change forever. In Edwardian Britain, the comfortable upper-middle-class lives of a relatively small cohort (it should be remembered that some eighty per cent of the population comprised the working-class) would have an immense impact on transport matters especially in the quickening of railway progress resulting in the delivery of many more comfortable trains for first-class, and indeed, all travellers.

Denis O'Donoghue, in writing 'Travel-de-Luxe at a Penny a Mile' in *The Railway Magazine* in 1912, suggested railway development over the previous thirty years had 'been a record of wonderful progress' where travel had 'come to be looked upon not in the light of a luxury or a serious undertaking, as it was a generation or two ago, but as a common, everyday occurrence'. The limit of railway advancement had not nearly been reached but it was something that had developed unconsciously; for the many smaller railway companies in the industry, it represented a summit of their involvement. It was the beginnings of modernity, speedier services and hints of change to meet customer demands of all social classes for improved, extended and multiplication of train services.

The Edwardian era correspondingly coincided with a rise in literacy of all classes and an interest in travel as railway companies (and shipping lines) jostled to capture public attention with reams of promotional output. Simon Bradley argues that the 'railways took some time to wake up to the potential of income from advertising' with the Great Exhibition of 1851 being an early-watershed. Certainly, at the time, excursion operators were active in promoting their wares. Railway company practice for most of the second half of the nineteenth century was to farm out tertiary activities such as display advertising at stations, in waiting rooms and booking halls and for this to be handled by specialist organisers such as the W.H. Smith company.

By the turn of new century, railway companies began to take greater control of activities. Travel literature development was stimulated by the considerable appetite for adventure which had followed the real-life exploits of explorers, pioneers and colonialists during the Victorian era. Travel-related literature was extremely popular, selling in vast numbers as writers sold the dream of exotic travel; hardly surprising that publishers and business owners placed trains and ships at the centre of a fast-developing industry. All this was facilitated by the railway companies adopting fluorescent gas mantle lighting technology in the mid-decade providing a much-improved carriage reading environment.

By this period, Britain's railway companies began to enhance their public images as progressive and self-confident businesses. In the years before the First World War, many of the pre-grouping railway companies had established dedicated publicity departments – the forerunner of the modern marketing function – to capitalise on developing business opportunities and a recognition that advertising was just one ingredient in managing the complex process of communicating with customers. But as Shin notes, Britain's railway officials came to 'regard advertising as the centrepiece of the railways' marketing efforts' and a greater acceptance by the companies as to the value of marketing with a need to create strong brand identities.

Railway poster advertising took great strides at the time, yet in its early development stages much advertising was ineffective, messy and disorderly, based on a collage of competing images trying to deliver too many messages, especially as progress in print technology now allowed posters to be produced in colour. By the inter-war years, the railway poster had matured into a distinct art form where good graphic design and taste was based on a creative brief process with implicit underlying commercial considerations. As a result, the 1920s and 1930s signalled wonderfully atmospheric posters and supporting marketing material designed to showcase glamour, speed and safety. This was all to come, but before the

Railway advertising became an important source of revenue for upmarket weeklies. Their value was noted by *The Bystander* in this editorial feature coinciding with the end of July 1907 summer tourist rush. The Great Northern, the Midland and Great Western were amongst the leading companies targeting affluent domestic holiday trade. (Illustrated London News Ltd/ Mary Evans)

The Poster Persuasive

HOW THE RAILWAY COMPANIES TRY TO TEMPT THE HOLIDAY-MAKER

"As Happy as a Sand-boy"

A clever G.N.R. poster advertising one of the many popular trips to the Northern districts

Days were when the railways of this country seemed to consider the traveller as a being provided by Providence for their especial benefit. He might be charged the highest possible prices, taken to his destination by the longest possible route with the greatest expenditure of time in the most uncomfortable of carriages. To-day, the traveller has come into his own, and the Companies, no longer acting the part of tyrant, now seek to tempt him to visit the chief places on their lines with every allurement they can devise, short of free travel, though in many instances the fares are so low that it almost amounts to the same thing. The three posters here reproduced are only typical of many others which are now giving us breaths of the sea and country on the hoardings.

"The Cock o' the North"

Since the first excursion was run by arrangement with Mr. Thos. Cook of Leicester in 1841, the Midland Railway have made a speciality of cheap and fast travel

England's Riviera

The similarities of Cornwall and Italy have been cleverly brought out by the above G.W.R. poster, and should tempt many to pay a visit to this delightful region

(Particulars of the railway arrangements for the holidays will be found on page 244)

Great War, Britain's non-integrated railway system was a highly competitive market.

The GCR had established a publicity function in 1902, widely regarded as being at the forefront of a new trend in railway marketing employing a dedicated manager in order to market the railway effectively. The LNWR set up a similar department some seven years later, as well as placing greater emphasis on the development of group travel initiatives whilst cultivating American visitors streaming off Cunard's new floating hotels, White Star's intermediate and Canadian Pacific's Liverpool liner business. One of the most visible aspects was the sheer volume of railway and travel related postcards generated by the company before the Great War. The exploits of the Great Western in expanding the leisure travel market is well documented.

By the early 1900s, the company had a centralised and fully integrated publicity machine having first staked out a sectorial claim for new tourist arrangements some thirty years before. The LSWR joined the commercial fray in 1913 with a publicity department reporting directly into the general manager's span of control. One publicity mechanism the railway companies did not pick up on at this period was the idea of talking directly to press editors (apart from new dedicated railway publications) even though the newspaper industry was the net recipient of much duplicated advertising expenditure. Such informal press conversations were invariably held at board level and usually in the surroundings of London's gentlemen clubs. The opportunity to put over the railway point of view was not always taken, even though they exercised a dominant commercial position in everyday life.

The notion of public or media relations and its integrated use by railway companies would have to wait until the inter-war years and the accomplished practitioners of the dark art of journalism such as Southern's John Elliot, as well as a raft of other 'sophisticated advertising and publicity techniques' that would be employed by the industry. Wolmar describes the Great Western 'as the most innovative of the companies in respect of publicity', producing a continual trail of quality holiday-related publications from 1904 until nationalisation. The management of the essential public image meant a strong relationship with the tourism system and in the development of joint publicity schemes at a domestic level between the railway and West Country (and Welsh) resorts but also, more importantly, in overseas territories with international trade bodies, shipping lines and in the continuation of its long-established contacts in the prosperous American market. All of this would gather fruit in later years.

By the turn of the twentieth century, the railway companies had really ratcheted up their promotional activities in the creation of up-to-date images of themselves, their services and in the creation of modern railway posters. As Bradley observed, 'The railways' increasingly active publicity departments joined in the display. Many of their productions are not regarded as classics of commercial art, but advertising moved from "informative" text-based formats into "creative" pictorial modes.' Much creative output would take the form of route and destination promotion, forming an intensification of rivalry between railway operators. Shin goes on to explain, 'As historians have noted, the competition between railway companies for passenger business did not lie down.'

Britain's railway companies could be construed as one of the original 'destination marketers', recognizing that passengers booked journeys for discovery and pleasure, rather than for purpose, safe in the knowledge that reasonable accommodation and things to do would await at journey's end. They established themselves at the forefront of a modern persuasion-based tourism industry in which, as Pimlott describes, 'All the resources of twentieth-century salesmanship were called into play by the holiday resorts, the transport undertakings, the travel agencies, the hotels, the amusement caterers'. Increasing ingenuity was displayed with the development and quality of advertising 'until in the end skilled practitioners were exploiting almost every human motive in propaganda which year by year grew in scale and intensity'.

By the inter-war years, tourism achieved an industrial accolade by economists. Middle-class workers now enjoyed paid holidays working five days per week rather than six and, for the first-time, started to attract the attention of sociologists where holidays with pay were a luxury that could be enjoyed commensurate with the appropriate level of income. Tourist traffic spilled over into what could be described these days as the leisure economy. Increasingly, ordinary workers had Saturday afternoons off, leading to a tremendous growth in sport-orientated rail excursion traffic as large numbers of fans were transported to away matches, especially for football. Most workers could travel and were keen to support their local team as, in the early years of the professional game, many clubs in the old first division were based in the north. Naturally, northern based railway companies did well with passenger footfall as most top tier clubs were from Lancashire, Yorkshire and the north east. In the south of England, cricket and rugby retained upscale followings made up of a narrower social and geographical constituency. The noisy excesses of alcohol-induced boisterousness associated with rugby union was something the railway companies put up with, particularly from partying supporters making their way to and home from respective rugby headquarters for international fixtures.

The GWR enjoyed its upmarket engagement with Edwardian life, delivering a smart West Country image for holiday business. In many ways, this was nothing new as, since 1876, the Great Western had initiated a policy of spending money on advertising, commissioning photography and engravings of West Country scenes. The south west counties, as pointed out by writer Matthew Engel, were 'seen as the most uniformly desirable part of Britain; soft airs, soft climate, soft countryside, soft accents.' Since the early days of the *Cornish Riviera Express* or the *Limited* as the GWR liked to describe the train, Cornwall's mild climate ensured the delivery of a county image as an alternative winter resort comparable to overseas rivals on the Azur coast. The county was positioned to be as attractive in winter as summer months, as the company created a steady stream of travel literature, promotional material and advertising posters initially under the guidance of the publicity officer, Felix Pole. The journey, the raft of destinations and the experiences helped GWR build Cornwall; for the first-time, an integrated consumer approach was recognised, noting the limited ways in which advertising had been used historically (merely to convey announcements) to one where subtle changes in approach were needed to persuade the consumer of the benefits of visiting the region. Felix Pole and James Milne were influential in this development, later becoming general managers of the railway and some of the most notable British marketing practitioners in the first quarter of the twentieth century. The first variation of a train name that generated huge public interest was for a new Cornwall schedule – the *Riviera Express* following an exclusive competition run in conjunction with *Railway Magazine's* readers and a name later adapted to the *Cornish Riviera Express* or the *Limited* in 1906.

By this time, travel organisations such as Thomas Cook had maintained offices in New York for the best part of thirty years. Ocean liners filled with prosperous passengers headed to Europe in great numbers and unsurprisingly, Britain's railway companies wanted a greater share of this lucrative business. The GWR and the LSWR attempted to cash in on lucrative Atlantic passengers by running rival boat train services to Plymouth which increasingly became more luxurious in nature. The LSWR first identified a niche with dedicated open Pullman-style vehicles in the early 1890s. Christian Wolmar captures the scene:

'Like Scottish sleepers, these special boat trains were exceptional and not run to a normal schedule. Once it was known that a liner was to arrive at Plymouth, a train was despatched as soon as possible, whatever the time of day, and it was a point of honour to run these trains at fast speeds.'

The two railway companies fought for the American traveller, fine-tuning regional representations in 'the railway race to the west'. These initiatives were designed to appeal to international audiences and in terms of place-making, something the two companies had been in competition with each other over since the late 1880s. International marketing commenced in 1904, with the Great Western's *Historic Sites and Scenes of England* targeting Americans. *The Sphere* magazine pronounced the publication as:

'a most admirable specimen of how a railway company can best utilise its forces. This is no mere puff. It is a handsome volume of 128 pages, very elaborately illustrated with everything of interest that can be seen on the great railway's excellently-managed system. The writer has a keen sense of those literary and historic associations which appeal with full force to the American pilgrim.'

The marketing material was also useful for tapping into their wealthy brethren disembarking at Plymouth on Norddeutsche Lloyd's (NDL) quartet of liners by using their high-speed Ocean Liner Specials for quick transit to London. By 1906, Hamburg America Line's (HAGAG) luxurious SS *Amerika* stopped regularly at Plymouth, generating a steady flow of well-qualified American visitors. The value of tourism had been well and truly grasped by Britain's pre-grouping railway companies and especially in the south west, where there was a far greater convergence of publicity effort but elsewhere in the country, the interests of the railway companies and tourist places did not entirely overlap. But the combined value of these initiatives came to an end at the outbreak of war.

The move towards railway consolidation was underway and quite naturally, the idea of travelling in style took a back seat during the war years. Until the Great War, railway companies generated a considerable level of publicity material aimed at the first-class market. Most early Pullman stock had been bought out by individual railway companies, who then set about developing their own bespoke services, especially carriage catering arrangements. As Bradley noted, the best railway carriages expressed 'the spirit of their age just as much as its ocean liners, motor cars and smart hotels'. This was the height of pampered luxury for prosperous passengers as railway companies provided beautifully designed and well-appointed carriages. Edwardian affluence was reflected on many train services and this was particularly evident on the three Anglo-Scottish routes, where eight or twelve-wheeled bogie coaches were now standard fare, enhancing day and night-time travel. Competition between the three sets of collaborative arrangements on the Anglo-Scottish lines was intense but the media at the time was enthused about the quality of experiences they received, especially that of the Midland who had first introduced dining facilities for first-class travellers with meals served in their carriage seats on Scottish trains in 1882.

The Edwardian period was characterised by newer, up-to-date trains. Locomotives were more powerful, incorporating the latest wheel-arranging developments available at the time ensuring a smoother and speedier journey. For first-class passengers, the Edwardian era was an age of travelling elegance with many high-roofed carriages that were seventy feet long. This provided the space for railway companies to create a more gracious way to travel, first-class railway carriages becoming sanctuary for the rich and well-behaved to feel perfectly at home. For those who had the time, leisurely and agreeable travelling experiences was there for the taking. In Britain, on-board train dining caught the imagination in a big way as the quality of fare and service started to mirror the best fine-dining restaurant and grand hotel establishments. Simon Bradley describes the period at the turn of the century as 'a sort of arms race in railway catering, as competing long-distance lines tried to outflank each other in the pleasures and amenities of travel'.

Similar developments were apace in Europe and north America. Technology which had brought about improvements in gas lighting was now applied to railway catering. Based on LNWR's *American Specials* and Dalziel's *Southern Belle* Pullman innovations, high-quality food could now be cooked on the move rather than merely keeping partially or previously-cooked food hot on the train with the introduction of the Fletcher, Russell & Co gas cooker. The company's gas stoves and water heaters were later to become a norm in the industry and were fitted to most railway kitchen and restaurant cars. Notwithstanding the vicissitudes of producing meals in cramped conditions and in moving carriages, the menu was often of the highest quality, particularly on Wagon-Lits' European services, although in Britain there were inconsistencies in both standards of quality and quantity. Despite the advantages of land-based operations, railway companies were unable to recruit top chefs in the way that leading hotels and shipping lines could. They did their best with pampered Pullman-style dining opulence taken up by most companies running long-distance trains. The GWR was no different when the *Limited* was introduced in 1904. Two years later, the *Cornish Riviera* established new standards of dining for travellers on the West Country run.

Whilst considerable attention is focused on Anglo-Scottish services, the other region where development was discernible was the south west of England, with both the GWR and the LSWR focusing on providing superior passenger services. Whilst the Great Western had an established foothold for holiday traffic, the LSWR did not hold back on their efforts either.

Given the competitive nature of West Country services, it is hardly surprising that Pullman, even under new management and clearly delivering significant travelling enhancements, could never crack either LSWR or GWR's premier regional trains. By 1906, the GWR had a new streamlined west of England route from Reading to Taunton, removing the necessity of going to Exeter via Bristol and the 'Great Way Around' or the 'elbow-joint' of the West Country journey as it was termed. But before this, Molly Hughes, writing as M. Vivien Hughes in her book *A London Family*, recounts a long-distance Paddington to Cornwall journey on Great Western's broad gauge in the late 1870s. She describes the trials and tribulations of travelling by train on a family visit to Cornwall in the days before the *Flying Dutchman*, the *Cornishman* and the *Riviera Express*. Molly noted that on such a long journey of twelve hours, they were confined to a non-corridor carriage where passengers usually sat six a side: 'much courtesy was needed for a long run when there was no escape from one another'. In those days, 'Luncheon-baskets had not been invented, neither was it possible to reserve seats'. But family-prepared food did have its merits as a sojourn from the tedium of carriage confinement which did get better once they had arrived at Bristol as the coach emptied providing the chance to move about more freely. She noted:

'A bulging basket had been eyed as it sat in the rack. Restaurant cars are boons, and luncheon-baskets have their merry surprises, but for food as a species of rapture nothing compares with sandwiches, eggs, pasties, and turnovers, doled out one by one from napkins.'

The Edwardian era saw continuing development of a consumer-focused luxury goods industry. Luxury travel is inextricably entwined and has been a permanent theme ever since. Luxury services were perceived as an extension of luxury goods and for the first-time were considered by the wealthy as necessities. Professor Bernard Rieger notes that first-class passengers 'formed part of an expanding market for luxury goods and services that, together with high-class hotels, spas and exclusive retail outlets, catered for a clientele of aristocrats, members of the European haute bourgeoisie, and American plutocrats'.[1]

Indeed, it may be argued that the French invented the notion of luxury products, a world which Fletcher, writing at the time, notes

By the early 1900s, LSWR could offer by way of two key arterial routes bank holiday excursions in four sets of seaside or rural destinations; Cornwall, Devon, Dorset and the Isle of Wight. Southampton, on the Bournemouth and Weymouth line, was also used to promote cross-channel trips to Cherbourg, St. Malo and the Channel Islands but the longer western sea passage reduced time ashore unless night-time crossings were made. The company cleverly positioned ideas of combined rail and sea trips, something that had been popular since mid-Victorian times. (Illustrated London News Ltd/Mary Evans)

'the art of providing edibles out of season, and more things to use than anyone can possibly want combined with the least exertion and the utmost physical comfort if anyone should want to use them'.[2] Certainly, a characterisation of the 'bloated luxuries' of Edwardian overindulgence that carried over into period transport for those with the ability to pay. Luxury goods manufacturers were keen to align themselves with appropriate upscale travel opportunities.

In the 1912 'Shakspere's England Exhibition' at Earl's Court, 'The House of Burberry' had their own wooden constructed pavilion stand to showcase their products to the general public which included garments, sleigh, and skis used by Sir Ernest Shackleton in his Antarctic explorations. This was all positioned within *The Tatler's* pages for August Bank Holiday travel arrangements provided by the railway companies.

The onset of the Great War saw monumental changes engulfing advanced societies across the globe. Things would never be the same again as a gradual crumbling of tradition for the leisured classes and the world they inhabited, only to be replaced by a brave new, uncertain world. Harold Perkin captures the end of the period rather eloquently:

> 'For the nostalgic rich and powerful, who felt they had lost so much, that earlier society inhabited an Indian summer of gracious living, the whirl of the London 'season' and country house parties, an endless round of pleasure based on low taxes, cheap servants and self-confidence which went with unquestioned status.'

Perkin goes on to suggest that the First World War has 'often been credited or blamed for a series of key social changes which, it has been countered, would probably have happened sooner or later anyway'. The gracious forms of the great expresses that took the rich and powerful in comfortable, luxurious first-class surroundings to their constant rounds of social engagements irrevocably altered. Some luxury trains simply disappeared, caught up as casualties of redrawn frontiers and the legacies of internal conflict. But occasions presented themselves. The Great Western opportunistically ran a late autumn/winter advertising campaign in a selection of leading titles that included *The Bystander*, *The Sphere*, *The Illustrated London News*, *The Tatler*, *The Sketch* and *The Illustrated Sporting and Dramatic News* highlighting the Cornish Riviera as an alternative society location for the forthcoming 1915 season, boasting that the county could hold 'its own with any Continental holiday ground' as trips to the French Riviera were frustrated by war. The Cornish Riviera suggested 'the season's programme, is just as attractive, and there is a social gaiety about all the resorts that is pleasant in the extreme' as well as the Great Western comparing the promenade at Torquay to that of Nice.

Summer holidaying in the fashionable Lakes of Killarney resorts was never quite the same after the demise of the *Killarney Express* in 1914. Other train services were reconfigured, the consequence of war-time running, whilst others lost part of their magic to the pursuit of speed and the modern customer mantra of getting to destinations as quickly as possible. The Midland Railway had always garnered a reputation for taking London society to the Highlands shooting season. *The Sketch* endorsed the company's services:

'In view of the Twelfth and the great march on Scotland, the tours of the Midland Company should be studied. Nothing can be more pleasant than to run down (or does the Scotch capital demand "up"?) to Edinburgh in a dining-car, leaving town three times a day. The night service is excellent. The Midland is especially useful for those who wish to go to the West of Scotland.'

In post-war days, the Midland's route to the Highlands for 12 August season lost some of its ardour as faster east and west coast day-time trains provided quicker access. For time limited Americans who wanted to combine grouse shooting with a round or two of golf in their itineraries, this was an important consideration. Continuing its broader based approach to attracting domestic tourists, the Highland Railway positioned the region as a destination for everyone. But like one last throw of the dice, the Midland proudly continued its upscale passenger association, declaring that St. Pancras was the natural starting place for all holidays north.

All the same, some great expresses were reborn in classic 1920s mode leaving as impressive railway lore traditions as did earlier great Victorian and Edwardian trains. In August 1919, the great holiday scramble came, as thousands of people headed towards the sea side on their first holiday for five years. Piers Brendon took a similar stance when continental travel restrictions were lifted, describing spring departures as a 'considerable exodus to Europe' whilst the summer presented a domestic 'staycation' orientation as 'the British made for the shores of their island like lemmings'.

Those railway companies that had had the foresight to invest in better services recovered quicker than other companies. In Britain, the Pullman company's ideas of comfortable and civilised travel at a price were re-established. Elsewhere, where railway companies possessed the appropriate carriage stock, they were turned out invariably on prestige long-distance and boat train routes. By the end of the year, it was possible to take continental holidays again as foreign travel restrictions imposed by the war were lifted. The return to peace saw something akin to a mass exodus of the wealthy. As Kidner cites 'everyone who was anyone

In the last summer season before grouping, the Midland Railway was actively courting passenger business to the north of England and Scotland, and all conveniently accessed through its central routes. By the early 1920s, *The Bystander* had adopted a close working relationship with travel sector advertisers as British, and later European railway companies, continued to be highly supportive of the publication for many years. (Illustrated London News Ltd/Mary Evans)

had to take much of their pleasure in Paris, and they needed a luxury train to the short-sea-crossing ports'. And it was not just Paris everyone was headed to; top drawer destinations of the Mediterranean were also on society's minds. So too was the Swiss Alps, unaffected by the inferno of war and back on upscale winter itinerary schedules. As Graves and Hodge comment:

'St. Moritz was popular for skating and skiing - as yet expertness in skating was more common than in skiing among society people. The illustrated weeklies during the winter of 1919-20 were full of photographs of Lord So-and-So's party on skates.'[3]

In time, skiing would overtake skating as the most popular winter pastime, and something recognized by Thomas Cook who presented a Ski Challenge Cup. Cross-channel steamers were returned for civilian use, even though French and Swiss train travel could be difficult due to severe coal-shortages – an endemic problem throughout Europe at the time. Thus began a twenty-year process for the Swiss to remove a reliance on coal for steam traction by electrifying the country's railway network powered by abundant hydro-electric schemes.

Come North !
Come North !

The Highlands of Scotland await you. See the glorious scenery, breathe the bracing air of the mountains, moors and lochs, play on the wonderful Golf courses, walk or drive over the well-kept roads. You *must* visit the Highlands to appreciate the beauty of your own country.

Easy and convenient to reach via

THE HIGHLAND RAILWAY

An ideal holiday haunt for every taste.

TRAVEL VIA WEST COAST ROUTE.

Write for Official A. B. C. Tourist Guide Free and Post Free from Traffic Manager, Highland Railway, Inverness, or from Messrs. D. C. Cuthbertson & Co., Ltd., 38, Bath Street, Glasgow, or 100, Princes Street, Edinburgh.

In this Highland Railway advertisement – the Scottish Highlands could be accessed by all three Anglo-Scottish routes but for passenger convenience, the company choose to emphasise its relationship with the west coast corridor. In this July 1922 *Bystander* advertisement, the company recognized the imminent changes taking place in the railway world as the region was portrayed as a destination for everyone. (Illustrated London News Ltd/Mary Evans)

By the turn of the twentieth century, most of Britain's railway companies had completed their hotel building ensuring that each terminus station had its own grand hotel. Five of London's eleven station hotels by 1905 were awarded five stars from Baedeker. Further afield, the NBR constructed a grand hotel at Edinburgh Waverley in 1902, named after its station. Many folk of an older generation still referred to the hotel as the 'North British', probably not realising the significance of its pre-grouping rail ownership. The Great Western continued its collaborative tourism forays, entering an agreement with the Irish Tourist Authority to enlarge the Lakeside Hotel at Killaloe, providing an additional lounge and rooms for a further fifty guests as part of the Duke of York tourist trail initiative.

Central London also had its non-railway owned luxury hotels providing stiff competition at the top end of the market. Many of these ventures were constructed during the late Victorian/ early Edwardian period such as the Carlton Hotel at the corner of Haymarket and Pall Mall, the Ritz Hotel in Piccadilly; the Savoy Group owned the Strand-based Savoy Hotel and the new Mayfair Claridges Hotel. The Ritz and the Carlton were designed by Charles Mewès and Arthur Davis. Their creations marked the interface of exquisite Edwardian space, opulent decorations and exemplary kitchen based culinary extravagance delivered in impressive new dining venues by hoteliers such as César Ritz and head chef Auguste Escoffier. Ritz and Escoffier were the gastronomic 'wow' factors of their day. Not only were new luxury forms to be found in hotels but also with the shipping lines operating increasing numbers of trendy ocean liners and railway companies running the most prestigious of railway trains across two continents. The firms responsible for blending design and carrying out the work were ground-breaking, resulting in cross-pollination of ideas bringing about novel approaches to design creation as the best ideas could be interchanged within different transport modes. Ritz, Escoffier, Mewès and Davis together with British decorators Waring and Gillow were part of a much-respected design grouping producing some of the most palatial luxury settings the modern hospitality industry had ever seen.

In 1896, Gillow of Lancaster, one half of the celebrated interior decorator firm, had already worked with the Midland Railway fitting out their most flamboyant Pullman style restaurant dining cars yet. A writer for *The Sketch* waxed lyrical about the new dining carriages. He said:

'While on the question of railway improvements, I must refer to the two new dining-cars which the Midland Railway are to place in the London to Manchester express service on the first day of the New Year. Built in the company's Derby workshops, they are designed to give the greatest ease, comfort, and safety possible to passengers, whether travelling at a low or high rate of speed. The bodies of the carriages, which are sixty feet long, eight feet wide, and eight feet high, rest upon bogie trucks with six pairs of wheels. A number of india-rubber springs of a new type are also interposed between the under-frame and the body of the car, the complete structure being so arranged as to minimise vibration and irregularities of motion. The floors, sides, and roofs have been built up with felt, india-rubber, hair, and vulcanite between the timbers, for the purpose of absorbing or preventing the conduct of sound and deadening the noise and rattle which usually accompany locomotion by rail; and to further this object the side and top windows are double glazed with plate glass. The decoration, which has been carried out by Messrs. Gillow, of Lancaster, introduces a new departure in railway upholstery. Each car is lighted by means compressed oil-gas (each lamp having four jets), and is warmed by hot water from the engine, the heat radiating from a brass grill. A ladies' and a gentlemen's lavatory is also provided at each end of the car.'

In fact, the Gillow relationship with the railway sector was already flourishing, as the firm had designed the interior furnishings of Pullman's *Prince of Wales* parlour car the previous year. Synergies were exploited as the long-established Gillows company had a background for over a century in the crafting of high-quality furniture for the wealthy. Nearby firm Waring, based in Liverpool, similarly began life as a cabinet maker, but during the 1880s, the company diversified to include interior decoration with contracts to furnish hotels amongst its interests. In the late Victorian period, the two firms started collaborating on projects, ultimately resulting in a 1903 merger. The enlarged business of Waring & Gillow continued their fine standing as a high-class decorating business for luxury environments including the *Victoria and Albert* Royal Yacht. Work with the fast-developing merchant marine sector continued and in a few short years, Waring & Gillow cemented their reputation providing the interiors for Cunard's new luxury express liner *Lusitania* as well as smaller high-end liners, *Heliopolis* and *Cairo*, which operated in the eastern Mediterranean sun spots.

In the last decade of Victoria's reign, similar approaches were beginning to be applied to British carriage design which were to become the norm in both third and first-class travelling environments and particularly with new luxury formats that were starting to evolve at the time. A writer for *The Sketch* captured the mood precisely:

> 'It seems a very remarkable thing that, with all our progress on the railways, half a century should have been allowed to elapse before journeys lasting from ten to twelve hours should have to be undertaken under conditions that have been allowed to prevail.'

He was alluding to the rather primitive state of affairs that had been standard for so many years. The writer went on:

> 'Everything comes to the man who can wait, and to such of us who have been permitted to wait until this year of grace (1893) the old order has given place to a revolution in third-class travelling, which consists in being able to pass the journey with as much comfort as if we were passing the day in a first-class hotel.'

Collectively, the railway companies had begun to appreciate what was needed to attract a high-class clientele, especially America's Gilded Age travellers. From the 1890s, trans-Atlantic steamers had for the first time begun to resemble the ocean palaces they were to shortly become. To complement strides in merchant marine development, Britain's main railway operators started to design carriages recognising the demands of their ocean liner passenger traffic, especially wealthy American customers who had long been used to superior railroad travelling. Three companies primarily involved in serving Britain's major gateway ports – the GWR, the LSWR and the LNWR – upped their game considerably with improved passenger services. For the first-time, ocean liner boat expresses were spacious, comfortable and instilled with a brand of romance and glamour linking the railway companies to the shipping lines. In 1889, the LNWR began a policy of naming nine of its Teutonic class of locomotives after Liverpool based White Star Line steamers. Joint promotion initiatives projected attractive corporate images to enhance trans-Atlantic services. By its very nature, integrated marketing activity was targeted at a diverse international customer base who could and would expect the best travelling services money could buy whether at sea, on land or on rail.

At the same time, Britain's railway companies also started paying attention to the real needs of their most prosperous domestic customers. In March 1892, the GWR ushered in what has been described as the country's first modern gangway express train for its Paddington to Birkenhead route, with a range of passenger comforts that included the steam heated radiators that shortly became the norm. The clerestory roofed stock allowed for additional height and light with the coaches according to Wolmar 'panelled with walnut and satinwood that would not have been out of place in a gentleman's club'.

It was the Midland though, as could be expected, who continued to be trend-setters in carriage development. 'The Midland Railway Company has started well on the race, as it has invariably done in every new development of railway business' accorded *The Sketch*. The prospect of the company accessing lucrative boat train passengers in Liverpool set alarm bells ringing at Euston. In 1898, the LNWR introduced the first batch of specially commissioned carriage stock to service to this aspiring market. As has been noted, the LSWR also had one eye on wealthy passengers travelling to or returning from the south west on express steamers stopping off at Plymouth. The company in 1907 felt it had to provide a more satisfactory service for prestige American passengers who were disembarking from early morning steamers with the LSWR constructing several high-quality boat train sleeping cars whose compartments were said to be exquisitely adorned with brass bedsteads and bed knobs.

Whilst this was an obvious luxury travel enhancement, they were not to everyone's tastes. The service proved to be unsuccessful as the coaching stock was eventually sold to GWR when LSWR withdrew from running Plymouth boat trains. By railway grouping, LSWR had no sleeping cars of its own, the position only changing with the introduction of the specialist Wagon-Lits *Night Ferry* sleeping cars in 1936. During Edwardian times, washbasins in compartments became a common feature in British sleeping cars but it took a further thirty-years or so for showers to be introduced to LNER first-class sleeping compartments – an on-board facility that US passengers had enjoyed for some considerable time. The term the 'American boat train' had come into common usage from the early 1900s. Whilst US passengers were not quite so keen on LSWR's early morning sleeping cars, a more relaxing experience was available from LNWR who in 1908 built their new *American Special* stock. One of the train's features was the provision of carriage armchairs and sofas which on the face of it might have appeared a perfect example of Edwardian decadence but in fact were designed for passengers who had suffered with the ship's crossing.

Crossing the north Atlantic in mid-winter could be notorious with literally days of seasickness endured by all liner passengers. What was never disputed was the research LNWR had conducted. When launched with a media fanfare, first-class passengers were eager to inspect the pleasures of LNWR's newest equipage clearly directed towards the prosperous American travel market. Railway writer Robert Hendry tells us, 'It was luxury and convenience far excelling anything that today's international traveller might dream of'. The carriages were built with 'intricately carved woodwork' and a 'degree of elegance' that craftsman presently are unlikely to deliver.[4]

Modern luxury rail travel in Britain was now clearly taking off. The Great Central together with the Metropolitan Railway in the London area entered the luxury sector, running all-corridor stock with restaurant cars to their new London terminus at Marylebone. Advertising carried banners of 'Rapid Travel in Luxury' and 'New Express Corridor Dining Trains'. Indeed, *The Sketch* noted in a travel feature that:

> '"Rapid Travel in Luxury" is a phrase that appears on the cover of the time-table issued by the Great Central Railway, and a perusal of its contents demonstrates that this enterprising Company is justifying use of the phrase.'

The Metropolitan Railway, too, used a couple of Pullman vehicles to attract prosperous commuters. The company ran two Pullman cars, known as *Mayflower* and *Galatea,* built to the underground's specific loading gauge requirements by the Birmingham Railway Carriage and Wagon Co. providing a morning and evening luxury service for its affluent City of London customers to the then rural backwaters of Buckinghamshire. These Pullmans lasted until London Transport days but were eventually withdrawn in 1940. These cars were also used for late night theatre goers, something the celebrated railway writer Hamilton Ellis described in *The Trains We Loved* (Pan, 1971) as 'a veritable godsend to various old bar-poppers who could now drink their way happily home on the midnight train from Baker Street after others had closed'.

South of the river, LBSCR was launching a new generation of handsomely-appointed Pullmans. The fundamental building blocks for railway companies to successfully compete in the luxury goods market had spilt over into the provision of luxury trains. Across the English Channel, European railways were employing first-class restaurant cars delivering high-quality dining on long-distance trains. Wagon-Lits' operations were forging ahead, with the company working with the continent's best designers and craftsman to build its luxuriant dining and sleeping cars, together with a fledgling hotel business subsidiary. Certainly, Wagon-Lits were well known for their gastronomic feasts by this time, widely reported on in Britain and America's specialist upscale press.

By the end of the 1800s, the Midland Railway had had the best part of thirty years' experience of running high-quality first-class clerestory style diners from London to Scotland, to Manchester and into Liverpool Central to attract a proportion of the blossoming Atlantic Ferry trade which was now reaching record numbers. Under the supervision of CME David Bain, who took on the design mantle in 1901, the company saw no reason at the time to ditch this coaching style having built up an outstanding reputation for its first-class train services. The use of smaller locomotives and the double-heading of express trains was a feature of Midland's operations at the turn of the century.

Whilst Midland had undoubtedly been the trail-blazer, Britain's other railway companies were beginning to catch up as the LNWR had introduced its first-generation of Liverpool *American Special* boat train stock in 1898.[5] Within ten years, the GWR was running classy high-speed restaurant cars on the *Limited* to Cornwall, the LNWR had its sumptuous second-generation of first-class *American Specials* whilst the British Pullman Car Co. was placing its first home contracts for seven lavish twelve-wheeled cars with Birmingham-based Metropolitan Amalgamated Carriage and Wagon Co. The new LBSCR *Southern Belle,* as the new Pullman train was named, was built with modern elliptical style carriages acquiring a label of the 'world's most beautiful train' embracing three historically eclectic design period styles. This all represented a fusion of the latest state of the art technology combining the best interior design and fittings of the day.

Improvements in carriage catering could be seen across the board. Light meals were associated with the Pullman Company on the London to Brighton route with the company providing a pantry buffet service offering tea and sandwiches since 1881. This ensured a good customer following and a decent working relationship with the LBSCR and other railway companies in the south of England. Indeed, such were the standards of some third-class restaurant cars, particularly those of smaller companies such as the GSWR, whose main competitor was the Caledonian Railway, that even passengers who could afford first-class fares deliberately choose to travel third-class. Some passengers spent most of the journey in the third-class restaurant carriage indulging in, to borrow from Dickens, a celebration of slap-up meals although the quality of some railway company third-class menus could be questioned 'with boiled this and that, cabbage, and custard, the best bet usually being a chop or steak, both of which were equally popular at the turn of the century'.

Equally, Stephen Crane described third-class lunching on the *Scotch Express* as 'an average menu of a chop and potatoes, a salad, cheese, and a bottle of beer' Whilst a number of railway companies had their eyes on the luxury segment, they also focused their attentions on a broader market with the ability to spend, particularly the prosperous middle-classes who were increasingly drawn to travelling further afield and sharing the luxuries of life. The ceremonies and conviviality of home life, built so successfully into the fabric of railway company hotels, were extended to the railway carriage. Afternoon tea was now an established ritual, with carriages manned by immaculately turned out attendants. The English preoccupation with the refined art of afternoon tea drinking was something that appealed to wealthy Americans, some genuinely perplexed by the formalities of etiquette found amongst members of Britain's rarefied and highly stratified class structures. Oliver Wendell Holmes was intrigued by the formalities of tea on a second visit to Britain and Europe in 1886 after an interval of more than fifty years. He notes:

'The afternoon tea is almost a necessity in London life. It is considered useful as "a pick me up," and it serves an admirable purpose in the social system. It costs the household hardly any trouble or expense. It brings people together in the easiest possible way, for ten minutes or an hour, just as their engagements or fancies may settle it.'

Specially adapted first-class dining cars provided a lounge type environment to sample the afternoon tea experience when travelling by rail. There was an ulterior motive too. Afternoon tea became part of a drive by railway companies to provide light meals and refreshment without the need to provide full-scale kitchen car catering and, from their perspective, a less costly exercise.

The LNWR in the years before the war targeted the northern business community with its through trains to the south coast, emphasising the quality of its luncheon and tea car trains. The idea of the tea car was not confined just to Britain. In the United States, the Great Northern Railway operated a luxury train to Seattle called the *Oriental Limited* and known for its afternoon tea service. Food historian Jeri Quinzio notes, 'Promptly at four o'clock, a dining car waiter served tea and a uniformed maid served platters of dainty cakes to passengers'.

In photographs, fashionably dressed ladies could be seen enjoying tea in the observation car. Seattle, like Vancouver in Canada, was the embarkation point for many trans-Pacific liners to Japan and China. The idea of the tea car bridged an increasing interest amongst prosperous customers in east/west food cultures. Relative to American and European operations, British railway journeys were comparatively short affairs, so the tea car was used by railway companies to bridge the food gap especially on some services where railway companies declined to offer full on-board dining. Whilst the idea of the tea car evolved ultimately into other on-board catering formats, in Britain it flourished into a long-standing tradition that was fast-disappearing elsewhere but lasting until 1990s railway privatisation. As Neil Wooler explains, 'At afternoon tea time, the restaurant car remains one of the last bastions of the toasted teacake'.

The jury was always out as to whether train catering was a benefit needed to retain passengers (and certainly competition existed on many routes) or whether it was viewed as a profit or loss centre; the experience of many US railroads was always more about managing the losses of on-board catering. The Lancashire & Yorkshire Railway (LYR) developed tea cars specifically for its shorter journey network but the new food service innovation at the time was the buffet car, which could supply a combination of light snacks and liquid refreshment as well as a limited range of hot fare. These facilities were considered especially beneficial for servicing passengers using the company's Irish Sea steamer operations at Fleetwood. The GCR first tried this food concept in the 1890s and, with their London extension, buffet cars akin to bars complete with handsome pictures of the highest saloon-lounge standard were open to all travelling passenger classes and were designed to provide light meals and refreshments outside of main mealtimes.

This was not the success envisaged, probably due to Edwardian reservation and the convention of not wishing to mix with different social classes. But when the new London line was completed, the GCR deftly moved upscale to target first-class customers with a luxury travel proposition. Notwithstanding, most railway companies were somewhat slow developing the buffet car concept, preferring to work with existing suppliers of warm food baskets collected from station platforms first introduced in 1884. This activity reached its height in Edwardian times as the first examples of 'fast-food' branded packaging appeared. The quality of station catering improved considerably as railway companies maximised passenger discretionary spending. By time of the Big Four creation, railway companies employed even more effort behind 'food on the move'.

As well as carriage catering developments, sleeping car standards significantly improved although varying considerably from company to company and their routes. It was very much the province of those operators of long-distance rail services, but improvements were discernible. By Edwardian times, bed linen became standard, appealing especially to lady passengers accustomed to better things in life. Why the idea of supplying fresh, clean sheets took such a long time to come to fruition in Britain is surprising, as this had been normal practice on Pullman's sleeping cars operating on the Chicago, Alton & St. Louis Railroad since 1865.

By the Great War, the trappings of new design styles were bonded in both shipping line and railway company thinking. Most railway operators elected for more modern looking styles of wooden carriage construction but maintaining ornate styles of panelling and colourful liveries that so characterised the period. When the Pullman company built new cars for the Caledonian Railway, it developed a particular Scottish-styled theme. Each car was named after the country's heroines and decorated in an individual style reflecting Scottish heritage. Standards included inlaid and veneered panelling, velvet carpets, silk curtains and dining chairs upholstered in morocco leather with the innovative *Maid of Morvan* observation car designed for tourist traffic incorporating a large circular-ended compartment and large observation windows kitted out by Waring and Gillow.

The new 1914 ECJS stock laid down the gauntlet for superior travelling on the east coast route characterised by first-class restaurant cars with polished-teak partitions. Further luxury adornments included green tapestry upholstered seats, leather-topped tables and rose coloured carpets. Pullman cars were regularly deployed on SECR's boat trains from Victoria, ensuring a seamless service for continental travellers. Platforms one and two at Victoria would have been a very typical period scene as R.W. Kidner points out 'Pullmans were boarded by top society'; the station platforms were conveniently located with just a 'short walk for royalties and notables of all countries between their Pullman Special and the Buckingham Palace landaus waiting in the yard'.

Railway companies deliberately planned their luxury services around more enlightened departure times, particularly post breakfast. At mainline stations, fast-track platform access to awaiting luxury trains was a highly organised affair, minimizing periods of waiting for fortunate first-class travellers. Professor Colin Divall notes 'it's interesting that the experience of *waiting* is rarely tackled by historians, despite the fact that most people hate hanging around'. Yet the station concourse could always be a gold-fish bowl for the rich and privileged eager to endorse their wealth. By the early 1900s, the quality illustrated weekly titles were always full of the latest fashion tips and the best possible dress for train travel. And if your party needed to loiter around before boarding the first-class carriage, then there was always a rich vein of appropriate titles in well-stocked station bookstalls to be surveyed together with all the other necessary travel accoutrements of maps, timetables and tourist guidebooks all designed to sooth the holiday journey by train. For women, how they looked and arrived would increasingly become a benchmark of civilized behaviour.

The end of the Edwardian period represented the zenith for Britain's pre-grouping railways. Change was looming but for a few brief years before the conflagration, luxury travel continued to thrive as company managements continued to make plans. As previously noted, Dalziel's Pullman Company in 1913 concluded a twenty-year agreement with the Caledonian Railway to provide all its dining carriages as a means of boosting its share of Scottish tourist business. Ten new first and third-class Pullman dining and buffet cars with opulent interiors were built for Caledonian's operations. Meals without a supplement payment were accessible to passengers elsewhere on the train. This was a logical development first seen with LBSCR in the early 1890s, when Pullman carriages were used to provide catering arrangements for standard railway train services. Luxury first-class cars ran between Glasgow and Aberdeen, whilst Pullman buffet cars were employed over shorter distances. Pullman's initiatives helped maintain progress towards more comfortable travelling experiences.

Soloman notes a commentary from Hamilton Ellis remarking, 'in Britain, the third class Pullman service introduced on the London, Brighton and South coast in 1915 offered greater comfort than first class carriages of ordinary design'.[6] First-class railway carriages, restaurant car and sleeping car development tended to evolve together in the early years of the twentieth century but such progress was not universal across Britain's disparate railway system. Whilst the Edwardian era and the period before the Great War was generally acknowledged as the period when railways were at their most profitable, this did mask inequalities across the industry sector. For some companies, the ability to invest in new coaching stock was simply not there because of falling revenues and profitability. Some routes were extremely profitable, helping to cross-subsidize other railway company activity. On the well utilised east and west coast routes between England and Scotland, first-class passengers would enjoy new day and night-time travelling experiences with the introduction of a succession of new ECJS and WCJS rolling stock.

For first-class travellers, the development of culinary service was a notable feature of Edwardian times. Seductive spaces were created for dining and entertainment in new hotels, on ships and within a British context on trains, where quality food provision at the turn of the century started to take a central role, becoming a uniform feature of many railway company offerings. By 1903, the Midland Railway had gained a particularly good reputation for high quality food provision. The company provided dining cars with day-long first-class catering on all its sixteen main St. Pancras departures. Passengers from Bristol could expect dining cars as far north as Bradford and Leeds.

But at the top end of the market, it was to shipping lines that first-class passengers would look. The cavernous steel spaces of large new liners allowed superstructures to be filled with class leading kitchens where chefs tutored by France's leading culinary artists could excel in creating the finest and most exquisite forms of early twentieth century gastronomic fare. The emphasis placed on food quality was typically exemplified by shipping industrialist

Alfred Balinn, who hired Ritz to train his HAPAG shipping line's catering staff to Ritz-Carlton standards. In 1905, Ritz and Escoffier opened a Ritz-Carlton a la carte restaurant on-board the German liner SS *Amerika*. The Ritz-Carlton hospitality brand was developed for the US market with the company's first New York hotel opening in 1911 and a second a la carte restaurant on-board the giant SS *Imperator* in 1913. Both ship's restaurants were closed when war broke out the following year, representing a high-point of maritime culinary excess in which the early luxury goods innovators ensured standards at sea were equal to those of the London Ritz-Carlton or the New York Waldorf-Astoria. Celebrity chef culture, now such a prevalent theme within the modern cruise line business, is nothing new.

And so, similar themes were seen on rail particularly on long-distance routes. The British Pullman Company's focus at the time was more on the quality and comfort of its surroundings than its food offer, since the clear majority of its operations were restricted to the short-distance SECR and LBSCR routes where light meals, snacks and drinks were considered more important to customers. It was only after grouping, when Pullman carriages

A crowd of passengers are awaiting the arrival of a train at Bournemouth Central station. Whilst not a main London terminus, stations like Bournemouth hosted many passenger amenities to soothe the Edwardian traveller's expectations. (John Scott-Morgan Collection)

started to be employed on long-distance LNER trains, that the company had to really start competing on the culinary front. Differentiating between the needs and facilities offered between standard first-class and railway company preoccupation with carriage compartments and that of the new open style of Pullman car occupied much company management time. Certainly, the convention at the time was for Pullman cars to be fitted out with individual seating. This undoubtedly influenced Great Eastern Railway (GER) when they employed Pullman cars on their most important boat trains immediately after the Great War. Open style carriages became a feature of new stock commissioned by the Big Four railway companies from the late 1920s.

The spill-over from Victorian home influence continued unabated into the Edwardian era. Women from the higher social classes found new freedoms. Not only were restaurants and hotels permitted playgrounds for individual women or for small groups of them, but a state of independence extended to what may be best described as an early form of retail or shopping culture. Not only were specialist suppliers and department stores springing up around city centres but also special Malls or Arcades of individual shops selling a variety of high-end products and services especially involving women's fashion. The world of fashion would occupy the minds of new publishing groups who would fine-tune titles targeting particular groups of women.

This also spilt over into the home. Firms such as Waring and Gillow who produced high-class luxury interior designs for hotels, ocean liners and railway carriages made a move into the retail sector. Hardly surprising Waring and Gillow opened a new London furniture gallery in 1906 described as a twentieth century shop deluxe 'where everything, so far as the edifice and decoration are concerned, is on the palatial side, and where even the millionaire can gratify his most ambitious tastes', according to *The Sphere*. This started a home decoration and furnishing trend where advertising space taken by firms such as Maple & Company was positioned alongside railway holiday arrangement details. Product association of this type continued during the inter-war years as furniture, textiles and ceramics played a central role in defining stylish homes. During this period, the Pullman Company produced an in-house publication entitled *The Golden Way*, with many upscale brands such as Maples, Smith's English Clocks and Sloan Square-based Peter Jones Department Store taking space in the

The village of Tarbet, meaning 'a place over which a boat can be drawn', is located on the Loch Lomond isthmus and accessed by the West Highland Line. This NBR poster placed the Scottish Highlands destination as a centre for outdoor activities designed to attract prosperous travellers and especially the weekend Edinburgh and Glasgow visitor. Caledonian Railway's poster from around 1920, locates the long-established Tarbet Hotel, built in an impressive baronial style, on the loch shores as its main focus. J.J. Bell described the hotel at Tarbet as 'a favourite with sojourners'. The earlier 1912 NBR poster highlights the nearby Trossachs and Loch Katrine areas to the east of Loch Lomond that could now be reached via the new Aberfoyle tourist route. Loch Lomond, the Highlands and the Trossachs, made famous by Sir Walter Scott's writings which in time formed part of a 'Scott tourist trail', progressively featured in inter-war and later British Railways advertising with familiar 'See Scotland by Train' themes. Experience - ambience, culinary, service and personal attention. (NRM Pictorial Collection/Science & Society Library – images 16 and 16B)

advertising platform, keen to maximise an association with Britain's luxury trains.

Having household names designing first-class hotel, carriage and liner interiors with whom their customers would be totally familiar was a sound and logical business decision. The Great War would place the luxury goods industry on hold as the McKenna duties of 1915 placed duties of thirty-three and a third per cent on luxury product imports whilst an ending of culinary excesses was signalled together with rules governing the 'flaunting of luxury foodstuffs' before the final German U-boat blitz on British shipping in 1918, representing an end of an opulent age. As Perkin wryly observed 'The rich could not but look back at the war as the beginning of their decline in lifestyle and prosperity'.

Before the Great War, Britain's railway companies kept a close watching brief on developments occurring on the other side of the Atlantic, particularly as many wealthy American visitors were reaching these shores and frequently travelling on their country's premier trains. As well as specialist interest publications such as *The Railway Magazine* and *Railway Gazette* drawing together many railway route, leisure travel, hospitality and destination threads, it was also fuelled by a travel writing industry becoming progressively more sophisticated in terms of author output on both sides of the Atlantic. In May 1891, William Smith, a Yorkshireman of Morley, was travelling aboard the *Chicago Limited* express train. His observations of the facilities aboard the twenty-two-hour journey to the Mid-West included:

> 'The smoking-car has a reading room for the passengers, library, easy chairs, writing and card tables and a barber's shop, for without the latter it seems as if life would be hardly worth living in the States. If the traveller desires to present a respectable appearance when met by friends at the end of the journey, he can have his hair cut, curled and shampooed for half a dollar (2s), a shave for a quarter (1s), or a bath at the rate of forty miles an hour for 75 cents (3s).'

This particular travelogue must have gathered a considerable amount of dust on Yorkshire book shelves before being unearthed again by LNER officials for inclusion on the new 1928 *Flying Scotsman* carriage stock.

Another travel writer who ventured to the Mid-West from New York was Ethel Alec-Tweedie, a successful authoress who wrote an extensive portfolio of travel titles and other works spanning the years 1889 to 1936. She penned as Mrs. Alec Tweedie, Mrs. Alec-Tweedie and in her maiden name as Ethel B. Harley. Well educated and having lived in modest luxury, her life was turned upside down following the unexpected death of her husband in 1896 and that of her father shortly afterwards. Having been left effectively destitute with two young sons to bring up, and with little income to draw upon, she turned to writing.

She made her first trip to the US at the turn of the century but later returned to America on holiday for a third time in the autumn of 1912, having made a name for herself, and completed her thirteenth book which was printed in several editions. *America As I Saw It: or, America Revisited*. Published the following year, it was an extensive recollection of her visit, portraying the country's fads, fashions and tribulations. Ethel was now well-connected, travelling on several occasions in the utmost of luxury, which she likened as being akin to royalty, as a guest aboard the owners of private railroad cars, but would also step on to trains in exactly the same manner as most passengers did. Travelling by train in America was not always the easiest of exercises, particularly for women with accompanying pieces of hand luggage or grips as Americans called them. At the latter end of the Gilded Age, the country was acknowledged to be the home of service culture, with many luxury hospitality-driven enterprises catering for the needs of a new wealthy elite. Railroad companies began to ensure passengers enjoyed better travelling experiences at the beginning and end of journeys and when they alighted to and from the train. She wrote:

'How delightful it is that America has instituted porters at last; and what a joy they have a high platform now in a station like the Grand Central. Let us drink to the health of high platforms, and hope they soon appear over the length and breadth of the land. Those acrobatic crawls up slippery steps in to Pullman cars were not only exasperating, but dangerous.'

On her most recent visit Ethel travelled on the *20th Century Limited*, a train de luxe service first run ten years earlier, remarking how impressed she was with the travelling experience:

'one travels a thousand miles between New York and Chicago, a journey which cost me forty dollars, or eight pounds. It is a marvellous train, and in the summer months only takes eighteen hours to run that long distance. There *is* class distinction in America; but it is not always in the right place.'

Whilst there were undoubted improvements which Alec-Tweedie recognised, she pondered about the Pullman sleeping car she had come across on her first visit in 1900/1901 and the problems it presented for even the most intrepid of lady traveller. In a chapter entitled 'An Englishwomen's First Night on an American Sleeping-Car', she described the Pullman as a veritable US institution, but considered it to be alien to the requirements of many British and European visitors. It was not a patch on what would normally be encountered back home. The idea of separate compartments for the first-class traveller on American trains seemed at the time to be a million miles away or at least the distance of the pond. Even the *New York Times* lampooned the Pullman sleeping car with its shared sleeping berths to be 'as terrible as ever.'

CHAPTER 3

1921-1945: A Golden Age of Luxury Travel and Austerity

The 1920s was a period of dramatic contrasts with deep-rooted social and economic change modifying the face of Britain, Europe and the Western world forever. The loss of so many menfolk on Europe's battlefields saw a decline in mass emigration but the legacy of the waste of so much human life brought about a gradual change in society's makeup. Despite the disparities of ugly city slums, unemployment and stark poverty the middle-classes were totally enthroned by mid-decade.

For the middle-classes, the inter-war period was a golden age where they were uniquely and economically favoured. Many never had to brave the deprivations of unemployment, providing the bedrock of a modern spending economy. At the upper end of the social scale, there was a transition from the closed structures of nineteenth century England to a more open elite no longer based on landed wealth. The upper-classes by this time were a relatively small group of people, only around 40,000 individuals, who wielded immense social and political power, but its glamour and showy display enchanted a mass electorate. The impact of the Great War had a massive effect on lifestyles and social attitudes everywhere and for the railways left a big hangover, as they had been totally worn down by the war effort. For hospitality and retail-led businesses reliant on affluent American visitors, four years of 'no doing Europe this year' impacted significantly.

War-time railway maintenance inactivity, plus a slow and meandering roll towards railway consolidation, did little to facilitate a rapid response to normality. The railways in several ways were representative of old-style industries, ultimately leaving Britain in a position of labouring its way in the modern world, something Perkin described as:

'mainly due to British industrialists and traders persisting in products like coal, ships, heavy engineering and textiles for which world demand was shrinking, and not investing enough in the new consumer goods like motor cars, radios and electrical appliances for which demand was rising.'

By the early 1920s, the backlog in track maintenance caused by war-years neglect gradually brought about improved journey times. When planned legislation was announced, the pre-grouping railway companies had several years to plan for integration. With railway 'grouping' in 1923, the newly established Big Four railway companies undertook a spring clean of their assets as the industry moved from a laissez-faire existence into one in which government would ultimately seek to gain greater control of ownership influencing administration and operation. The creation of the Big Four private companies did invoke a process of modernisation which by mid-decade did much to improve the public's perception of train travel. To the outside world, the railways appeared revitalised and fresh looking, progressively introducing many new classes of locomotives and rolling stock. In the final summer of the pre-grouping era, the railway companies really pushed out the boat to capture first-class passengers. In noting railway arrangements for holiday travelling, *The Tatler* said:

> 'Some people imagine that their holiday does not begin until they arrive at their chosen pleasure ground. No greater mistake could be made; let your holiday begin at home, and the journey, whether to the sea or the mountains, the North or the South, the East or the West, should afford one of the brightest days of the summer. There is an old adage that "the passage perillus makyth a port pleasant"; to-day, however, the "passage perillus" is as delightful as the "port pleasant". If it is not so, the fault rests with the holiday maker, for by a little care on his part his journey can be made one of luxurious comfort.'

The travelling experience might have been well and truly on the railway agenda but for all their efforts the companies increasingly faced stiff competition from the relative freedoms the internal combustion engine provided for consumers as well as diesel technology for the conveyance of haulage and road-based bus and coach passenger transport. From mid-decade, the private motor car was beginning to be far more accessible as mass-production moved ownership of vehicles beyond the confines of the wealthy towards the meritocracy of the professional middle-classes who would soon buy them in their millions. Cars and taxis were ideal for short journeys but the tarmacking of hundreds of miles of country roads opened longer distance travel by car. Railways thus suffered from a general decline in the number of passengers they carried, despite their strenuous efforts to begin marketing train travel as an exotic and luxurious experience, but class-differentiated travelling and accommodation persisted and was something that made car travel so appealing.

Despite road-based competition, well-heeled first-class passengers witnessed impressive developments making rail travel far more pleasant especially on longer journeys as inspiring new steam locomotives and carriage stock were introduced during the mid-1920s. On the Anglo-Scottish routes, the LMS with their *Royal Scot* and the LNER with their *Flying Scotsman* named trains immortalised inter-war glamorous long-distance rail travel. This was not just confined to day-time operations, as night-time services also received luxury treatments with the introduction of the company's respective *Night Scot* and *Night Scotsman* sleepers. And the Scottish Highlands were not neglected as the LMS introduced the *Royal Highlander* sleeping car train on 26 September 1927, with Aberdeen and Inverness portions together with a breakfast restaurant car attached at Perth. At the height of the summer, separate night-time sleepers would run fuelled by LMS sleeper advertising extolling 'A smooth run for the 12th'. The company used the annual society trek to the Scottish Highlands to target the fashionable set in a range of selected upmarket titles highlighting alternative Euston and St. Pancras departures. LNER also adopted similar advertising themes for 12 August promoting their *Highlandman* and *Aberdonian* sleepers amidst moorland and gamebird imagery. Yet by the end of the 1920s, the Scottish Highlands, despite the best land having been turned over for a giant game reserve, felt the first ill winds of destination competition. The two railway companies could no longer rely on their upscale field sports constituency for Anglo-Scottish traffic. Tourism collaboration in a bid to attract a broader customer base was evident; LNER promoted Aberdeen, north Berwick, Dunoon and Rothesay under a banner of 'Scottish Holiday Resorts' in upmarket press with a call to action that involved resort local authority town clerk offices. The company also introduced a series of Scottish holiday handbooks for its routes carrying an advertising banner of 'So far...and yet so near'.

RONALD GRAY. 1924

LMS   # READY FOR "THE 12ᵀᴴ"
ARRIVAL OF A LONDON EXPRESS AT PERTH
By Ronald Gray

Previously, pre-grouping railway companies had had a haphazard approach to the naming of locomotives. Some were ambivalent, others were more coordinated but the policy tended to change with grouping as the widespread naming of locomotive classes, individual locomotives together with the naming of train services was recognised for its publicity value. The Southern Railway, for instance, named all of their inherited H1 and H2 class locomotives – long associated with the prestigious *Southern Belle* Pullman service – after coastal locations to create a better travelling image. Growth in naming locomotives and express services was firmly taken on board by railway company publicity

Above and opposite

The grouse season was always big business for the Anglo-Scottish carriers as LMS investment in this 1924 poster clearly indicated. Targeted primarily towards domestic audiences, selective promotion always ensured active interest from across the Atlantic. Wealthy Americans since late Victorian times rented well-known Scottish moors with the opening of country houses and shooting lodges always attracting a large influx of international visitors with interests in deer stalking, shooting game and stag and fishing for salmon and sea-trout. Special arrangements were made for trans-Atlantic passengers disembarking liners at Southampton with guns destined for Scotland carried in special secured vans. In 1928, a large number of Americans were recorded for 12 August whilst a year later, the LMS reported record business for the *Royal Highlander* sleeper with over six hundred sleeping berths booked to go out in six portions with duplicate running trains. LNER similarly chimed 'an exceptionally large number of Americans shooting in Scotland'. London visitors often demanded a plentiful supply of grouse to be on luncheon menus the day after commencement of the new season at many West End restaurants and hotels courtesy of a quick dash by train and road from the Highlands. In the 1930s, aware that hung birds acquired a better taste, enterprising London eateries would arrange to send generous supplies back across the Atlantic for American customers. (Illustrated London News Ltd/Mary Evans)

departments. Almost every main line would have its named expresses signposted in railway time tables and station and platform boards. Naturally, they invoked a variety of emotions. *The Times* reported on the LMS centenary:

> 'Sentimentality, snobbishness, romanticism, call the weakness by what you please, will always make the passenger prefer to travel by a train with a name, rather than the 9.15. Though few of us except boys small enough to travel on half a ticket, bother our heads much about the engine which draws us.'

Another element of railway promotion the Big Four companies took to heart was the publicity value of their liveries as modern branding tools. Prior to grouping, each of the main nineteen pre-grouping companies was different but their individual livery colour schemes ensured locomotives and coaches were instantly recognised by the travelling public on their local patch and routes. Elsewhere, their identification would have been more difficult beyond a small group of Edwardian 'railwayac'; the forerunner of the modern railway enthusiast. A limited number of liveries adopted by the Big Four ensured a consistency could be applied to promotion and especially with prestige large locomotives hauling specially named train services. Similar approaches were adopted by shipping lines for branding as consistent and distinctive shades of colour were used in the painting of funnels and hulls to enhance liner images: red and black rims for Cunard; buff and black for White Star; the lavender coloured hulls of the Union Castle Line and so on.

Whilst the term 'marketing department' might yet not have appeared on company head-office doors, the modern practice of marketing was now clearly in evidence, with a handful of skilful practitioners in each railway company who did much to change public attitudes towards the railways. Their actions created customer touchpoints as modern named locomotives were bestowed with personality; a process Matthew Engle suggests the Big Four 'showed some skill at putting their best face forward' and received by the public with considerable enthusiasm. Thus locomotive classes and name train services were synonymous with glamour, generating real excitement across large swathes of British society. In 1927, the non-stop long-distance runs of the rival *Flying Scotsman* and the *Royal Scot* trains attracted large crowds at stations and all along the lineside near population centres.

Ninety years later, the unadulterated power, speed, style and glamour of the nation's favourite locomotive – the restored *Flying Scotsman* – still does.

By the 1930s, the Big Four really started to understand their customers better in both trade and business to business markets but more particularly in the consumer arena with the identification of commuter, business travel and tourist customers. This was sometimes not the easiest of tasks, since railway routes were the product of an historical legacy of Victorian laissez-faire and minimal state intervention. Lines connected main cities, regions and countries of the home union but were not necessarily planned in the most appropriate way, growing out of many local initiatives often originally connected to the movement of extractive materials and industrial products with such inheritances marring the development of fast passenger services to and from London. The 1930s streamliner luxury expresses were a case in point. A.J. Mullay noted that joined up thinking was not always present, suggesting little consideration was given to where the LMS *Coronation Scot's* clientele might come from, including the LNER's failure to extend the down service of the *Coronation* in and out of Glasgow, resulting in unsatisfactory patronage of some services:

> 'Effectively, the LNER was offering a businessman's service to and from Edinburgh, which was a tourist, not a commercial, centre. The LMS was squaring the equation by offering a service timed for the casual traveller to and from a northern destination which was simply not an attraction for tourists. Glasgow was not then the cultural centre it is now; indeed the LMS did not even illustrate it in the train's introductory brochure for the US tourist market.'[1]

The *Coronation Scot* may have performed better if it had been timed as a late afternoon departure from both cities serving the business customer and in all likelihood would have established a durable market. Other railway companies knew their markets better, especially in terms of tourist demand as there were serious attempts to coordinate tourism opportunities at both national and regional levels as well as the active involvement of the major parties involved in travel activities. The International Union of Official Organisations for Tourist Propaganda was founded in 1924. During this period the railway industry, and in particular the

Great Western, was prominently involved with attracting overseas tourists to Britain. This was some of the earliest efforts of integrated destination marketing efforts with the 'Come to Britain Movement' founded in 1926.

Some of the Big Four were key stakeholders, united in the aim of promoting tourism in the country. The 'Come to Britain Movement' was later to become known as the British Tourist Authority and its latest incarnation VisitBritain. Of all the Big Four companies, the GWR took a leading role in marketing Britain internationally, something it had been doing since the turn of the century. As Dr Alan Bennett noted, 'Felix Pole was the only general manager from the four railway companies to attend the first meeting of the provisional meeting of the Travel Association on 26 February 1929'.

America was identified as the primary overseas market and a seventy-two-page booklet called *Seeing Great Britain by Railway* was issued by the Railways Information Bureau in 1928, providing American and overseas visitors with details on 200 around Britain and Ireland railway tours covering popular literary destinations associated with Shakespeare, Scott, Dickens and other authors. By the mid-1930s, GWR had really upped their game by appointing a US General Agent based on 505 Fifth Avenue in New York. The Travel and Industrial Development Association of Great Britain and Ireland took a slightly different approach at their pavilion at the 1939 World Fair in New York by using models of Britain's foremost trains (the real life streamlined LMS *Coronation Scot* was actually at the fair in a different location) to provide a complete tourist picture highlighting the main Big Four railway routes. British railway posters featuring the country's railway flyers suggesting themes of speed and destination identification had been in great demand, having sold several thousand in previous years.

Before these marketing-led initiatives, the base railway product had changed too. The first benefit many passengers saw in the mid-1920s was upgrading of coaching stock and a wholesale conversion to carriage electric lighting when coaches went into shop for overhaul. Although this proved a costly exercise for the companies, there was a gradual phasing out of old antiquated pre-grouping coaches from the Victorian and Edwardian eras, being replaced by new first and third-class steel panelled stock. Whilst the main line routes facilitated fast-running, the situation on secondary, local and suburban routes was less impressive as transport infrastructure on a day-by-day basis was still dependent on large numbers of manual workers responsible for keeping the railway running safely. Relationships between railway management and an increasingly volatile trade union movement were strained almost beyond breaking point.

The country was brought to its knees by the 1926 General Strike as Britain's railway system was largely immobilised by industrial strife, although valiant attempts by management and volunteers ensured some trains ran. The emergence of the middle-classes as strike-breakers was a phenomenon of the 1920s. By the end of May 1926, a degree of normality had resumed but the strike bitterly divided society; respite was desperately needed. Within a week or so of the launch of the *Atlantic Coast Express (ACE)*, Saturday, 31 July marked the start of the holiday season and a national mood change. Regional newspapers talked up the rush to the coast; mainline stations in London and the country's industrial centres reported big business as popular destinations on the continent, Scotland and resorts on the east coast and in the west were as busy as ever. Many trains were run in duplicate with several extra portions of the *ACE* put on.

During weekend working, the Southern Railway had laid on an extra 500 train services. Heavy weekend loading was not new to the railway companies as moving large numbers of people to chief sporting events had been a Saturday feature for many years. Holiday traffic was different and concentrated particularly with through train workings that might entail return trip workings of many hundreds of miles for carriage stock. For railway companies this presented problems as unutilised carriages hung around in sidings for long periods. Keeping hold of better conditioned old stock was one partial remedy, as they would have sufficient resource as and when required but it was still an expensive exercise. For some railwaymen, depending on shift patterns, heavy holiday workings might begin on Friday afternoon and end in the early hours of Sunday mornings. This phenomenon would not disappear (apart from the Second World War years) until the privately-owned car took over as a form of mass transportation in the late 1950s.

Apart from more luxurious stock on long-distance routes, which included a mix of Pullman services and new developments brought in by individual companies, there was also the reintroduction of more well-appointed trains for liner and cross-channel ferry/steamer services. With the dawn of the civil aviation age, the specialist travel firms began to fuse interests between land-based railways, short sea crossing, ocean voyages and emerging long-distance travel by air. Since late Victorian times, boat train services had become more luxurious for first-class passengers, many running with Pullman cars and progressively adapted to provide a seamless travel experience.

Prior to railway grouping, only a few regular luxury trains were ever bestowed with a name, although the informal use of naming individual services had gone on for decades before. In France and elsewhere on the continent much the same occurred, as luxury rail travel returned with speedier services coupled with even more style and panache. The Roaring Twenties changed luxury travel on land and sea. In Britain and France, this was a period of rail consolidation as the new companies plugged a gap in the market, developing a range of specialist train services for a new age of business, leisure and holiday travel. In Britain, much of this association was closely entwined with the Pullman Company, who jointly developed a raft of newly upscale services principally with two of the Big Four railway companies. In 1925, the LNER introduced a variety of Pullman services to the east coast route – the *West Riding Pullman* (renamed *Yorkshire Pullman* in the mid-1930s), *Queen of Scots* and on the East Anglian routes, Pullman cars for the *Hook Continental* boat trains.

The Southern would not be outdone by LNER's Pullman involvement. In the 1920s, the company launched a series of prestigious named trains; some branded as Pullman services, others not. The Southern Railway was managed by Sir Herbert Walker with a leadership style much respected by fellow railwaymen. Arguably it was the best managed of the Big Four railway companies, successfully introducing an expensive programme to electrify its commuter network. At the other end of the scale, Walker had worked with a variety of partners to establish luxury train services over its metals including the Pullman Company and its chairman Davison Dalziel, whom he had first met in the early 1920s. Dalziel's other interests included Chair of the Wagon-Lits Management Committee, providing a firm command of the requirements of running international luxury train services on both sides of the English Channel. The two men fostered a good working relationship since the inauguration of the new glitzy *Calais-Méditerranée Express*, better known as *Le Train Bleu/the Blue Train* in Calais on 9 December 1922. *Le Train Bleu* effectively provided new ground rules for modern steel-sided European luxury trains following a succession of new services introduced by Wagon-Lits and the German operator MITROPA. Wagon-Lits, Pullman, Southern Railway and their French partners NORD would eventually create two of the world's best-known integrated luxury train services linking London and Paris with a variety of other international routes through the *Golden Arrow/La Flèche d'Or* in 1929 and several years later the *Night Ferry/Ferry Boat de Nuit* services. Dalziel and Walker worked closely in developing all-Pullman services on other Southern routes, including Pullman carriages for specific Southampton-based *Ocean Liner Expresses* as well as for new developing long-haul aviation services in the 1930s. The new decade saw new Southern Pullman services; the *Bournemouth Belle* in 1931 (picking up Pullman rolling stock from the failed GWR initiative) and the new electrified *Brighton Belle* in 1934.

Like LNER, Southern did not place all its eggs in one basket with Pullman but looked to create its own new luxury named trains. The company established the *Atlantic Coast Express (ACE)*. The new train was an exemplary marketing tool and part of a trend increasingly adopted by all four railway companies. Southern Railway's promotional approach was seen as an expression of modernity reflecting historical traditions but perceived as more accessible and less exclusive than Great Western's style. The *ACE* was a direct competitor to the GWR's prestigious *Cornish Riviera Express/Limited* service, and its promotion was managed with a degree of enterprise and zeal under the direction of a new broom following the appointment of Southern's first public relations (PR) guru J.B. (later Sir John) Elliot. The *ACE* name was adopted following a staff suggestion scheme run in the July issue of the *Southern Railway Magazine*. When the *ACE* service launched, Southern had a certain degree of catch-up to play as Devon and Cornwall had been consistently promoted by GWR's agile Paddington publicity department for the best part of twenty-five years. Part of GWR's strategy was to deliberately position itself alongside the region's premier destinations where it was seen very much as a co-operative partner in developing the visitor economy. The company also paid attention to creating enhanced travelling experiences, recognising that holidaying families were a core constituent of the customer base. Even children of well-to-do families needed to be kept amused on the long holiday journey to the West Country. From the GWR's perspective, building the brand amongst the next generation of travellers was seen as a crucial move

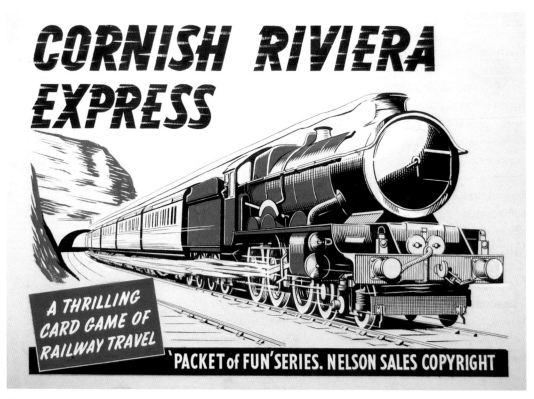

Having pioneered a series of highly successful jigsaw puzzles with Birmingham based Chad Valley Co Ltd, GWR and later British Railways Western Region extended the game format with the Nelson card game of railway travel. Railway illustrator A.N. Wolstenholme was known for his meticulous attention to detail in the quality of artwork he produced; his skills were very much on display in the creation of original artwork for the *Cornish Riviera Express* branded game. (Travelling Art Gallery)

and, from the mid-1920s, the company introduced a succession of 200-piece jigsaw puzzles where all the pictures contained references to the railway's locomotives, trains and activities.

Elliot was faced with a long-established and adroit competitor in having to counter a well-oiled Great Western machinery. This required the company to create a completely new identity for the train but, more importantly, the establishment of an *ACE* destination image that was fresh but at the same time in sympathy with the region's natural assets, Cornish Celtic heritage and the need to portray north Cornwall as King Arthur Country. The business logic was sound with an imperative to prise customers from the GWR's *Cornish Riviera* service by driving thousands of new middle-class passengers to the Southern's upmarket routes and destinations as tourist traffic to the south west of England grew substantially.

The new image could be wrapped up by the word 'Adventure' – a frisson of excitement and anticipation associated with visiting King Arthur's Kingdom.

Elliot had already sown the seeds by recommending to Southern's general manager that the company's express engines should be named. As with railway convention the world over, it was found people simply liked trains that had names. Malory's *Morte d'Arthur* became the inspiration for the designation of the 'King Arthur' class of locomotives due to the railway line's proximity to Tintagel and north Cornwall. The approach was liked by Walker, generating consensus amongst the company's senior management that themed locomotive naming would benefit Southern's business. Elliot describes in his chronicles that he 'felt sure we could cash in on the old legend' and was somewhat surprised when CME Maunsell liked the idea too, instructing a nameplate to be made up and placed over the locomotive splashes. It was a sensible counter to Great Western's long-held occupation of the media agenda. With their succession of Castle and King expresses, Hall, and later Grange and Manor mixed locomotive classes that created a lasting and majestic signature of Englishness and West Country landscapes.

So the first stage in the creation of the *ACE* storyline began when the King Arthur Class engine heading up the 11.00 am west of England express steamed out of Waterloo in the company of press photographers and reporters. The Arthurian theme as Walton notes 'was particularly associated with plans to develop tourism in north Cornwall, around Tintagel' maintaining the 'romantic associations with Tennyson, Malory and the early mists of British history' which had wide currency at the time.' Hardly surprisingly, therefore, Elliot sought to maximise Arthurian fable by developing this West Country district as a special place aided by the works and contributions of the future Poet Laureate, John Betjeman, who was well-versed for his support of architecture, heritage, landscape and the railway system. Mortenstow, writing in *The Sphere* magazine, penned an article on Arthurian Cornwall. 'Bude, Boscastle and Tintagel! They are names which stand for the Arthurian legend and so for the Arthurian land of England.'

A jam-packed publicity industry was now in full play. Betjeman and Jack Beddington, the publicity manager for the British division of Shell-Mex, were responsible for developing the Shell Guides, a series of highly successful county-based motoring guides catering for Britain's growing numbers of car drivers

ARTHURIAN CORNWALL.

The Land of a Great Legend and Beautiful Holidays

By MORWENSTOW

Bude, Boscastle, and Tintagel! They are names which stand for the Arthurian legend and so for the Arthurian land of England. If you want to find it you go, any morning, to Waterloo Station, across the most

ON THE NORTHERN COAST: Chapel Rock, Bude, one of the features of the popular resort on the borders of Devon and the Duchy

beautiful bridge in London, and you ask for the Atlantic Coast Express.

If you are curious you will discover that the Atlantic Coast Express is drawn by an engine of the King Arthur class: the Sir Tristram, the Sir Bors de Ganis, the Sir Lancelot, or the Sir Something-else. Therefore you are an Arthurian knight before you leave London and you are a much-belted one before you run through the beautiful country which lies between you and Bude in North Cornwall. Miles before you get there you feel the tang of the ozone coming in from the Atlantic, for there is nothing to speak about between Bude and the other side of that ocean. The Coast Express gets to Bude from Waterloo well within six hours, which is mighty good running and most smooth. It might run on into the late autumn if holiday folk would only recognise that that is a very perfect time in North Cornwall.

Bude has a real sea, blue and clear and wonderful; the sea of which Tennyson was thinking when he wrote in the "Idylls of the King":
" But after tempest, when the long wave broke
All down the thundering shores at Bude and Bos'
There came a day still as Heaven, and then
They found a naked child upon the sands
Of Wild Tintagel by the Cornish seas;
And that was Arthur, and they fostered him
'Till he by miracle was approved King."

Tintagel is not far from Bude, and the walk can be so inspiriting and inspiring that one hesitates to do more than dream of it, as Tennyson dreamed of his poetic Arthur. But the charm of Bude is the first thing, its wonderful bathing and sands are the next thing, its tennis lawns and its golf are other things, and the Coombe Valley, which comes in freshly, beautifully for the visitor, is always a thing by itself. A summer sun, warm but never oppressive; an azure sea, cool to the eye, invigorating to the body; a country of character and picturesqueness—could Bude stand for more? Anyhow, who wants more?

But even Tintagel thinks of the morrow and so there is a campaign in hand called the Tintagel Cliff Preservation Fund. Its object is to purchase as a public open space, to be vested in the National Trust, some sixty acres of land lying between Tintagel Church and the sea. This cliff land commands a view from Hartland Point to Trevose Head which all lovers of the beautiful and the romantic will like, and which, therefore, they should put their hands in their pockets to preserve. Otherwise Tintagel Cliff

MODERN TASTES ARE CONSIDERED: The magnificent tennis courts at Bude, which exert a powerful appeal on those left cold by glorious scenery as well as those catholic enough to enjoy both

may get built upon, and that would be sad news for Arthurian knights of all sorts, Eastward gleam the warning lights of Lundy Isle and Hartland Point, and south-by west is the ruby glow of Trevose Head, and all is poetry, in this the Arthurian land of England, of one corner of which Hawker of Morwenstow sang:
" And shall Trelawney die?
Here's twenty thousand Cornishmen shall know the reason why!

WHERE THE SEA COMES FOAMING IN: Bude cliffs seen from Upton

John Elliot's hand was clearly visible in this *Sphere* travel editorial from July 1929, being the first stage of image development where north Cornwall was positioned as a different and magisterial land but easily reached from London in under six hours. The Arthurian legend and Southern's close association would be finely-tuned by the company's Waterloo promotional team over the following decade. (Illustrated London News Ltd/Mary Evans)

forming a highly structured communications process using PR initiatives, film, celebrity endorsement and widely distributed marketing materials to reach consumers. Having shaped Shell Guides for Devon and Cornwall, Betjeman asked Paul Nash – a graduate of the Slade School of Art and one of Britain's most renowned artists of the period – to produce a Dorset guide in 1935, utilising a remarkable output of paintings and photographs he produced as an Isle of Purbeck resident. Thus, fuel suppliers, car makers and the Big Four railway companies by mid-decade were using the country's considerable artistic talents to mould domestic inter-war travel. Betjeman et al became celebrities of their day – a kind of 'Bloomsbury Set' of destination image makers – guaranteed to garner public attention for their big budget commissioners.

In the 1920s, British car manufacturers focused their attentions at the top end of the market with expensive, prestigious vehicles that were still regarded by many in the upper-classes as 'horseless carriages'.

By the mid-1930s, car prices fell in real terms with the average cost of a new vehicle almost half of what a car was some ten years before, resulting in the motorization of the middle and lower middle-classes. By the end of the decade, the majority of those with a household income of £500 a year owned a car. Car ownership, like home-ownership, together with the gradual suburbanisation of much of greater London and the south of England, established a consumer culture where the accumulation of possessions became the outward sign of success and thus a defining characteristics of 1930s middle-class life.

Both the GWR and Southern in the mid-1920s took up the cudgels to reopen holiday traffic to the far south west of England, reigniting a pre-war tourism boom. The Great Western was very much in the vanguard of promoting tourism and was always a significant register of cultural activity and focus. Their mass market *Holiday Haunts* booklet formed the backbone of their yearly publicity drive, with resort marketing teams selling in large numbers over a long-period between 1906 and 1948 apart from wartime interruptions. The tourism trade expanded considerably during the inter-war years, providing employment for large numbers of people working across Devon and Cornwall's hospitality industries. The Great Western had a good idea who their customers were as Medcalf suggests they were 'probably middle- and lower-middle-class holidaymakers who enjoyed increased incomes and lengthier holidays with pay'.

It is not always easy to identify the middle classes in this era. The economy hinged on the relative successes of the 'profiteers' in society, who could range from rich industrialists to the village greengrocer or the high-street butcher. Many in non-manual jobs representing the army of office workers in lower and clerical professions saw themselves as part of the middle-classes but in effect they constituted many households in the country earning less than £400 per annum, where life could still be very difficult.

Whilst holiday traffic was undoubtedly seasonal, the Great Western placed efforts behind a desire to make the far south west a year-round operation. The idea of 'Winter in the West' was developed by British author, journalist and broadcaster S.P.B. Mais in various GWR pamphlets but the company's publicity team possibly took an extreme view developing a 1923 poster suggesting the idea of Bathing in February on the Cornish Riviera. Mais was a productive writer who over a ten-year period wrote more than twenty pamphlets and tourist guides which ultimately grew into best-selling books. Such titles included *England's Character*, *England's Pleasance*, *Glorious Devon* and *England of the Windmills* but directed to an audience of car owners. According to Juliet Gardiner, he 'revelled in the title of "Ambassador" of the British countryside'. Mais also worked for the Southern Railway producing a free booklet called *My Finest Holiday*. Whilst the Great Western took every opportunity to foster a broader travelling public, the company eschewed the truly luxury end of the market by concentrating on sharing with its first-class customers the discovery of Cornwall's natural and cultural assets; effectively the GWR way of doing things.

Whilst the Southern concentrated on promoting links to Arthurian legend, the GWR took a broader county perspective in their promotional communication as their routes extended to the far reaches of the south west peninsula. Gardiner notes that by the 1930s, 'Cornwall became the summer destination of choice of several artistic, literary and generally "bohemian" types – though with its "reputable light" Cornwall had been attracting artists challenged to paint its everchanging seascapes since before the First World War.'[2] The company could concentrate on providing improved services based on speed and style with a consistent image of middle-England at its heart, but perhaps without the same veneer of gloss and glamour perpetuated by the Anglo-Scottish carriers. The GWR clearly understood its strategy and its middle-class customer base giving it some degree of prominence over its other Big Four competitors. As Medcalf concludes 'the GWR men were not as conservative as painted.'

The yearly editions of the well-known booklet *Holiday Haunts* set the tone for the company's marketing to Devon and Cornwall but including other West Country and Welsh resorts. And getting there was never a problem; the Great Western in the post grouping period continued to evolve its locomotive development with high-speed and efficient Castle and King Classes providing record breaking runs over the company's metals. Throughout the late 1920s and 1930s, the GWR built better and more up-to-date rolling stock. The company's most prestigious service, the *Cornish Riviera Express*, received new carriages in 1929 and again in 1934 and 1935 with the centenary stock issuing. But whilst the GWR introduced a raft of new named trains during the inter-war period, including the *Cheltenham Flyer*, *Cambrian Coast Express* and the *Cornishman* amongst others, and undoubtedly milked for their marketing value, these new timetabled trains did not receive the same consistent level of marketing investment as LMS and LNER put into their premier luxury streamlined services.

In effect, the GWR approach towards the first-class market was piecemeal; the company never really thought through each longer-term business case especially at the premium end. Tim Bryan suggests that James Milne (the GWR general manager) 'tried to emulate his predecessor, Felix Pole, in pursuing new ventures that provided some publicity for the company' but the 1930s were difficult trading times.[3] The short-lived *Torbay Pullman* and *Plymouth Pullman* boat train are probably classic examples of where the GWR thought it knew best by then introducing its own expensive and heavy-weight Super Saloon carriages that were plagued by seriously restricted operational route capabilities.

When the *Bristolian* non-stop, high-speed service was introduced to mark the GWR's Centenary on 9 September 1935, lack of investment meant that six of the seven carriage train ran without any special new stock apart from the latest type of mid-1930s buffet car which had a full-length counter, complete with pedestal seats. This was really fast-food on the move and whilst considered innovative by the railway press, the buffet car inclusion masked a general level of investment in new service development designed for the lucrative business market. Bryan also takes a swipe at the GWR, suggesting that the company got it wrong regarding its timing with a 11.00 am London departure that 'reflected some conservatism and a lack of understanding at Paddington, for few business travellers with appointments in Bristol would wish to leave the capital so late'.

Whilst the destination might not quite have been the city of a thousand trades, its unique mercantile position rendered the GWR decision a strange one, given Bristol was the GWR's second most profitable area after London. The company might have made a mishmash of the business travel market, but it revelled in its position of providing profitable passenger-focused West Country holiday travel services. So much so, the Great Western boasted it was the 'Nation's Holiday Line' as by 1939, more than fifteen million Britons enjoyed the privilege of some type of paid holiday away from home.

For those in society fortunate enough to live a leisurely life style, the marking of a new decade in 1930 heralded permanent change on the horizon. The thirties would be very different from the twenties as the western world became increasingly technology-based, delivering perceived benefits for all. The decade oversaw a loosening of class structures and hierarchies which was particularly evident in the ways consumers of all classes partook of leisure activities. Michael John Law suggests this was 'seen in the frequent and large-scale attendance at luxury super-cinemas and in many private and municipal facilities that welcomed customers from both the working and lower-middle classes.'[4] Society would continue to be dominated by industry- led middle-class capitalists but much of the traditional power base of the landed aristocracy and the county shires had ebbed away. This very much fitted with inter-war railway glamorisation as some luxury trains simply tailored the cut aided by sophisticated marketing and communication practice that created an illustrious image of domestic and international travel. The upper-class smart sets frequenting the *Flèche dÓr* and *Le Train Bleu* helped to maintain that impression.

Prosperity returned by the mid-1930s as trade revived. Those in full employment, and especially the burgeoning expertise of the professional middle-classes, would do well in the decade, although those at the other end of the spectrum suffered immensely in the depression years just as the dispossessed had done in years before. As with other forms of leisure open to everyone, the middle-classes oversaw an expansion of leisure travel with the family unit described as the 'enduring lifeblood' of English resorts until the emergence of overseas package holidays in the 1950s.

Writing in *The Sphere* magazine, Charles Graves noted that each railway company had its 'stunt' train and in case of the LNER this was the *Flying Scotsman,* with its cocktail bar, hairdressing saloons, shower baths and wireless (radio) headphones all designed as a means to keep the passenger occupied on longer journeys. He went on to describe the lengths railway companies would go to steal visitor and traveller 'road traffic from the road traffic kings themselves' by appreciating 'the fact that what used to be considered relaxation is now taken as boredom, and it is necessary to think up new ways to beguile the passenger who has not the concentrated fun of a steering-wheel in front of him and a klaxon beside his right wrist'.

For the well-off, choice of destination, things to do and new experiences to try out expanded significantly with the luxury end of the market, fuelled by the travel writings of the likes of Balfour, Fleming, Huxley, Leigh Fermor and Waugh. L.P. Hartley in his 'Literary Lounger' column in *The Sketch,* reviewed Evelyn Waugh's *Labels: A Mediterranean Journal* work. But first, he questioned why we travel, noting:

> 'Travellers of all kinds, and even writers of travel-books are many and various – sentimental, amorous, interested, bored, with as many moods and temperaments, perhaps more, than they have motives for their voyages. Indeed, the reasons why one goes on a journey are perforce limited. Pleasure, health, profit, these are most frequent. Such as travel to satisfy a *Wanderlust*, or to promote the cause of science or archaeology, or to flee from justice, are more rarely met with. But it may be generally assumed that a traveller is of a romantic disposition, and able to disregard discomfort and fatigue; for these (I need hardly say) are inseparable from travelling, however luxuriously conducted.'

Scotland continued to weave its magic. J.J. Bell's travel book *The Glory of Scotland* received critical acclaim when published in 1932, targeted at readers who had never visited the country. Modern destination building enterprise came to play as the LMS and LNER developed a joint poster campaign featuring Bell's travel literature, encouraging visitors to come north. Several years later, the two rail companies undertook a similar marketing exercise with Harry Batsford and Charles Fry's *The Face of Scotland* travelogue. Originally published in 1931, a third edition in March 1937 used the same trick as Bell with Scottish author John Buchan writing the foreword. Buchan remarked that the book had 'the supreme merit that it interprets its purpose generously' tracing Scottish 'national history, character and literature' to the landscape.

Intended as a visitor introduction, the exercise received extensive coverage. Despite these types of coordinated initiatives, which by the end of the decade were produced in significant numbers by the Big Four companies, place making rivalries were never far away. Travel agents, and Thomas Cook in particular, together with the shipping lines, provided the period mood music as they packaged old and new destinations in the form of exhilarating cruise itineraries and with short and long-distance air travel. Luxury

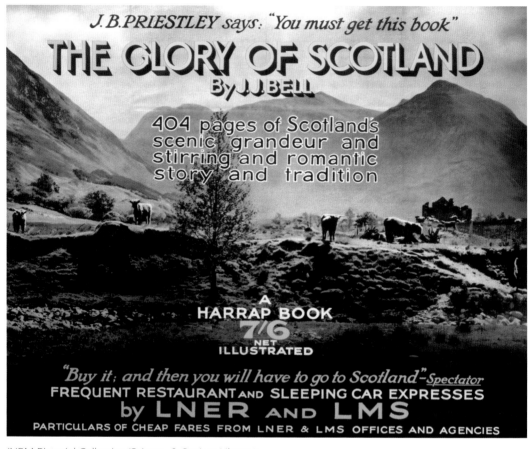

(NRM Pictorial Collection/Science & Society Library)

Rural dimensions with cows in fields, ruins and mountains provided the backcloth to this jointly promoted railway destination poster. Bell's book *The Glory of Scotland* emphasized the country's scenic grandeur, romanticism and traditional qualities and was infused with the support of literary luminaries of the period such as Compton Mackenzie and J.B. Priestley. The later 1937 'The Face of Scotland' poster and book illustrations were designed by Brian Cook, a nephew of Harry Batsford, showing a typical Scottish setting of a loch overlooked by a castle and mountains representing one of the few examples of his work not produced for the Batsford publishing house.

rail travel had its place but by 1937, Cook's handbook of services and tours featured air travel on its front cover as the company dominated the travel market, and by the time the brochure had been printed, Thomas Cook & Son was official agent for fifty-seven of the world's major airlines. Competition at the luxury end of the travel market was now sitting firmly in the railway company's own backyard but aviation represented a gap in their activities which they were already planning to fill with their own air services.

At the beginning of the 1920s, luxury forms of travel were special places and the bridge where this infusion of human interaction was most noticeable. None was more evident than the world of the exclusive hotel that witnessed further development in the inter-war period. In London, the Savoy company was almost unequalled in the elite and international market. Before the Second World War, the group was made up of three hotels including Simpson's restaurant, with a focus on American audiences that made up a high proportion of customers staying in the company's establishments. The organisation saw increased competition from other new enterprises and from the introduction of high-end service apartments.

Elsewhere in the capital, the Dorchester Hotel opened its doors in April 1931, setting new standards of luxury consumption. The old patrician round of the London season was not as it was as private houses in Pall Mall and Park Lane were either torn down or sold off to new owners. Formerly the homes for the aristocracy and nobility, they were replaced by vast hotels on the American model where rooms were seldom empty. Marketing writer Mark Tungate noted nineteenth century style and grandeur was never ever again attained; he says 'the future of hotels was industrialization: a corporate template to cater for the jet-borne business class' – a move in transport terms only a generation away. Former elegant city-centre railway hotels, now managed by the Big Four railway companies, slipped down the ranks of smartness. At the end of the 1930s, the LMS had the largest hotel estate of any of the Big Four, including ten sites which the company positioned as 'first-class' but with only three, the Midland in Manchester, the Adelphi in Liverpool and Gleneagles in Scotland, which opened its doors in 1924 complete with golf courses, indoor swimming pool, tennis courts, bowling green, croquet lawn and an expansive ballroom, were considered to be of international repute. Despite the care and attention given to planning Gleneagles, it lacked many facilities we would now take for granted.

LMS GLENEAGLES HOTEL
PERTHSHIRE
BY NORMAN WILKINSON.

Originally conceived by the Caledonian Railway to great acclaim in 1910, the two golf courses in the grounds of the Perthshire based hotel eventually opened for play almost a decade later with construction interrupted by the Great War. By 1924, the Gleneagles Hotel had opened its doors and immediately cemented itself as the LMS's flagship hospitality establishment outside of London. Built to luxury standards with the latest resort facilities, the country house style hotel was expected to attract international visitors of repute; it quickly established itself as a fashionable high-society holiday destination especially with wealthy American visitors. Described variously as a 'Riviera in the Highlands' and 'the eighth wonder of the world', LMS around 1927 used the services of Norman Wilkinson to create a draft image of the King's Course before committing final oils to canvas artwork.

When the Midland Railway's Manchester hotel was opened to great international acclaim in 1903, although considered lavish at the time, the 500 roomed establishment only possessed 100 baths. Whilst the Midland got many things right in attracting upscale clientele, its successor did not. The LMS Midland Hotel, an Art Deco building built at Morecombe in 1932 and designed as a substitute for the former company's Midland Hotel in the resort and another nearby railway hotel at Heysham Harbour, it was mistakenly positioned as a luxury establishment. Initially, the new establishment cultivated a 1930s A-list celebrity pack but it quickly fell out of favour. Its proximity to the north's industrial heartlands though made it a preferred location for working-class holidaymakers from the west of Yorkshire.

Whilst not a folly as it has been restored to its former glories, perhaps it was an early indication of LMS not really understanding the needs of wealthy customers? North American hotel chains were establishing high standards where en-suite facilities were taken for granted. Britain in the inter-war years generally lacked the great hotel chains created by the Statler or Biltmore companies and perhaps lacked a level of management expertise that was required to pay greater attention to the needs of its customers. Customer expectations of the hotels they stayed in had risen sharply in the 1930s, so no small wonder if they and other inferior establishments were surpassed by a new generation of quality hospitality organisations who had their fingers firmly on the pulse of new emerging consumer trends.

Similar situations occurred in Paris when the French railway system was nationalised in 1939. Nevertheless, the problems with their city-based estate and a general period 'of some difficulty for the railway and hotel industries alike', the Big Four railway companies in Britain looked to enhance their leisure portfolios as they 'expanded their operation at the top end of the resort hotel market' as there was a growing capacity and demand for leisure. The Great Western in 1929, which had a reputation as the most cautious of the railway companies involved in the hotel trade, acquired the Dartmoor located Mortonhampstead Manor House. Together with its Tregenna Castle Hotel in St. Ives and the Goodwick-based Fishguard Bay Hotel – known for its renowned luxuriant exotic gardens – the GWR had a small collection of upscale hotels that conformed to general American expectations of England being both traditional but modern. The company's hotel portfolio was probably the closest match of any of the other railway owned hotels in the high fashion of British genteel circles.

Exclusive golf orientated resort hotels such as Gleneagles and Turnberry received significant make-overs to create deluxe accommodation standards. They, the home of golf at St. Andrews and north Berwick, received the full marketing kitbag. The LNER, LMS and later British Railways, blessed Scottish golf resorts with

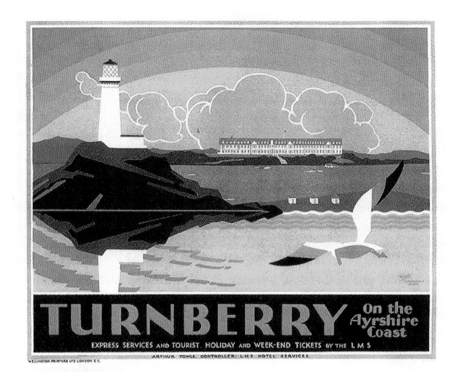

A palace of the Western Ocean

The waves come all the way from Nova Scotia to look at Turnberry. Imagine a great hotel looking nearly as big as Ailsa Craig, that stands on the Ayrshire Coast where the best soil in the world and the best sea breezes have made the turf more firm and more elastic than a golfer's conscience.

Imagine it, the last word in comfort and modernity, full of golfers by day and dancers by night, all lighted up and looking from seaward like one of the new Cunarders that are not built yet. Come to Turnberry, the Guest House by the Atlantic.

Accommodation should be reserved early. Apply to the Resident Manager, Turnberry Hotel, Ayrshire, Scotland; or to Arthur Towle, Controller LMS Hotel Services, St. Pancras, London, N.W.1

LAWN TENNIS TOURNAMENT—JULY 20th—25th.

TURNBERRY hotel

Express Services from London and the principal Provincial Towns served by the LMS

GOLF ● TENNIS ● DANCING ● SWIMMING

A New LMS Hotel: **WELCOMBE HOTEL STRATFORD-ON-AVON.**

England's Latest Country Guest House. Opens July 1st. Tariffs and particulars from the Manageress

TURNBERRY HOTEL

ON THE AYRSHIRE COAST
BY THE SHORES OF THE GULF STREAM

Atlantic breakers — Atlantic breezes . . . . Magnificent golf beside the seashore — beach and indoor bathing—tennis on perfect courts—riding over the sand dunes—fishing —sailing — and, the ideal background for a holiday, the luxurious hospitality of Britain's finest seaside hotel.

Open all the year. Full particulars from Central Bureau (Dept. 23), Midland Grand Hotel, London, N.W.1. Express Services from London and the principal provincial Towns served by the LMS.

ARTHUR TOWLE. CONTROLLER LMS HOTEL SERVICES

By 1929, Turnberry's railway hotel for golfers had been transformed into a destination of world-wide repute, enlarged and re-equipped with modern luxuries including sea-water swimming baths. Turnberry could warrant its own poster whilst LMS advertising positioned the hotel as offering 'its distinguished guests all that a connoisseur could demand' and on a par with 'the most celebrated hotels of London and the Continent' easily connected from the capital by express restaurant car service trains. In turning an eye to the American market, the May 1931 *Bystander* advert used enticing copy surrounding the planned Cunard super liners, whereas the May 1934 advertisement from the same publication used imagery of the range of bespoke activities guests could avail themselves as the hotel geared up for year-round opening aided by the benefits of its proximity to the Gulf Stream. In the final *Sphere* advert from January 1961, Turnberry was facing stiff competition for the visitor pound, offering longer-term residents special winter terms. The resort was renamed Trump Turnberry when acquired in 2014 by the 45th US President's commercial organisation. (Illustrated London News Ltd/Mary Evans)

TURNBERRY HOTEL
Ayrshire

Overlooking its championship Ailsa and Arran Golf Courses on the sheltered Ayrshire coast.

Pitch and Putt Course. Tennis. Sea-bathing. Indoor Swimming Pool. Dancing. Private Cinema.

OPEN ALL THE YEAR

✳

Guests met at Kilmarnock Station on request.

The Resident Manager will be happy to send coloured brochure and give full details.

TELEPHONE: TURNBERRY 202

During the 1930s, the LNER made sizable efforts to promote Cruden Bay as a golf resort. Styled as 'The Golfer's Hotel', this 1933 interpretation by Gordon Nicholl shows a meeting of guests in the hotel's reception and lounge area. Despite the company's best endeavours, the Cruden Bay Hotel did not live up to its original promoter's expectations.

The Golfers' Hotel

CRUDEN BAY HOTEL ABERDEENSHIRE

OWNED AND MANAGED BY
THE LONDON AND NORTH EASTERN RAILWAY

FOR PARTICULARS OF TARIFFS APPLY RESIDENT MANAGER

an array of high-quality poster advertising.[5] But long-term railway company investment in first-class and luxury resort hotels was not an automatic recipe for success. Profitability was questionable as many of the resort-based hotels were long distances from main areas of population whilst 'demand from the rich was stagnant' as the volume of overseas visitors declined sharply. Apart from the railway companies' comparatively deep pockets, operating a luxury hotel outside of London was tough going. Despite LNER's poster advertising in the early 1930s with various luxurious golf hotel executions, the loss-making Cruden Bay Hotel on the east coast of Scotland did not fare so well, facing closure and eventual demolition in the early 1950s.

The Big Four railway companies found themselves in a competitive environment having to seek ways to differentiate from other alternative travel and hospitality options. Notwithstanding, they attempted to sell themselves to an exclusive first-class set and met with a measure of success once the ill winds of depression had subsided. The new 1930s named trains provided speed, comfort, increasing levels of luxury and on-board facilities. According to Antony Ford, the *Brighton Belle* and Streamliner super-trains were 'the first really modern trains to run on British railways.'

Prestigious named expresses became the bedrock of Britain's Big Four to a greater or lesser extent. R. Barnard Way was an accomplished writer on railway matters. In May 1936, he released a book entitled *Famous British Trains*, tapping into both a traveller and railway enthusiast readership. *The Illustrated Sporting and Dramatic News* described the new express trains of the period as 'fire-breathing monsters' that had 'a strange fascination for most of us.'

In Britain, ideas surrounding speed, romance and glamour on rail services reached its zenith in the decade as both the LNER and LMS launched their own versions of luxury streamlined expresses. The Southern and Pullman Company with the introduction of new electric trains upped the ante. The *Sphere* described the cars thus: 'Luxury is the keynote of the new line. The third-class compartments excel in comfort and opulence of appointment many first-class carriages.' Marketing, promotion and PR (*The Sphere* piece is a good example in point) invited first-class customers to a world of exclusivity and glamour involving carriage construction on a grand scale with coaches possessing elaborate and luxurious interiors, dining cars with fabulous menus together with a non-stop programme of entertainment for longer Anglo-Scottish (and continental) journeys. This involved significant capital investment for railway companies and particularly for LMS and LNER as the competitive operational requirements of running long-distance Anglo-Scottish services dictated significant commitment to developing the most modern locomotive and carriage stock to enhance the passenger travelling experience.

This did not come without problems as, by the late 1920s, there was a reduction of the volume of first-class passengers. The old Midland route from St. Pancras was still favoured by many but its inclusion was not to last. Initially, the new LMS operation promoted both its west coast and central routes together offering the traveller alternative routes to come back with. These advantages were slowly lost as the speedier west coast line dominated as the businessman's route to the west of Scotland. The former Midland route could not compete with the 1930s speed fixation and was increasingly viewed by LMS management as a duplicate line, much in the same way as LNER had with the former Great Central line. Despite its importance as a route in the Second World War, the Midland route faced gradual rundown quickening in the British Railways era.

At the March 1929 LNER Annual General Meeting, Chairman Mr William Whitelaw, announced the numbers of first-class travellers had decreased by 227,000 in the previous financial year. The railway companies had lobbied government hard against the five per cent levy on all tickets priced over the minimum third-class fare which they argued was a 'relic from the old coaching days' and a 'disability' and 'liability' on train travel. Some respite was at hand in the April 1929 budget as the 100-year-old tax, originally introduced in 1832, known as 'Railway Passengers' Duty' which brought in between £400k and £½ million per year was abolished by Chancellor Winston Churchill. According to the *Scotsman* newspaper, this was a 'present' to the railway companies, in return for which they were required 'to make certain improvements in equipment' as an aid to relieve unemployment.

The sweeping away of the longstanding tax on first-class fares undoubtedly helped to improve the financial climate for railway company investment, of which the inclusion of modern new first-class carriage stock formed part of the 1930s carriage replacement programmes. This measure paved the way for the electrification of the Brighton line and many other south east commuter routes, as well as the eventual introduction of the

Pullman Car Company *Brighton Belle* (5-BEL) service and a fleet of new express electric six-car trains, (6PUL and 6CIT twelve-car formations) which incorporated a single composite kitchen/parlour Pullman car to provide on-board catering targeted at an upscale commuter in the busy hours. No fewer than twenty-three sets designed for electric traction alone were built in 1932, with a total of thirty-eight cars built of high-grade steel eventually delivered to Southern Railway. Specification was focused on the prosperous morning business traveller. The express 6CIT units accommodated 138 first-class seats (120 third-class) whilst the 6PUL formations had seventy-two in first-class (236 third-class). Later additions in the mid-1930s to Southern's three-rail network did not include a Pullman specification, making do with a pantry car instead.

With these fiscal inducements, the 1930s represented a period of optimism for railway companies as well as specialist tour operators as a degree of allure was added to the image of railway operations through the naming of glamorous specialist trains and services including many new named expresses unashamedly showcased to the luxury end of the market. Again, some were Pullman services others not. As well as the electrified *Brighton Belle*, the remainder were steam-hauled services that greatly fascinated the public.

Highly persuasive railway marketing targeting privileged social groups, connected with people travelling both first and third-class, creating for many a feeling of romance and an aspiration to something better that was very reassuring in persuading both men and a growing number of women with time and money to travel by train more frequently. There was something about the named train and nowhere was this more visible than with the Art Deco styled LMS and LNER streamliners plying the east and west Anglo-Scottish routes as well as new Pullman steel-sided stock. The A4 locomotive was highly distinctive, attracting tremendous publicity value especially as Mallard had broken the world speed record for a steam locomotive. LMS and LNER conjured images for a media-conscious age that so helped define the decade before the war providing a valid counterweight to the elitist perception of air travel between England and Scotland.

As previously noted, a personal transport revolution was taking place in the inter-war years that would ultimately impact on the railways in a serious way. Increased car ownership altered railway travelling patterns from the 1920s onwards, despite being a relatively expensive exercise even for the well-off at first.

Cheap Summer Tickets to SCOTLAND

Golf in Scotland's not a sleepy afternoon saunter. It's sport of a kind that stirs your spirit. The courses are magnificent in themselves and they lie by mountain and moorland and sea-coast unmatched for beauty.

With a Summer Ticket (come home any time up to a month) you travel to Scotland for only a penny a mile. You can break your journey anywhere—both on your way there and on your way back.

When you arrive in Scotland ask for one of the Holiday Contract Tickets. They cost very little (from 7/6) and allow you to travel about the district by any trains for a whole week.

With a return ticket to Scotland, you now have the choice of travelling back by the East Coast, West Coast, or Midland routes, with break of journey at any station.

The following holiday guides are obtainable from L·N·E·R or L M S offices and agencies:

L·N·E·R—
"The Holiday Handbook"
   (in the bright red cover) 6d.
"Scotland" (Free)

LMS—
"Scottish Apartments Guide" (3d.)
"Scotland for the Holidays" (Free)
"The Romance of Scotland" (Free)

MOTOR CARS accompanied by one first-class or two third-class adult passengers are conveyed to include outward and homeward journeys at the reduced rate of 4½d. a mile charged on the single journey mileage for distances not less than 50 miles. Single journey charges at 3d. a mile.

L·N·E·R
LONDON AND NORTH
EASTERN RAILWAY

LONDON MIDLAND & SCOTTISH RAILWAY
L M S

Stay at L·N·E·R and LMS Hotels

SCOTLAND
NEARER YET

EDINBURGH IN 6 HOURS

GLASGOW IN 6½ HOURS

NEW TRAINS SPEEDS COMFORTS

"The Coronation," leaving King's Cross for Edinburgh at four o'clock, and "The Coronation Scot" from Euston to Glasgow at 1.30 p.m. each weekday (except Saturdays), will carry you swiftly northwards and across the Border. To enjoy their luxury, you have only to pay a small supplementary fare. (The seating capacity is limited).

Scotland, with its ever-attractive charm, has never been reached by rail so quickly, has never been so near in point of time. "The Coronation Scot" and "The Coronation" present complete comfort, offering you perfect cuisine and unexcelled staff service. "The Coronation" has an observation car.

"The Coronation"
Leaves King's Cross at 4 p.m.
arrives Edinburgh at 10 p.m.
Leaves Edinburgh (Waverley)
at 4.30 p.m. arrives King's
Cross at 10.30 p.m.

"The Coronation Scot"
Leaves Euston at 1.30 p.m.
arrives Glasgow at 8 p.m.
Leaves Glasgow (Central) at
1.30 p.m. arrives Euston
8 p.m.

For those who prefer to leave London earlier in the day there are "The Flying Scotsman," taking only seven hours to run from King's Cross to Edinburgh, and "The Royal Scot," running from Euston to Glasgow in 7½ hours. These, too, offer comforts that completely dispel travel tedium.

"The Royal Scot"
Leaves Euston at 10 a.m.
arrives Glasgow at 5.30 p.m.
Leaves Glasgow (Central) at
10 a.m. arrives Euston at
5.25 p.m.

"The Flying Scotsman"
Leaves King's Cross at 10 a.m.
arrives Edinburgh at 5 p.m.
Leaves Edinburgh (Waverley)
at 10 a.m. arrives King's
Cross at 5 p.m.

These and other Day and Night Services to Scotland are yours for the booking. With a return ticket you can travel out by one route and have the choice of returning by the East Coast, West Coast or Midland routes, with break of journey at any station.

PENNY A MILE MONTHLY RETURN TICKETS
Ask at any L·N·E·R or L M S Station or Office for details of Penny-a-mile Monthly Return Tickets (1st class 1½d. a mile), Tourist Tickets and Circular Tours.

MOTOR CARS accompanied by one first-class or two third-class adult passengers are conveyed to include outward and homeward journeys at the reduced rate of 4½d. a mile charged on the single journey mileage for distances not less than 50 miles. Single journey charges at 3d. a mile.

STAY AT L·N·E·R or L M S HOTELS

IT'S QUICKER BY RAIL

LONDON MIDLAND & SCOTTISH RAILWAY ● LONDON & NORTH EASTERN RAILWAY

By the mid-1930s, Anglo-Scottish tourist travel was managed by LMS and LNER in a more co-ordinated fashion. These two examples of railway advertisements from *The Sketch* demonstrate the comfort, flexibility, speed and cost-effectiveness of train travel, together with the range of summer holiday themes, activities and hotel accommodation available throughout Scotland. (Illustrated London News Ltd/Mary Evans)

The railway companies made strenuous efforts to ensure they were fully part of the mechanisation of road transport running their own haulage operations but one element they could not control were the fleets of private cars, taxis and buses conveying passengers to and from railway stations in ever greater numbers. In the second half of the twentieth century, as vehicle reliability and the quality of the country's road network increased, Britons in their droves would forsake the railways for the comfort of the personal car.

That was not always the case as, in the pre-war days, the motor car represented an opportunity for the railway companies as closed vans transporting motorised vehicles had been introduced some time before grouping. Indeed, Midland Railway's four and six-wheeled motor car vans had been envisaged by the company as a means of maintaining its prosperous customer base especially on its routes to holiday locations in Yorkshire, the Border Country, the Scottish Highlands and in the other direction south to Bournemouth, Swanage and Weymouth via the Somerset and Dorset line which it had co-managed with the LSWR since 1875.

Other pre-grouping railway companies in Edwardian times such as the Caledonian, the LYR and LNWR went out of their way to encourage passengers to take the 'new-fangled motor car' on holiday by rail. The rail-haulage of motor cars in special covered vehicles was a feature of the Big Four era. Joint advertising between LNER and LMS on the Anglo-Scottish routes targeted at upscale customers promoted circular ticketing and special arrangements for the transportation of motor cars on outward and homeward journeys. The transportation of cars continued well into the nationalised period, culminating in the British Railway's modern open vehicle long-distance 'Motorail' business of the mid-1950s.

Whereas motorised vehicles brought competition at the end of the Great War, especially lorries for the transit of freight, the Big Four railway companies in their early days started to use new commercial freedoms to run bus, coach and charabanc operations to help retain holiday passenger-carrying business, especially to more affluent and traditional customers who were used to spending longer periods of time at holiday destinations. The concept of increased dwell time and new mechanisms to extract visitor cash followed as the two-week summer holiday for wealthier households was still very much part of the domestic calendar.

Classless motor coaches or charabancs were the ideal mechanism for day trips away from resorts, especially to places unaffected by inclement weather. In time, the day trip market became self-selecting. Thematic excursions to places of interest and specialist attractions featuring history and nature were more appreciated by middle-class customers whilst working-class 'trippers' who were conveyed from their homes chose resorts where excitement and immediate gratification were on offer rather than the contemplative enjoyment of more high-brow trips. The railway companies had a direct role in these activities, either running day-trips themselves or sub-contracting arrangements to new and emerging specialist coach-hire businesses but always seeking to keep the visitor pound (and shilling), or a proportion by way of commission, firmly in their pockets. Managing secondary spend as modern cruise companies now so well do is nothing new.

In 1927, the GWR expanded upon these ideas by introducing something new called the 'Land Cruise'. Publicity leaflets extolled the virtues of the company's integrated train and bus operations to provide the means to explore off the beaten track places of interest which would enhance the mind. These holiday trips included transport, accommodation, meals and entry costs to special places in the rural heartlands of the West Country and Wales, where, since grouping, the GWR had run its expanded network of routes. The Land Cruise was a means of preserving the first-class ticket market as it employed first-class train travel, luxury motor coaches and the best of hotels, en route.

The cultural and heritage theme was increasingly utilised by Britain's Big Four rail operators in different forms. It proved popular, as by 1934, the Great Western was promoting land cruise options of thirteen days' duration. All-inclusive holidays were some of the earliest examples of organised adventure and countryside tourism targeting the affluence of Britain's middle-classes who were looking for something different for leisure time enjoyment. As well as educated tourists boosted by Britain's new civic universities, there were many who would give the coastal resort hotspots a miss, opting for different rural and market town experiences. Stratford-upon-Avon with its 'Shakespeare Country' historical England themed holidays would offer further alternatives, proving to be particularly attractive to American visitors of an Anglo-Saxon lineage. The GWR's advertising and marketing machine was never likely to miss a trick or two with this important target market where, since the early years of the 1900s, the company had placed considerable promotional investment.

A further variation of the land cruise was to be a rail-based cruise product. One label the Big Four railway companies could not be accused of was lack of imagination and innovation. By the 1930s, luxury ocean cruising was well entrenched. Shipping lines were up-to date organisations understanding changing patterns of consumer demand. They developed the concept of 'single-class ships' with plenty of deck space and outside pools. Accommodation, designed for warm-water cruising, was spacious, airy and well ventilated in the days before air conditioning and, significantly for guest experience, a reduction in overall passenger numbers but with the ability to charge a premium for exclusive holidays.

LNER took a leaf out of the shipping companies' book, creating a similar product based on railway travel but covering longer distances with a variety of different itineraries than GWR's land cruise which geographically was more restricted. In 1933, the *Northern Belle*, a 'five-star hotel on wheels' concept, was launched. As one correspondent to the *Scotsman* noted at the time, the travelling hotel was presented as a challenge to ships, resembling a self-contained luxury liner. It was, perhaps, one of the earliest examples of modern planned tourist constructions where luxury trains, destinations, guests and the experience economy met under the same roof. Comprising dining and kitchen cars, lounge and writing room car, wardrobe car, post office, newspaper shop, hairdressing saloon, first-class sleeping cars described as cabins and with fresh linen, food and water delivered to the train every day, the *Northern Belle* was unashamedly pitched towards an affluent audience.

Ingeniously designed shower cubicles, first introduced in 1930 to around eight sleeping cars, were expensive to install. Likewise, the hairdressing saloons cost LNER money operationally but their inclusion was considered essential for the luxury nature of a rail-based cruise product. They were popular too, as June tours sold out almost immediately on release. Variously described, the rail cruise was a 'wonder train', a 'magic carpet' and 'as the only train of its kind in the world', covering some 2,000 miles visiting a combination of rural and urban destinations that could be modified at the last minute to avoid any operational line hiccups.

Itineraries included Edinburgh, the east coast city of Aberdeen, the Grampians, the Western Highlands, the Border country, the English Lake District, the Yorkshire coast and the fashionable centres of York, Lincoln and Cambridge. Restricted to just sixty fee paying guests, the week's holiday cost £20.00 covering all essential day and night-time needs. The *Northern Belle* initiative attracted considerable favourable press coverage comments; typical of 'the railway company, in arranging this new means of sightseeing, have chosen well'. In the 1930s, literary tourism may well have been considered a niche interest but the 'land of the poets' themed inclusion to the tour schedule was well received by the party. Its innovative itinerary across LNER metals with dedicated tour manager, motor coach tours and receptive locals to add destination flavour provided a blueprint twenty-first century luxury dining trains still pay homage to. Everything came to a shuddering halt at the end of the decade (although well anticipated) for all companies involved in bespoke travel activity. As Brendon observed, 'Whereas the lamps had gone out slowly in 1914, the blinds came down at once in 1939.' For all aspects of luxury travel the blackout was complete as Wagon-Lits fell into Nazi hands.

The inter-war period marked the first real decades of consumerism, whereby style and image increasingly replaced factual product information in marketing communication. For Britain's railways, this process had started some thirty years earlier with the advent of modern printing technologies and the widespread adoption of poster advertising. An increasingly liberated society sought affordable products and services that made home-life easier; homes could now be filled with time-saving electric gadgets. Personal products and services were now for the first time also associated with consumer lifestyle and aspiration. Railway companies who had 'well developed' policies to advertising and publicity practices lost no time in enticing potential customers aboard their long-distance trains, especially the middle-classes who were the main targets. The Big Four frequently worked 'in an intuitive rather than a systematic way', mirroring approaches similarly adopted by other mainstream British advertisers, that were generally speaking not 'as complex, sophisticated and self-conscious' as found in American advertising and marketing practices at the time.[6] Marketing activity began to be built around the modern phenomenon of social class market segmentation which first appeared in Britain in the second and third decades of the 1900s. With an increasing range of freely-available life-style products and services at a price, the middle-classes sought to emulate those of a higher social standing. Women of all social classes were now a target for manufacturers and leisure industry suppliers but especially the middle-classes,

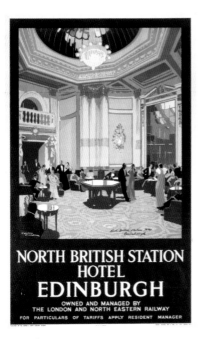

NORTH BRITISH STATION HOTEL EDINBURGH

OWNED AND MANAGED BY THE LONDON AND NORTH EASTERN RAILWAY

FOR PARTICULARS OF TARIFFS APPLY RESIDENT MANAGER

(National Railway Museum/ Science & Society Picture Library)

(Illustrated London News Ltd/ Mary Evans)

LNER adopted different creative themes in order to attract the right kind of clientele to its Anglo-Scottish luxury trains. Part of this strategy included the increasing use of women's images in advertising and promotion. This 1932 poster places the North British Hotel at the heart of civilized Edinburgh life. Illustrated by Gordon Nicholl, the establishment provides a relaxed evening environment to be enjoyed by travellers complementing an earlier approach taken in a *Bystander* advert from September 1925.

who had savings and disposable family incomes to be able to buy in greater numbers. Leisure and travel products and services could be targeted by social stratification and promoted exclusively to a female audience. Nowhere was this more prevalent than in the world of fashion which underwent a huge change. Arriving in style suddenly became de rigueur.

Fiona McDonald, in *Britain in the 1920s* (Pen and Sword, 2012) captured the 1920s spirit, commendably noting 'a dramatic lifting of ladies' hemlines'. She goes on, the 'era heralded in a shifting of attitude towards fashion that saw women being able to just about bare all and get away with it.' This undoubtedly influenced women from the upper echelons of society who were the decade's party face, but the main impact of these changes for both men and women was a trend towards looser fitting, more comfortable and casually styled clothes that made travelling so much easier. For ladies in particular, this meant an end to the 'constricting and prudish fashions that had ruled women's lives' for many years before. Fashion and the new vigorous forms of dancing helped to characterise the period, but there was similarly a change to social etiquette and the way one behaved that so defined the age. On one level, there was a new vibrant degree of informality and manners that threw off the shackles of the past and for women this was especially so. The way they conducted themselves was important but there was also another dimension that was more traditional, requiring a more modest approach that so determined social positioning and in the case of young ladies of a certain social class, the qualities that were needed to secure a decent marriage, as in the workplace, despite the advances in women's university education, interesting and fulfilling job opportunities were still rather limited.

Long-distance train travel in Britain, Europe and America was set to become up-to-the-minute, aided by fleet-footed railway company efforts to enhance passenger experiences with exciting ranges of new on-board facilities as part of the part of the luxury travel brand fabric. Travelling was a means to broaden the mind and the opportunity to meet new people. The inter-war era presented the railway companies with the chance to solidify a new luxury travel segment. Women and their travelling experiences for the first time were put at the heart of much linked marketing activity. In the mid-1920s, LNER ran a series of advertisements in *The Bystander*, placing women on the centre stage commending 'When Beauty Travels'. Fashion and luxury train travel were to become firmly embedded. Norman Hartnell, in spring 1930, launched a tweed outfit called the Flying Scotsman which matched a tweed golf bag, hatbox and suitcase.

In 1933, *The Bystander* magazine ran a 12 August fashion feature aimed at 'those lucky people who are about to board the Flying Scotsman on their way to moors and glens' who were assured that they 'would do well to visit the showrooms at Marshall and Snelgrove before they leave for the North'. Travelling and entertaining was a key feature of upper middle-class life during the second half of the decade. Glamorous trains, liners, and in time, aircraft would become essential luxury settings for new films surrounded by starlets clamouring for parts. The cinema was the most potent image of the age, with the early 1930s Hollywood parodying London society.

Thus, a modern media celebrity industry had been born, driving a market for luxury consumer goods with vigorously protected brands for perfume, handbags, stockings and haute couture. Society continued to be dominated by the upper middle-classes, but it was the vast numbers of Britain's lower middle-classes, comprising clerical workers, salesmen, insurance agents and shop assistants amongst others, who had fixations on society's activities, ably reported on by a proactive middle market press comprising the *Daily Express*, *Daily Mail* and *Daily Sketch* newspapers. Britain possessed a national 'comfortable middle-class' whose social horizons were similar to those of the upper-middle-classes but possessing growing occupational and residential mobility. They bought property around Surrey's stockbroker-belt areas whilst Sussex and surrounding counties played host to many stylish architect-designed houses with quick London access provided by electrified routes and the new Southern Electric Pullmans. The Metropolitan Railway's extensions beyond north London became home to John Betjeman's celebrated 'Metroland' living maintaining

Not the *Brighton Belle* but this carriage print by Richard Ward, titled 'Direct Electric Services, London-Brighton', highlights the importance given by Southern Region management to the selection of first-class services between the capital and the south coast, and in particular, the integral Pullman carriage designed to attract regular morning and evening business commuters. (Travelling Art Gallery)

ELECTRIC SERVICES   LONDON—BRIGHTON

From a Water Colour by RICHARD WARD

standards in dress and diet as well as where they choose to live. Hardly surprising that twentieth century trains, boats and planes would play a central stage in these proceedings.

Britain's Big Four railway companies made strenuous efforts to meet increased traveller expectations. Whilst larger and deeper carriage windows had become the norm, the GWR and LNER dabbled with the notion of Vita-glass and its 'health giving' properties allowing natural UV light to filter through as well as early developments in coach air conditioning. Whilst LNER had its high-profile trains, GWR maintaining its usual air of superiority, despite the white elephant *Ocean Specials*, LMS as the biggest of the private railway companies quietly just got on with some of the most significant coach development and improvements of the inter-war period. Their later carriage production covered the years from 1933 to 1948 and well into railway nationalisation as LMS's superior designed coaches (building on the Midland Railway's Derby heritage) continued to be built for several years before the gradual introduction of British Railways Mk I stock. Stanier created his Period III coaches to a new standardised format and style which was to last for the remaining lifetime of the company. Often referred to as 'Stanier stock', many of their robust examples lasted until the late 1960s and in their final form helped pave the way for the British Railways standard coach. Period III coaching stock was characterised with windows having well rounded corners with a sliding ventilator incorporated in the upper part of the window and ribbed roof styles. The vast bulk of LMS designed stock was constructed to a fifty-seven feet length chassis but most of the passenger full brakes and kitchen cars were built to a fifty feet chassis. But the key was comfort with padded and sprung carriage seating and in first-class compartments with just four seats whilst the open stock in first-class would incorporate one and two abreast seating arrangements.

From the 1920s, there was significant innovation in the way food was presented on trains. Luxury train operators set the bench mark as restaurant carriage meals were comparatively lavish; some railway companies used them as loss-leaders to lure the right type of high-spending customer. Carriage and station food service, like the railways' hotel operations, were always difficult to identify. Precise trading patterns and any loss was invariably absorbed by the business. With railway grouping, the LMS not only inherited Midland's grandiose stock but also the LNWR and Caledonian Railway WCJS that included the splendid twelve-wheeled dining

From grouping, the newly-formed LMS organisation commended the quality of its dining cars for its long-distance routes. Leonard Campbell Taylor's depictions of a carriage interior was one of a series of new poster designs commissioned by the railway in 1924, representing a radical new approach that moved old-style copy-led advertising to the province of the outside gallery in a bid to capture the travelling public's imagination. Produced by sixteen Royal Academy artists, LMS's new designs raised the status of poster art as the company gave established artists like Campbell Taylor free artistic expression. His portrayal showed the lavish dining accommodation, fashion and tastes expected by passengers with period deluxe train travel. (NRM Pictorial Collection/Science & Society Library)

and sleeping cars, the *Corridor* and the *American* stock. Likewise, the LNER took on the ECJS stock before embarking on new carriage building programmes for its premier expresses that included specialist dining car sets using safer electric cooking. LNER similarly inherited some 200 dining cars plus the former GER Pullman stock now deployed on longer-distance routes.

Old-fashioned wood-panelled dining cars gave way to more modern eating environments for both first and third-class passengers, combining new approaches which would include buffet cars and an acceptance by management that by the late 1920s, more casual eating styles in Britain had started to appear. The railway companies set about creating new boundaries for deluxe railway catering as well as maximising opportunities for third-class eating options by extolling the quality and convenience of their restaurant and buffet cars. On the GWR, third-class passengers could enjoy an excellent, modest priced meal service in separate dining cars as part of a deliberate attempt to popularise restaurant car services with 2/6d luncheons available on all of their routes and for the less well-heeled passenger, this was undoubtedly part of the holiday treat travelling west.

Nevertheless, the inter-war period was characterised and renowned for travelling and eating in style. Gloriously appointed restaurant cars were to be found on most luxury train expresses serving classic five-course table d'hôte menus. Most prestigious trains would be manned by uniformed stewards in starched jackets ready to fulfil every passenger's culinary whim. Immaculate and impeccable service was always the norm for GWR staff, especially to deliver the on-board dining magic. Stewards would walk the length of the train, sliding open the compartment doors to advise passengers that a white napkin and silver service lunch experience was awaiting them, to be served in the restaurant cars. Timings ensured lunch aboard GWR's world-famous *Cornish Riviera Limited* would invariably coincide with the additional luxury of the beach and sea vista as the train sped alongside the walls between Dawlish and Teignmouth. But this was nothing new, as Molly Hughes narrated her experiences from almost fifty years previously for *Railway Magazine*:

> 'Then, with magnificent gesture, the Great Western swept up to the sea side, indeed almost into the sea. Mother remembered a day when the waves had washed into the carriage. The bare possibility of such a thing made this part of the run something of an adventure, and we almost hoped it would happen again.'

In 1929, a new style kitchen car was introduced on the *Limited*, delivering sumptuous, gourmet culinary experiences to first-class passengers having already introduced articulated stock for comfort in 1925.

All Big Four companies experimented with new ways to provide fresh ideas for customers to enjoy food and drink experiences on railway journeys. As well as the traditional restaurant-car market and new buffet car formats, GWR introduced other food on the move, concepts including new styles of catering baskets and a quick lunch bar at Paddington station targeted with more sophisticated and adventurous customers in mind with their 'Paddington 3-deckers' consisting of smoked ham, lettuce and mayonnaise and half the price of a restaurant meal. The LMS conjured new formats for railway catering as the company was regarded as a pioneer 'in improved food innovations'. *The Sphere* magazine wrote:

> 'they [the LMS] recently started a buffet car where light snacks were served, and then improved on this with a cafeteria car where a genuine "help yourself" service is installed between Liverpool and Manchester. The passenger comes in at one end of the dining-car, slides his tray along, fills it himself from the various dishes, and then has it checked up by the cashier before paying for it and eating it at one of the tables.'

Even upscale passengers used to being waited upon viewed such approaches as novel.

Period advertising and poster imagery was based on the middle-class couple concept and an indication perhaps of where railway companies still saw their main market-place. By the late 1920s, Britain's Big Four companies moved to broaden and enhance culinary experiences introducing food formats and menus possessing a little more flair, imagination and choice although sometimes difficult to deliver in the confined kitchen car spaces of fast-moving trains. In July 1928, Gresley had introduced a brand-new triplet restaurant car set with its renowned first-class car decked out in Louis XVI décor, designed by Sir Charles Allom whose company was synonymous with the fitting out of inter-war luxury liners. By 1932, LNER brought in buffet expresses and cocktail bars on its premier east coast trains, first appearing on the *Flying Scotsman*. The company even ran 'Discretion in Mixing Cocktails' posters with waiters having 'regard for passengers' eupeptic welfare'.

The GWR had their café cars, whilst the Southern in the immediate post-war days dabbled with Tavern Car formats which proved unsuccessful as a travelling bar concept. The inter-war years were truly the pinnacle of long-distance railway dining as by the end of the 1930s, the impact of the comparative luxury aviation offer based on speed and access was felt on both sides of the English Channel as the proportion of Pullman style cars on both British and continental expresses started to decline. Despite having some of the

With glamorous expresses plying the east coast, LNER placed significant effort on the quality of its culinary offer in a bid to capture and retain first-class custom. Illustrated by Tom Purvis, who was one of the company's five leading designers, and who for a while worked exclusively for the LNER, his sophisticated style poster from 1935 epitomized the trendy and decadent first-class food and drink experiences afforded to passengers on Anglo-Scottish expresses. Special new kitchen vehicles, sandwiched between first and third-class restaurant cars, provided high-quality food preparation areas to deliver the kind of high-class hospitality environments mirrored by their own grand hotels. Interestingly, railway companies choose to glamorize women smoking in public spaces, deemed perfectly acceptable at the time, and amongst certain social circles, quite a stylish pursuit.

most glamorous cross-channel trains, the Southern Railway was losing some of its continental passenger volumes to nascent aircraft operators.

For twenty-five years, the railway companies and specialist providers such as Pullman and Wagon-Lits had had it their own way in a period that Kidner remarked as 'the matching of 'beautiful people' to 'beautiful Pullmans' as nowhere else'. The proportion of first-class tickets sold on Britain's railways was subject to competitive forces as fewer people travelled first-class especially families taking two-week holidays to the continent where taking the car by cross-channel steamer/ferry offered more sensible travel solutions.

With the outbreak of war, the glamorous way of life was brought to an end. For many at British society's top end this was a repeat of a generation earlier as the country hurtled towards another period of national belt-tightening. There was an immediate curtailment of luxury travel in Britain and especially in Europe where large parts of the continent came under Nazi occupation. As Andrew Martin says, 'It wouldn't do to promote certain elite, luxury trains when the nation was supposed to be pulling together.' The most prestigious coaching stock was taken out of railway operations and stored for safety's sake at remote locations considered less likely to be bombed.

When war was declared in September 1939, catering was reduced almost immediately as Pullman, restaurant car and buffet cars were withdrawn from service ceasing operating on most routes. Public outrage led to limited services being resumed on 1 January 1940, but respite was short lived. First-class carriage stock was initially retained on mainline routes, albeit with reduced catering facilities, but by May 1942, all catering was removed from the LMS and LNER routes. At the same time, some Pullman cars were assigned to NAAFI operations and a few aging Pullmans used on LNER lines were kept for wartime use, though second-class open and end door carriages were kept in traffic and designated first-class. In the south of the country, following the 'phoney war', the *Brighton Belle* was reinstated in January 1940, when the 5-BEL car sets operated with 6-PUL or 6-PAN units to provide a mix of Pullman and non-Pullman operations until bombing at Victoria station on 9 October that year caused damage to unit 3052. All three sets of the *Brighton Belle* stock were removed until services resumed in May 1946.

The ageing LNWR royal train became a mobile palace on wheels for the duration of the war, painted in LMS livery to make it look like one of the company's old-fashioned and unobtrusive trains for security reasons. Special trains were established for important personages to support the war effort. One such train, comprising mainly LMS stock together with a number of vintage clerestory roofed 'semi royal' carriages for private office and living arrangements, was put together for the use of Prime Minister Winston Churchill.

From time to time, Pullman cars would be added to form special VIP trains as and when required, for which a limited number of Pullman cars was stationed just outside London in conveniently quiet locations where they were to be made available at a moment's notice. On one such occasion, Churchill and Field Marshall Smuts were travelling from Waterloo to the coast to survey newly installed sixteen-inch guns capable of shelling German positions on the other side of the English Channel. The previous night routes to Portsmouth had been bombed but rapid permanent way repairs allowed the Prime Minister's train transit via the Guildford line. Another special train was created by LNER for General Eisenhower, becoming the General Headquarters for the Allied Military staff before the D-day landings from the south coast. Pullman cars would be added to specially convened trains with fully blacked out carriages carrying VIP passengers from London to Bournemouth West for Air Ministry/BOAC flights to and from Poole Harbour, and also Hurn Airport, which was little more than an airfield at the time. The flying boat station would ferry a succession of high-ranking military personnel as well as political leaders including Charles de Gaulle and a certain eighteen-year old singer 'Forces Sweetheart' Vera Lynn. On one occasion, General Montgomery was credited as bringing her back rationed luxury black bananas.

CHAPTER 4

1946-1975: A Second Golden Age and New World Change

Post-war euphoria was short-lived as austerity began to bite. Even the upper-classes were not immune as the traditional role of society waned; with the role of media increasingly occupying a central role defining the glamour of travel. Railways lost some of their traditional sheen. With an increasing accent on business, many travel establishments failed to adapt. Golf hotels such as Gleneagles modified and conferences became part of the venue's customer offer.

In the next decade, the middle-classes redefined society. For a start, there were now more of them and they were the nation's brains, providing leadership and organisation in a mixed private and public sector economy that included the newly nationalised railways and an evolving travel industry. In much the same way that Victorian Britain had been transformed by their energies, post-war recovery would be dominated by their actions. The landscape of the country changed too – television aerials could be seen on every roof.

The working-classes adopted broad strands of middle-class life as well as standards, values and life-styles which impacted on how people travelled and to where, yet it was the middle-classes who had a love of travel; they had the money, inclination and the social horizons to holiday abroad. In the immediate post-war days, the lack of available foreign currency and general affordability prevented many Britons from venturing beyond these shores but by the early 1950s, European rail travel was back on track. Overseas travel conferred an immediate label.

Rail had been the traditional mode of holiday transport but by the mid-1950s, it was defined by the personal car or the coach offering real competition to rail, being both cheaper and more convenient with flexible, drop-off points. Whilst Butlins dominated the holiday camp industry, smaller resorts still retained their upmarket niches, social gradations and individual characteristics

The 1960s were different; a dazzling age of consumerism and rapid social change – the swinging sixties – and a movement towards rampant avariciousness, lavish living and personal material advancement. Hardly surprising that these developments filtered into the leisure and holiday sector and a travel industry largely concentrated in the hands of a few powerful industry players. Yet within a decade, there were initial signs of a move from the collective experiences of the holiday camp and the package holiday towards a more individual design of leisure and holiday taking that gathered pace in the last quarter of the twentieth century. It was a period where mainline steam tours would also establish a niche on Britain's rail network with the first rumblings of a return of private sector deluxe train travel.

Prior to the Second World War, the railways had held an important domestic tourism role, but this would irrevocably change as a result of aviation industry developments and greater numbers of people acquiring a car. Within a few short years of the cessation of hostilities, Britain's railway system was in state hands, leading to profound changes in transport policy. The importance of military aviation had seen Britain through the war. Quite understandably, the development of civil aviation was an essential tool to help guide future prosperity and security of the nation and its new European allies. The railway's proportionate share in all forms of transport and the tourist system would shrink considerably from 1950 onwards.

However, in the immediate post-war period before railway nationalisation, the Big Four companies considered that they had an important role in shaping civil aviation, due to their active pre-war involvement in the industry. The Southern Railway, the LMS and the GWR had made serious proposals for a separate board to establish a new short-haul airline to be known as British European Airways (BEA). Cash-strapped LNER was only nominally involved as they had no resources to invest at the time. The other partner was BOAC, created in July 1939 following an amalgamation of Imperial Airways and British Airlines; strategically, a bold move as the intention was for the airline to be free to concentrate on long-distance services. But the business ideas for combined rail and air involvement for short-haul traffic was unfortunately to founder with a change of government so the first real and only opportunity for an integrated rail and air operation in Britain was lost. In his 1982 memoirs, Sir John Elliot remarked:

'I have often wondered to what extent the future of British civil aviation would have been different if the British air network had been closely linked to the railway; certainly, a great deal of money lost in wasteful competition would have been avoided'.

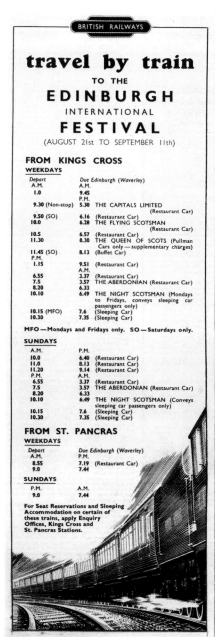

British Railways promoted train travel to the 1949 Edinburgh International Festival with both King's Cross and St. Pancras departures. *The Illustrated London News* still had an upscale readership to tempt with the Eastern Region's improving post-war services appearing alongside a Rolls Royce Motors endorsement together with a Pan Am advertisement. Perhaps an indication of the new luxury transport order to come; flying the Atlantic aboard double-decked Clippers would have been the height of sophisticated glamour. (Illustrated London News Ltd/Mary Evans)

The railway companies believed that short-haul air traffic played very much into their hands as not only were they seen as providers of integrated cross-channel shipping and rail-based transport solutions, but increasingly they felt they had an important role in redefining new and novel transport technologies. Impending railway nationalisation was on the horizon and dampened everything, so plans were comparatively short-lived. Whilst their portfolio of activities was seen to add to and shape domestic and European aviation services, the creation of BEA as a separate business entity effectively ended railway company involvement in air transport. By the end of 1947, the aircraft, routes and staff of Railway Air Services had been subsumed into the new European airline.

Although post-war austerity had well and truly kicked in, the arrival of a newly branded national airline signalled a partial return to a glamorous European travel style. This in turn would include, for a few short years, services provided by a new generation of British aircraft specifically designed and manufactured to meet the needs of BEA's short-haul operations and real competition at the top end of the market for domestic and continental travel services. The fact that business and industry increasingly powered the economy inevitably meant that there was a change in how people travelled. The traditional luxury travel environments were increasingly modified for the requirements of the business community which, by the early 1960s, was to dominate first-class rail travel agenda in the shape of the new Blue Pullmans. Since the 1940s, British business had begun to pay its senior employees not just by taxed income but by way of the 'perk'. Managerial expensed first-class rail travel became a norm and British Railways responded to such opportunities.

Initially, British railway nationalisation represented a period of optimism providing an opportunity to look to the future. It was a chance to recover from the ravages of war but suffered from a lack of maintenance and serious under investment as resources had been poured into the war effort. Britain's railway infrastructure had been left totally neglected. Nationalisation, nonetheless, was a difficult wicket to bat on as British Railways struggled to establish a cohesive identity under the unwieldly structures of the British Transport Commission (BTC).

From an image perspective, British Railways launched an initiative to name many train services to try and recreate a degree of glamour associated with travelling by train and to mask delays and cancellations as track and signalling were gradually restored to facilitate faster running of passenger trains. Pullman services were back on and at the top end of the market standards were maintained wherever possible. The early 1950s represented a period of nostalgia, signifying a new but brief golden age of rail travel. Much work had been already been done to restore the luxury cross-channel services of the *Golden Arrow/La Flèche d'Or* and the *Night Ferry/Ferry Boat de Nuit*. Despite a limited level of governmental shenanigans surrounding ownership, the French were grateful for the efforts of Southern Railway, who undertook to re-establish links at the earliest possibility, giving Pullman and Wagon-Lits a near monopoly again of the upper end of continental passenger traffic before the short-haul airline operations of BEA and Air France began to swallow the business.

The aerial assault on Britain during the war-years left Southern with a considerable programme of on-going permanent way work to restore lines; the company's key boat train routes had sustained substantial damage. So much so, in 1952, Sir John Elliot and colleagues were presented at SNCF's Paris boardroom with a medal and certificate of an Officer of the *Légion d'Honneur* in commemoration of the work they had done to facilitate normal working. The mid-decade heralded the beginnings of an up-to-date railway system, despite Britain's preoccupation and 'undoubted widespread emotional attachment to steam, for all its dirtiness.' The £1.24 million *Plan for the Modernisation and Re-equipment of British Railways* was designed to transform the railway system to be comparable with anything European railways were offering in terms of speed, punctuality and efficiency. Certainly, a tall order, as railways in France, Germany and the Netherlands were net recipients of large scale American investment in the form of the Marshall Plan and the rebuilding of Europe.

The naming of train services proved to be a short-lived affair as by the 1960s, new diesel locomotive hauled expresses became far more utilitarian and down-to-earth in nature. Restaurant cars became buffet cars as British Rail considered the traditional Pullman train to have lost its glamour and to be an outmoded concept in need of rejuvenation, limited to just a few dedicated services primarily for the business traveller. Certainly, the umber and cream liveried cars came out of operating service as they appeared to represent a bygone age. Newer Mk II stock brought forward significant strides in superior passenger comfort and ride with new bogie technologies allowing 100 mph running, but ultimately re-badged in British Rail's corporate blue and grey. For a brief period, discriminating passengers could still enjoy a luxury and personal service as the nationalised railway tried to update the Pullman concept with a more appealing and distinctive experience with the introduction of the Nanking blue liveried diesel-powered *Blue Pullman* trains as well as the later electrified Manchester and Liverpool Pullmans. They were a response to a view held by British Rail that they should compete with other transport types, especially air. But the old Pullman company was shortly to disappear as new livery standard formation trains did away with most of the remaining locomotive hauled expresses. The named train was the end of an era – the commissars at British Rail's headquarters in London's Marylebone deemed they no longer fitted with an image of a modern railway.

Luxury rail travel still had a limited market, but its composition was changing due to aviation competition on Anglo-Scottish routes. The *Bournemouth Belle*, designed for holiday-makers, was now predominantly of a third-class seating specification. The *Devon Belle*, a corresponding luxury Pullman service from Waterloo to the West Country, was less successful, eventually being withdrawn after the summer of 1954. How people paid for holidays and short breaks was changing too by the early 1960s, particularly in the luxury travel sector with its focus on European holidays and increasingly intercontinental air travel, with deposits being taken to spread the economic load. Domestic holidays and travel by train were for some now seen as a little dowdy and down market for those who could afford better. Yet the railways with speed and access still formed part of the promotional efforts used to draw upscale international visitors to the country. In a feature on 'The Visitor to Britain' *The Sphere* commented:

'Despite the occasional moans of the inhabitants, this country possesses a rail system second to none. There are several mile-a-minute-expresses, including the "Bristolian" (London-Bristol, 108 miles in 105 minutes), the "Atlantic Coast Express" (non-stop to Salisbury, 84 miles in 83 minutes), the "Elizabethan" (London-Edinburgh, non-stop 393 miles in 395 minutes), and the "Midland Pullman" (London-Manchester, 187 miles in 192 minutes).'

And first-class Pullman cars were still part of a luxury travel agenda. Yet for Britons, international travel was aided by the comparative ease of taking money abroad, together with the simplicity of the travellers' cheque. For those firms operating in the sector, such mechanisms delivered healthy financial returns. Thomas Cook turned down the opportunity to launch a joint credit card with American Express who had an established niche in the upscale travel market. In 1963, American Express went to launch their own card in Britain, establishing a dominant position in an increasingly lucrative market. Travellers cheques, however, continued to provide Thomas Cook, still in state hands, with a favourable cash flow that 'was the envy of competitors' attracting the attentions of would be suitors including the Midland Bank, who recognised the firm still offered the only effective competition to American Express.

In 1972, the Midland, together with a consortium that included Trust House Forte and the Automobile Association, landed their catch. Five years later, the Midland bought out its junior partners until the Thomas Cook Group was eventually sold to Germany's *Westdeutsche Landesbank* and charter airline LTU following Midland's acquisition by HSBC and a following series of corporate off-loadings, acquisitions, mergers and consolidations to create the modern-day travel group.

At the top end of the market, the post-war period saw changes in the way rail travel was presented, largely brought about by consolidation and nationalisation. Travelling in style in terms of décor and surroundings changed as streamliner carriages were no longer run as fixed express rakes. British Railways did their best to present the kind of pre-war culinary and service experiences associated with train travel. In the immediate post-war period, restaurant cars reappeared on premier train services but the Big Four railway companies in their last days looked to broaden the non-luxury culinary experience they had begun in the 1930s. Some 600 buffet, kitchen and restaurant cars went into storage during the war-years, but their temporary disappearance ensured an extended operational life well into the British Railways era with some east coast wooden panelled restaurant car stock introduced in 1933 lasting until the 1970s. Consequently, the manufacture of new catering carriages was not of the highest priority when standardised Mk I coaches were introduced in the early 1950s; Britain, after all, was still experiencing food rationing.

New catering stock did eventually start to appear in 1957, with the second round of Mk I carriage construction as different formats were trialled such as combined 'buffet restaurant cars' and all this coinciding with a rush to diesel and electric modernisation as a means to raise rail travel from its low ebb. Even in the 1960s, British Railways were experimenting with different catering coach formats such as the conversion of old LMS Period II third-class sleepers, rebuilt mixing different design styles to create a 'cafeteria' car. A further development at the time was the 'griddle car' of which just three were built for evaluation by British Railways, Scottish and Western Regions. The kitchen on the griddle car was located in the centre of the vehicle with a buffet saloon at one end and a bar saloon at the other. With most restaurant cars, the kitchen would normally be placed at one end of the carriage. The idea of the griddle car was to produce a mix of hot food from the griddle and the serving of drinks manned by a crew of up to three in busy times. The concept was not a million miles from the new kind of hospitality brands such as the Berni Inns steakhouse operation which had achieved considerable prominence by the late 1960s brought about by a change and the shifting habits of consumers powered by an explosion in television and press advertising influencing the way we behaved. In a trend that started in the 1920s, the country's leading food producers became food brands maintaining a vice-like grip, dictating our habits and the way we consumed food. Whilst there were fast-changing food cultures, Pullman did manage to pull out of the bag new kitchen car variants with the batch of new Metropolitan-Cammel Mk II Pullman cars used on the east coast routes. Brian Haresnape described developments:

> 'The kitchens of the 1960 cars were models of compact efficiency, and one always marvelled at the quantity and variety of foods prepared in such modest areas often whilst on the move, and at speeds of up to 90 mph.'

Pullman might have been considered an odd throwback to the golden age of train travel, the late 1950s and 1960s progressively saw the railway culinary experience based on a new utilitarian dining concept as railway operators across Europe gave more prominence to speed rather than providing high quality dining. Chris de Winter Hebron sums it up admirably. 'The dining now was no longer a key experience of the journey, simply an added-value service.'

Whilst trains were getting faster, the London-Manchester trip would still take just over three hours – it nonetheless provided a receptive audience for a full table d'hote breakfast or a-la-carte lunches or dinners served at their seats by blue uniformed attendants matching the new Nanking blue and white livery of the train. British Railways (shortly to become British Rail) and other travel companies began to address us as consumers – no longer termed passengers – as society moved progressively from set styles of dining to a modern culture of branded food on the move. This was facilitated by changes in food technology, transforming the railway kitchen from a place of art to a serving hatch for food prepared off-site and heated up in microwave ovens. Ultimately, the freshly cooked breakfast in most parts was a vanishing culinary form as British Rail saw great economies to be had by doing away with the restaurant car, although in the InterCity branded 1970s, the great British breakfast was still a regular feature of the journey experience whilst travelling on the east and west coast routes. In the twenty-first century, this has manifested itself with an airline imported concept of a railway equivalent of an aviation 'trolley dolly'. Manned by attendants who board trains at selected stations, they sell hot and cold drinks together with unappealing snacks as they move up and down the central alley of the train; that is in the rare moments when the carriage is not so overcrowded to restrict access and movement. On everyday rail travel, there is little to enhance the overall journey experience, apart from a few selected routes where onboard dining is still a regular feature. The sheer numbers of passengers travelling by train at the moment invariably means standing for part of the journey whatever class one travels in.

If railway modernisation was in full swing in Britain by the late 1950s, much the same was also happening on the continent of Europe where cross-border developments across several different countries saw the launch of the TEE network recognising the importance of business as a revenue-earning upscale travel segment. Perhaps luxury travel was no longer the most apt description, but Britain's railway companies had always used their first-class provision to move away from focusing on individual wealthy customers but evolving new products to cater for a steady stream of well-funded company and public sector travellers particularly the armed forces – officers almost exclusively travelling on first-class warrants. Britain's *Blue Pullmans* were angled towards the passenger flows of business and commercial travel, representing a response to changing times. Under modernisation plans, they were part of a brave new world destined to shape the British railway system in the second half of the twentieth century, together with a recognition that fast, modern trains could offer a competitive response to the onslaught of the private car, the extensions of the motorway system and domestic aviation routes.

After ten years as a nationalised institution, the railway system very rarely received plaudits for breaking new ground, but the innovative *Blue Pullmans* would draw on Anglo-French heritage, combining luxury elements and naming of the trend setting *Blue Train* of 1922 and the later sleek, modern styling associated with the coaches of the post-war *Mistral* launched in 1950. With diesel-powered end cars running in fixed carriage formations they also borrowed ideas from the initial batches of TEE expresses. The British *Blue Pullmans* were one of the last throws of the die for Pullman travel under British Railways ownership before the brand was eventually discarded in 1997 by private sector operator Virgin Trains. The federal nature of the British Railways structure afforded regional management a degree of slack. Some were more receptive to the notion of Pullman than others, particularly Eastern Region who had followed the LNER signature by continuing with a tradition of running premier-class luxury dining services.

Pullmans had returned to Western Region with the week day running of the *South Wales Pullman* on 27 June 1955. The limited accommodation train was designed for the business traveller, with an 8.50 am Paddington departure calling at Newport, Cardiff, Bridgend, Port Talbot, Neath and arriving at Swansea at ten past one. South Wales's reliance on traditional heavy industries provided a regular supply of expense account business passengers. The return journey to London would leave Swansea at 4.30 pm, arriving back at Paddington at 8.45 pm. The *South Wales Pullman* stock had been made available with the demise of the *Devon Belle* Pullman service in September 1954. *Blue Pullmans* were operating on Western territory by 1960, quickening the end of premier steam-hauled services. On 11 September 1961, the steam-hauled *South Wales Pullman* was replaced by the new *Blue Pullman* on the South Wales route, although the rake of traditional Pullman cars was always at hand in the event of diesel failure. The *Blue Pullmans* would run on the South Wales line until May 1973. In its early days, the South Wales service helped cement the Gower Peninsula's reputation on the tourist map. 'Ganymede', writing a piece on good living in *The Sphere* commented, 'The journey from London by the blue Pullman train which leaves Paddington at 4.45 every afternoon is quite painless. The train is air-conditioned and quiet enough to converse in a lower than normal voice. The service is impeccable.'

British royalty's long-term association with Pullman travel also continued with the *Blue Pullmans*. The diesel-powered expresses were an indulgence product incorporating significant advances in railway technology, but they had a comparatively short operational life of just thirteen years. Their mainline introduction in 1960 was accompanied by prior industrial unrest which threatened the project. Yet they exuded a carefully constructed smart new image of streamlined modernity, running over a selected small number of main city routes. Indeed, *The Coventry Evening Telegraph* described the new train as 'airliner comfort, luxurious' with 'swift, smooth and silent' running.

Their look was ahead of their time; as Charles Fryer noted, they were 'a cross, one might say, between the forward end of the *Brighton Belle* and that of a present-day High Speed Train'. Given a few InterCity 125s are still running on the GWR branded franchise, they are a remarkable testimony of design durability. The high-speed diesel multiple-unit (DMU) *Blue Pullmans* exuded a prestige and undoubtedly the Design Panel showcase. But they were totally in tune with the time, representing the hopes and aspirations of a new decade of operation as the railway system moved from steam to the alternative power traction of diesel and electrification. The DMU *Blue Pullmans*, capable of a top speed of 90 mph, were the first railway vehicles with two sets of powered cars, one at each end, and totally different from earlier multiple train formations where engines or motors were incorporated below decks

The London, Birmingham and Manchester axis was an important revenue source for British Rail but due to long-term line electrification construction work, an alternative fast route had to be devised to counter increasing competition from airlines targeting the domestic business traveller. The *Midland Pullman* was launched on 4 July 1960, running from London St. Pancras to Manchester Central with a first-class-only train formation as well as an additional London and Leicester train. Manchester was on the extreme of a daily return service with the DMU Pullman units capable of putting in sustained periods of 90 mph running even on uphill stretches, but it was pitched at business usage. British Railways in their reporting railway progress series announced,

The New **MIDLAND PULLMAN**

First Class de luxe travel — Supplementary fares

8.50 am	Manchester Central ↑	9.21 pm	Mondays to Fridays from 4th July	12.45 pm	St. Pancras ↑	4.00 pm
9.04 am	Cheadle Heath	9.07 pm			Leicester	
12.03 pm ↓	St. Pancras	6.10 pm		2.10 pm ↓	London Road	2.33 pm

The last word in rail comfort. Limited accommodation, book in advance

This British Railways London Midland Region poster from 1960, illustrated by A.N. Wolstenholme, shows the new state of the art *Midland Pullman* thundering through a rural setting whilst Western Region adopted the benefits of a more luxurious high-speed diesel Pullman promotion on their Birmingham and Bristol routes. (NRM Pictorial Collection/Science & Society Library)

'The diesels de-luxe form a new precedent of passenger service… This is the executive suite on wheels.'

Two six-car sets were built for work on the Midland Region route, comprising 132 first-class seats, whereas Western Region's three sets were made up of eight-car units incorporating 108 first and 120 second-class seats. By 1962, St. Pancras journeys had been speeded up, providing the Midlands and the North West with the 'Finest Main Line Rail Services'. The London to Birmingham runs were comparable to speed times achieved by the fastest steam services before the war.

At the time, Birmingham could still be reached by former LMS and GWR lines. The city was served by a London Paddington to Birmingham and Wolverhampton (low level) *Blue Pullman*

New Pullman Services

Commencing
12 SEPTEMBER 1960

DIESEL PULLMAN

HIGH SPEED LUXURY TRAVEL
FIRST AND SECOND CLASS

AIR CONDITIONED ›

SOUND INSULATED ›

SMOOTH TRAVEL ›

MEALS & REFRESHMENTS ›
SERVED AT EVERY SEAT

LIMITED ACCOMMODATION ›
(SUPPLEMENTARY CHARGE)

BRITISH RAILWAYS
WESTERN REGION

between
WOLVERHAMPTON & BIRMINGHAM
and LONDON (Paddington) also
BRISTOL and LONDON (Paddington)

FULL DETAILS FROM STATIONS, OFFICES & AGENCIES

until electrification in 1966 and the commencement of the new Manchester and Liverpool Pullman service. The requirements of a new breed of business traffic was translated with *Blue Pullman* carriage layout and its 1970s successors, the InterCity 125. *Blue Pullmans* incorporated 2+1 sets of sumptuously comfortable seats placed between off-centre coach gangways designed to facilitate business meetings. Significant numbers of first-class travellers could still enjoy high-quality on-board dining as meals were served in the new business-like settings. Meal costs were high but aimed at the executive suit market where the expense would be met by employers. Michael Williams captures the scene perfectly; 'crisply dressed stewards served the finest railway cuisine of the day at every seat.' Travellers instantly knew the unique *Blue Pullmans* trains as they sported the definitive Pullman Car Company crest (now fully owned by British Rail) on the nose of the front and rear power cars, much in the same style as the original *Brighton Belle* Pullman of thirty years before.

There was nothing vintage, however, about the new Pullmans, designed with one eye on the domestic aviation market which was now providing a fast and efficient London Heathrow and Manchester service. Pullmans formed part of an overall British Railways package of incentives to tap into the business traveller market. Regional advertising initiatives emphasised how express trains maximised the working day in London. The new Pullmans were the first British trains to incorporate full carriage air conditioning, which also included double-glazed fitted windows with adjustable blinds inserted between the panes instead of old-fashioned dusty curtains. Another new feature at the time was a public-address system which in the twenty-first century is very much the bane of many frequent train travellers. Although sleek and modern, the *Blue Pullmans* were not without their operational problems so, from time to time, a substitute standby set of traditional brown and cream coloured made up of new Mk II Metropolitan-Cammell stock, together with elderly Pullman brake coaches, were always on hand at Old Oak Common in case of failure. They would be hauled by any available diesel.

On Western Region, the Birmingham and Bristol Pullmans were the premier express services. The Bristol Pullman initially had competition with the prestigious new Warship-hauled diesel-hydraulic *Bristolian* and *Merchant Venturer* services but by June 1965, these named trains were dropped in favour of an additional West

Country Pullman service when the Midland Region pair arrived. However, as late as May 1965, a *Bristol Pullman* could comprise traditional Pullman cars together with Hawkesworth brakes in reinstated Western Region chocolate and cream livery when diesel sets were out of commission.

In 1967, a Paddington to Oxford service was introduced, with additional capacity brought by the transfer of the original Midland Region sets which were painted in a new livery of grey with a blue window band. The pace of corporatisation sadly took over and the bespoke *Blue Pullman* services ending by 1973 on Western territory, to be replaced by new InterCity 125s and the railway operator's vision of the changing shape of passenger rail travel. InterCity 125s from Paddington could reach Bristol in ninety-two minutes, Cardiff in 113 minutes and Swansea in 175 minutes. Gone was the Pullman proposition, the quiet and attentive, smartly dressed waiter and his carefully choreographed welcome honed over many

Old and new railway technologies combine west of Paddington. A rather poignant view for many but it came to symbolise luxury rail travel progress on Western Region in the early 1960s. (Harry Luff/Online Transport Archive)

years of successful on-board working only to be substituted by a completely new and different hospitality proposition; self-service, the microwave and a simpler and easier to manage buffet fare.

On the lines to the north west, the swinging '60s brought the commencement of the electrified Manchester and Liverpool Pullman service. Electrification, described as virtually a complete line rebuild, whilst having to continue to run existing services, was eventually completed early in 1966. The new *Manchester Pullman* service commenced duties on 18 April as part of celebration plans for the major British infrastructure project, cutting thirty-five minutes from existing fastest journey times.

An overhead catenary system supplied power for Class 81 and 86 electric locomotives hauling the much quicker Manchester and Liverpool Pullman trains. The new service operated from London Euston to Crewe and Manchester Piccadilly and to Crewe and Liverpool Lime Street, whilst the existing Manchester Central Blue Pullmans were transferred to work on Western Region providing additional route capacity. The WCML route was now very fast (relative to British mainline standards) with sections of the line running more than 100 mph hauling the Manchester Pullman service in around two and a half hours. The electrified *Manchester Pullman* service was still a prestigious and sought-after train, garnering a following amongst the north's business elites. A total of twenty-nine carriages comprising kitchen, parlour and brakes were built using British Rail's Mk II specifications.

The 1966 Pullman stock included a range of extras designed to offer travellers an at-seat restaurant experience. New ideas at the time included carriage automatic opening doors and reclining seats as well as features first introduced on the *Blue Pullmans* with air-conditioning and double glazing with integrated Venetian blinds. Weekday only morning departures left Manchester at 7.50 am and Liverpool 7.45 am with an evening return journey considered ideal for the business community. A travelling secretarial service was trialled on the *Manchester Pullman* with little advance publicity. The *Birmingham Post* reported, 'Take an express letter, Miss Smith' – 23-year-old Gilly Yendall had 'travelled north in the morning and returned to London on the afternoon Pullman. Equipped with a typewriter and shorthand notebook, she has been available to work for businessmen at £3 per hour.'

CHAPTER 5

1976-2000: Preservation and Restoration Projects

Towards the end of the century, Britain moved towards America's concept of a classless society. Travel was open to everyone: In a world of homogenised travel products, ideas surrounding niche tourism began to take hold and with a middle-class market place dictating a more sophisticated tourism mix, the concept of the luxury dining train, amongst a raft of new lifestyle travel and tourism products, emerged. Traditional destination zoning and of particular hospitality establishments has always been a phenomenon of the leisure and travel scene where specialist groups of people came together. Ideas surrounding social tribes may be anthropological in essence, but they increasingly crept into the luxury lexicon as ideas defining 'smart-sets', 'in-crowds' and 'badges of membership' – often determined by new forms of fashion label – started to roll off the tongue.

The first rumblings of a backlash against highly organised and prescriptive tourist packaging was noticeable. For those at the top of social orders, exclusivity and the need to be away from prying eyes was clearly evident as modern celebrity destinations emerged dictated by wealth and social access. A form of discreet luxury pervaded selective destinations, allowing wealthy guests to get on with what they wanted to do. Some choosy destinations were prone to 'posh brand' commodification hunted down by aspirant outsiders who sought identity with upscale associations. And international travel at the end of the 1900s was very much a 'club scene', dictated by social tribe conventions one associated with. Queueing for the loo aboard Concorde was almost celebrity ritual and a telling marker of the symbolic shift where "posh" was now democratized. For those of wealth, partying to holiday destinations in style was still part of the ritual but the nature of travel was beginning to change from public visibility to private access.

If Thomas Cook had difficulty in defining his middle-class travellers in the 1860s, then what was the position at the turn of the twenty-first century when boundaries had seeped into more complex structures where traditional middle-class associations were now the common ground for all? This process started in the 1950s but thirty years later, some eighty per cent of Britons were taking holidays involving European travel. But this new-found legitimacy started to unleash serious interest for luxury culture touchpoints and progress up the social rank. And luxury travel was something most aspirant consumers could tap into, broadening horizons as new and exciting long-haul destinations were increasingly reachable and in greater numbers, with the middle-classes seeking identity in their worldview establishing clear blue water between themselves and lower social orders by backing luxury consumption and demonstration. As established travel agents had found in the past, affluence and select clientele were always good measures for business as healthy visitor interests in luxury and adventure identified a mark of differentiation. The emergence of the internet economy focused attention on individualised and quality holiday experiences. An aspirant generation, broadened by higher education, demanded access to new destinations, languages and cuisines finding budding niche tourism businesses waiting in the wings and ready to fulfil customer aspirations. New-style travel organisations proliferated - the most successful snapped up by big acquisitive tourism groups.

On Britain's electrified northern lines Pullman trains continued to run twice daily but the less successful Liverpool service, made up of just four Pullman cars, ended in 1975. The look of the new northern Pullman cars was a reverse of the standard grey and white livery with pearl grey with blue window surrounds to provide the service a degree of visual differentiation. To reinvigorate what was still one of British Rail's premier services, the carriage stock was refurbished with a lavish marketing make-over and relaunched as a *new* first-class-only *Manchester Pullman* on 5 October 1983, being the national rail operator's last all-Pullman express. A second attempt at a dedicated Liverpool Pullman service began on 13 May 1985, but only with a limited number of first-class carriages; the remainder being second-class stock. The so-called Pullman element could only be found in the first-class carriage. Some twenty-two Pullman coaches received the names of notable northern luminaries, appearing as a red band below the window. The rebranding exercise included well-known historical women figures such as Emmeline Pankhurst and Elizabeth Gaskell but most carriages were renamed with what was considered to be more up-to-date northern celebrities such as Sir Stanley Matthews, L.S. Lowry and Arnold Bennet.

In May 1985, as part of British Rail's last-dance with the Pullman marque, most of the life-expired stock was withdrawn and replaced with *pretend* non-Pullman Mk IIIB open firsts. The not so refined InterCity attempt at an up-market business travel brand left little time for the subtle and finer things in life. The Pullman marque now equalled the first-class carriage running on selected train services in and out of London. Targeted at the business customer, the new brand was positioned as an alternative to domestic short-haul air travel and the company car. In 1986, British Rail tried to introduce a culinary upgrade with on-board Pullman chefs and a Euston-based Pullman Club but it was business like and had no sense of the romance and style that the Pullman name had for so long delivered. But some of this undoubtedly rubbed off. The *Illustrated London News,* in a double-page spread on 'London's Best Breakfasts', described the 8.00 am *Manchester Pullman* from Euston as a place where a 'notorious splendid grill' could be had for £7.95. Yet despite these enterprises, Maurice Bray reflected on the changing face of the British railway system, where speed had replaced the old-values of superior service. He described images of the modern *Manchester Pullman* used in marketing literature thus:

> 'A formally attired attendant stands by the door inviting the brief-cased executive in a hurry to board, while another colleague makes notes of the requirements of another distinguished passenger who clutches at his newspaper. Unlike the Pullmans of fifty years ago, there is no mystique about the train, no hint of elegance and luxury.'

The 1990s Pullman concept was no longer about the aura of another age. The new reality was travelling comfort, where first-class Mk III and Mk IV carriages provided a roomy and ergonomic adjustable seat, with a table wide enough to spread out. The double-glazed windows and sound insulation reduced interior noise so passengers could talk to each other or work in comfort. The long-distance InterCity Pullman express services, described as sporting an executive livery, continued until quietly dropped in 1997 by Virgin Trains. Whilst the Pullman concept had been discarded by scheduled rail operators, something special was stirring in the leisure world of luxury train travel. Proper Pullman services using fully-restored heritage Pullman carriage stock was reintroduced to Britain's main line railways but this time under private ownership. Since 1982, the *Belmond British Pullman* provided one half of the world's most celebrated dining train; the *Venice Simplon-Orient-Express*.

Whilst the Pullman concept could attract much media attention, a need was identified for high-speed diesel trains that could run on many non-electrified routes which would provide a blue print for fast and efficient train travel for the next forty odd years. In the 1970s British Rail introduced their InterCity 125, a train (not dissimilar to the earlier *Blue Pullmans*) formed of a rake of passenger carriages sandwiched between two power cars, one at each end, providing sufficient power to sustain speeds of 125 miles an hour over long periods. The power cars could accommodate sets of between six and nine Mk III coaches. As such, the InterCity 125 had the capacity to provide a section of the train that would be a modern replacement for first-class Pullman cars and carriage dining of the past representing an evolution from all-luxury trains, amongst a stable of regular trains, towards an homogenous product – that is, hourly departures using a consistent fleet of rolling stock – forming the essential bedrock of today's mass mobility rail market. What was happening in Britain was also mirrored in Europe as the French constructed their prestigious high-speed *Train à Grande Vitesse* (TGV) networks. Despite the undoubted success of the InterCity 125 project, which saw increased passenger volumes as a result of speed and frequency of services, prior to the arrival of rail deregulation, Britain's railways underwent a protracted period of decline whereby passenger travel by rail represented a shade under twenty per cent of all distance travelled in 1952 to around five per cent in 1995. But the latter years of British Rail also saw other changes, altering the dynamics for luxury forms of rail travel. Deluxe trains of decades past were repackaged, leading to the emergence of what is recognised today as the luxury cruise train and an entirely separate phenomenon designed to fulfil different consumer needs as a leisure experience product. Pullman and Wagon-Lits cars gained a level of glamour and prestige not known in post-war days, largely driven by film and television output fuelled by the writings of the late Agatha Christie. Elegant marquetry and décor of period coaches made up of sumptuous dining car seats, cosy carriage compartment furnishings and comfortable sleeping car bunks were suddenly de rigueur again.

In to this mix, British Rail and its InterCity brand did their best to stimulate Anglo-Scottish traffic with a host of marketing initiatives to attract visitors to Scotland. In 1988, steam trains were reintroduced on the Highlands route between Fort William and Mallaig, a service that continues to this day run by private sector operators. In tandem, the railway preservation market became highly visible as groups of individual steam enthusiasts banded together to become serious and highly organised affairs creating long-term projects to restore locomotives, carriages and relaying heritage railway lines. But more importantly, there was also a whole new railway paraphernalia moving in to the province of a broader based leisure world, where dedicated businesses would run vintage style mainline train services recapturing the glories of the past. Coupled to this was a constant stream of wealthier customers who would pay good money to experience up-market, premium-priced dining trains hauled by steam locomotives restored to run on either the British main line network and/or heritage lines.

Despite a common wisdom that deluxe rail travel was dead, developments that were scheduled to take place in Britain and Europe, rejuvenating the luxury train concept, were also mirrored elsewhere around the globe. Regarded by many travellers as the most luxurious period train in the world, Rovos Rail in South Africa has been setting an agenda few firms can parallel with their *Pride of Africa* train launched in 1987. In Canada, the *Royal Canadian Pacific* was resurrected in 1998 and was typical of the Canadian approach to be something a little different from their near neighbour. American railroads and wealthy individuals had had Pullman and private varnish cars but the Canadian Pacific Railway (CPR) had its own special luxury passenger cars known as business cars. Given the vast geographical spread of the country, CPR executives before the age of the plane required specialist carriages in order to work and travel huge distances around the country. The business cars were built specifically for transporting senior railway management in a certain degree of comfort and style. The Austrian *Majestic Imperator* train de luxe was the last *new* train in the 1990s to be developed as a deluxe rail concept. This luxury train had its roots in Austria's royal trains of the past and even managed to use original period bogie and chassis from vehicles from the turn of the twentieth century when it was built. The reconstructed Habsburg court train is now one of Europe's most individual and distinctive of luxury trains. Despite the accent on leisure-based train travel, the overall railway sector became big business again. By the mid-1990s, with a new epoch of private sector railway operator, Britain's mainline railways underwent the first stages of a continuous modernisation process coinciding with significant growth in the number of passenger journeys by rail. The scale of this transformation is still with us currently, as record numbers of passengers are carried on Britain's railways.

In Britain, the leisure-based luxury dining train era began in earnest on 25 May 1982 when the *British Pullman* and the *Venice Simplon-Orient Express (VSOE)* was launched. Lodged in popular consciousness as the *Orient Express,* it was one train but split into two halves. James Sherwood recounts why he never had any doubts about the project's ultimate success:

> 'Trains have an extraordinary romantic aura about them, and the Orient-Express conjured up an image of the lost era of luxury train travel, when elegant and beautifully dressed passengers journeyed across Europe on mysterious missions to exotic destinations.'

It was a significant media event but carried a cautionary notice. In an editorial, *The Railway Magazine* wrote:

> 'James Sherwood has invested no less than £11 m in this venture, gathering together old coaches from all over Europe and having them lovingly restored by craftsmen at workshops in three countries. He also has a firm belief that his faith will be upheld by the customers who will be prepared to pay the equivalent of first-class air fares to sample the gracious atmosphere of this recreation of the world's most famous train, not just for the first year of operation, but for the foreseeable future. The hard-economic fact that to recoup his investment and pay his way, James Sherwood must carry about 120 passengers on every train – and in its latter days, the old "Orient Express" only averaged a payload of 80 passengers. However, by then the old train was but a shadow of its former glory, in addition to which more people than ever are travelling nowadays. Like Georges Nagelmackers before him, James Sherwood is taking a gamble. We wish him well.'

The reincarnation of the golden age of luxury rail travel required two distinct portions for the first twelve years of operation with the establishment of new infrastructure on both sides of the English Channel. James Sherwood's initial intention was to concentrate on the continent:

'Our original plan was to operate the train only from Paris to Venice, but the British were the most frequent visitors to Venice going back to the Grand Tour days, and they were also lovers of historic trains. I felt we should re-create the entire journey starting in London.'

The London Victoria to Folkestone section used superbly refurbished first-class British Pullman dining cars. The twice weekly exercise of crossing the English Channel by sea to continue the journey was a relatively short-lived affair though; the opening of the Channel Tunnel in May 1994 saw the Boulogne to Venice leg relocated to Paris, freeing up the *British Pullman* cars to concentrate on providing upscale excursion tours for which there was a healthy market. James Cousins, writing an appreciation of the work of Brian Haresnape in 1987, captured the spirit of the *British Pullman* in its early days. 'Certainly, the true essence of the Edwardian grandeur of the experience can perhaps only be achieved by the attention to accommodation and service offered by such special trains as the revived *Orient Express*.' At the time, the *British Pullman* carriages recaptured a rich and romantic history that was almost in touching distance for many people.

The carriage stock came from a variety of places, including former *Brighton Belle* and *Golden Arrow* origin cars. Such vintages ensured a degree of authenticity in the re-embodiment of luxury travel. In addition, the task was made easier as railway enthusiasts in Britain had preserved more of the former first-class stock. James Sherwood recollects:

'We acquired [the Pullman cars] from all sorts of unexpected sources, including a master at Eton College, railway historic societies and restaurant owners who were using the cars to serve guests … In France we found General de Gaulle's private car, which he had used in Britain in the war. We bought it, only to be informed the French government was about to impose an export ban on the following Monday. So, over the weekend we got a road-haulier to transport it to the Channel, load it onto one of the Sealink ferries and spirit it out of France.'

Restoration to mainline standards of operation was not always straightforward. 'Rusting was particularly bad around the toilets, where water had sloshed around for decades. British law required that we strengthen the horizontal integrity of the UK train to ensure it wouldn't concertina in a collision' admitted Sherwood. But artisan specialists were near at hand at the Carnforth Steamtown Railway Museum where the Pullman cars were carefully undergoing renovation. The Waring & Gillow furniture factory had recently closed, providing a bank, as Sherwood remembers, of 'excellent craftsmen only too willing to work and soon we had our woodworking and French polishing shops and repair yard'.

As a result, the *British Pullman* is now made up of a rake of gracious ladies meticulously restored to their former glories: former 1933 electric cars that were part of the *Brighton Belle* sets; kitchen firsts no. 81 *Gwen*, no. 83 *Mona*, no. 84 *Vera*, always paired with no. 80 *Audrey* as a two-car unit and motor thirds no. 92 and no. 93 and trailer third No 86 which are all in storage awaiting full restoration in due course.

In addition, the company also owns a variety of steam-hauled cars from a 1923 to 1951 heritage, namely *Agatha, Carina, Cygnus, Ibis, Ione, Lucille, Minerva, Perseus, Pheonix* and *Zena* and third-class cars nos. 76 and 83. Whilst all of these Pullman cars are imbued with history two of them – *Carina* and *Perseus* – have special significance since they formed part of the special 'Operation Hopenot' Pullman Funeral Train carrying Winston Churchill's body from Waterloo to Oxfordshire on 30 January 1965 for burial.

Steam-hauled traction has always been part of the *Belmond British Pullman* offer, especially for the increased programme of domestic luxury train excursion tours to an assortment of destinations which by and large are from and returning to London. And a variety of mainline steam locomotives have been used over the years including *Clan Line*, a Southern Railway Merchant Navy Pacific and for a four-year period the world's most eminent steam locomotive, no. 4472 *Flying Scotsman* made regular appearances until the engine was acquired in 2004 for the nation by the National Railway Museum. After some thirty-five years of almost continual operation, the *British Pullman* has a highly successful non-sleeping luxury train format providing a mix of mainline day excursions and trip combinations from London to a variety of destinations and events. The train has a total of ten operational Pullman coaches at one time in four different carriage styles with seating for between twenty and twenty-six passengers in each carriage with a maximum capacity of 226 guests.

CHAPTER 6

2001-Present: The Era of the New Luxury Dining Train

Society at the turn of the twenty-first century is dominated by a small elite who enjoy wealth and privilege on a grand scale. This group could afford to travel, opening up areas of the world to a high-class tourism market their ancestors would not have believed. The middle class, always rising, tried, where cash permitted, to do the same. This elite, a cohort of entrepreneurs and business people, in effect formed a new aristocracy. Today, known as the uber-rich, they attract world-wide media attention. The travel industry, based on state-of-the-art luxury modes of transport, has expanded recently, creating a world of jets and ocean-going yachts owned by millionaire individuals or mega-corporations. We are now on the edge of leisure space travel.

Despite the extension of democracy in western society and huge advances in economic consumption, health care and justice, in some ways, society is as divided and divisive as ever. The rich have got richer and the poor, poorer, in some ways exacerbated by the digital and media age and the rise of a truly global economy.

In this modern society, the traditional concept of class has all but disappeared. Thanks to economic growth and the widely held view that 'Jack is as good as his master', the middle-class is now bigger than ever, with a huge variety of identities and lifestyles. They are the success story of today – well educated, in good jobs with a comfortable situation in which they are happy. The financial crisis of 2008 caused hardly a ripple in this group, protected as they are by a hedge-fund mentality and clever accounting.

As the media revolution has seen a shift towards digitalization and the phenomenal power of the Internet, there is nevertheless still a market, arguably a growing one, for quality newspapers and specialist magazines. A social revolution, which began under Margaret Thatcher in the 1980s and characterised by Harry Enfield's 'Loadsamoney' led to leisure and travel becoming available to the middle-class 'baby-boomer' market who inherited wealth and enjoyed gilt-edged pensions. These silver-haired globe trotters, who reinvented the once-elite cruise industry, will, however, disappear in the next generation. Travel industries will need to change their mindset to offer services to a younger, poorer clientele; the good times do not last forever.

So far, we have followed the evolution of luxury train travel and the markers that make it so special to consumers. So where does the luxury train concept now go? Everyday railway travel in Britain (and the rest of the world too) is now something rather mundane, where the fusion of all the elements that once made train travel so unique are all but lost in pursuit of modernised schedules and the bean counter's abacus of a standardized service. Despite railways having powerful supporters, there is little to differentiate the on-board experience of most train operators. Even first-class travel on British scheduled train services may be under threat too. In the summer of 2017, there was an expectation amongst transport policy-makers of the need in the future for fewer first-class carriages on inter-city trains mirroring changing work-place patterns. As the *Daily Telegraph* laconically commented in an editorial, 'Will a cooked breakfast on the Scotland to London sleeper become the preserve of the super-rich?'

Nevertheless, the demands of modern railway operation in the early Noughties saw the birth of many new luxury trains straddling the four corners of the globe. James Sherwood observed, 'By the turn of the century the pattern for the super-luxury railcar had developed.' The business model was leveraged, and the luxury train asset sweated; de luxe trains were fast becoming mature travel products with new entrants emerging. Belmond's first foray into extending the *British Pullman* franchise came with the *Northern Belle* in 2000 with a twenty-first century tourism product heralding from the original opulent 1930s 'Belle' Pullman rail cruise concept. The *Northern Belle* has a total of seven carriages in the style of Pullman dining cars, rebuilt from British Rail Mk I and II stock offering 2+1 dining experiences for up to 260 guests. The train did not include guest sleeping accommodation but provided day trip, short tour itineraries and weekend excursions focused on the north of England, often with different departure points. In addition, London and Scotland, together with circular tours of the country over scenic routes were offered. With the addition of staff sleeping cars, the train was able to provide extended journeys just as its LNER predecessor did, starting and ending with alternative points of departure around Britain. One of the problems of the extended tour format was the requirement for overnight tour guests to move into hotel lodging before returning to the train the following morning. It was a move, according to Sherwood, that met with mixed fortunes over the years, as in the autumn of 2017, Belmond divested itself of the luxury train operation selling it to parties connected to the West Coast Railway Company consortium.

The *Royal Scotsman* was a further extension of the company's UK train business when acquired in 2004. The train was described as a 'revival' product with its make-up of nine exclusive post-war Edwardian-style cars making trips to and around Scotland (though not exclusively) for a small group of just thirty-six guests. The *Royal Scotsman* is of 1960s vintage, with rebuilt British Rail Mk II carriages providing two restaurant cars, an observation lounge car and cabin sleeping cars but reflecting an early twentieth-century heritage of varnished woods, polished brass and fine fabrics. Sherwood noted:

> 'Scotland has its own very special charm, and the train operates very much like "Afloat in France", with a minibus following it around, taking passengers on day excursions to famous castles, Scotch whisky distilleries, salmon smokehouses and lunches with famous locals and chiefs of clans. Every night the train pulls into a remote siding so guests sleep undisturbed in the fresh (sometimes very fresh) Scottish air. The standards of food and service on board are superb, and every compartment has its own private bathroom.'

The *Royal Scotsman* has developed into a very special travel product according to Sherwood. 'I expect it will be enlarged by having more sleeping cars and another restaurant car, which can be added when needed to meet demand.' The *Belmond British Pullman* and the *Belmond Royal Scotsman* remain the company's flagship UK luxury trains representing timeless values of luxury construction.

De luxe trains in many ways have mirrored the growth in luxury consumption taking place across the world largely driven by new wealth. Luxury train travel has become the antidote to mid-life crisis fuelled by a rapidly growing over-40s market. Postponed family formation changes bring a younger, professional and well-educated customer base to the market as well as the millennial demographic happy to look cool with mum and dad recording remarkable journeys and places – a manna for the Instagram generation. Whilst these younger groups are important, the market place nonetheless has been characterised by post-war baby boomers, many now in retirement, who finished their careers with an earnings peak and defined pension schemes bringing disposable monthly incomes free from debt.

These demanding wealthy retirees demonstrate a growing appetite for frequent adventurous travel experiences. In tandem with this dynamic, many baby boomers possess keen specialist and hobby interests helping to shape and drive demand across many leisure industries. Growth in tourist passengers for luxury trains and the sheer numbers of heritage railway operations (in most western countries authentic organisations connected to industrial landscape of the past), signified a range in customer types from whole family groups, to couples and the individual enthusiast. The modern-day railwayac or train buff may be a customer of a certain age who not only remembers the last days of steam on British railways but experienced it in miniature too with their table-top die cast and tinplate model railways. They are the 'Hornby Dublo Generation'; 1950s and 1960s school boys (and girls) whose childhood memories and touchpoints are reawakened by the evocative sights and smells of ancient suburban stock with their cosy compartments of dusty padded seats and carriage windows adjusted by leather straps and the smart melamine finishes of Mk I second generation coaches. Hardly surprising, then, in August 2017, when the Royal Mail brought out a classic toy special stamp edition featuring an iconic image of a period Hornby Dublo train set.

Such connections are likewise imperative for the luxury products sector. Sound, emotion and taste, such important marketing tools for luxury car marques, are part of our sensory system connecting products to both the past but also to the future with current customer aspirations, desires and wants. When a mainline certified steam locomotive is coupled to a luxury dining train, the sights and smells of steam traction are so often compelling experiences, thus forming an integral component and element of the luxury products' fabric. For upscale customers, slow-paced luxury trains are part of a new age of leisure rail travel as integrated culture tourist packages combine hospitality, culinary excellence, relaxing environments with fellow likeminded travellers to engage in specially planned itineraries that provide a host of excursions and things to do wherever the trains' metals go. Undoubtedly, they are tough audiences who know good service culture. In short, they tap in to a world of good taste and are part of a surreptitious shift in travel landscapes and changing symbiotic relationships between consumer and tourism providers that have transformed the industry over the past thirty years.

One of the most significant developments currently shaping the luxury train industry is the level of collaboration taking place between operators and stakeholders around the globe. In some countries, the national rail authority is developing new upscale and mid-market tourist trains. This is particularly evident in Spain, where RENFE have introduced four separate train services catering for different market segments with offers across broad and narrow gauge rail routes. Whilst the focus might be on the luxury segment, some specialist train operators have identified profitable niches pitching at a level below luxury occupying a high-quality travel segment appealing to specialist markets. RENFE has been successful in creating a mix of both luxury and value for money tourist train operations. India, with its long-established British relationship, had one of the world's greatest railways systems built during the period of empire. Hardly surprising, therefore, given this heritage, that the country in the past twenty years should have attempted to really grab a portion of the luxury train agenda by exhibiting a form of private/public sector collaboration that has worked very successfully. Indian Railways, the national rail authority, has in tandem with state tourism and development agencies and private companies, segmented the market to create luxury train services to maximise the regional tourist potential. *The Maharajas' Express* is now one of the most imperious of trains, exploring the rich cultural heritage of India's fabled destinations. Japan, a relatively late entrant to the luxury train market, has now a host of new tourist market services placing it at the top table for international travellers in terms of destination choice.

Another approach that has been developed is for specialist tourist exploration trains to contain a variety of different travelling class specifications. These trains, often with communal approaches to dining and foodservice based on local and regional cuisines, effectively provide luxury, first, second or even third-class offerings meeting the needs of every pocket with different entry requirements. This is a type of luxury three-star market comprising old style sleeping cars that are not en-suite with separate toilets and may or may not have separate shared showers. Some operators believe that such a mixing of classes in one train does not work, even where they incorporate specialist sections that are insulated from the rest of the train to cater for the high-end customer.

Luxury travel providers need to be nimble to differentiate between affordable luxury and those customers seeking life-changing customised experiences built to specific traveller needs. This is highly important, since there are many distinctive traveller groups who thirst for different things from international train travel. They may be the train enthusiasts ticking off locomotives, carriages and freight wagons seen at remote railway locations of the world, or the adrenalin chasing explorer junkies craving for adventurous pursuits en route but the one thing that unites them all is the special magnetism of train travel to previously unknown destinations and stop-overs. The customer base is changing, and they too have distinctive requirements where perhaps luxury surroundings and gourmet food is not of the highest priority but instead prefer the immersive experiences of discovering new peoples, cultures and landscapes in less proscribed and packaged formats. With these types of product offerings, railway travel providers are able to straddle the notions of affordable constructs where ideas of 'everyday luxuries' and 'value for money luxuries' fit with the modern interpretations of bespoke and individualized approaches found in ultra-luxury travel.

Main line ticketing of steam locomotives and carriages opened a new market for luxury travel. Diesel locomotives, with their relatively short and highly intensive lives, also moved into the preservation movement, becoming attractive means of traction to haul luxury trains and all tapping into a reawakened consumer choice of new experiences. On scheduled services, first-class rail travel based on social stratification no longer held sway, swept away by the needs of the business community who were the primary shapers of everyday 'trains, boats and planes' travel products. Sherwood's visions of recreated luxury rail and hospitality travel products based on the Pullman tradition provided living nostalgic connections and fitted perfectly into the requirements of the modern world. Suddenly, the train had become a synonym for character and luxury and was beginning to spread throughout the globe.

Sherwood's endeavours in rekindling the magnetic attraction of the *British Pullman* also spilt over to the post British Rail privatised world and the awarding of the east coast franchise to Great North Eastern Railway (GNER) which as a trading name found considerable favour with rail enthusiasts cultivating a traditional image of on-board dining. GNER was the last operator of proper dining cars on the east coast line with carriages adorned by the words 'The Route of the Flying Scotsman' and 10.00 am departure slot. Andrew Martin reports, 'His (Sherwood's) trains on the ECML had warm-hued interiors and liveries created by design professionals, as opposed to the man with a paint pot who seems to have been kept so busy during privatisation.'

Running anything other than a utilitarian service now seems to be the order of the day in the first decades of the twenty-first century. The best customers can expect is a take on premium or added value service offering. Train operating companies appear to deliberately shy away from any modern interpretation of the luxury concept. Corporate bean counters cite it simply cannot be achieved within the boundaries of today's modern scheduled services.

But everything is not entirely lost in the modern British railway system, particularly where train operators manage longer distance routes. A limited number of scheduled service providers are involving themselves in the delicate areas separating business and leisure markets but also where the two interface. These include *Eurostar*, the new GWR franchise and Serco's *Caledonian Sleeper* service. As non-competing organisations, they recognise the subtle distinctions of service offering, particularly with the provision of food on the move. *Eurostar* offers Business Premier guests travelling at speed through the tunnel themed meals designed by their celebrity chef culinary director Raymond Blanc, whilst GWR's day-time Pullman car dining uses locally sourced ingredients to provide a flavour of West Country and Welsh foods on selected GWR lines including the routes to Cornwall. Old style Pullman dining is described by the company as one of Britain's best kept secrets, with menus originally designed by consultant chef Mitch Tonks. And a degree of romance can still be found with Britain's two sets of sleeper trains. GWR is introducing new style cabins and an on-board lounge bar on its London to Penzance *Night Riviera* sleeper, whilst exciting new food and accommodation developments are coming with the new *Caledonian Sleeper*. Undeniably, signature led food initiatives by GWR and Serco help to shape customer experiences where many multifaceted and different slants to culinary product development can clearly been seen. *Belmond British Pullman* now offer new fine dining and sommelier-selected food and drink experiences with an array of celebrity chefs preparing exclusive on-board tasting menus and then later joining guests on the train's itineraries.

Other private sector companies such as *Golden Eagle Luxury Trains* are responsible for a new generation of long-distance deluxe trains sprouting around the world, offering an increasingly sophisticated take on rail travel to destinations possessing unique, spectacular settings and vistas with itineraries and stop-overs providing access to extraordinary places of immense historical, cultural, natural and built-world significance. Real stories of the world's remote places, their peoples and the foods they eat reach out to visitors. It's a strong message and clearly based on emotional connectivity and understanding that can be so wholly imparted in the vast outback and rich surroundings of Russia, Asia Minor, Australia and Canada.

Yet there is a customer base attracted to the deluxe or ultra offer requiring an all-inclusive, fully en-suite, long-distance fine-dining luxury train experience. Whilst some luxury train providers concentrate on western style food presentation, increasingly the infusion of culinary twists to reflect local and regional aspects has gained prominence. Local food sourcing, the inclusion of fresh produce collected en route and food sustainability remain high on the agenda for many long-distance operators and their guests. Another trend has been the creation of luxury trains to maximise the heritage value of historic dining, lounge, bar and observation cars, whilst at the same time, either through converting existing coaches or building completely new carriages, introducing different grades of high-quality air-conditioned sleeping accommodation with varying degrees of quality in terms of en-suite bathrooms that may include power showers and even bath tubs in the specification. For some passengers, gone are the days of traipsing down the corridor to the lavatory and bathroom even if they are travelling on one of the world's most renowned trains. Some guests, such as on *Belmond's VSOE* sleepers, are perfectly happy to put up with mild inconveniences of a small cabin and modest washbasin for a day or two to top-drawer European destinations as it undeniably forms part of a highly memorable foot in the past experience.

For more wealthy travellers and despite the train's hallowed reputation, the awkwardness of bumping into a fellow traveller in the corridor wears thin. Respite is at hand as *Belmond VSOE* enters the twenty-first century where three super-spacious Grand Suites cars providing the opportunity for limited numbers of guests to celebrate significant anniversaries or milestones in life position *Belmond VSOE* at the very top end of luxury worldwide travel market.

Stirring new product development ideas recreate the concept of the private varnish cars of the past. Such initiatives position rail

Belmond's impressive VSOE Grand Suites carriages – named *Paris, Venice and Istanbul* – containing living areas, double beds and en suite lavatories and bathrooms with showers were introduced to the train's 2018 operating season. Private accommodation mirrors the rest of the train's 1920s style, with exquisite hand-carved timber interiors capturing French life at its period best. (Belmond)

Golden Eagle take a similar path with a dedicated carriage for luxury private hire on a lavish scale with their *Trans-Siberian* tours. Known as the Romanov Suite, the car contains a double Imperial style bedroom, an integral kitchen and personal chef, lounge and dining room for private dining and an individual travel guide for itinerary visits. The same exclusive carriage also contains a Silver Class compartment. (Golden Eagle Luxury Trains)

travel at the centre of the luxury travel industry as purpose-built luxury trains deliver highly sophisticated culinary and travel experiences. Managed by renowned hospitality operators, the market has consolidated, with innovative ideas surrounding new build luxury trains transferring from the boutique cruise market and the world's best hotels. Luxury river cruising and small ship ocean cruising are both growth markets but their success as holiday experience products gradually swells the market for luxury train travel. The décor, setting and surroundings of travelling in style require different approaches and change is certainly afoot as the broader luxury travel and tourism sector notes consumers beginning to focus away from the physical elements that define its composition. Design and exclusivity are important elements built around real craftsmanship, personalised service and delivered with exquisite little touches. These are the hallmarks of ambience and elegance that new twenty-first century luxury trains deliver. But no longer is it measured just by accommodation quality determined by the bed linen thread-count, or specially designed spaces that cater for hospitality indulgencies where caviar and fine wines are central to the brand message, but it is one where the sophisticated traveller now demands a new softer form of luxury construction.

The material components remain central to the fabric of luxury indulgence, but travellers seek something that is extraordinary. Personal experiences are multidimensional, determined by authentic engagement and interaction that unburden and unleash guests' senses of travel. Such types of travel experiences may be high-end ticket expenditure, but they now attract younger and affluent multinational audiences. Not necessarily time rich but as a group determined to squeeze the last fruits of unique destination explorations. At the top end of the market, the range of personalised offers built around the train, the route and its itinerary loom large, but there is also an additional legacy transforming the luxury sector with creations and experiences assembled around a series of Ps – pedigree, premium, privilege, prestige, persona, public figures and privacy. The exact number of Ps might be open to debate by marketing academics and luxury industry practitioners these days as privacy might be combined with the letter S for seclusion which has become a highly important element sought after at the premium/ultra-travel end, but nonetheless, capturing an approach that requires the building of special structures of uniqueness. A hundred or so years ago, social classes were clearly segregated and none more visible than on the floating palaces.

First-class isolation was rigidly enforced by shipping lines anxious to preserve the inviolability of their best fare paying customers. Yet yesteryear constructions are still with us nowadays on the world's largest passenger vessels but in subtler forms masqueraded as a ship within a ship concept. New words are used to describe personal service. At the truly luxurious end larger cabins or staterooms command premium prices, butlers replace stewards and the first-class dining room is rebadged as the grill as with Cunard's White Star Service offering. Such customer approaches spill over in to the luxury train market and in particular those exclusive offers with small numbers of highly valued guests.

Apart from operating on selected geographical routes that are different wherever possible, the key aspect for specialist providers is the need to avoid homogeneity; in the luxury segment service differentiation is vital, with tour operators delivering top of the range VIP arrangements with specialist meet and greet airport transfers and tour managers acting as key points of contact throughout the period of travel. Another trend borrowed from the cruise ship sector is for professional operators to create bespoke and highly tailored sightseeing experiences built around expert lectures and commentaries of highly informed and engaging celebrities and not available to other guests travelling on the same train. The academic historian and expedition leader imbued with television appeal has suddenly become big business. And indeed, the opportunity to crush that last element of secondary tourist spend has not been lost with the retail dimension as luxury train operators such as Belmond add to the luxury travel experience with expertly managed on train boutique shops providing ranges of smart clothing, jewellery and accessory branded goods as mementoes to record the train and destination experiences. Such activities form a distinct subsection of retail, since luxury shopping in tourism recognises the power of branding in travel where 'glamorous, classic and elegant' luxury products fit the bill.[1] The demands of a global luxury market place means luxury train owners, particularly the largest companies in the sector who have the capacity to invest heavily in marketing support, need to deliver a high level of visibility for their luxury train portfolios. In effect, many services have become luxury train brands in their own right, imparting instant recognition amongst would-be travellers in much the same way as the great named trains and luxury liners of the past have done. In what is a competitive and fast-moving milieu, the earliest entrants now command significant market presence.

In summing up the many different explorations this book on luxury railway travel has sought to capture is the essence of time. From the Victorian and Edwardian eras to the twenty-first century, one thing safe and sure is the knowledge that luxury train travel remains a highly prized and fashionable tourist pursuit with trains, their routes and destinations the world over now firmly placed in the ticket-list of must do travel experiences. Luxury rail travel has been rediscovered, taking consumers in exciting new directions with slow paced, luxury dining sleeping trains linking vibrant and exciting themed destinations. Long-distance luxury trains open up new opportunities, providing non-pressurised ways to experience the world's wonders in far more environmentally friendly ways that to some consumers still matters greatly. Gary Franklin,

Vice President, Trains & Cruises at Belmond explains his company's position in moulding the market:

'Belmond has a long and rich history rooted in luxury rail travel. Our Venice Simplon-Orient-Express train is formed of several vintage carriages that made up the original Orient Express train, known as the "king of trains and the train of kings". Today, our iconic train features traditional sleeper cabins, three restaurant cars and recently added ultra-luxury grand suites, all with meticulously restored wood inlays and Lalique glass that see the "golden age of travel" brought back to life and safeguarded for generations to come … Belmond remains at the very forefront of this exciting sector of the rail industry. Demand for authentic luxury rail travel is ever-increasing and our portfolio is continually expanding and evolving to keep pace. In the three decades since the Venice Simplon-Orient-Express debut, Belmond's fleet has increased to seven trains, spanning Asia, the United Kingdom and South America, where Belmond introduced the Belmond Andean Explorer in 2017, as the region's first ever luxury sleeper train. As a Company that has long been considered a pioneer in its field, we remain committed to expanding our luxury travel offering and to taking our luxury train experiences to exciting new frontiers.'

One of these new twenty-first century limits for the global luxury train travel phenomenon is managing operations and providing class-leading experiences over long-distances. Golden Eagle Trains is one of three specialist operators in Russia providing a variety of itineraries and destinations with differing Trans-Siberian routes. The company operates at the top end of the market and could be regarded as the world's leading exponent of long-distance sleeping car trains, providing luxury rail cruises with tours normally lasting between ten to twenty-one days but with the occasional forty-two day long tours. The *Trans-Siberian Express* is Golden Eagle's flagship operation. Such schedules entice guests with adventure travel in comfort and safety with off-train excursions and visits that are unique and memorable and often providing travel experiences that guests could not experience in any other way other than by train. In other words, trains and their itineraries are planned with huge attention to detail, instilling a company chant of a customer 'Wow' factor at least once a day. Golden Eagle's market offerings are variously described as hotel on wheels, hotel trains and land cruising using a strap line of 'Voyages of a lifetime by Private Train'. The company commenced running land cruises in 1989 using existing Russian rolling stock which was non en-suite but improved substantially by the attachment of purpose built shower cars and restaurant cars essential for long-distance sleeping car trains. Such was customer interest and demand in the opening up of the country following the demise of the Soviet Union, the company over the next ten years improved the quality of all aspects of the service they offered.

Golden Eagle's Tim Littler notes, 'Around 2000, we started investigating the possibility of having a purpose built luxury train in Russia.' In 2003 a prototype luxury car was first produced. By 2007, Littler went on, 'We were able to launch the Golden Eagle brand, a half km long twenty-one car purpose built fully en-suite train with restaurants, full kitchen car, bar car, staff accommodation, generator car and twelve sleeping cars with two classes of en-suite accommodation, Silver and Gold.' The sleeping car accommodation was further upgraded to three classes with the addition of 'Imperial' suites, giving the train a maximum 128 guest capacity. The Golden Eagle *Trans-Siberian Express* is now Russia's premier luxury train, having celebrated its tenth anniversary, whilst in 2017 it passed its first million miles in service. At the core of the travel experience is its distinctive culinary and fine-dining offer.

> 'Because of the remote areas that we travel to, it is sometimes difficult to find exceptional restaurants in areas that have little or no tourism, but that is why we are there. Onboard we have a very high standard with two teams of chefs, the main team works during the day and the second team works during the night preparing different breads, pastries and desserts for the following day as well as some prep work for the day chefs.'

Menus are mainly western in style but produced with a local twist and using as much local fresh produce as can be sourced throughout the journeys, together with a balanced wine list from Old and New World vineyards but also including quality wines of Hungarian, Romanian, Russian and Georgian origin.

Russia in many ways is an unique destination for rail enthusiasts, maintaining up until 2000 a huge pool of around 9,000 workable steam locomotives which made part- or all-steam traction

Golden Eagle's comfortable Bar Car provided the perfect location to watch Russia's winter landscape glide by. (Golden Eagle Luxury Trains)

Dedicated personal cabin attendants are at the heart of the Golden Eagle hospitality offer. (Golden Eagle Luxury Trains)

tours possible. Golden Eagle has its own steam locomotive, a 4-8-4 Class P36 which was orginally built in 1954 and restored to full mainline operating condition in 2001. Locomotive No P36.0032 is frequently seen hauling departing or returning *Trans-Siberian Express* tours in and out of Moscow and St. Petersburg. Partial steam haulage of luxury trains is the icing on the cake for many guests. In the past, the company has run three Trans-Siberian tours with steam haulage throughout using up to seventy-two different steam locomotives on each tour. Tim Littler goes on:

> 'We will be running from Moscow to Sochi in the North Caucasus (the destinantion of our first tour in Russia twenty-five years ago) which will also visit Grozny in Chechnya and Gagra in Abkhazia. The tour will be steam hauled throughout it's 6,000 km journey using twenty-one ex Soviet era locomotives!'

Nevertheless, in the luxury train arena authentic and period-setting carriages are not always essential. Littler describes the unique snags of running tours across the Russia and Asia:

> 'We undertake long and arduous journeys in sometime hostile environments (minus thirty-five to forty-five degrees plus centigrade), desert sandstorms and occasionally less than perfect track; for this we need rugged and modern equipment that is easilly maintained in the countries we operate. And of course, these carriages are fitted out to the highest possible standards.'

In tandem with other luxury train operators around the globe, the company in 2014 diversified by taking over operation of what is now known as the Golden Eagle *Danube Express* for services in the Balkans and to Iran. The train originally was limited to four deluxe sleeping cars, currently has five and by the end of 2018 will have seven, with a total guest capacity of sixty-four. The company also charters other luxury trains for journeys in India, China, Southern Africa and the UK. In addition, Golden Eagle runs luxury tourist trains to Asia Minor's Silk Road lines which are now very much back in vogue since the commencement of a new railway container freight trade route linking China, Russia and intermediate countries to the West. The new Silk Road allows twenty-first century nomads to reconnect with travel literary connections of the past; James Elroy Flecker's 1913 poem 'The Golden Journey to Samarkand'

P36 AWAITING ITS FATE

Eric Bottomley

The pencil sketch by Eric Bottomley is of the locomotive residing in the Kadala lumber plant where it was discovered by the Golden Eagle team in 1996. Eric's sketch is based on photographs taken at the time before the restoration process began.

Eric Bottomley's evocative depiction of a Russian 4-8-4 P36 Class express passenger locomotive was commissioned by Tim Littler of Golden Eagle Luxury Trains. No. P36.0032, one of 251 class locomotives was restored to mainline operating condition and painted in the company's distinctive blue and red livery. Fitted with a Lempor exhaust system in 2004 which resulted in increased power, the locomotive has since hauled the first 100 km of many Trans-Siberian Express departures. (Eric Bottomley/Golden Eagle Luxury Trains)

reportedly encouraged Thomas Cook to create post Second World War luxury adventure holidays. The *Golden Eagle's* Moscow to Beijing route is truly enigmatic. In the Russian territories the *Trans-Siberian Express* is used then switching to the *Shangri-La Express* train on Chinese metals. Straddling five evocative countries, the Silk Road rail tour crosses areas that are only accessible by rail, and as a travel experience draws heavily from that early twentieth century inspiration.

In conclusion to our story, where does one look for future inspiration for leisure-based train travel? Perhaps the answer is Japan, a country that has been at the forefront of railway technology development for over half a century. Its new network known as the Shinkansen – translated in English as new trunk line – allows Japan Railways Group companies to operate 'Bullet Trains', providing high-speed services across the country's mainland and islands. Whilst speed has been at the forefront of scheduled service

Whilst the *Fujisan View Express* might not technically be of luxury specification, the train nonetheless is positioned at the high-end of quality Japanese travel experiences. With a scenic route linking Otuski to Kawaguchiko, at the foot Mt Fuji in about forty-five minutes, the specially designed three-car train introduced in April 2016 allows visitors to engage with the natural world heritage site's unforgettable vistas. As an authentic rail excursion, the train is indicative of the kind of unique train travel explorations that makes Japan like no other place on earth.

railway advance, it also possesses a suite of the latest generation of the world's most luxurious new-build trains. As a nation, Japan surpasses at slowing down, and nowhere is this more evident than in the luxury train sector.

The country excels in its reputation for five-star hospitality demonstrated through the sensory embodiment of *Omotenashi* – making guests feel valued and respected, together with a characteristic desire by specialist tourism providers to fulfil every customer need and is deeply rooted and pervasive in the travel and hospitality sectors. Japan also has its own words describing its new deluxe excursion and charter trains – *Joifuru Torein* translated as the 'Joyful Train' – a concept that had its roots from the early 1960s when a vintage dining car was converted to include tatami floors and windows shielded by shoji paper screens. Carefully crafted themes have been built into the fabric of a succession of new luxury trains gracing the country's islands in recent years. An army of specialist railway engineers, designers and artisan workers have taken the modern train in new directions, mirroring the luxury twentieth century traditions of British and European rail travel, by showcasing the new tourist trains with the best quality materials available whilst marrying old-style craftsmanship. Carriages on these new generation of luxury trains have been built with hand-finished interiors, utilising the finest of décor fabrics capturing the look and feel of Japan's rich culture, heritage, wisdom and expression. Two trains, the *Kyushu Seven Stars* and the *Royal Express* were designed by Eiji Mitooka, who was also responsible for the design of the Type 800 bullet train. His use of wooden materials has been imitated in other luxury trains.

The *Kyushu Seven Stars* is a specially designed diesel locomotive-hauled train running on 3ft 6in narrow gauge lines. When debuting in 2013, the excursion train represented Japan's first serious foray into the luxury cruise train sector. Operated by JR Kyushu, it has seven beautifully constructed carriages with a total of fourteen suites accommodating a maximum of thirty guests. Operating two-day, one-night and four-day, three-night itineraries starting and finishing at Fukuoka, the former concentrates on routes around northern Kyushu whilst the latter tours the whole of the island in southern Japan providing scenic rural views and of the South China Sea. The *Seven Stars* comprises dining and lounge cars including piano, bar counter and observation areas with the rest of the train given over to five sleeping carriages incorporating a variety

The Kyushu *Seven Star* luxury train in all its glory. (Kyushu Railway Company)

of specifications but each en-suite room has a sleeping and seating area and private bathroom with shower and toilet facilities with one car located nearest to the dining and lounge car allocated to less mobile guests. The two luxury suites, accommodating up to three persons each, are located at either end of the train with the rear car having an extended rear window across the width of the carriage providing private scenic views much in the style similar to British Pullman observation cars of the past. The dining car is named *Jupiter*, representing a connection to Pullman car heritage encompassing a culinary approach reflecting the island of Kyushu's countryside and sea food culture together with local sourcing of ingredients and produce. Most meals are taken on the luxury train, but the region's unique restaurants also provide guests with eating out options. Yet the cost of travel on the luxury train is not cheap, as a four day journey on the *Seven Stars* currently costs between 300,000JPY and 950,000JPY (£2-6,000).

According to Dr Hiroki Shin, the business impact of the *Kyushu Seven Stars* has been significant. He ventures:

'JR Kyushu's railway business has been running a significant deficit of late, partly due to its operating in a disaster-prone area with earthquakes and floods. The luxury train was part of an effort to increase local tourism, thereby salvaging local lines. The *Seven Stars* train is closely linked with the Kyushu Shinkansen, opened in stages between 2004 and 2011, with JR Kyushu aiming to cultivate tourism demand, including inbound foreign tourists, rather than relying too heavily on business demand with the bullet train service. Much of JR Kyushu's income comes from non-railway business activity such as restaurants, hotels, retail and real estate. The undoubted success of the *Seven Stars* is said to have boosted the company's brand value and forming part of a company holistic development plan.'

The *Train Suite Shiki-shima* is a cutting-edge hybrid diesel and electric powered DMU sleeping car excursion train able to run on both electrified and non-electrified narrow-gauge lines extending its route and itinerary capacity. It was introduced on 1 May 2017 by JR East, using Tokyo as a home base and travelling to the Tohoku region and Hokkaido's northern reaches. Spring to autumn itineraries cover both two and four-day durations, mostly comprising onboard accommodation but the second night of the four-day trip includes a hotel stay. Similarly to the *Kyushu Seven Stars*, the new train will carry just thirty-four passengers in a luxury interior and service setting that rivals Japan's best luxury hospitality focused businesses. The ten-car train incorporates diesel generator observation power cars at either end, lounge and dining cars as well as six carriages given over to a total of seventeen sleeper units accommodating different suite combinations but all possessing showers and toilets. Five sleeping cars contain three private suite rooms to each carriage whilst the sixth car includes two high-end deluxe suites that have Japanese-style baths built of aromatic hinoki cypress wood. Cuisine is a focus of Japan's new luxury trains with elegant restaurant cars providing different themed settings. The *Train Suite Shiki-shima* menu reflects a French style infusion with local produce sourced from along the route but all designed by Japanese Michelin-starred chefs. The company's English language website and Tokyo base reflects a more international traveller base.

The Train *Suite Shiki-shima* luxury sleeping car excursion train in its hybrid diesel and electric powered DMU format. (East Japan Railway Company)

Continuing the Japanese trend for luxury trains to accommodate small numbers of high-end guests, the *Mizukaze Twilight Express* is a hybrid DMU luxury sleeping car cruise train running on narrow gauge metals and launched in June 2017 by the JR West railway company. Based in Kyoto, Japan's cultural capital, the state-of-the-art hotel train carries guests in 'nostalgic modern' settings across western Japan. The ten-car train incorporates six sleeping cars with retractable beds providing day-time seating and space, two observation cars with outdoor viewing platforms, a lounge and a dining car with interiors finished in luxurious art deco-styles. The train caters for a maximum of thirty-four passengers with one carriage providing a single suite featuring a double bed, bathroom with a roll-top bath and private balcony. Undoubtedly positioning the *Mizukaze Twilight Express* amongst the world's most elite luxury trains, Japanese cuisine is produced by the country's leading signature and Michelin-starred chefs. Itineraries include a mix of two-day/one-night or three-day/two-night combinations with day-time activities including bespoke cultural sightseeing excursions with initial emphasis firmly placed on Japanese language travellers.

Taking the luxury day excursion market in a new direction with the wave of new luxury trains is the country's *Royal Express,* launched in September 2017. Operating a variety of short tours, the train includes a three-hour jaunt to the Izu Peninsula, the seaside retreat of Shimoda popular for its beaches and hot springs, plus longer cruise plan itineraries with overnight hotel stays and tours included along the train's route. The rugged southern and western coastlines of the Izu Peninsula are less developed providing rural weekend retreats in relatively close proximity to Tokyo. The region has a close identity with Commodore Perry's 1854 landing and the opening of Japan to the outside world, with organised travel plans including sightseeing tours in a replica of one of Perry's ships. The opulent surroundings of the eight-carriage train accommodating up to 100 passengers take in features such as relaxing armchairs, a bar car with piano and an additional multi-purpose carriage for exclusive private party chartering. Overall the *Royal Express* is a child-friendly experience as it contains a dedicated children's area including a library and ball pond to keep youngsters occupied. The *Royal Express* is currently targeted at the domestic market with an undoubted focus on the train's culinary dimension with menus prepared by leading Japanese celebrity chefs together with local artists providing live musical performances.

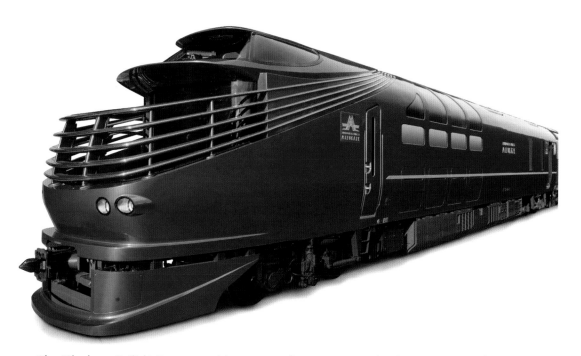

The Mizukaze *Twilight Express* combines twenty-first century modernism as an integral component of its unique luxury travelling experience. (J R West)

Japan's vistas are unique travelling experiences. Such developments ensure luxury rail travel is now recognised as a unique hospitality industry possessing powerful characteristics and constructions not easily replicated. There may be a limit to the number of luxury trains the global tourism market can sustain but there appears to be room for more, although missing links and different track gauges make this mission difficult. The Cape to Cairo rail link in Africa may have been a lofty ambition of Victorian explorers but as Golden Eagle's Tim Littler points out. 'It would be as an evocative route as the Trans-Siberian but north of Dar es Salam or Angola there is a 1,500 km gap with no rail connection and also two different gauges.' Thus far we live in an age where almost nothing is considered to be technologically impossible; bridging this geographical gap may yet be on the agenda, since the creation of new rail routes for combined freight and passenger movement has proven economic justification. This foray to another world has brought readers within touching distance of luxury train travel. It has been, and continues to be, an exciting journey which at the top end of the market attracts the world's high net-worth travellers. Luxury trains worldwide are big business and open to all wealth creators with the relevant imagination, resources and deep pockets. Who knows where the luxury train industry may yet go?

The Royal Express takes the modern-day luxury train in different directions catering for different traveller needs.

Three Routes to Scotland

The East Coast Route

The *Special Scotch Express* story goes back to 1860, when three separate railway companies – the GNR, NBR and the North Eastern Railway (NER) banded together to create a dedicated long-distance Anglo-Scottish passenger service. What was new from a passenger perspective was a standard railway carriage design exclusively for ECML use, representing significant improvements in the way travellers were conveyed over longer distances. The *Flying Scotsman* is a direct descendant of the *Special Scotch Express* – a train name first devised by George Bradshaw. As a business imperative, it was deemed necessary to create more comfortable ways to travel long-distances – memories of tortuous journeys involving the horse drawn stage coach were still fresh in many passenger's minds. Developing carriages of the same type would be easier to maintain, encompass the demands of all-day and all-night travel, through coach working and would meet the specific requirements of the east coast route. The idea for such a service covering around 393 miles, considered pioneering in mid-Victorian times, was masterminded by the GNR's Walter Leith, the company being the senior partner in the east coast collaboration.

The inaugural running of the *Special Scotch Express* was recorded on 18 June 1862, with fixed departure times set at 10.00 am from both King's Cross and Waverley stations. The idea of regular timetabled services based on a uniform British time zone (Greenwich Mean Time) was something still comparatively new to Victorians. Coupled with the notion of a seamless passenger journey, such novelties had yet to really gain a foothold. Passengers had never been guaranteed the most pleasant travelling experiences even though the line between London and Doncaster and the company's London termini at King's Cross was completed in 1852. Journeys were slow, taking some ten and a half hours for the expedition north due to engine slowness; locomotive design was still in its infancy.

Yet GNR's Chief Mechanical Engineer (CME) Archibald Sturrock maintained engines that were reliable and reasonably fast for the time until the company's second CME Patrick Stirling was appointed holding the post until he died in office in 1895. During his tenure, speed and power were at the forefront of engine advancement, catering for the needs of the company's premier London to York section with its testing and continuous gradients, as well as new routes which the GNR were opening. By 1870, Stirling, regarded as a locomotive design pioneer, built one of the nineteenth century's best-known engines, the elegant-looking 4-2-2 Stirling eight feet Single. Known as 'Single Wheelers' it provided a locomotive class whose engine performance was so good that it was openly copied by other British railway companies. The locomotive's innovative look and style was an industrial image which was representative of the second half of Queen Victoria's reign.

The Stirling single wheelers provided for a rapid acceleration of services, taking some two hours off journey times. They went on to establish speed records in the 1888 and 1895 Races to the North, when rivalry between the west coast operators – the LNWR and the Caledonian Railway – and the east coast companies was fierce. Locomotives on the King's Cross and Edinburgh east coast could cover the route in under six and a half hours but because of an accident and subsequent enquiry in 1896, a speed limit was mutually agreed by both sets of railway companies. The speed obtained by British locomotives at the time matched the best of Europe and America. William Smith, who travelled extensively across the US and Canada in late Victorian times and wrote of his travels, commented, 'The *Scotch* express between London and Edinburgh follows closely (like that of crack American trains), 'with a speed of 51.6 miles an hour' although faster speeds were recorded on the New York City to Buffalo section of the Chicago line; a route according to *The Sketch* was 'in much favour with travellers from the Old World.' But journey times between London, Glasgow and Edinburgh took a minimum of eight hours with agreed speed restrictions. In 1900, the GNR introduced more first and third-class dining cars to its 11.20 am Anglo-Scottish express departure for Edinburgh, Glasgow, Perth and Aberdeen. Speed limitations remained in place until 1932, despite significant advancements in steam locomotive technology that took place in late Victorian and Edwardian times where 'Atlantic' 4-4-2 wheel configured engines became the dominant form of express traction. The sight of grandiose engines pulling the *Special Scotch Express* into York station prompted the North Eastern in to action.

The NER was the second company in the east coast railway collaboration but saw its primary business in moving coal. However, due to existing agreements, the company had to provide suitable engines for passenger traffic on their York to Newcastle section. From the 1890s, express passenger traffic grew on the east coast route as restaurant, kitchen and sleeping cars were added to more frequent trains but never ran Pullman cars apart from one York rebuilt carriage designed as a first-class tea car for use on its day-time Leeds to Scarborough services. The introduction of heavier carriage stock allowed Thomas Worsdell the freedom to address issues designing the NER's own 4-4-2 Atlantic engines. His Class V locomotives were built to haul the heaviest of east coast express services. Worsdell was succeeded by Sir Vincent Raven as CME, continuing big engine policy.

The final railway company in the trilogy was Edinburgh-based NBR who built the ECML's Newcastle to Edinburgh section which established the east of Scotland to London route. The NBR, was set to become the largest of the Scottish companies. The company's network grew steadily but at different times it was hampered by financial improprieties, hassles and commercial rivalries with, amongst others, the Caledonian Railway. The *Special Scotch Express* had been subject to the 1862 Border Counties arrangements, which saw several amalgamations of local railways across the English and Scottish borders. From July 1869, the NER began running through passenger trains from Newcastle to Edinburgh as part of a revenue sharing scheme.

Scottish railway historian P.J.G. Ransom suggests that the NER came out on top of these negotiations as their east coast expresses could be seen running into Edinburgh until grouping. The NBR similarly expanded its network south west from Edinburgh through the Borders to Carlisle but for many years the company was frustrated by the Caledonian Railway, who refused adequate access in Carlisle for Waverley line freight traffic. The Caledonian Railway had entered a pact with the LNWR in 1867 to further west coast line development and used this mechanism to frustrate NBR's commercial plans, leaving relationships between the two companies at an all-time low.

By 1876, the position had improved as the mighty Midland Railway completed its Settle & Carlisle route providing the commercial muscle for trains to operate from St. Pancras through Carlisle to Glasgow but also the route through Scott Country between Carlisle and Edinburgh dubbed the Waverley Line. Such developments forced NBR to become more customer focused. To the north of Edinburgh, the NBR, through amalgamation and eventual agreement with the Caledonian Railway, extended its network with a circuitous line to Aberdeen. The booming city was served by two routes by the NBR and Caledonian Railway thus becoming the northern terminus in the Races to the North contests and acting as a catalyst for developing 'Royal Deeside' tourism promotion. In 1879, NBR was rocked by the Tay Bridge disaster rendering its future far from certain for some time. Yet NBR maintained good relationships with both the Midland and the NER, who were to become key strategic partners in building the Forth Railway Bridge later in 1890. With the Forth and the rebuilt Tay Bridge, a fast-direct route from London to Edinburgh, Dundee and Aberdeen was established inserting the last piece of the east coast railway jigsaw. Central route competitor the Midland Railway was ironically the most enthusiastic supporter of the Forth Bridge project, contributing some thirty per cent of construction costs as the company saw great opportunities to push its Highland luxury tourist expresses as well as business traffic from the Midlands and the West Country. By 1893, Thomas Cook featured the bridge on the front of their Scottish tour travel brochures.

Dugald Drummond took over NBR's CME helm in 1874. A combination of 4-4-0s were produced for the next forty years under two successive CMEs. In common with its ECML partners, 4-4-2 Atlantic classes were built for the NBR in the early twentieth century for its principal main lines whilst smaller 4-4-0 locomotives were primarily used for provincial routes. By the end of the Edwardian period, all three railway companies had various elegant, fast and efficient Atlantic Classes hauling the east coast. *Special Scotch Expresses* always had their own coaches since its first running in 1862 with specialist through carriages becoming key features of the east coast route. In pre-grouping times, these dedicated coaches were termed as East Coast Joint Stock (ECJS). Railway author Michael Harris (*LNER Carriages*, Noodle Books, 1994) writes 'the ECJS set consistent standards for design and construction' and their supply for the east coast run as 'la crème de la crème'.

But for the first thirty years and despite a dedicated carriage specification, the standard ECJS coach was predominantly a six-wheeled carriage, representing a railway policy lasting almost to the last decade of the 1800s. Collaborative working delayed railway infrastructure development. Railway historian David Jenkinson criticises the GNR for being 'a distinctly arrogant railway' full of self-satisfied complacency and as an organisation having to be pushed into providing something better[1]. Taking a similar view of the necessity to look after passengers – or lack of it as far as the GNE was concerned – railway writer Maurice Bray says 'in catering for its commercial passengers the GNR did not seem to pay much attention to advertising its hotels' service to them.'[2] Carriage change came 1893, when the *Scotch Express* received new coaches ushering in a new era where longer wheel-based corridor or gangway carriages together with dining and sleeping cars delivered much improved passenger comfort, satisfying the demands of late Victorian travellers. All passengers had access to the dining and separate kitchen cars considered a novelty at the time.

One surprise is the time it took for the three consortium companies to commit to creating ECJS carriages fit for luxury travel purposes. With competition on the west and central routes intensifying, GNR and the NER were forced into action. Despite introducing new specialist stock in the 1890s, the GNR's role as the lead partner in the consortium had been lackadaisical in terms of carriage design, development of interiors and of passenger comfort. Competitive pressures forced the GNR to take a lead in laying a firm foundation in ECJS carriage design and building for the best part of half a century under the supervision of Edinburgh born Nigel Gresley. Better known and knighted for services for locomotive design in 1936, Gresley originally came to GNR in January 1905 as assistant carriage and wagon superintendent. His impact was to last well into the LNER era until his unexpected death in 1941. However, within a year of his arrival, he had introduced elliptical-roofed, steel-framed and teak panelled coach designs that became a carriage standard. The period between 1900 and 1914 was regarded as a carriage revolution; innovations adopted by GNR were closely followed by the other partners with their own individual coach building programmes at York (NER) and Cowlairs (NBR) becoming the blueprint for future LNER thinking.

Gresley's influence on carriage design below decks was particularly significant especially with four-wheeled bogie suspension providing passengers with a superior ride. Designs impacted on future developments of dining and sleeping cars

NEWS AND VIEWS.

Travel Comfort.

THE Great Northern Railway offers to the tourist such facilities as make travel a veritable luxury. With restaurant cars, bedrooms on wheels, and every other equipment necessary to one's comfort, the carriages are indeed travelling hotels.

At Sir John Bennett's, Ltd.

At this well-known Cheapside house is to be seen some fine examples of the jeweller's art together with a most comprehensive display of its well-known watches and clocks. Those in search of Yuletide gifts

A NOVEL MOTOR MASCOT

may find every want satisfied in a gratifying manner. Some exclusive designs in watches suitable for both sexes are worthy of one's mature consideration. Many fine designs in jewellery too claim one's attention.

Motor Mascots.

Motorists, propitiate the fates and have a mascot! Illustrated above is a "quaint conceit" which is one of several designs made by the well-known firm of Dunhill.

LUXURIOUS HOTELS ON WHEELS

Speed & Comfort

NEWS AND VIEWS.

Care of the Teeth.

I have been recently giving Calox Oxygen tooth powder a very lengthy trial, and have nothing but praise for this dainty and efficacious toilet accessory. Calox is not only a powder for polishing the teeth but it is a scientific dentifrice that meets every requirement. The use of Calox produces a sense of freshness and purity only possible as the result of a chemically-clean mouth.

A "Joke" Prize.

Illustrated here is a miniature prize cup which forms a capital "joke" prize for

A "JOKE" PRIZE CUP

losers in all sorts of games, cards or otherwise; its size is exactly as reproduced. This useful little cup is sold by Henry Brown of Kensington High Street for 2s. 6d.

A Useful Diary.

The new edition of "Welcome's Photographic Exposure Record and Diary" is now obtainable, and its publication will be welcomed by every photographer inasmuch as this book is a perfect encyclopædia of photographic information.

The Tatler was another key publication for railway promotion. The title's editorial in December 1907 coincided with the GNR's 'Luxurious Hotels on Wheels' initiative. Apart from dedicated Anglo-Scottish ECJS railway carriages, GNR's stock served many Yorkshire and east coast resorts keen to attract well-off visitors. (Illustrated London News Ltd/Mary Evans)

which were the essential components of civilised long-distance travel. Gresley experimented with articulated bogies, where two carriages share a single bogie and this form of arrangement became a corner stone of future triplet kitchen and dining cars putting the emphasis on amenities for the long-distance *Scotch Express* and the future *Flying Scotsman* train. Gresley's work created a distinctive carriage look with dome-ended elliptical roofs, new electric lighting systems where new GNR carriages quickly replaced four and six-wheeled clerestory stock that had been in widespread use – the comparatively slow take up of bogie coaches on the ECJS was partly down to the fact that the east coast line had been so well engineered. The train was effectively divided into two halves as a separate kitchen car with no gangway access was added followed by high-quality eight wheeled bogie third-class dining carriages which the *Railway Magazine* in August 1897 suggested were some of the best in the country, but created an awkward problem since they were unmistakably better than the first-class 'diners' on the same train. Improvements did not appear overnight, as Wragg tartly advises us 'until 1887, the fastest east coast trains did not allow second or third-class passengers'. Early *Scotch Express* carriages were relatively primitive affairs until higher specification stock eventually appeared in 1893 where new teak-panelled stock design was to remain sound for many decades, standing the test of time. However, rapid developments in carriage design made the then new ECJS double bogie twelve-wheeled gas lit clerestory stock 'old fashioned' within ten years of being built.

By the early years of the twentieth century more sophisticated forms of carriage appeared. In 1914, modern rolling stock was allocated that saw the premier east coast train gradually evolving its name from the *Special Scotch Express*, to the *Flying Scotchman* or *Scotchman* to ultimately the *Flying Scotsman*. New ECJS stock was a comparatively late development but the term 'luxurious railway travelling' was fastened to the *Flying Scotsman* together with a gradual speeding of the route as, by the turn of the century, the ECJS partners were building a variety of larger and more efficient boilered Atlantic Class locomotives. Gresley had taken over the CME role at the tender age of 35 on Ivatt's recommendation. Bigger and more powerful engines were on the design boards and by 1922, the first of a new generation of 4-6-2 A1 Pacific Class of express locomotive appeared from Doncaster works no. 1470 *Great Northern*.

The east coast route was popular with relief trains having to cater not just for the leisured classes but also the demands of business travellers. London and Edinburgh were Britain's two largest financial centres, their well-being central to the ongoing success of the Empire. Naturally, passenger demand drove investment in modern rolling stock. New carriages introduced before the Great War were well received but this was to be the last significant improvement in travelling comfort and innovation in pre-grouping days. Luxury travel developments had to wait until the mid-1920s and a brand-new railway era as the ECJS companies morphed to an enlarged business operation. Style and service on the east coast run would now be joined by a new seduction; speed, courtesy of the new 4-6-2 A1 Pacific Class locomotives. By 1924, passengers would speed along the east coast route to Scotland courtesy of powerful

This east coast railway consortia marketing initiative probably dates from the Edwardian period. The poster highlighted Scotland's natural assets with a rural night-time setting with a village beside a moonlit loch, the promotion of the line as the quickest of the three Anglo-Scottish rail routes as well as access to other parts of the Scottish countryside reachable with Edinburgh departures. (NRM Pictorial Collection/ Science & Society Library)

new engines with a brand-new named train. *The Flying Scotsman* would be endowed with comfort and luxury facilities.

What can be said about the *Flying Scotsman* train that has not already been written? It is certainly deep rooted in British psyche, embedded across several railway eras and a direct descendant of the *Special Scotch Express*. The service's longevity extends to the current day as a scheduled early morning service commends a same name running daily from Edinburgh Waverley to London King's Cross. Whilst the first running of the famous named train may be charted from 1923, it was the progressive development of pre-grouping railway companies providing long-distance rail travel, offering travellers to Scotland a host of diverse leisure and holiday attractions together with a link from the Scottish capital for the business and financial community to the Empire's London markets. It was a popular and premier route exemplifying a highly civilized yet exclusive travel experience across all carriage classes.

Speed, luxury and ultimately glamour were class mates to an emerging brand, and all wrapped with a quality food experience where expert cuisine was produced in modern hygienic settings and delivered to guests with faultless personal attention. New ECJS stock comprising a total of ten carriages carried sixty-eight first-class and 225 third-class passengers, including for the first time the introduction of thirty-six ton steel-sided kitchen cars, a development new to most railway companies at the time, comprising a central kitchen galley with pantries located at opposite ends serving the separate first and third-class restaurant cars attached to the kitchen car. *Railway Magazine* considered 'the whole arrangement being most commodious and up-to-date in all respects'. According to other press reports at the time, the first-class restaurant car was truly luxurious, seating twenty-eight guests at any one sitting with a glass door partition dividing smoking and non-smoking sections. The dedicated *Flying Scotsman* train from 1 July was now part of a new media agenda making travelling 'more pleasurable every year' and a train 'of much magnificence, wherein the traveller will find the last word not only in rolling stock but also in the commissariat'. *Flying Scotsman* was promoted as a showcase extending the Scottish holiday season where 'the employment of the cars will be watched with interest by many of the railway authorities and the travelling public' to a specially invited press party of some 200 journalists gathered on the train including thirty to forty from London and representatives from America and Japan.

By the summer of 1914, *Flying Scotsman* entered the east coast's advertising language. GNR lost no time endorsing its latest luxurious restaurant and sleeping cars allocated to new ECJS rakes. Interestingly, car-carrying traffic would evolve with railway operators with this advertisement positioned alongside a *Bystander* feature on the latest motor cars available at the time. Whether this was intentional remains a moot point. (Illustrated London News Ltd/ Mary Evans

FOR
SCOTLAND
TRAVEL
EAST COAST ROUTE
the SHORTEST and QUICKEST way to
EDINBURGH, DUNDEE, PERTH, ABERDEEN, INVERNESS AND WEST HIGHLAND RESORTS.

First Class Dining Car on " Flying Scotsman," which leaves London, King's Cross, daily at 10 a.m, Sundays excepted.

10 through Restaurant and Sleeping Car Expresses which enjoy the highest reputation for comfort and punctuality, and form the finest series of long distance trains in the world, are run each week-day from

King's Cross Station
G.N.R. the starting point of the "FLYING SCOTSMAN."

The Entirely New Carriages and Restaurant Cars composing this Train from July 1st represent the latest word in luxurious accommodation.

Write to Superintendent of the Line, Dept. B.S., G.N.R., King's Cross Station, for time tables and illustrated booklets, especially for "On Either Side," which pictorially describes the interesting places seen from the carriage window.

GNR advertising described the *Flying Scotsman* as 'the latest word in luxurious accommodation'.

On group formation, east coast Anglo-Scottish trains were symbolised by powerful new and fast mainline locomotives; the third of the 4-6-2 A1 Pacific Class introduced in LNER livery was named *Flying Scotsman* after the GNR's premier express train. A total of ten large A1 locomotives made up the new class, the first of which actually debuted in GNR colours. They were ground-breaking, long and lean-looking machines, with larger boilers than the preceding Atlantic classes and built for speedy, long-distance rail travel. It could be argued the new Pacific classes and in particular no. 1472 *Flying Scotsman* were always destined to be media personalities. Exhibited on the Palace of Engineering stand at the British Empire Exhibition, Wembley 1924, the Gresley A1 Class locomotive attracted considerable press and public attention, pitched alongside GWR's equally revolutionary Castle Class engines in a quest to portray the country's most powerful express passenger locomotives. The A1s provided a consistent motive power image on the ECML as LNER sought to maximise to good benefit. The inaugural nonstop run of *Flying Scotsman* was on Tuesday, 1 May 1928, having been usurped by LMS's *Royal Scot* nonstop run a few days before. Whilst LMS's act was clearly designed as one-upmanship, the LNER position was to garner additional sustained passenger traffic. The combined north and south nonstop running created substantial press coverage and huge crowds were present at King's Cross and Waverley. And as *Railway Magazine* reported 'similar scenes of enthusiasm were witnessed at the principal intermediate stations, notably York and Newcastle'.

Nonstop running implied speed but the east and west coast Anglo-Scottish routes were bound by agreements made in the previous century to restrict journey times to eight hours following the Races to the North excesses. There were also absurdities, as the *Night Scotsman* was half an hour faster than its famous day-time service. This ultimately ended in 1932 as archaic rules looked ridiculously sedate. As author Andrew Martin wrote, 'it was said that dead fish (on trains from Aberdeen docks) were travelling to London faster than passengers from the north.'

By 1932, the journey was quicker, taking around seven hours and fifteen minutes. Two years later, the *Flying Scotsman* was the first LNER locomotive to have officially recorded a speed of 100 mph but by the mid-1930s the train had to share the limelight with new streamliner expresses. Post-war, when Britain was at last getting back on its feet, the new British Railways *Flying Scotsman* lost its non-stop accolade to a newcomer service the *Capitals Limited* which itself a few years later was renamed the *Elizabethan* when a new queen ascended the throne. This was all part of a process where streamliner non-stop traction on the east coast brought improved passenger facilities. Yet speed will always be connected to the *Flying Scotsman* as the name lives on. In 2019, a train carrying its title is still the fastest train service running between Edinburgh and London.

The *Flying Scotsman* had an unparalleled image and an intricate component of the twentieth century social history narrative of England and Scotland. It was a product of the new public relations operation keen to maximise and weave storytelling in a bid to stimulate the travel market. The positive thinking, publicity conscious unit seldom lost the opportunity to promote the company. Throughout its lifetime until railway nationalisation, this was something the company became extremely adept at. No. 4472 *Flying Scotsman* was used by the LNER publicity machine for the first non-stop running to Edinburgh on 1 May 1928. It was a significant media event that would see the peaking of the *Flying Scotsman* brand, cementing the locomotive's reputation and the gaze of the travelling public. Interestingly, no. 4472 was used in an earlier high-speed trial between King's Cross and Leeds to assess whether a short four carriage steam train could match the performance over a similar distance of the *Flying Hamburger* diesel-electric train. As a result, no. 4472 became a firm favourite for public relations initiatives.

From grouping, the LNER's image came under the responsibility of the company's dynamic advertising manager, W.M. Teasdale. Teasdale was at the forefront of publicity-led developments such as the naming of no. 4472 after the LNER's premier Anglo-Scottish service, its inclusion at the British Empire Exhibition and the trialling of a cinema carriage all designed to establish a 'brand' visibility that would drive east coast revenues. From 1928, Cecil Dandridge took over as LNER Advertising Manager and he would invest further in *Flying Scotsman* publicity-led initiatives such as non-stop runs, the almost continual updating of luxurious carriage stock and the quality of onboard service that would enhance its reputation and travelling experience for the public.

North-from King's Cross by the *"Flying Scotsman"*

AMONG the Expresses which leave King's Cross for Scotland by the East Coast Route is the "Flying Scotsman," the oldest and most famous train in Great Britain.

It travels through country richer in glorious scenery than any other between England and Scotland—Abbeys, Castles, Cathedrals and Historical Remains—and along some sixty continuous miles of English Seaboard.

The "Flying Scotsman" departs at 10 a.m. each week-day. Other Restaurant Car Trains, a Pullman Train and Sleeping Car Trains take the same route at intervals during every twenty-four hours.

East Coast Route to Scotland

Shortest and Quickest for

EDINBURGH   DUNDEE
ABERDEEN   PERTH   INVERNESS

Write for full information to the Passenger Manager, L.N.E.R., King's Cross Station, London, N.1, or enquire at any L.N.E.R. Ticket Office.

In the early years of the Big Four era, the Anglo-Scottish east and west routes were marketed individually. This 1925 summer season LNER advert from *The Tatler* used the increasing awareness and reputation of the *Flying Scotsman* to promote a range of Highland and east coast destinations easily reachable from Edinburgh. (Illustrated London News Ltd/Mary Evans)

The company invested heavily in all forms of media, particularly with the use of iconic posters and postcard advertising that used LNER's new standardised lettering to enhance the train's image. This helped create a popular culture that similarly utilised marketing initiatives firmly targeted at children with branded toys and books that ensured that by the end of steam traction in the early 1960s, *Flying Scotsman's* brand was firmly embedded in the public psyche.

What the company was doing was used as publicity strategy information with Dandridge writing regularly under 'Advertising Notes' in the LNER staff magazine, helping to maintain a perception the company was one of the industry leaders. Interestingly, the ultra-modern image of the A4 was also used on *Flying Scotsman* luggage labels which until 1937 were normally hauled by A1 and/or A3 Classes. Luggage labels were highly effective forms of advertising, effectively mini creative translations of larger railway travel posters, that helped to develop the *Flying Scotsman* brand heritage that would continue into British Railways days, mixing a combination of modernity together with nostalgic representations that last to the present.

By 1924, to help publicise the east coast route service, a new twenty-four carriage set with roof boards sporting the *Flying Scotsman* legend was introduced. By the end of the decade, the service was at the forefront of LNER's product and service development, but its 1924 new coaching stock was considered 'mildly innovatory' but in terms of interior design and décor was nothing that could be considered outstanding. In a space of just four years, the Anglo-Scottish travelling experience underwent thoughtful change. With the start of the flamboyant 1930s, *Flying Scotsman* had it all, with new train stock demonstrating LNER's commitment to carriage travelling experience on its long-distance prestige expresses all designed with the intention of securing a prosperous travelling customer base.

On the initial 1 May down run, the hairdressing salon was well patronised. *Railway Magazine* reported that the attendant had 'all necessary equipment and a cabinet and cupboard for requisites and articles for sale'. Likewise, the newspaper and book service was much appreciated as W.H. Smith's travelling newsman was 'able to supply newspapers, periodicals and the latest books, including those published for the first on the day of travel.' LNER advertising in July 1929 emphasised '393 miles of luxury travel' whilst the following summer the culinary offer of 'the Louis XVI restaurant with its all-electric kitchen assures you of perfect food' became the focus.

By 1930, Gresley had now really gone to town on the design stakes but more importantly, in terms of delivering improved passenger comforts for longer-distance day travel, the inclusion of two super first-class carriages with winged armchairs with adjustable seats and backs, footstools, and pressure ventilation.

Glamour and comfort were key components of the inter-war *Flying Scostman* product but more improvements were to follow that would make the service the most renowned luxury train of its day. In 1932, advertising in the *Bystander* was captioned by '45 minutes off the run of the *Flying Scotsman* emphasising the Louis XVI restaurant, the cocktail bar, ladies retiring room and hairdressing saloon'. Most notable, however, was the claim 'It is an "Imperial Palace" in miniature'.

The train's carriage innovations now included listening to the radio over headphones, the previous ladies retiring room carriage space had been shortened to include a dedicated cocktail bar for pre-lunch drinks at one end and a hairdressing salon run by B. Morris & Sons. Despite LNER's undoubted carriage advances on *Flying Scotsman*, the Pullman company operating in Britain and Ireland was slow on the uptake, even though all of these ideas had been pioneered by the American organisation many years before. The British operation opted to retain its recognised role. French-style first-class carriages were added to the *Flying Scotsman* in 1935 whilst three years later the train received new and more luxurious carriages, the fifth generation of new stock, including a buffet-lounge car and very much in keeping with other carriage developments taking place on LNER's streamlined expresses. On amalgamation in 1923, new thinking was required for the Pullman relationship. Most of the former GER Pullman stock from East Anglian routes (apart from specified boat trains) was moved to the east coast main lines as they were not earning their keep. In so doing, Pullman became a long-term feature of Anglo-Scottish expresses. The reason for this switch, according to Chris de Winter Hebron, was that 'Both the LNER and Dalziel [Pullman] were looking for a more cost-efficient use of the cars, but it is uncertain who made the first move'.

As a result, several Pullman services were created very early on, running out of King's Cross with the intention of aligning facilities to upscale tourist and business customers. One such route was to the north Yorkshire spa town of Harrogate, England's most northerly spa, possessing an affluent retired residential community as well as being a destination attracting the right balance of visitors drawn to the town's distinctive cultural life and in close proximity to the outstanding Yorkshire Dales countryside. In theory, the exact kind of destination attributes needed for a successful luxury train. More importantly, it likewise acted as a traveller signpost, a gateway signalling a Pullman association that would grace the LNER and later British Railways Eastern Region rails for many years. Initial running of the upmarket *Harrogate Pullman Limited* required a four-car train to be reversed out of Leeds with a new locomotive attached to the rear of the train before continuing its journey to Harrogate and Newcastle. A London to Sheffield businessman's Pullman train out of King's Cross was trialled between 1924 and 1925 but the service was not destined to be a success, and perhaps a pointer to successful Pullman services requiring a mix of resident, visitor and business traveller traffic. It was withdrawn after the 1925 summer season, with specialist cars allocated to a new Pullman service beginning on 21 September specifically serving the key commercial centres of Leeds and Bradford as this passenger route paid. Such was the success of the Harrogate and Edinburgh route, the *Harrogate Pullman Limited* no longer had to stop and reverse out of Leeds but continued partially over LMS metals with an ultimate Edinburgh destination. With its popularity, the number of Pullman cars was increased to six-car and then seven-car rakes. By 1927, LNER solidified its offerings with the Leeds and Bradford service being officially named as the *West Riding Pullman* with an additional stop at Wakefield where Pullman cars specifically for Bradford and Halifax were detached, ensuring Newcastle and its industrial hinterland was served with appropriate connections.

In the weeks prior to the 1925 12 August Highlands sojourn, *The Tatler*, in its railway notes, congratulated LNER:

'on the inauguration of a new train, composed of first and third-class Pullman cars, running between London and Scotland. The coaches, designed to provide every measure of safety, are luxuriously appointed, containing movable armchairs which ensure every possible comfort.'

The Harrogate-Edinburgh connection in 1928 was officially renamed as the *Queen of Scots* with the service receiving new steel-sided Pullman stock as well as four additional third-class cars in 1930, which LNER decided to lease from the Pullman Company following the ending of the GWR *Torquay Pullman* fiasco. The route was also extended in 1928 to include Glasgow as a final stop with a total journey of 440 miles. With additional carriage resource, Yorkshire in addition received an extra weekend Pullman service when the popular *Sunday Harrogate Pullman* calling at Bradford was introduced.

When LNER brought in their own super trains in the mid-1930s, Newcastle was served with a direct luxury train service. The *West Riding Pullman* no longer called at Newcastle, with the service renamed as the *Yorkshire Pullman* with the south bound morning departure allowing Pullman car connections for York, Hull and Doncaster passengers and a return afternoon north-bound service via Leeds. Further variations of Pullman services would occur with new LNER streamliner super trains of 1935 and 1937. Of all LNER's pre-war Pullman services, the *Queen of Scots* offered a real customer experience valued by passengers, although the advent of streamliners, according to some commentators, left it somewhat in the shade. As Charles Fryer's sentiments commendably captured, 'More than any other Pullman train in Britain the *Queen of Scots* offered train-timing excitements as well as journeying comforts.'

Perhaps this was down to a familiarity many upscale customers preferred as the Pullman company continued to reinvent its traditional offering based on furnishings and décor as well as by its external appearances. Although the Pullman Company had introduced many new cars by the early 1930s, they were instantly recognisable and by mid-decade benefited considerably as, on the east coast routes, Gresley A4 Class locomotives were introduced bringing a further dimension of power and speed to Pullman services as well as the glamorous new K Class steel-sided stock designed for sustained periods of ninety to 100 mph running. But staying on the train was part of the fun experience as, even with A4 traction, the journey could still take nine hours.

The 1930s was the decade of Britain's super trains when a brief four-year period between 1935 and 1939 exemplified the romance of streamliner rail travel. And nowhere was this more evident than on the Anglo-Scottish main routes re-igniting the so-called mythical Race to the North competition, this time run between the consolidated LNER and LMS railway company consortia that had an eye on the premium sector, which for most part could deliver a profitable operation. The *Flying Scotsman* service had been running over ten years as well as a batch of east coast route Pullman services when the first of the LNER streamliners appeared, initiating a classic age when steam hauled expresses captured the public imagination. Streamliner rail services were a deliberate attempt by the country's main railway companies to push steam traction efficiency to the then limits of technology, but it is difficult to establish how successful they were for both LMS and LNER. In 1936, the *Northern Daily Mail* and a host of other regional newspapers reported on how Britain led the world with steam technology as 50,000 minutes were saved on rail speed-up. The paper cited:

> 'Four years ago, the railways of the world replied to the challenge of our services with railcar trains capable of much higher average speeds than the regular steam trains. The success of these railcars encouraged designers to develop steam locomotives capable of similar speeds … Recent events have shown that the steam locomotive is by no means a back number [as] streamlining gives a saving on coal consumption at high speeds, and attention is now being given to climbing power, with the object of attaining higher average speeds.'

David Wragg suggests that many observers believed 'they were in effect "loss-leaders" due to poor utilisation of costly locomotives and rolling stock, as well as high staffing and maintenance costs, not to mention the extra fuel consumed by high-speed running and the need to maintain track at the highest standards.' Having gained a worldwide reputation for quality express services, Britons fell in love with streamliner services. A period of a few short years, when LMS/LNER integrated marketing activity was so successful that it garnered public attention in a big way as their developments commanded the media landscape.

Such were the publicity-led initiatives between the major companies, they made front page news in Britain's national press, reported extensively around the world and subsequently written into railway folk lore. As Jenkinson noted, 'Even the engine drivers' names were as much part of the common currency as are the Grand Prix drivers of today.' Streamliners were central to the promotional agenda since Gresley's revolutionary LNER A4 engine designs produced the fastest steam locomotive in the world but from a commercial perspective delivered a successful and efficient construction format that ensured the class would remain operational until the end of steam haulage on British Railway's Eastern and Scottish Regions. LMS's bold attempt with streamline casing on their new generation of Duchess Class locomotives ended with the adoption of more traditional engine construction facilitating easier maintenance for shed crews.

GWR trialled streamline locomotive adaptations but this was to be a short-lived, half-hearted experiment, as mainline benefits were not proven.

In Britain, streamliner expresses grabbed imagination like nowhere else as the LNER and LMS set about a new Race to the North with a series of technological leaps in steam-hauled locomotive and carriage traction. Renewed competition for passengers between London and Scotland was brought about by the impending threat of aviation services at the top end of the market, prompting the LMS and LNER to end their truce not to compete on speed. *Silver Jubilee* was the initial streamliner express service introduced in 1935, running from London King's Cross to Newcastle and the first dedicated high-speed luxury train with a four-hour timing between the two cities. The *Silver Jubilee* was a single articulated set of seven (eight from February 1938) carriage luxury non-Pullman train that built on developments introduced with the 1928 *Flying Scotsman* carriage stock. They very rarely failed in service and there was no back-up stock of carriages.

But the LNER streamliner was a new type of prestige train, considered more stylish, in keeping with a period of change, providing extra comfort as well as being the first hauled by the latest generation of A4 locomotives. Evidence of its success was noted even in its first week of operations with some passengers having to be seated in the restaurant cars from the beginning of the journey.

Image was important, with the Silver Link locomotive 'clad in silver-painted metal to make it look like a streamlined, aerodynamic bullet' says Juliet Gardiner commenting on the 27 September 1935 run. She considers that Gresley thought little more of the A4 cladding than a marketing device, suggesting that the 'train's performance was minimally enhanced, if at all, by the new design, but it gave the desired impression of speed, modernity, technological progress'. This was the chic 1930s and for those who were prepared to pay extra for the first-class service, the journey north to Newcastle was something to savour. The *Silver Jubilee* likewise had a superb restaurant car service, incorporating a bespoke, state of the art kitchen car sandwiched between two sets of restaurant cars creating outstanding meals. A single table d'hôte menu consisting of a five-course luncheon as well as a two-course joint luncheon with varied options well above the ordinary of the period proved that

Tom Purvis' work from 1937 highlighted LNER's 'Its Quicker by Rail' series. The new streamlined Anglo-Scottish *Coronation* service crossing the Royal Border Bridge at Berwick on Tweed exemplifies speed and style working perfectly in tandem. (NRM Pictorial Collection/Science & Society Library)

Britain's Big Four railway companies could match the very best of European railway cuisine. Chris de Winter Hebron provides a snapshot of the culinary experience aboard the *Silver Jubilee* with a luncheon that:

'had many more choices than were available on the LMS "namers" – three fish courses, entrées and sweets. Even the "joint luncheon" allowed you to choose a main course from any fish or entrée option, and a dessert from any of the sweets or cheese. And the à la carte offers included most table d'hôte items as well as anything from a complete mixed grill through a cold buffet to snacks, pastries and sandwiches.'

LNER's *Silver Jubilee* proved to be a commercial success demonstrating that a moderate length high-speed train could be lucrative delivering for its owners a handsome profit.

"THE CORONATION"

CROSSING THE ROYAL BORDER BRIDGE BERWICK-UPON-TWEED

IT'S QUICKER BY RAIL

FULL INFORMATION FROM ANY L·N·E·R OFFICE OR AGENCY

"THE CORONATION"
ON THE EAST COAST ENTERING SCOTLAND
IT'S QUICKER BY RAIL
FULL INFORMATION FROM ANY L·N·E·R OFFICE OR AGENCY

With the success of the *Silver Jubilee* operation, it was only a matter of time before a streamliner service was extended to Scotland. In fact, LNER had announced an intention for such a service at a planning meeting in July 1936. The *Coronation*, introduced on 5 July 1937, was the first direct Anglo-Scottish streamlined high-speed luxury train designed to operate on the line throughout winter with the obvious implications of the A4 locomotives pulling a much heavier train than *Silver Jubilee* whilst dealing with headwinds and coal consumption.

Equally as visually distinctive as the *Jubilee*, the stylish lines of the *Coronation* hauled by A4 locomotives – all named after British Empire countries – were finished in a deep garter blue colour whilst the streamline carriage sets were in a two-tone blue livery. Jenkinson describes the *Coronation* as a brand-new train in concept and décor and a speedier service, as the east coast route to Edinburgh was half an hour faster than the LMS

Frank Henry Mason's evocative Quad Royal poster of the *Coronation* entering Scotland is one of the lesser known images of the luxurious LNER train. Produced in the late 1930s, it was also part of the 'Its Quicker by Rail' series.

train to Glasgow. The eight-car formation of stainless-steel carriages made up of twin articulated sets contained the latest developments in air conditioning and sound proofing. The train in summer carried a 'beaver tail' observation coach which was not used in the winter as the train's timetabled schedule – departure 4.00 pm from King's Cross and 4.30 pm from Edinburgh Waverley – meant that most of the service ran in the dark, arriving late in the evening, hindering its commercial success. Two sets were built for the *Coronation*, one additional set as a backup and a fourth set for the new *West Riding* train all gorgeous and deservedly popular.

It was a full restaurant car service, with two kitchen cars replacing the dining cars providing meals served at customer seats in open carriages combining a hospitality approach planned to outdo Pullman. The first-class seats arranged 2+1 had lateral wings that preserved privacy as well as double hinged tables that could be put up for the serving of meals or for work but also folded down to provide greater space for passengers. Variously described as fine-dining at speed, the *Coronation* accorded travellers a super train status that was to only last a few short years before the war. Other on-board services used to entice customers included a women's hairdressing saloon and for businessmen the provision of secretarial support. The final running of the luxurious train was 31 August 1939 and they were never to return as a dedicated streamliner service after the war.

The *West Riding Limited* was the last of LNER's streamlined service, introduced on 27 September 1937 and replacing the *Yorkshire Pullman*. Like the *Coronation,* the streamlined service had been planned since 1936 with LNER targeting the West Yorkshire business community returning to and from London on a regular basis. The *West Riding Limited* accommodated up to forty-eight first and 168 third-class passengers and, like other streamlined services, passengers in both first and third-class were charged a supplementary fare. The service had a late 7.10 pm departure from King's Cross but the LNER had firm sights on its catering provision to serve evening meals and thus taking profit in-house that otherwise would have gone to Pullman.

Post-war considerable thought was given to how fast express services might be resurrected. In the interim, railway managers had to deal with low line speeds as a result of a catalogue of permanent way backlogs and improvements to the east

"THE CORONATION"
DESIGNED BY SIR NIGEL GRESLEY CHIEF MECHANICAL ENGINEER L·N·E·R IN HONOUR OF THE CORONATION OF KING GEORGE VI 1937
KING'S CROSS - EDINBURGH IN 6 HOURS
LONDON AND NORTH EASTERN RAILWAY

Doris Zinkeisen's unconventional depiction of the *Coronation* train running through a rural setting was part of an avant-garde approach to poster design adopted by some of the Big Four railway companies in the late 1930s. (NRM Pictorial Collection/Science & Society Library)

coast track and signalling in order to facilitate high-speed traffic. Trying to rekindle some of the glamour associated with pre-war trains was not easy but as LNER morphed into British Railways Eastern and North Eastern Regions, the new structures inherited a tremendous legacy to build from. A bigger threat, however, particularly at the top end of the market, came from aviation and the benefit of quicker Anglo-Scottish and regional short-haul flights. With the establishment of British European Airways (BEA), domestic aviation was making inroads on north eastern and Scottish routes, attracting the railway's prosperous first-class travellers and business passengers. Into this breach stepped the *Flying Scotsman* which started flying again as a head boarded service in the summer of 1946. Despite the war years, it was one of the first of LNER's premier services to receive new coaching stock in 1946.

Two years later, it received a raft of food on the move innovations with a new style of buffet car with bar counter and display case as well as an accompanying modern lounge in the carriage to seat eight passengers. These were introduced as part of the train's carriage formation and perhaps, for the first time, a modern servicescape now familiar with all regular train travellers and accessed by all passengers. The buffet car had a compact kitchen filled with the latest catering equipment designed to allow chefs to deliver large volumes of convenience-style meals every day as well as mod-cons for light refreshments that included a coffee machine, an ice cream refrigerated cabinet and toaster. With these developments, the *Flying Scotsman* service by the summer of 1954 was in the position to haul passengers in style again between Edinburgh Waverley and King's Cross with the fastest of non-stop runs recorded in six and a half hours.

Post-war motive power for the train was made up of a combination of rebuilt A3 and A4 Class locomotives as well as the new A1 Peppercorn Class introduced from 1948. The *Flying Scotsman* was no longer a direct train but relegated to a stopping service. During this year, British Railways ran a summer advertising campaign, highlighting improvements to services with more holiday trains running with restaurant and buffet cars but warning of overall carriage stock problems that were likely to involve some passengers having to stand at peak periods.

The use of A4s on the summer runs during the last three years of the 1930s reduced journey times to seven hours, with Aberdeen being reached in ten hours despite a lengthy stop at Waverley. A4 use was required because the non-stop service was regularly heavily laden with thirteen or fourteen coaches, including a full brake carrying luggage at the front of the train together with a restaurant car triplet set. The sight of long raked Anglo-Scottish services on the east coast line was to become a dominant feature of the early years of British Railways. Their power ensured that despite speed restrictions caused by ongoing repairs to the permanent way on the east coast line, the engines could catch up with minimal delays with remarkable ease. The streamlined A4s were used on British Railways' succession of new named trains, including a non-stop service to Edinburgh. By 1952, the *Capitals Limited*, thanks to corridor tenders allowing crew members to change without stopping, was almost as fast as the

Although relegated to a stopping service – albeit with just two halts at Grantham and Newcastle – this *Flying Scotsman* poster cements the importance of British Railways increasing portfolio of east coast expresses. (NRM Pictorial Collection/ Science & Society Library)

pre-war *Flying Scotsman*. But it was not until 1954 that the *Flying Scotsman* service could carry passengers between the two capital cities non-stop in six and a half hours.

In 1958, the first hauling of the *Flying Scotsman* came as the gathering pace of railway modernisation kicked in as A3 and A4 Class steam locomotives and others would begin to see out their days. New Deltic (Class 55) diesel-electric traction was gradually introduced to the ECML in 1961. On 18 June 1962, British Railways Eastern Region celebrated the centenary of 10.00 am *Scotch Express* with a special Deltic-hauled train, retaining a steam-age *Flying Scotsman* headboard. These images, heralding a march of progress, were used by British Railways to promote the long-established route, despite losing business travellers to air services. The image, however, was used to capture the hearts of a younger audience with Hornby Dublo producing a *Flying Scotsman* set featuring a die cast manufactured locomotive together with tinplate maroon carriages in a move replicating the company's first Gauge O train sets in 1927.

The new Deltic 3,300hp locomotives were built by the Newton-le-Willows based Vulcan Foundry. Extremely powerful beasts, they brought down the journey time (with many stops) of the stopping service to seven hours and twenty minutes with 100 mph running along many parts of the route. Deltic specific *Flying Scotsman* headboards were created for the 1961 summer season which initially appeared below the head code panel. This was then re-positioned on to the upper lamp iron above the head code panel until 1964, when a winged thistle style was introduced. The modern looking Deltic image defined the *Flying Scotsman* service in the first half of the 1960s, with two tone green livery locomotives pulling new Mk II maroon stock. Progress was not appreciated amongst all; a minority of steam locomotive enthusiasts did not like new style traction with the words 'Sod the Deltics' daubed on tunnel entrances along the east coast route. By the mid-1960s, the *Flying Scotsman* service gave way to British Railways corporatisation with its yellow-ended blue-painted Deltics and blue-grey liveried carriages. Whilst still timetabled, the Deltic-hauled train lost its headboard and coach boards (in common with most named trains), the only identification of the 10.00 am service being paper printed coach window stickers.

Between 1976 and 1982, the Deltics started to be replaced by diesel InterCity 125 sets and with it the *Flying Scotsman* lost its 10.00 am departure slot to another King's Cross service, the *Aberdonian* which by the mid-1990s was one of the last remnants of the named train era vanished from the timetable. The ECML route continued to be improved with the Selby diversion that saw journey times further reduced. On a couple of occasions (May 1978 and June 1981) the front InterCity 125 power car was adorned with a *Flying Scotsman* headboard sticker resembling a design from steam-days. The last piece of the railway modernisation jigsaw came in 1990 when the Edinburgh ECML route was eventually electrified with InterCity 225 sets, with Class 91 power cars capable of 140 mph running with Mk IV carriage stock, but on the ECML the train is restricted to a maximum speed of 125 mph. In 2011, a speeded up four-hour service was introduced, with sets incorporating a special livery. It remains to be seen what will happen to the *Flying Scotsman* train brand with the newly created LNER franchise under state ownership.

We have briefly touched on Pullman's east coast activities. Post-war Pullman was back on LNER tracks. In November 1946, the *Yorkshire Pullman* resumed. Two years later the *Queen of Scots* Pullman was back on Anglo-Scottish metals as well as the introduction of the *Tees-Tyne Pullman* creating what de Winter Hebron describes as 'two distinct on-train catering markets'. These long-distance services were only part of the story, as the *Tees-Tyne*

One of the 1946 Thompson LNER/ British Railways production of A2 4-6-2 Pacifics, Heaton shed based No 60512 *Steady Aim* is seen in control of the recently reintroduced *Queen of Scots* Pullman service. (John Scott-Morgan Collection)

In an effort to rekindle a degree of magic surrounding post-war Anglo-Scottish train travel, British Railways restored the *Queen of Scots* Pullman, a weekday stopping service between London, Edinburgh and Glasgow. The tartan theme was retained in Reginald Mayes poster but some of the 1930s trappings that distinguished deluxe services in the glamour days were lost to austerity. (NRM Pictorial Collection/ Science & Society Library)

THE QUEEN OF SCOTS
PULLMAN - EACH WEEKDAY
(KING'S CROSS) LONDON and GLASGOW (QUEEN STREET)
calling in each direction at
LEEDS   HARROGATE   DARLINGTON   NEWCASTLE   EDINBURGH

Pullman was officially termed the successor to LNER's pre-war *Silver Jubilee* streamliner when introduced on 27 September 1948. Deemed to be a quick response to post-war blues, these new Pullmans re-introduced some degree of normality for the travelling public.

The *Queen of Scots* resumed post-war working with extra Pullman cars on 5 July 1948. It was given the full marketing treatment with dedicated poster advertising, stylish luggage labels and a brake car tailboard supplied by the Pullman Car Company. The train was hauled by an assortment of locomotives including rebuilt A1, A3, A4, British Railways Standard Class 4-6-0s, and in later years before being withdrawn in 1964, by Deltic diesels.

The *Tees-Tyne* was an all-Pullman train with usual supplementary charges but incorporating well-known standards of comfort and targeted at the business community as a limited stopping service running between King's Cross and Newcastle. It was particularly popular amongst upscale travellers for its Hadrian Bar car with its early evening 5.30 pm departure from London. One of the business service innovations on the up service was with the arrangement of the Pullman conductor, so it was possible for passengers to be provided with a car on arrival at King's Cross which would remain at their disposal throughout the afternoon if they so wished. Initially the nine-car train took an hour longer than the pre-war streamliner express, due to line speed restrictions, but timings gradually improved. By the late 1950s, the *Tees-Tyne Pullman* was one of a quintet of Pullman services running from King's Cross noted for making good time, loading well but the near life-expired stock required replacement, particularly as faster and sustained high speed diesel running services involving quick acceleration were just around the corner.

The *Tees-Tyne Pullman* was one of the Pullman services receiving a total of forty-four new Metropolitan-Cammel Mk II Pullman cars which would run with vintage 1928/1929 parlour brakes at each end. The *Tees-Tyne Pullman* now had the capability for speedier services when new Deltics were introduced and was one of the services selected to receive the ten pilot scheme diesel locomotives from 1958 onwards. New Pullman stock was a significant coup for British Railways as Haresnape noted, 'Sir John Elliot evidently produced a convincing case for the BTC to finance construction of a batch of replacement cars, quite apart from the forthcoming diesel luxury trains'.

The train, with simplified lining on its umber and cream livery, lasted well into the new corporate British Railways era. By 1961, the *Tees-Tyne Pullman* had an earlier down departure from King's Cross at 4.50 pm and consistent with the trend towards business people requiring earlier starts and finishes to their working days, resulted in the once heavy demand for lunch (south-bound) and dinner (north-bound) falling away considerably. The last running of the *Tees-Tyne Pullman* as a titled train was on 30 April 1976. New post-war innovations came when British Railways introduced a brand-new east coast non-stop summer time service on 23 May 1949. The *Capitals Limited,* was launched by Edinburgh-born film actress Anne Crawford taking part in the King's Cross naming ceremony. The train was allocated an eight-hour travelling slot between London and Edinburgh, replacing *Flying Scotsman* as a direct uninterrupted service. The *Capitals* was given a 9.30 am departure from King's Cross, designed to improve early evening connections from the Scottish capital. In the morning, a connection from Aberdeen would leave at 5.55 am with the non-stop *Capitals* departure from Waverley at 9.45 am ahead of the *Flying Scotsman*. The launch of the new *Capitals Limited* service did not entirely meet with everyone's approval. Writing to the *Dundee Courier and Advertiser*, one infuriated passenger took pen to paper, venting his annoyance:

'Dear Sir, – It is rather surprising to find it is impossible to book from Dundee to London on any of the daytime trains. The much-publicised new "Capitals Limited" might be alright for those people fortunate to join the train at Aberdeen or Edinburgh, where booking is permitted, but the poor old Dundonian must take his chance of a seat, or resign himself to standing on the run down to London. Surely it is not beyond the wit of our "planners" to devise some way of providing the facility for trains from Dundee. The excuse is that trains do not start from Dundee, but one notices that two coaches of the London trains begin at Aberdeen and are bookable there – why not attach one at Aberdeen and one at Dundee? Yours faithfully Pro-Rationalisation.'

Carriage stock for the *Capitals Limited* was ex-LNER exclusively air conditioned. The new non-stop service was not constructed as a luxury train, initially running with only limited first-class seats in a heavy thirteen car formation with at times the rake exceeding 473 tons gross. In terms of passenger experience, it borrowed the

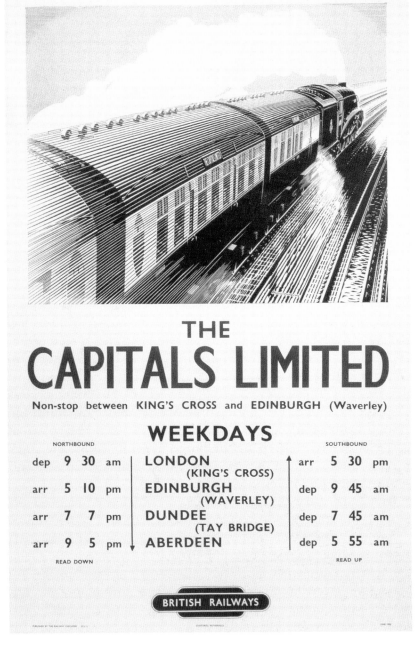

THE
CAPITALS LIMITED

Non-stop between KING'S CROSS and EDINBURGH (Waverley)

WEEKDAYS

NORTHBOUND					SOUTHBOUND		
dep	9	30	am	LONDON (KING'S CROSS)	arr	5	30	pm
arr	5	10	pm	EDINBURGH (WAVERLEY)	dep	9	45	am
arr	7	7	pm	DUNDEE (TAY BRIDGE)	dep	7	45	am
arr	9	5	pm	ABERDEEN	dep	5	55	am

READ DOWN

READ UP

BRITISH RAILWAYS

The June 1950 British Railways execution was part of a four poster set designed to showcase speed and modernity. Devised by A.N. Wolstenholme, his illustration endorses the newly established non-stop *Capitals Limited* east coast King's Cross and Edinburgh train. (NRM Pictorial Collection/Science & Society Library)

best ideas from pre-war running, accommodating ex-LNER kitchen car, buffet car, two restaurant cars and a ladies' rest room stock; initially run in its original teak finish livery but later painted in British Railways blood and custard finish.

The allocated steam motive power was almost entirely A4 Class fitted with corridor tenders. During its launch year, British Railways also experimented with early examples of alternative traction with a diesel-powered locomotive providing the longest non-stop diesel run at the time taken. Yet the new service in some quarters did not receive universal endorsement, being labelled a 'show train' similar to the pre-war streamliner expresses designed to show Britain could run non-stop trains further than the Americans, whilst at the same time demonstrating to everyone the popularity of rail travel as a quick and comfortable means of transport. The *Capitals Limited* did get progressively faster, with the journey time coming down to 440 minutes in 1951, with a further acceleration of service the following year almost matching *Flying Scotsman's* 1939 seven-hour running.

With British Railways' tendency to introduce named trains, the 2.00 pm departures from King's Cross and Edinburgh Waverley were allocated the title of the *Heart of Midlothian* in May 1951 as part of the Festival of Britain celebration. The modern dining car train was allocated brand new Mk I coaching stock, giving British Railways a trio of day-time expresses that were packaged together on speed and service. The non-stop *Capitals Limited/Elizabethan* was the fastest, the *Flying Scotsman* stopped at Newcastle whilst the *Heart of Midlothian* was the slowest of the three services stopping at York, Darlington, Newcastle and Edinburgh. In 1953, a Coronation Year exhibition of royal trains took place at Battersea Wharf station, highlighting for the first time the effect royal journeys had on the development of more comfortable and sophisticated rail travel

With impeccable timing, the *Capitals Limited* was renamed the *Elizabethan* in honour of the Queen's Coronation, a move Mullay noted was 'much acclaimed at the time'. The new *Elizabethan* was a summer time service too, beginning life on 29 June 1953 linking the two capitals with the fastest non-stop normal fare service. Maximum speed limits on the ECML were now ninety mph in places, with Coronation year heralding the 'most comprehensive speed-up of passenger services' in the recovery period following the war, but it also marked the beginning of the end of the non-stop running era between London and Edinburgh. A4 Pacific steam traction rose well to the challenges of all-round acceleration of services on the east coast, particularly as non-stop *Elizabethan* was a heavy 400 ton plus train with eleven carriages. The train was part of a big planned ECML summer-time speed up, with twenty-nine expresses achieving an average of 60 mph with maximum permitted speeds of 90 mph achieved at times. A comparison was made with the pre-war *Coronation* service which was 100 tons lighter than the new service. The non-stop service *Elizabethan* would rise to a heavily laden thirteen coach train for the busiest points in the summer season but still achieving a six and three-quarter hour trip. Special correspondent to the *Yorkshire Post and Leeds Mercury,* Mavis Landen, wrote of the maiden running:

> '*The Elizabethan* is a crack train to join the series which includes the *Flying Scotsman* and the *Queen of Scots*. It showed what British Railways can do in speed and service. And how the railway officials (and the Press party aboard) loved it…There was hardly a man among them who did not get a thrill in saying: "She's doing 90 m.p.h." or consulting a watch to say: "Six minutes early at Doncaster…five and half minutes early at York. Not bad".'

A4s dominated for the foreseeable future, providing a fast, efficient and speedier service between the two capitals. Mrs J Bailey wrote in the *Milngavie and Bearsden Herald* about the first stage of a journey to Denmark in the mid-1950s. 'We left Edinburgh on the *Elizabethan* non-stop train for King's Cross and thought how quickly the train had gone, as we only took six hours.'

But change was on the horizon in February 1959, as the prototype of the Deltic diesel in its distinctive early blue, silver and yellow livery would haul the train. The end of the non-stop era came with the last steam-hauled *Elizabethan* on 9 September 1961 as steam was phased out in favour of new diesel traction, which ironically had no corridor facility to change locomotive crews thus involving a stop at Newcastle. Throughout its life, the *Elizabethan* predominantly used the old ex-LNER stock which was now repainted from blood and custard to maroon livery, together with the inclusion of some Mk I carriages. The culinary offer on the morning train departure would include luncheon and afternoon tea delivered through a kitchen car, two restaurant cars and a buffet car. As British Railways moved towards the uniformity of 1960s operations, the menu service became progressively standardised. Its final running as a named train was 7 September 1962 when the days of the other named expresses on the east coast line were also numbered.

The *Talisman* was the final incarnation of pre-war Anglo-Scottish east coast glamour expresses when introduced on 17 September 1956. The named train, steeped in Sir Walter Scott's literary novels that had so inspired railway company promotion since the 1860s, was a completely new winter time service running Monday to Friday with simultaneous 4.00 pm departures from King's Cross and Waverley. It was pitched as a 'restoration' of the short-lived high-speed LNER *Coronation* streamliner express; *The Railway Magazine* described the train as 'outstanding' among the new winter timetable although at this stage still forty minutes longer than the much lighter streamliner express. However, the new train involved a stop at Newcastle. It proved to be so popular that in addition a morning service in both directions was introduced in 1957, effectively creating a *Morning* and *Afternoon Talisman* in the timetables. Rebadging the morning service as the *Fair Maid* and extending to Perth was not a success, leading to its withdrawal. The *Talisman* was reinstated the following year and as with other premier east coast expresses was predominantly A4 hauled until the Deltics came on the scene, progressing a gradual acceleration of train times.

Invariably, the *Talisman* was made up of a range of carriage stock from both pre-war heritage and newer British Railways Mk I coaches, with early train formations including an original streamliner first-class twin set instilling a touch of luxury and reconnecting with the inter-war days of fashionable travel, although no surcharge was made for travelling. It was the first long-distance service to use maroon liveried carriages. On-board catering was extensive, with breakfast, luncheon and dinner menus as well as morning coffee, afternoon tea and light refreshments with a corridor service whenever possible. In 1964, the first-class section of the *Talisman* morning departure was made up of Pullman cars, whilst the remainder of the train was made up of the new corporate blue and grey liveried carriages capable of ninety-100 mph travel for the summer timetable that were part of British Rail's 'Train of Tomorrow'. The new coaches provided 'a smoother and quieter ride' and had 'panoramic windows and forced-air ventilation'. The Pullman initiative proved to be a short-lived experiment even for hard-nosed businessmen and first-class travellers who still revelled in the style east coast trains could deliver rather than travel by air. The *Talisman* and the *Heart of Midlothian* were both withdrawn in May 1968, thus bringing an end to two of the many prestige Anglo-Scottish expresses that once traversed east coast metals.

The West Coast Route

The Scottish west coast route was built in stages reflecting many local railway company developments. At the dawn of Britain's railway age, with the launch of the Liverpool and Manchester Railway (LMR), the north west of England found itself at the confluence point of an Anglo-Scottish route. A Birmingham and London portion had been eventually completed in 1838, followed by a flurry of commercial amalgamation around 1845 as the Grand Junction Railway joined with the Manchester and Birmingham Railway and the London and Birmingham Railway to form the LNWR. Its establishment created a British railway bedrock and a standard bearer for one of Victorian Britain's foremost and most progressive transport businesses.

The western route had to contend with difficult topography to reach Scotland. A northerly route from Preston to Lancaster had been built in 1840 and a decision was then taken to construct the route to Carlisle along the Lune Valley via Shap, dispensing with the need for tunnelling, rather than building an easier and meandering route around the Cumbrian coast. Until 1848, Scotland-bound passengers had to make do with disembarking at Fleetwood and taking a boat to Ardrossan with rather inadequate services, before the Caledonian Railway's southerly route from Glasgow to Carlisle connected to the west coast line in its original form. Further south, over the years, improvements were made to minimise traffic congestion and to speed up the west coast route. By 1848, the LNWR and the Caledonian Railway were set to become the principal operators of west coast trains to and from Scotland. The line's visibility was aided over the years by Queen Victoria's frequent visits to Scotland with LNWR's royal trains ensuring many journeys north would be conducted via the west corridor in conjunction with the Caledonian Railway. From the 1860s, long-distance running became the norm with the LNWR, and Caledonian Railway spurred into action by developments taking place on the east coast route. A competing 10.00 am departure from Euston was set in stone in 1862 and, apart from a brief interlude for the First World War, this remained in place for many years and well into LMS times. Euston became the 'gate to Scotland' with the 10.00 am departure known as the *Day Scotch Express*. Quite simply, with quality new stock, the train heralded a more gracious way to travel. Making known the new service in the *Evening Standard* on 9 July 1862, the company's general manager, W. Cawkwell, described the service as providing 'improved communication with Scotland' with first and second-class fares available as a 'new and more rapid express train to Scotland now leaves London (Euston Station) at 10.00 am, arriving at Carlisle at 6.00 pm, Edinburgh at 9.20 pm and Glasgow at 9.50 pm'.

Entrenched attitudes towards rolling stock were difficult to shift though, as the LNWR in the 1880s was still running new eight-wheeled non-bogie carriages on long-distance routes. The company dabbled with Pullman sleepers – described as drawing-room sleeping cars – on its nightly London to Liverpool services in the mid-1870s. Whilst well-received by the travelling public, this initiative was not to last as the LNWR emphasized more reliance on ferrying day-time passengers to its newly constructed prestige hotel in Liverpool for onward transmission to awaiting ocean liners. On the west coast route, better bogie-built carriages did not materialise until after 1888 to enhance customer comfort. Whilst the LNWR occupied the premier and quickest route to the Port of Liverpool by the early 1890s, it was experiencing considerable competition from the Midland for both freight and passenger traffic.

LNWR motive power in the early days of the *Day Scotch Express* would have been courtesy of 2-4-0s, often hauled in pairs. Typical of this wheel arrangement would have been F.W. Webb's Precedent Class locomotives which were used extensively in high-speed running on the west coast line, aided by the introduction of water troughs so that locomotives could pick up water en route. No. 790 *Hardwicke*, now preserved and part of the national collection, achieved a degree of celebrity status with its exploits, running in the 1895 Race to the North with its ECML competitors. By the 1890s, 4-4-0s were more prevalent, hauling express services in a period when the first designs of 4-6-0 locomotives started to appear. In 1891, new joint stock arrangements were initiated between the Caledonian and the LNWR with 'New Corridor Trains with Refreshment and Dining cars attached for First and Third Class Passengers' as announced in the *Sketch* of 12 July 1893. This ensured that stock was 'well-built, cushioned, heated and lighted carriages, both first and third class'.

More powerful locomotives were required to haul WCML trains. In 1897, three pairs of purpose-built joint stock dining cars made up of a kitchen/third-class diner together with a first-class dining car were added, ensuring the west coast Anglo-Scottish service was now a complete train with vestibule connections and the first in the country to have middle-gangways. The west coast 'Corridor Train' had entered the dictionary on both sides of the Atlantic by this time. Dining stock mirrored the latest improvements in carriage construction providing passengers with coal-fired stove heating and gas lighting which remained in service on the prestigious west coast line until 1905, while awaiting the significant carriage developments that would take place for the most important LNWR train services.

In 1904, LNWR CME George Whale introduced a locomotive building programme that was to transform the company into one of the twentieth century's most powerful businesses. Based on a 4-4-0 format, Whale introduced the Precursor Class in June 1904, helping to reduce the need for double-heading of trains and providing an improvement in punctuality. Whale developed an extended 4-6-0 version of the Precursor with smaller driving wheels known as the Experiment Class which was ultimately to prove a successful locomotive class when provided with superheating arrangements by Whale's CME successor Charles Bowen-Cooke. A total of 105 locomotives were built between 1905 and 1910.

Bowen-Cooke's great WCLM express performers were an improved passenger version of the 4-4-0 known as the George the Fifths and a superheated 4-6-0 locomotive known as the Prince of Wales Class introduced in 1911. The Prince of Wales class, together with the new four cylinder 'Claughton' 4-6-0 class of locomotives, hauled the LNWR's heaviest expresses. The Claughton was the company's first large express class locomotive and although considered not to have been totally successful due to weight and line restrictions, a total of 130 were nonetheless built from 1913 to 1921 only to be replaced on premier line duties by LMS's iconic Royal Scot 1927 class. The Claughton was featured in 1909 as part of a LNWR railway picture postcard series depicting the *Scotch Express* at full speed. In 1911, the Caledonian Railway introduced a new 4-6-0 locomotive known as the 'Cardean' Class; this distinctive looking locomotive was synonymous with Glasgow and Carlisle running.

By Edwardian times, business travel had increased substantially; the city of Glasgow was at the forefront of the country's locomotive and ship building industry equipping the industrialisation of the British Empire. The west coast expresses were gaining greater visibility as the *Day Scotch Express* also became known as the *Flying*

Scotchman or *Scotsman* (synonymous with the east coast route name), a term LNWR did little to dismiss in promotional literature. The name was purely a marketing ploy as no company train on the west coast line possessed the name officially. Customer demands forced the company to bring about change. Since the early 1890s, the most luxurious LNWR carriages had been destined for Liverpool's *American* boat trains as the collection and departure of international mail and passengers was considered of primary importance.

In 1904, CME George Whale, introduced a carriage building programme transforming LNWR travelling. WCML carriage construction changed for the better as passengers were presented with more comfortable and better-appointed coaches as the 1904/06 clerestory dining and sleeping cars were considered above average. For the first time under the LNWR initiative, the WCML received what could be genuinely considered as luxury stock. These carriages were appointed to the 2.00 pm *West Coast Corridor Express* or *The Corridor* as nicknamed by railwaymen. The famous 1907 and 1908 Liverpool Riverside *American Special Stock* had their origins in this carriage design. Joint LNWR and the Caledonian Railway working ensured the 2.00 pm *Corridor* was a fast express and a precursor to the well-known LMS *Mid-Day Scot* service. The mid-day dining expresses (as well as the similar services on the east coast route) were heavy trains often requiring double-heading on some parts of the route. Jenkinson considered the LNWR 2.00 pm coaches to be not as lavish as the *Americans,* although externally they were very similar but they represented a mid-Edwardian high point for both first and third-class passengers.

Before the Great War, the WCJS received another new batch of fifty-seven feet eight-wheeled stock specifically for the ten o'clock morning departure. In addition, LNWR's Wolverhampton works turned out a new set of sixty-eight feet twelve-wheeled luxury sleepers designed by H.D. Earl, the carriage superintendent for WCJS night-time duties. Each saloon contained ten berths, one smoking compartment that could be transformed into a berth and an attendant's compartment. There were communication doors between each berth which could be converted into double-berthed compartments to cater for couples and families. There was no doubting their pedigree and antecedence as the railway's copywriters ran riot promoting the new stock.

North of the border, the Pullman Company in 1914 secured a significant coup with the Caledonian Railway to provide a fleet of new Pullman vehicles including a total of seventeen carriages as well as four dining and twelve buffet cars to run on a variety of routes in Scotland. Deliveries were interrupted by war but by 1922, Pullmans were being added at Carlisle as breakfast cars on overnight WCML services from Euston. Day and night-time travel on the west coast was now quite elegant and with it came

The Maximum of Luxury
at the Minimum of Cost.

"PULLMAN" and "PERFECTION"

are synonyms when they refer to Car Building, in which art the Pullman Car Company leads the world. In elaborate design, substantial construction, and luxurious finish, Pullman Cars represent the highest standard of excellence.

Ingenuity and skill are constantly being applied to the improvement of details with a view to adding to the comfort of travel. Every Car is in charge of an experienced well-trained Conductor, whose services are always at hand from start to finish of a journey, and invalids and ladies with children can always rely upon ready attention to their comfort and convenience.

Cleanliness is also a special feature, coupled with perfect ventilation and good lighting, thus making travelling a real luxury.

Pullman Drawing Room, Buffet, Dining, and Observation Cars are in operation on the following important lines :—

Observation Car, "MAID OF MORVEN"

Southern Railway :
L. B. & S. C. Section ; Victoria and London Bridge to Brighton, Hove, Worthing, Eastbourne, Bognor, Newhaven, Portsmouth, &c.

S. E. & C. Section ; Victoria and Charing Cross to Dover and Folkestone in all the Continental Services. Also Deal, Ramsgate, Margate, and Kent Coast Towns.

London and North Eastern Railway :
Gt. Eastern Section ; Buffet Cars (First and Third Class) between Liverpool Street and principal stations, also First and Second Class on Continental Trains.

London Midland and Scottish Railway :
Caledonian Section ; Glasgow & Edinburgh to Aberdeen, Oban, Perth, Stirling, Gleneagles, Dumblane, Forfar, Callander, Lockerbie, Loch Awe, Carstairs, Beattock, Carlisle, &c.

Highland Section ; Blair Atholl, Newtonmore, Kingussie, Kincraig, Aviemore, &c.

Metropolitan Railway : Buffet Cars are run between Aldgate, Liverpool Street, Baker Street, Aylesbury, Chesham, and Verney Junction.

"The Southern Belle"

The most Luxurious Train in the World.

Daily (including Sundays).
Pullman Train de Luxe.
Running between
LONDON AND BRIGHTON.

THIRD CLASS "PULLMAN" CARS between LONDON, BRIGHTON, EASTBOURNE, PORTSMOUTH, &c.

Refreshments. Breakfasts, Luncheons, Teas, Suppers, and other refreshments can be obtained on the Cars.

Reservations. Reservations can be effected through the Station Superintendents at the various termini, either by letter, telegram, or telephone.

Special Facilities. Cars for private parties can be specially reserved, under certain conditions, upon application to the various Railway Companies.

The Pullman Car Company, Limited,

Chief London Office—

VICTORIA STATION (S. E. & C. R.), PIMLICO, S.W.1.

Telegraphic Address—" Pullman, Phone, London." Telephone No.—Victoria 9978 (2 lines)

Branch Office—CENTRAL STATION (Caledonian Railway), GLASGOW.
Telephone No.—Central 7473.

Thomas Powell, Secretary and Manager.

In the early days of railway grouping, the Pullman Car Company was seeking to enhance their promotional image with a tag line of 'the maximum of luxury at the minimum of cost' as shown in this advertisement from the 1924 Railway Year Book. (James S. Baldwin)

morning and afternoon named train departures. The WCML companies put up a fight to secure prosperous customers, something it continued to do so post-war with Pullman for the Caledonian and Highland sections of LMS Scottish operations.

Prestige services on the Euston WCML received a makeover with the launch of the new *Royal Scot* service on 11 July 1927. It was followed by considerable press interest. Like *Flying Scotsman* on the east coast that combined the name of an individual locomotive and titled train service, the *Royal Scot* was bundled with the naming of a locomotive class, an individual engine together with a long-established service with simultaneous 10.00 am departures from London and Glasgow.

As in the case of the *Flying Scotsman*, the *Royal Scot* could trace its antecedents back to 1862. The Fowler-designed *Royal Scot* became LMS's prestige Anglo-Scottish daytime service. On 27 April 1928, it too became a non-stop service, matching LNER's *Flying Scotsman* with a 400 hundred mile run by two separate locomotives, one

Despite the competitive nature of Scotland's three mainline routes, in this July 1933 *Bystander* advertisement, the LMS and LNER jointly sponsor the luxury elements of non-stop Anglo-Scottish train schedules with flagship *Flying Scotsman* and *Royal Scot* services. This coincided with the development of air services with its comparative speed and convenience that started to eat in to the top end of the market. Joint ticketing arrangements offered passengers the choice of east and west routes on return journeys. (Illustrated London News Ltd/Mary Evans)

NON-STOP TO SCOTLAND
The Flying Scotsman

Last year The Flying Scotsman brought down its non-stop time for London to Edinburgh (393 miles) to 7½ hours—an acceleration of 45 minutes. That is the World's Record. It is now the regular time during the summer. It is amazing how much of elegance and luxury has been squeezed into The Flying Scotsman—buffet, salon de coiffeur, Louis XVI restaurant, ladies' retiring room, vita glass windows. A world-famous train worthy of the world-famous cities between which it runs.

The Royal Scot

Every day (but not on Sunday) at the little Border station of Gretna Green there comes out of the South a flash, a roar and, it may be, a whistle. The Royal Scot has passed from England into Scotland. London to Glasgow in 7 hours 40 minutes! That was the new record set up last year. That is the time the Royal Scot is maintaining throughout the holiday season this year. A magnificent achievement to be ranked amongst the greatest of all railway feats.

With a return ticket to Scotland, you now have the choice of travelling back by the East Coast, West Coast, or Midland routes, with break of journey at any station. Ask at any L M S or L·N·E·R Station or Office for details of Summer Tickets (penny-a-mile), Tourist Tickets and Circular Tours.

MOTOR CARS accompanied by one first-class or two third-class adult passengers are conveyed to include outward and homeward journeys at the reduced rate of 4½d. a mile charged on the single journey mileage for distances not less than 50 miles. Single journey charges at 3d. a mile.

L M S
LONDON MIDLAND
& SCOTTISH RAILWAY

LONDON & NORTH
EASTERN RAILWAY
L·N·E·R

bound for Glasgow and the other for Edinburgh. The *Royal Scot* was never destined to emulate the non-stopping arrangements of its east coast competitor, as even with a powerful bank of locomotives, the train had to undergo a break in proceedings at Carlisle for crew changes. In 1933, Stanier introduced Pacific wheel arrangements to the west coast with Princess and later Coronation and Duchess Class locomotives on a route that had previously not seen anything larger than a 4-6-0.

When the *Royal Scot* commenced service, it was a deliberate attempt by LMS management to respond to the *Flying Scotsman's* status as a household word with faster summer time trains with names designed to capture public attention, thus becoming as familiar as ocean liners. On commencement of the service, the new train received the most up to date passenger coaches available, with particular emphasis on new first and third-class carriages collectively known as the '1928 *Royal Scot* Stock'. The coaches reflected a more open style with three luxury first-class semi-open carriages that had 'large single picture windows in both the compartments and the dining bays' as well as spacious 2+1 seating whilst recognising the needs of lady travellers separated 'by a quite splendid toilet compartment of almost 'powder room' size.'[3]

In addition, the *Royal Scot* set included a first-class lounge brake that included settees, armchairs and occasional tables with picture window vista and a real acknowledgement by LMS to counter the superior carriage developments on the east coast. In 1930, the *Royal Scot* was again updated with new carriage stock where semi-open first, corridor composite and brakes had deeper windows that improved the passenger experience, which Jenkinson considers 'were altogether some of the most stylish carriages ever offered to the non-supplementary passenger'.

By 1933, the *Royal Scot* received its first Stanier-designed rolling stock of steel-panelled coaches. The carriages, together with a brand-new locomotive, no. 6100 *Royal Scot* (in fact, a swapped engine identity of no. 6152 *The King's Dragoon Guardsman*), were transported to America for the 1933 Chicago World Fair and then a 11,000-mile tour of Canada and the USA. On its return from north America, the entire train went on a UK exhibition tour but despite the massive publicity derived from the entire marketing initiative, the *Royal Scot* was never perceived to be quite as fashionable and luxurious as LNER's trend-setting east coast trains.

LONDON MIDLAND & SCOTTISH RAILWAY
OF GREAT BRITAIN

THE "ROYAL SCOT"
LONDON(Euston) to GLASGOWand EDINBURGH

By 1931 the LMS *Royal Scot* received the full poster treatment in this creative execution by P. Irwin Brown highlighting the company's premier Anglo-Scottish west coast train. (NRM Pictorial Collection/ Science & Society Library)

Pullman was never part of the west coast scene in LMS days; even the former Caledonian Pullman stock was destined to be repainted first in LMS colours and later British Railways blood and custard livery. Undoubtedly, the *Royal Scot* was the company's crack service and with new rolling stock upgrades, including open stock and kitchen diners added over a four-year period up until 1937. New LMS Period III coaches set benchmarks for sumptuous quality comfort standards on their trains but despite the elevation, the *Royal Scot* was never allocated with fixed carriage sets. Of all the LMS Anglo-Scottish inter-war expresses, the *Mid-Day Scot* launched on 26 September 1927 assumed a lower profile than other glamorous Scottish trains. The Glasgow portion of the Anglo-Scottish express retained its former celebrated twelve-wheeled West coast 1908 '2 pm' carriages and a certain sense of style as a restaurant car express.

At their February 1937 AGM, LMS announced their intention to join the streamliner ranks. In May of that year, an announcement was made that the new train would be called the *Coronation Scot*, incorporating a brand name that was a perfect strategic fit with the company's other *Royal Scot* and *Mid-Day* Anglo-Scottish premier services. The *Coronation Scot* ran on the Euston to Glasgow west coast route and was to be LMS's answer as a high-speed streamlined service, but there were some suggestions that the company was slow to join the streamliner age, taking some twenty-two months to introduce the train after LNER's *Silver Jubilee*. Powered by newly built locomotives – they were officially given the classification of Princess Coronation Class in September 1937 – and given numbering 6213-7, they were quite different from their predecessors.

The carriage stock for the *Coronation Scot* was also to be something special, with three sets of nine coaches in each making a total of twenty-seven vehicles. Each train consisted of fixed carriage sets that were a feature of the east coast route. Twenty-one of the carriages were effective conversions but they were built flush-sided and finished externally in a luxury finish in a blue-and-silver livery with seating for eighty-two first-class and 150 third-class passengers. Seating was in blue, brown and green upholstery and finished superbly with timbers from around the Empire providing a luxury passenger feel. The train had a simultaneous up and down departure on 5 July 1937, drawing large crowds to Euston and Glasgow Central stations. As Mullay succinctly noted in *Streamlined Steam*, 'Here at last was the LMS's reply, and a distinctive looking one it was, too'. Yet despite the colourful birth, LMS was still smarting at LNER's ascendancy in the streamliner stakes. Privately, the company felt that the train did not succeed in generating the same level of excitement from railway journalists in the way the LNER streamliner services did.

In 1937, the company accepted an invitation to exhibit a complete *Coronation Scot* train at New York's 1939 World Fair and set about designing a completely new train. The management plan was to build three new-style sets for the *Coronation Scot* with the intention of introducing them in 1940. Mullay records that the

The American *Coronation Scot* sporting cow bell and pilot light could always be relied upon to guarantee an audience. The second photograph shows the eight-carriage train in full flight on US metals. (John Scott-Morgan Collection)

decision to build new sets was 'puzzling' since there had been no adverse customer reaction or operational downsides to the 1937 vehicles, resulting in trouble-free running until the outbreak of war in September 1939. They were planned as truly luxurious carriage sets that would be a real 'show-stopper'. Not that the 1937 sets were not up to the job. David Jenkinson makes the point that, 'Once inside the LMS train, one had a feeling of *déjà vu*; the luxury and quality was there, but one rather expected this from the best LMS trains'. As it turned out, the later carriage set sent to America in January 1939 – three articulated pairs, a first-class sleeping car for staff and for decorative purposes a brake club car – were a 'sensation' at the New York Fair and a fair reflection of what the British run streamliner train would have looked like if war had not intervened.

The new crimson lake and gold liveried streamliner sets would have retained a mixture of open and corridor styling but with a longer frame of just under sixty feet and designed to be extremely spacious. Because of hostilities, twenty-five partially completed carriages existed and remained in an unfinished build state at Derby for the duration of the war, only being completed in British Railways days and then to a much-reduced specification. The 'American' set was marooned in the States, deteriorating to some extent but eventually coming home once there was a cessation of conflict. With austerity led post-war times, the *Coronation Scot* carriage sets were never run together as originally intended but released back into general service as individual coaches.

Despite LMS's best endeavours with pre-war expresses, there was a feeling that the company never really got to grips with creating the glamourous image that the east coast route appeared to enjoy. A combination of factors was at play. The industrialised nature of the west coast route was less visually attractive, whereas the east coast route was always festooned as the Anglo-Scottish tourist trail. The west coast route also suffered from the lack of Pullman services which LMS (and GWR) management disliked. In addition, the company never seemed to latch on to the full potential of the prestige groove which the former Midland Railway and its Scottish allies had carved out with their central route.

Nevertheless, the *Royal Scot* was reintroduced on 16 February 1948 as British Railways' west coast line's flagship train. With its restart came limited onboard catering as dining car operations came under the new Hotels Executive structure. Similarly, with Pullman

This **1937** LMS Bryan de Grineau poster shows off the powerful new locomotive class leading the *Coronation Scot* train. The style is similar to that used by leading American railroad companies at the time, showcasing their new streamliner technology heading prestigious express services. (NRM Pictorial Collection/ Science & Society Library)

The Royal Scot effortlessly hauled by Coronation class 7P Pacific No 46227 *Duchess of Devonshire.* Based between Crewe and Glasgow Polmadie sheds, the locomotive was often photographed working the difficult inclines of the Cumbrian Fells and at Beattock Summit, in south Scotland. At 1,016 feet above sea level, Beattock is the highest point of the west coast Anglo-Scottish route. Shown here in early British Railways livery with a heavy rake of blood and custard carriage stock. (John Scott-Morgan Collection)

services the *Queen of Scots* and the new *Tees-Tyne Pullman*, the train was one of the few places travellers could expect a reasonable food offer, although with food rationing it was not as extensive as pre-war. But long-distance travellers could still rely on *Royal Scot* whisky, the best-known of railway drinks.

By the mid-1950s, Britain's railway catering and food on the go was not the problem of earlier years. The *Tatler and Bystander* reported, 'British Railways have one of the most comprehensive cellars in the country, the wine list at the Great Western specializing in vintage clarets.' And this could be enjoyed in the most modern of surroundings as the correspondent noted. 'Take the new lounge bar "The Royal Scot" at Euston: a smart affair with not only a bar to lean on but waitress service for light meals at the table, where you can choose your own steak and watch it being grilled if you wish.'

Anglo-Scottish rail travel could still be an occasion. In 1950, the premier west coast train was draped with highly distinctive Hunting Stewart tartan designed locomotive head boards as well as being one of the few London Midland services, along with the *Caledonian,* to carry a carriage tailboard. During the 1950s, British Railways Mk I stock was progressively introduced as the service lost some of its élan. The *Royal Scot* was one of the country's longest-running train services having survived Big Four, British Railways and the new privatised era of Virgin Trains until its last titled run on 1 June 2002 when the name was dropped.

Interrupted by the war, the *Mid-Day Scot* resumed running again on 20 September 1949 with a direct service to Glasgow only – the Edinburgh and Aberdeen split was not revived. It assumed the status of a prestige service in British Railways days, being heavily loaded with up to fifteen carriages in the 1950s, often hauled by the sole 4-6-2 Class Pacific locomotive no. 71000 *Duke of Gloucester,* a regular performer on this service. The *Duke* still runs as a mainline locomotive in preserved format. The *Mid-Day Scot* lost its powerful Pacific class haulage to diesel in the early 1960s with the final running of the service on 13 June 1965. In its final period of running, the *Mid-Day Scot* was marred by a fatal train crash on Boxing Day 1962.

The pre-war *Coronation Scot* was never run again as a streamliner service. Its eventual successor, the *Caledonian,* was introduced on 17 June 1957 and, whilst the east coast route retained some of 1930s streamliner allure with the A4 Pacifics, the Princess Coronation Class locomotives were already shed of their streamliner casings. Despite this, due to passenger demand, the *Caledonian* restaurant car express was run with both morning and afternoon departures from 1958. The west coast line now had a fleet of crack 400 minutes schedule expresses with both the *Royal Scot* and the *Caledonian* sporting very distinctive Anglo-Scottish branding. Advanced seat reservations were always advised as passenger traffic increased. The last running of the *Caledonian* came in September 1964 and with the departure of the *Mid-Day Scot* the following year, the prestige of travelling aboard one of the west coast line named expresses was lost in the pursuit of line electrification and modernisation.

This December 1950 British Railways poster again produced by A.N. Wolstenholme promoted the newly revived direct and prestigious Glasgow west coast service. The early British Railways posters often used images of two-tone blood and custard liveried carriages that formed of the new rail image. (NRM Pictorial Collection/ Science & Society Library)

THE
MID-DAY SCOT

WEEKDAYS

NORTHBOUND				SOUTHBOUND		
dep	1 0 pm	LONDON (EUSTON)		arr	10 9 pm
DOES NOT STOP		WATFORD JUNCTION		arr	9 A 40 pm
dep	2 37 pm	RUGBY (MIDLAND)		*DOES NOT STOP*	
dep	4 14 pm	CREWE		arr	6 59 pm
DOES NOT STOP		PRESTON		dep	5 B 45 pm
DOES NOT STOP		LANCASTER (CASTLE)		dep	5 B 16 pm
arr	7 17 pm	CARLISLE		dep	3 48 B pm
arr	8 53 pm	CARSTAIRS		dep	2 27 pm
arr	9 23 pm	MOTHERWELL		dep	1 B 50 pm
arr	9 45 pm	GLASGOW (CENTRAL)		dep	1 30 pm
READ DOWN				READ UP	

A Stops to set down passengers only
B Stops to take up passengers only

BRITISH RAILWAYS

The Central Route

The third route securing Scottish access came with the Midland Railway extending its interests northwards, completing the Settle and Carlisle line in 1876. The Midland, which had been formed by the merger of three railway companies in September 1843 with a combined share capital of £5 million, by this stage had become Britain's third largest pre-grouping railway company through a policy of absorbing smaller lines and expanding its own network, creating a series of routes to the north of England reaching both Leeds and Manchester and in the south of the country where Bristol and Bournemouth were within its operational orbit. It possessed a portfolio of routes the envy of other competing companies. In 1897, *Railway Magazine* describes the company's position as follows. 'Certainly, the Midland commands a greater variety of romantic lengths of line and pleasant and attractive holiday and health resorts than almost any other of the British railways.' The net effect of building the Settle and Carlisle line was a through-route to Scotland connecting with NBR's Waverley Edinburgh route. The Midland now had a firm grip on the Victorian tourist's quest for health and wellbeing, attributes which many Scottish destinations possessed in rich abundance. In addition, by concluding an alliance with the GSWR, the Midland gained two bites of the cherry, running expresses from London St. Pancras to Glasgow. This largely came about because of LNWR's refusal to allow the Midland access to the WCML as the company had already entered commercial arrangements with the Caledonian Railway, the dominant Scottish carrier on the west coast, in 1867.

Midland Railway sought government permission to build the new route but before the Settle and Carlisle line had been constructed, the dispute between the LNWR and Midland had been resolved. Parliament granted the necessary powers for the line and under considerable pressure from both the NBR and the GSWR, who looked to the futures of their traffic revenues, refused Midland permission to withdraw from their undertaking. The company was obliged to go ahead with the new Settle and Carlisle route which proved to be one of Victorian Britain's greatest achievements. With today's modern construction techniques, it is difficult to grasp the scale of human enterprise necessary to spring the line to life. Some 6,000 men endured deprivation almost beyond comprehension over a six-year period, operating in the most extreme, bleak winter conditions in an unforgiving terrain to build the line between Leeds and the Borders.

Anyhow, there was an upside as England's highest main line provided arguably the most scenic and picturesque of the Scottish main line routes with iconic rural stations littered along the line and imbued with marketing potential. Whilst Queen Victoria's Balmoral trips were largely confined to the east and west coast routes, there was something about the Settle and Carlisle connection that caught public imagination. Whilst the seventy-two-mile line was designed for fast express-running, it was the slowest of the three routes north with many services stopping at stations in the heart of England and Yorkshire's urban conurbations. Yet the line, with its remote natural landscape properties, became central to the Midland's subsequent promotional activities. The company packaged its services by tapping into England's travelling aristocracy and new wealthy upper middle-classes. The Scottish Highlands had catered for English pleasure-money since the early 1840s. But by the end of the decade, the Highlands of Scotland were seen as an instrument of mainstream tourism made up of a middle-class market comprising serious-minded clergy, doctors, schoolmasters, governesses and the business community for whom partaking in organised tourism travel was a learning experience. Queen Victoria's royal patronage made the destination highly fashionable, facilitating a growing visitor economy.

From the mid-1860s, the Highlands had been well and truly opened with Aberdeen and the Grampian regions reached and the railway link from Perth extended to Inverness opening up visitor traffic in a substantial way. P.J.G. Ransom noted that 'all three Anglo-Scottish routes fed into the Highland Railway at Perth, and in summer it was possible to see East coast, West coast and Midland sleeping cars from London all included in the same Highland train between Perth and Inverness'.

American essayist Henry James wrote of his 1878 Scottish travels when he detected 'still plenty of members of the large class which has autumnal leisure to spare, hurrying northward. The railway-carriages were occupied, and the platforms of the stations ornamented, by ladies and gentlemen in shooting-jackets of every pattern and hue.' To James, Scotland was regarded as 'a highly convenient playground for English idlers'. Mocking the shooting season, he concluded, 'For the last six weeks this annual current has been irrigating (not to say irritating) the Scottish moors and mountains; and it is hardly too much to say that at this period you must come to Scotland to see what England is about'. James, in his musings, noticed rituals and behaviours foreign and puzzling to him and not present in American society. Likewise, *The Scotch Express*, written some twenty years later by Stephen Crane, reflected his experiences of British life at the turn of the century. Crane, too, similarly noted James's observations:

> 'If one stands at the gate in August particularly, one must note the number of men with gun-cases, the number of women who surely have Tam-o'-Shanters and plaids concealed within their luggage, ready for the moors. There is, during the latter part of the month, a wholesale flight from London to Scotland which recalls the July throngs leaving New York for the shore or the mountains.'

These writings portrayed a certain kind of England to an American middle-class readership who had grown up on a steady diet of familiar English authors. Such reflections stirred the travel desires of tens of thousands of Americans, and Britain at the tail of the Victorian era became what is today referred to as a 'must do' destination. The custom of a late summer sojourn to the Scottish Highlands, where London society decamped en masse, continued for another half century. This established convention, courtesy of the three railway routes, would be interrupted by European conflagration changing the nature of things.

Perkin quotes David Cannadine's view of the impending fate of the leisured classes concluding, 'in the towns as in the countryside, the period from the 1870s until the outbreak of the Second World War saw the aristocracy under attack and in retreat'. A changing of the guard was on the horizon as Perkin observed; 'The old order was not doomed, however, it was simply changing' witnessing the rise of the professional society and a new moneyed middle-class society.

James and Crane's writings, inspired by East coast intellectual and literary circles making residencies in Britain and Europe, were a timely reminder that a new world order (America) could be expected, ultimately fine-tuning the luxury travel sector through the sheer volume of its travelling numbers. Yet by the end of the Edwardian period, the Scottish Highlands were already changing, attracting a broader democratic base. The Highland Railway, before its disappearance with grouping, promoted the region

Inverness, the Highland's hub, had routes running to all points of the compass. To the east, the Grampian region was covered by the GNSR. Actively endorsed as an alternative to the western Highlands, this *Tatler* advertisement from August 1910 shows the destination's royal connections. Modern-life 'stress' must have been evident even in Edwardian times as north east Scotland's therapeutic qualities were noted as the ideal sanctuary for 'For Health and Nerves'. Ideas surrounding 'Wellness' and 'Wellbeing' were set to become dominant tourism themes in the twentieth century. (Illustrated London News Ltd/Mary Evans)

as 'The Call of the Hills' with rail services to the 'Heart of the Highlands' in its advertising in the *Bystander,* running 'through carriages and sleeping cars from London to Inverness nightly'. The company also produced its *A.B.C. Guide to the Highlands of Scotland*, advising would-be travellers of the ease of reaching the railway's wide-ranging destinations in a 200 page publication.

The Scottish railway routes at the end of the nineteenth century were big concerns. The Midland Railway made sure it was going to secure a sizable proportion of the cake, with the third Scottish route providing an alternative and leisurely way to reach the country. The company's active promotion almost incited a further round of races to the north. Sir Walter Scott's Borders, Trossachs and Highlands romanticised writings had made the country's 'landscape and history familiar to readers across the world'. J.J. Bell later took a similar view writing in the 1930s, saying, 'It is no small wonder that every year thousands of people come to look at Melrose Abbey, the most precious jewel of the Borders; no wonder that Scott, who loved its every gleam and gloom, was inspired to tell the world about it'.[4]

Scott's literary borderlands were an area rich in natural beauty that had few equals in Scotland and as Lawrence James noted, his romantic Gothic world 'was dear to the heart of the middle-class tourist who wanted to see the buildings and countryside where the high drama of history had been staged'. The North British similarly did their bit for travel promotion by naming locomotives that 'celebrated Sir Walter Scott's characters and Scottish topographical features (Glens, Lochs), with obvious connections both to the tourist industry and to a sense of Scottish identity. The route to Scotland with its backdrop of awesome scenery, castles and ruined monasteries became important attractors providing an historic theatre that 'captivated the Victorian middle class'.[5] Such attributes were important conduits to the Midland's fortunes, a railway operation originally built on freight operations, with a profitable development attracting a steady stream of travellers mesmerised by spectacular and remote countryside and a visual experience second to none.

For the Midland, traveller interest was not just confined to Scotland as the recently completed Settle and Carlisle's Ribblehead Viaduct, considered to be one of the engineering marvels of the age with its remote, moor side and country stations, became an icon on its own merit and an influential topic of passenger conversation.

By the time of its construction, Midland's general manager James Allport had already abolished second-class passenger traffic by ensuring third-class passengers were carried in well-fitted carriages, ultimately enhancing the company's profitable revenue streams. First-class fares were also reduced and the standard of offer enhanced. The business model of first and third-class fare structures was to become the norm until nationalisation of the railway system many years later. As noted, the Midland Railway in 1874 pioneered the idea of luxury travel services by experimenting with Pullman sleeping cars and longer twelve-wheeled carriages for its middle country services. Pullman catering was restricted to the serving of light refreshments only.

When Midland's superior Scottish service commenced in 1876, it was branded the *Midland Scotch Express,* running with a mixture of six-wheelers and twelve-wheeled composite bogie stock. The evening run would have incorporated a Pullman sleeper for good measure. The Midland and its Scottish partners never attempted to sell the central route on speed, preferring to promote itself on the premium service it offered and with its connections. The initial Pullman surcharge made Midland's Anglo-Scottish services more expensive, but their trains were the most comfortable and cultured way of travelling longer distances. A stop at Sheffield allowed coaches to be attached from the Bristol morning departure. Speed and Race to the North rivalries were left to the respective east and west coast consortia. By the time new ECJS carriages appeared on the east coast route, the Midland Railway had been offering superb comfort and a quality dining service on the most picturesque Anglo-Scottish route for almost twenty years. Before the introduction of corridor stock, Midland's first-class passengers had been happy to reserve seats in the dining car, remaining seated for the duration of the journey. The Midland then upped the competitive ante with their east and west coast rivals when in August 1897, the company introduced quality third-class dining carriages to the *Midland Scotch Express* formation; a move which *The Railway Magazine* described as 'luxurious'. In addition, the company added a through carriage on the 10.00 am St. Pancras Scottish departure catering for holiday passengers joining steamers at Greenock for the Firth of Clyde and Western Highlands of Scotland.

Midland Railway continued to set the pace for innovation to attract high-spending passengers on its Anglo-Scottish route. The company promoted its Leeds-based luxury-furnished Queens

Hotel as Yorkshire's premier hotel, providing passengers with a suitable and convenient location to break their journeys between England and Scotland. In 1896, the Midland introduced first-class dining car 361 specially fitted out by Messrs Gillow, one of the most celebrated and renowned interior decorators of the late Victorian and Edwardian period. Its night-time offer was enhanced by the introduction in 1901 of four new twelve-wheeled sleeping cars built by the Pullman company. By the summer of the same year, the Midland and the NBR, through collaborative arrangements, could offer a faster service as the *Midland Scotch Express* was rebranded as the *St. Pancras Express* running from London to Edinburgh over the Settle to Carlisle route. Specially built engines were introduced to the service for the purpose of reducing journey time. Leaving at 9.30 am (only half an hour earlier than its ECML and WCML competitors), its scheduled arrival at Edinburgh Waverley was only marginally later than that of the *Special Scotch Express*.

Unfortunately, poor timing was a feature of combined Midland and NBR running so the new initiative did not ultimately trouble its faster east and west coast rivals. In Scotland, the NBR relished the benefits of the two routes, especially to the north Scottish routes beyond Edinburgh. By the early 1900s it was promoting long-distance travel and actively extolling the virtues of corridor trains with through dining and sleeping car arrangements, carriages with lavatories with passengers enjoying the benefits of steam heating in winter.

The Races to the North attracted huge media and public interest at the time although widened public awareness did not immediately translate into incremental traffic volumes for both routes. Carriage improvements and the numbers included in rake formations increased the weight of long-distance expresses leading to much of the locomotive development already discussed. What was much in evidence though, by the end of the Victorian era, was considerable progress in the development of the railway infrastructure across all three routes to Scotland. Railway companies overcame capacity issues by putting on more Scottish bound trains, thus providing better facilities for all passenger classes. As railway historian Dr David Turner notes, 'By 1890 the experience of railway travel had become unique, and passengers could read in full illumination, smoke, dine in luxury, sleep and relieve themselves if necessary.'

For first-class travellers, day or night-time travel to Scotland was a much-discussed adventure. One of the key benefits of the third route

At the height of the Edwardian period, the Midland Railway was making the most of its extensive network and connections, attracting well-to-do passengers to use the company's through rail routes for Scottish autumn holidays. Stock phrases such as 'the best route', 'comfortable travel' and 'picturesque scenery' were the bedrock of Midland promotion until the 1923 amalgamation. (Illustrated London News Ltd/Mary Evans)

was the option of through workings to either Edinburgh or Glasgow. In the pre-grouping period, the Midland for a time ran more trains than its WCMS rival as passengers were attracted by the superior comfort of the carriages, the general service it provided and the extensive range of quality hotels the company had at its disposal. In 1913, some forty-one per cent of all English railway company expenditure on hotels was incurred by the Midland. The railway company had garnered a fine reputation as a caterer and hotelier using prestigious hotels as a means of promoting the company's name more generally. The Midland's London hotel was managed to high international standards featuring in Bedecker's *Guide* with services comparable to the Ritz. Indeed, Midland advertising from the period featuring their clerestory first-class dining cars would carry a headline as the best route for comfortable travel and picturesque scenery.

Likewise, the North British added their contribution to travel promotion with an advertising sign-off of the 'direct and picturesque route between England and Scotland is via the Midland and Waverley Route'. In addition, the NBR in 1907 developed a poster entitled the 'The Home and Haunts of Sir Walter Scott' extolling the picturesque benefits of the direct Midland and Waverley line connecting the countries. Similarly, timetable leaflets from the same year for express trains to the north would carry the stock phrase 'The most interesting route to Scotland'. The Midland and the NBR were a formidable combination prior to the Great War.

With railway amalgamation from 1923 and despite considerable coordinated marketing activity between LMS and the LNER to promote Anglo-Scottish traffic, the central route from London St. Pancras to Glasgow and Edinburgh was effectively relegated to secondary line status. The route was populated by many standard Midland designed 4-4-0 locomotives which, according to Roy Williams, would do 'sterling work for years'. In later years, Jubilee class locomotives would also feature but the quest for speed and more powerful and larger locomotives by the all-powerful LMS running department ensured west coast line dominance. On the central route, the through working of glamorous day and night-time expresses with dedicated joint carriage stock which the Midland Railway and its Scottish partners had so assiduously built up over their tenure was effectively wasted in the inter-war years. The *Thames-Forth Express* between St. Pancras and Waverley was a half-hearted attempt at joint company working between LMS and LNER when introduced in September 1927. The service did not last when war curtailed the named train just twelve years later in 1939.

Downgrading of the line continued. In 1958, British Railways undertook a half-hearted attempt with a *Waverley* named train summer service. Express it most certainly was not, taking the best part of half a day's travelling time from St. Pancras to Edinburgh with an interminable number of stops. These hangovers crept into post-war operations as the east coast picked up the prestige baton again. As Christian Wolmar observed:

'British Railways lost the central control that had been enjoyed during the war when it was split into regions which continued to act independently, without common standards or working practices, and the fierce rivalries little different from the competition between the old companies.'

In the latter years of British Rail, the line almost closed for good. The cost of maintaining the Ribblehead Viaduct was cited as the primary reason. Yet in 1989 extensive public lobbying ensured the line was saved. Today the route (and the Viaduct itself) remain a major visitor attraction accommodating not only scheduled services but many steam-hauled specials.

As we have discussed, night-time sleeper services have always been part of the Anglo-Scottish railway story whichever route they followed. Today, there are few things in modern, everyday life warranting a real sense of occasion. One of those rare travelling experiences that sets emotions tingling is *Caledonian Sleeper's* overnight service to Scotland. Whether it is to vibrant, must-do city destinations or the awesome tranquillity of the Highlands, the train now echoes to the great Anglo-Scottish expresses of the past. A new *Caledonian Sleeper* with modern twists

A more conventional approach to showing the *Coronation Scot* at full speed was used by Norman Wilkinson as the train ascends one of the steepest parts of the west coast line at Shap Fell. (NRM Pictorial Collection/Science & Society Library)

THE CORONATION SCOT
ASCENDING SHAP FELL
by Norman Wilkinson, P.R.I.

The Coronation Scot, blue and silver express of the LMS Railway, runs each weekday (except Saturdays) between London and Glasgow in 6½ hours, leaving Euston Station and Central Station at 1·30 p.m. The trains consist of nine air-conditioned coaches, internally panelled in decorative woods. The locomotive Coronation Scot (No. 6220) is one of five high-speed streamlined engines designed to maintain high average speeds in all weathers over the famous West Coast Route to Scotland, which includes such difficult ascents as Shap Fell (915 ft.), and Beattock Summit (1,014 ft.). Coronation Scot attained on a test run with the train in 1937 a maximum speed of 114 miles an hour, creating a British railway record.

exude the kind of quality train travel rarely found elsewhere, serving as an elusive reminder that first-class rail travel was once the epitome of glamour and sophistication. Recreating the romance of Scottish rail travel is a tall order but this can all be found aboard the outstanding new midnight teal-liveried train. The *Lowlander Caledonian Sleeper's* gleaming new carriages meet the needs of a predominantly business class customer travelling between London, Edinburgh and Glasgow. Yet it is the company's *Highlander* sister service with its meandering single-track routes to the wilds of Scotland which infuses a sense of feeling of escape and excitement that long-distance rail travel brings.

The Anglo-Scottish *Highlander* with its unique combination of Aberdeen, Fort William and Inverness routes straddling an immense outdoor terrain, seamlessly connects with the region's vast cultural, heritage and natural history wealth. Window gazing from the sleeper's Highland summer evening departure induces soporific sleep-inducing qualities. And all this is buried in the past century and a half of travel exploration that captures the endeavours of Scottish Victorian railway companies – the real trailblazers and pioneers of their day who made access to the hills far easier. Overnight train travel interlaces subtle connections of yesteryear that are still important today. 'We took over running the sleeper three years ago and as part of our bid we knew that to safeguard the legacy of the service we had to build new trains.' The voice belongs to Ryan Flaherty, Managing Director who subtly recognizes how this history feels. The train now reflects a carefully constructed rail travel experience; enhancements have been continually woven in, providing significant improvements to the guest journey. The mission, quite simply, is to reposition the train as a modern and true symbol of Scotland. And in a move that has resonance with bygone days of London society collectively moving to the Highlands for the grouse season, the company is highly supportive of Scotland's field sports tourism economy allowing the ferrying of shotguns and gun dogs on its night-time trains.

In Spring 2019, a new *Caledonian Sleeper* train came into being, heralding a fresh era of Anglo-Scottish rail travel delivering a truly timeless guest experience. Partly funded by the Scottish Government, the investment of over £100m in the new trains delivered seventy-five new Mk V carriages featuring developments not seen in Britain before and all designed to usher in a new standard of overnight travel between London and Scotland. Luxury may be a subjective notion when it comes to everyday travel but similar to the segregated areas found on long-haul flights, the *Caledonian Sleeper* delivers both a luxury and standard tier service, providing the modern-day traveller with a range of accommodation options to cater for both business and leisure travel markets. Overnight accommodation options include Comfort Seats, Classic Rooms (twin or single), Club Rooms (twin or single with en suite) and Suites (double bed with en suite). Ryan Flaherty says:

> 'When you look particularly at how we've developed the new train there's quite a broad range of accommodation offers, so we've kept the seats there. We've always got one coach in each train and they're busy, proving there's a market, be it students, backpackers so you can still get up there on budget … The seats provide the most leg room you get in the country and we have spent a lot of time making sure this seated coach is right because, and I've been quite passionate about this, for me it's about offering the best quality whatever category of accommodation you offer and I feel very proud that *Caledonian Sleeper* looks after our seated guests just as well as we look after the people who are paying the higher prices.'

But it is at the top end of the market where aspiration becomes a reality as the Club Cabins include ensuite loos and showers, whilst the Suite Cabins are more spacious including a double bed replicating real hotel-style accommodation:

> 'Sixty percent of the accommodation on the train is ensuite and then above that we've then got the double rooms which is a first for a scheduled UK service … We're really excited about that as it's a fabulous product. The double room concept was a bit of a leap of faith, but people are booking ahead not just because of the special occasion but research shows people just want a bit of space when travelling.'

He expands further on how the company developed the concept:

> 'There are people who are travelling with their husbands, or wives or partners and just want that extra bit of comfort so there is definitely an appetite. We are building the product to make sure that it is not just a double bed and the accommodation reflects a lot more.'

Recognising the travel problems many disabled and reduced mobility guests have to endure, the Classic, Club and Suites are fully accessible rooms for guests with reduced mobility including hotel-style key card entry, convenient access, charging panels and Wi-Fi throughout the train.

In recreating a portmanteau of the 'hotel on wheels' concept first coined by journalists in 1893, there will be a return to old-style, tasteful onboard dining. The restaurant car of old will be replaced by a classic modern new brasserie-style interpretation known as the Club Car. One of the key dining features will be the provision of high-quality culinary experiences with onboard chefs preparing meals from locally sourced Scottish food and drink producers. There is a separate area within the Club Car which is the dedicated galley/kitchen space. The galley design has focussed on making full use of space to increase refrigerated capacity and equipment for food production. Ryan Flaherty sums it up admirably:

'For me it's about bringing Scotland to a plate and that's what we try to do. If you take someone travelling to the Highlands, a large number of them will have dinner with us as we leave London. What we want to do is to bring a Scottish restaurant on wheels to London every night delivering a real and an authentic taste of Scotland. We do the haggis on board and the Scottish salmon but cooked slightly differently.'

This is no sudden transformation as, over the past three years, the Serco-owned franchise has responded to the Scottish Government's request for onboard catering to reflect all that is good about food and drink in Scotland. Ryan Flaherty adds:

'From my point of view developing the menus and the proposition was so easy because there's so much really good stuff in Scotland that it was not a challenge. What was interesting was all the food produced previously was done by a flight catering company so there was nothing Scottish about it. Almost all our food comes from suppliers in the Highlands and the quality is spectacular, so we've won awards and have a Taste of the Best accreditation from VisitScotland.'

No doubt a heaven for foodies but perhaps a little throwback to the decadence of the Wagon-Lits French Riviera bound *Blue*

Train celebrity bar cars. Local sourcing and food provenance have become vital components for many hospitality organisations, but the transfer of such food related ideas is again nothing new as *Railway Magazine's* correspondent discovered on the *Rome Express* way back at the tail end of the Victorian era. After a good night's sleep, a Scottish breakfast is available to all guests on the *Caledonian Sleeper* although the full range of products vary depending on the travelling accommodation.

The outlay made by the company's parent Serco suggests an expansion of the market is on the cards as consumers rediscover the delights of travelling aboard the Anglo-Scottish carrier. As Ryan Flaherty notes:

> 'We may not be the cheapest way to get to Scotland, but we will be the most civilised way to get you there and certainly if you're trying to get to the regions, we will be the most convenient way. Undoubtedly customers are making a choice to spend a little bit more and come with us and I think when we talk to those people my team on the train are pushing peoples' buttons with a service customers' actually want.'

Quality train travel on a scheduled service is not entirely lost on Britain's twenty-first century railway system.

West Country Allure

The Cornish Riviera Express

The routes to the West Country always engendered a touch of enchantment as the Great Western and the LSWR, through a series of local railway amalgamations, engineered the south west of England into the country's premier domestic holiday destination. Our story details how the two leading express trains of their day sought to capitalise on this blossoming romance. Great Western's *Cornish Riviera* London to Penzance train is still providing an on-board Pullman style train dining experience with direct ancestry to the 1904 express, where period advertising informed readers for the first time that West of England services embraced the charming 'Cornish Riviera'.

Cornwall was a place that uplifted hearts, yet it was slow seeing no significant quickening of service until 1890. But from late Victorian times, long-distance trains stopped in the county courtesy of the company's new fifty feet corridor stock, with individual compartments, lavatories and the still novel development of a dedicated smoking saloon. It proved popular, as in 1896 double section morning trains were run from Paddington in the summer months. Whilst the journey was better with bogie carriages, the travelling offer was still rather crude as a restaurant car was only added in 1899. Why the GWR should venture beyond its points west heartlands placing such emphasis and investment behind a prestigious train to the far south west has never received adequate explanation; suffice to suggest it was in response to the long-distance exploits of competitors on Anglo-Scottish routes, together with the commercial value of running luxury services piloted by LBSCR, the Midland and SECR. Yet in the far south west, railway management was slow to respond to opportunities.

But access and travelling time to the West Country did improve significantly with the *Cornish Riviera* launch, or the *Limited* as GWR preferred it to be known. The new service provided significantly improved travel opening up a virtually unknown holiday district. Even with numerous well-to-do county families, Molly Hughes pronounced Cornwall during the last quarter of the 1800s as an 'enchanted land' with tiny whitewashed 'native' cottages. Of all Britain's pre-grouping railway companies, the GWR used the company's natural resources to develop a panoply of promotional literature working with resorts to celebrate rural traditional England and becoming a prime mover in jointly developing the south west England visitor economy. The notion of successful destination development took hold here at the end of the nineteenth century as active collaboration between the railways, hospitality owners and local authorities created an infrastructure for an emerging tourist industry with records suggesting that these types of initiatives may have taken place in Cornwall as early as the 1860s. Nevertheless, new hotels were sited in quality locations with sea views close to railway stations and other amenities in a Cornish landscape so similar in many ways to the shape of Italy.

Through careful and selected image creation, tourism quickly flourished and with it the idea of short-breaks and the luxury travel experience. Nowadays, the visitor economy is made up of myriad providers collaborating, but this has not always been the case. From late Victorian times, railway companies (and shipping lines) existed in highly competitive environments where fierce commercial rivalries were always present, requiring more sophisticated approaches to attract a prosperous clientele. Railway involvement in new tourist arrangements was fast developing. Cornwall was transformed but for much of the 1800s, the county had remained isolated, initially only accessible by packhorse and viewed almost like a foreign country. Pimlott recounts a Cornishman visiting London at the beginning of the century 'as a kind of outlandish curiosity'. A hundred years later, there was still some something rather distinctive about the Cornish character. C. Lewis Hind, writing in *The Tatler* about the arrival and resulting milieu of a Cornish express at Paddington:

'As a Briton I turned for sympathy to the man who had been jostling me. He was a postman off duty and communicative. There was 6 ft. of him and he was dark-featured. I listened eagerly, for the voice of this haunter of the London end of the gleaming metals that stretch to the beloved Duchy had the Cornish ring, and he had the face that you only see on the shoulders of the "foreigners" beyond Tamar.'

Cornwall's seclusion gradually eroded as the county was now reached by coach and coastal steamer. Yet it was still comparatively unknown except for a small minority of visitors with a love for the picturesque and romantic. But with its connection to the main railway network in 1859, Cornwall, like the English Lakes, became firmly planted in the tourist gaze. O.S. Nock, in *The Limited* (George Allen and Unwin, 1979) described the mysterious destination as a land where the 'Cornish themselves lived in isolation and referred to the occasional tourists as visitors from England'. The introduction of the *Cornish Riviera Limited* train service transformed the county as GWR and later British Railways' Western Region's flagship service.

Cornwall was on the tourism vista; as a place name, it was quickly subsumed into language usage. Professor Jack Simmons summarised the position rather eloquently: 'Cornwall became accessible to tourists and popular with them, as it well deserved to be from its own merits – as idiosyncratic as those of Switzerland'. Cornwall was different; as early as 1908 the county's benign climate that encouraged distinctive flora and vegetation was featured in upscale newspaper coverage.

The GWR had quietly gone about planning the *Cornish Riviera* as a non-stop service of some 245 miles, combining length of operation with the new century's infatuation with speed, pushing locomotive technology to its limits. When launched, it was considered a marvel of Edwardian ingenuity. At Paddington, palpable excitement could be felt as travellers headed west. The Great Western was on to a winner, worthy to be mined for its long-term publicity value. Even when the Westbury and Castle Cary short cut shaved twenty miles off the distance when opened two years later, regular and sustained performance achieved almost daily set the barometer reading for British long-distance railway running. For the next twenty-five years, the company was second to none in its operation of long-distance, non-stopping expresses, creating in time a teeming artery of intense holiday traffic which was to change the face of Cornwall.

At its inception in July 1904, the *Cornish Riviera Express* comprised just six coaches, five Dean clerestory carriages and a single elliptical roofed Dreadnought dining-car open to all travelling classes. Initially, it was far from luxurious but new more comfortable stock was added a few years later with well-appointed coaches and restaurant car services. These advances ensured that the service found favour with long-distance travellers and became synonymous with a developing *Cornish Riviera* brand. Improvements in coaching stock, delivered by Churchward who took over as GWR's CME, introduced new sixty-eight feet length bogie dining coaches.

These were spacious, built to 9½ft width – the very limit of the loading gauge – with one end of the coach allocated to first-class passengers separated by a central kitchen and equipment. The other end of the dining-car was set aside for third-class travellers. The GWR could compete with Anglo-Scottish operators for comfort and on-board train services. As de Winter Hebron comments from a 1909 Great Western *Railway Magazine* entry, 'Non-stop services have necessitated the provision of well-equipped dining cars on all long-distance trains…'

At the same time, the Great Western's hotels and refreshment rooms department was running a tariff structure with differing prices for the same menu to first, second and third-class customers. For much of the twentieth century, the first-class offer on the *Limited/Cornish Riviera Express* was luxurious and *the* way to travel to Cornwall. Apart from a very brief period at the end of the 1920s, GWR never required the services of Pullman. Certainly, the company was a comparative latecomer to providing superior travelling facilities to its flagship trains – this largely determined by the ramification of its switch from broad to standard gauge running in 1892 – but over the following decades, GWR took the view that their premier train services consistently matched or were superior to those of Pullman. The *Cornish Riviera* name became an all year-round train and with the new Westbury short cut in the summer of 1906, it really did establish important trends chiming with the travelling public. Whereas Cornwall's holiday industry had a sense of bravado, its resident population was comparatively small; Newquay was the county's only notable resort with around 3,000 inhabitants. Whilst GWR put considerable effort into raising awareness of its traffic to Plymouth Atlantic liners, Cornwall was still as a foreign land to many Victorian holiday-makers.

When the *Cornish Riviera* brand launched, it was a relative latecomer to highly-organised travel literature but its primary role over the following decades was as the key facilitator to an enlarged West Country holiday market. In March of the same year, the GWR had lost no time in promoting the *Cornish Riviera* experience. Its early advertising and printed communication talked about the 'Delightful Cornish Riviera' as 'England's ideal winter, health and pleasure resort'. The company positioned Cornwall in regional and national press as an alternative destination with advertising actually questioning the merits of incurring 'the trouble and expense of a long foreign journey'.

The Isles of Scilly similarly received attention as did motor-vehicle services for exploration, together with the availability of handy maps to aid visitors. By December, the company was using customer testimony in its advertising stating 'thousands of delighted travellers acknowledge (Cornwall) to be the ideal home'

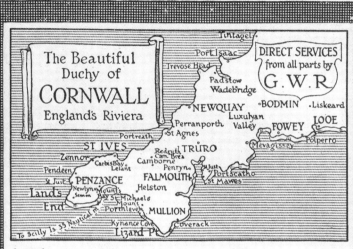

The Cornish Riviera

For your Summer Holidays.

Cornwall offers the most lovely coast in England —rugged moorland scenery—luxuriant valleys. Sea and sky alike have Mediterranean hues. Picturesque villages, almost foreign in their quaintness, vie with the better-known resorts in urging unique claims upon the holiday-maker.

Learn more of the "Delectable Duchy." An illustrated travel book, "The Cornish Riviera," will be sent post free for 6d. "Holiday Haunts in West of England," (descriptions and apartments list) post free, 2d. Write Mr. J. Morris, Supt. of the Line, Paddington Station, W., or apply G.W.R. Bookstalls and Offices.

G.W.R.—The Holiday Line.

Cornish Riviera Limited Express leaves Paddington daily, 10.30 a.m. Numerous other fast trains; see time tables. Week-end, Tourist, Excursion Fares to all parts. JAMES C. INGLIS, General Manager.

By late Edwardian times, the whole of Cornwall was promoted as an alternative to Mediterranean resorts. In this 1910 August bank holiday edition of *The Tatler*, the Great Western described itself as 'The Holiday Line' with direct services to the main towns of Bodmin and Truro and a raft of coastal destinations. The LSWR Withered Arm lines in the north of the county conveniently covered by a GWR banner. (Illustrated London News Ltd/ Mary Evans)

as well promoting Cornwall as 'The British Riviera' and an ideal location to spend the Christmas holidays and the winter months. The market for sophisticated Edwardian tourists was competitive, with high-class hotels on the French Riviera and leading hospitality establishments in Europe's capitals actively promoting their wares. It was into this market that Cornwall pitched itself for upscale tourist traffic.

The *Limited* introduced a new travelling generation to the delights of West Country train travel with haute cuisine provided in the palatial and convivial surroundings of its new restaurant cars and the country-house style Tregenna Castle Hotel at St. Ives. The company promoted the *Cornish Riviera* in the north east of England alongside adverts for regular steamer sailings from Newcastle to London whilst further afield the destination was styled in the Scottish press as the 'old-world country'. With new offices in New York, GWR progressively maximised these themes for the American market. Cornish residents were now writing to newspapers waxing lyrical about their 'sleepy hollow' and the punctual nature of the new expresses that served the county.

Fast access to Cornwall aided the growth of tourism. As Simmons comments, it was 'the one new business that offered any hope of replacing, even in part, what the county had lost' from the demise of its extractive industries. The county's residents responded positively to the newly found economic prospects tourism presented through the creation of new business practices where the influx of pleasure-seekers would create new forms of livelihood. Simmons notes the role of railway inclusion: 'Cornish men and women who set themselves to exploit the new opportunities they offered'. Despite advantages tourists brought, there were many who saw themselves as insular in nature and culturally distinct. Even by the 1920s and 1930s, numerous Cornishmen refused to describe themselves as 'English' but the GWR managed tourism programmes provided a little respite to the local economy that experienced economic decline and mass emigration.

GWR train advertising focused on Cornwall's accessibility, using fast and luxury themes used on its Plymouth ocean mails and boat train traffic. Yet for many visitors, Cornwall was not totally familiar, adding to the allure with romantic imaginations, being perceived by travellers as a far-off place catching their fancy. Aside from any Devonian route deviations, Cornwall remained the company's primary focus of attention as, once in to the county, the *Limited* would stop at Truro, Gwinear Road and St. Erth as they were junctions for important branch lines serving the burgeoning holiday destinations around the Lizard and St. Ives. From the summer season of 1909, GWR recognised Falmouth's attractiveness by running a special through coach to the Cornish destination. *The Bystander* in its Editor's Box noted the through coach arrangement as:

'indicative of the growing popularity of Falmouth, which is not only beautiful for situation, but enjoys a salubrity of climate which has led to many recommendations from eminent medical and public men. Penzance is, of course, the natural terminus of the Cornish Riviera, and has striven to rise to the opportunities which the rent booming of the West Country has brought about, but Falmouth is a strong rival and has many claims to the popularity for which it caters.'

Cornwall's other large towns – St. Austel, Camborne and Redruth were left to other train services.

From the outset, the train was gustily promoted as an exclusive service combining not just luxury features to sooth travellers in their seven-hour sojourn to the far south west, but by creating a journey experience built on distinctive cultural heritage. The journey, where no aspect of convenience and comfort was left undone, was an integral part of the overall destination experience. Departure from Paddington was a carefully orchestrated affair with a 10.30 am departure time and always from Platform 1. Gleaming chocolate and cream liveried carriages (except for their brief crimson lake period) with carriage headboards left the traveller in no uncertainty of where they were heading. Suitable reading material was part of the travel experience.

Penzance had well and truly positioned itself on the tourist map, creating an official guide book as early as 1860. By 1908, joint marketing initiatives took place between the railway and the local authority. The Corporation of Penzance printed *The Official Guide to Penzance* with a strapline added later – 'A Gem of the Cornish Riviera'. But it was Cornwall's romantic ideas that stirred the public's imagination. By 1912, the company was actively promoting the *Cornish Riviera* as Britain's national winter resort. As Cornish holiday resorts grew more popular, the load of the *Limited* had to

In the early days of the Cornish Riviera brand, Penzance was a flourishing resort. With this GWR poster illustrated by Alec Fraser from around 1909, the Queen's Hotel is depicted as a place for the fashionable yet budget-conscious. By late Victorian times, the town had established itself as the far south west's major cultural centre. In 1908, the Queen's Hotel had been extended for a second time, boasting modern amenities increasingly expected by high-end tourists, including the provision of bathrooms with hot and cold running water together with a high-class restaurant and wine cellar. (National Railway Museum/Science & Society Picture Library)

be increased with through coaches for Falmouth and St. Ives. Such initiatives marked a change in the way that the GWR thought about promoting its services to achieve a degree of competitive advantage over its rival LSWR's metals to north of the county.

The *Cornish Riviera Limited* was so popular that it ran in two portions on summer Saturdays until the Great War when it was suspended. Cornwall, though, was perceived as a relatively safe destination free from any thought of invasion. In the early stages of the war, passenger traffic to the far south west was heavier than ever. Post war there was a gradual acceleration of day and night-time West Country trains when services resumed in 1919. The Paddington to Penzance train was restored to a 10.30 am schedule as the service began to resemble the pre-war service but there was to be no formal launch of the company's pre-eminent express for the time being. By the early 1920s, the *Cornish Riviera Limited* was firmly established again as one of the country's leading luxury train services. Cornwall was altering as a destination, reflecting the changing habits of leisure and holiday taking attracting the interests of a new generation of adventurers addicted to speed and the new fashion for surf-riding the Atlantic rollers of the north coast. Surfing was part of a broader outdoor agenda which included camping, hiking and caravanning pursuits.

The Cornish Riviera in 1922 was promoted in *The Tatler* as the 'Best Climatic Conditions for Winter Holidays in the Homeland' reachable by 'magnificent trains and restaurant cars'. The following year, the Great Western were hammering home Cornwall's advantages as the 'English County pre-eminently suitable for Winter holidays or residence' by listing three important destination attributes: the ability to rival the mildness of the climate found at the Mediterranean's Riviera resorts; the quality of scenery to leave long-enduring impressions; and the pure air of the Atlantic ocean breezes. Advertising mentioned these attributes 'to have a wonderful bracing effect upon the human frame'.

The train's reputation was further enhanced with the gradual introduction of the iconic-looking Castle class locomotives and new seventy feet length coaches. GWR could maximise revenues as the longer length third-class coach had ten compartments with lavatories at both ends and safely seating up to eighty passengers. The company's policy was to design coaches to carry the maximum number of travellers with a minimum of tare weight. Of all the railway companies, the GWR was the leading exponent of the art of the 'slipped coach' which allowed carriages to be dropped without stopping at intermediate points for other destinations en route to the west. Typically, during this period, train formation would have three two coach sections at the rear of the train to slip the carriages for Weymouth and the Channel Islands, Ilfracombe and Minehead and Torquay. During the summer months, the *Cornish Riviera* would run as two separate trains to accommodate passenger demand.

For
Health Scenery & Sport
(the constituents of an Ideal Holiday)
go to the
Ocean Coast
(cool in Summer)
(warm in Winter)

"Ocean Coast" Booklet and all information of Train Services, Fares and Cheap Facilities, obtainable at principal G.W.R. Stations and Offices, or from the Superintendent of the Line, G.W.R., Paddington Station, London, W.2.

G.W.R. Paddington, W.2.   FELIX J. C. POLE, Gen. Manager.

Almost pre-empting the Southern's new ACE service promoting the north of Cornwall, the GWR brought out a new 'Ocean Coast' holiday booklet in 1924 highlighting routes to 'well-being' destinations facing the Atlantic. With a blend of ancient, traditional and yet modern styles, its imagery appealed to well-heeled *Tatler* readers many with families. The Ocean Coast was one of a list of ten free booklets supporting *the Handy Aids* series of 1920s publications. By the early 1930s, this had evolved with a 'Race to the Ocean Coast' children's puzzle produced in conjunction with the Chad Valley Company. (Illustrated London News Ltd/Mary Evans)

THE CORNISH RIVIERA

Does it rival the Continent for **WINTER?**

*T*HE *claim of the Cornish Riviera to a high winter sunshine record is supported by official statistics; it is considerably warmer than other parts of the British Isles, and there is little variation between day and night temperatures. No claim is made to continuous daily sunshine, but you can often sit out of doors in glorious sunshine without an overcoat.*

Many of the famous holiday resorts of Cornwall are officially referred to in the medical directory as being beneficial for winter residence.

There are no Casinos in the Cornish Riviera and no hotels de luxe for which luxury prices are charged, but there are many comfortable and homely hotels where charges are moderate, and one in particular, the Tregenna Castle Hotel, in picturesque old-world St. Ives, where the winter terms range from 4½ guineas to 5 guineas per week only.

For a sum less than the fare to the Mediterranean Riviera you can journey to the Cornish Riviera and pay all expenses for a week at a leading hotel.

The train service of the Great Western Railway has brought the Cornish Riviera within a few hours' journey of any of the great centres of industry and the fame of the Cornish Riviera Express (10.30 a.m.) from Paddington Station is world-wide. Compare this with a journey to the Continental Riviera taking up to 24 hours or more.

The Superintendent of the Line, G.W.R., Paddington, will post to you upon application, accompanied by sixpence in stamps, a handsome illustrated guide to the beautiful Cornish Riviera and information on how to get there.

Paddington Station,
London, W.2.

Felix J. C. Pole,
General Manager.

ST. MICHAEL'S MOUNT
Penzance

THE CORNISH RIVIERA

*T*HE wonderful coast scenery of romantic Cornwall, with its rugged rocks, delightful coves, and old-world villages, affords material for the type of holiday that no other travel experience can efface from the memory. Apart from its unsurpassed scenic attractions, the climate is remarkable for its mildness and equability both in Summer and Winter: it is even more equable in winter than the French Riviera.

"CORNISH RIVIERA"

a beautifully illustrated travel book (price 6d.), also train service and fare information, can be obtained at G.W.R. Stations and Offices, or from the Superintendent of the Line, G.W.R., Paddington Station, London, W.2.

G.W.R., Paddington Station   FELIX J. C. POLE, *General Manager*

In the 1920s, Cornwall was positioned as a year-round destination by the Great Western and as a viable alternative to spending the Winter season on the French and Italian Riviera. These two examples are pitched towards *The Tatler's* affluent readership but recognizing a value for money element as incomes were squeezed as well as southern France rapidly became more expensive in the inter-war period. (Illustrated London News Ltd/Mary Evans)

The inter-war years were the *Cornish Riviera* heyday. The introduction of the even larger King class locomotives in 1927 allowed the service to reach Plymouth non-stop in just four hours; speed and exclusivity became the by-word. The company's spin doctors worked hard to promote the 'English Riviera'; a destination adage ultimately adopted by Devon's Torbay resorts. *The Sphere* magazine wrote:

'At this season, (early December) when so many people are seeking suitable venues for wintering away from London and the great industrial centres, it is fitting that the claims of Cornwall be brought prominently to notice. When, in addition to the climatic advantages of Cornwall, one adds that the beauty of the county is of such a nature as to amaze all who witness it for a first time, and that the hotel proprietors and authorities are now bestirring to provide more amenities of a recreative character, it is clear that Cornwall is bound to attract an increasing share of the patronage of those who, from whatever motive, are in the habit of spending the winter away from the murk and smoke of large towns. The historical associations, no less than the geographical beauties, render it a veritable storehouse of beauty, while the means of access – the Great Western Railway – ensures a pleasant journey to and from the selected resort.'

By the early 1930s, GWR was emphasising the quality of the *Cornish Riviera Express* travelling experience aboard 'the World's most famous train!' and in particular the dining service, as advertised in the *Bystander*. 'What can be more delightful than taking the perfectly served all-British luncheon in the spacious dining car as the train glides at high speed through Britain's glorious countryside. The ideal prelude to the perfect holiday.'

The company was now seeking to broaden middle-class markets. GWR Cornish Riviera advertising in 1927 made direct comparisons to the French Riviera in winter which was progressively becoming more expensive as it evolved into a year-round destination.

'There are no Casinos in the Cornish Riviera and no hotels de luxe for which luxury prices are charged, but there are many comfortable and homely hotels where charges, and one in particular, the Tregenna Castle Hotel, in picturesque old-world St. Ives, where winter terms range from 4½ guineas to 5 guineas per week only.'

The Great Western heavily endorsed its own country house hotel to attract prosperous customers who would otherwise have had plenty of alternative destinations to consider. Tied to the Cornish Riviera brand, the St. Ives based hotel became a fashion icon in the inter-war years attracting a certain younger London set in the summer whilst adopting a more genteel customer in the winter months attracted by the hotel's standards of style and elegance. (NRM Pictorial Collection/ Science & Society Library)

The GWR by 1935 had to introduce another named train to satisfy traveller demand. Summer-time usage was so intensive that a sister service, unofficially known as *Cornishman*, was introduced in 1935 leaving Paddington five minutes after the *Limited*. *Cornishman* was, in fact, a reincarnation of another former unofficial premier named train used by the company previously in Victorian times as a broad-gauge train ran from Paddington to Penzance via Bristol. On 20 May 1892, a Rover Class 4-2-2 locomotive hauled the very last broad-gauge *Cornishman* service. Ironically, 'The Cornishman' was only afforded an official title in British Railways Western Region timetables in June 1952, running a service initially from the Midlands (Wolverhampton low level) with the route extended to Sheffield and Bradford in the 1960s. The 1935 GWR *Cornishman* was, therefore, an additional relief train designed to cater for the sheer volume of holidaymakers providing a passenger service heading directly to the company's intermediate stations at Weymouth and Plymouth. Torquay, Paignton and Brixham now had their own individual train which, for a short period in 1929 and 1930, was a Pullman service. But in Cornwall, the *Cornishman* stopped at Newquay, St. Erth and Helston as these stops served branches to other important holiday haunts before reaching Penzance. Interestingly, visitor interest in south west England was so intense that Southern Railway's multi-portioned *Atlantic Coast Express* similarly suffered problems of excess passenger demand. The company, too, had to run additional relief services to Dorset, Devon and Cornwall.

In the years before the Second World War, to say that the *Cornish Riviera* (and the *Cornishman*) were busy services was an understatement. By the 1939 summer season, the train had swollen to eight separate portions, the main part of the train with restaurant car for Penzance and one through coach for destinations to St. Ives, Falmouth, Newquay and Kingsbridge. More easterly destinations such as Ilfracombe and Minehead were serviced by the Taunton slip and two Weymouth and Channel Islands carriages were slipped at Westbury. Many West Country coastal resorts became highly dependent on both the GWR and Southern Railway.

In this period, a greater degree of co-operation and friendly rivalry existed between the two companies as they promoted their respective trains. During the war years, there were alterations to the *Cornish Riviera* service as it was initially re-routed via Bristol and Bath. The train later returned to Westbury but for several

The Great Western invested consistently over the years in Cornwall's image as a premier tourist destination. This 1928 Cornish Riviera poster, illustrated by L. Burleigh Bruhl, featured one of the ever topical GWR booklets by S.P.B. Mais on the Cornish Riviera and Glorious Devon, initially published in August 1928. Some 10,000 copies of the Cornish Riviera publicity booklet were printed with the publication enjoying a longevity lasting the best part of a decade. The holiday mood, from the same 1920s period, is captured perfectly in Alexander Stanhope Forbes classic interpretation of Penzance station. (NRM Pictorial Collection/Science & Society Library)

By the mid-1930s, railway artist Frank Newbould had acquired a celebrated status working for three of Britain's Big Four railway companies but also for the country's leading shipping lines. This Cornish representation captures the county atmosphere with rugged coastline, beach coves and tiny harbour settlements potted with white washed cottages. The GWR's coastal branch lines made holiday connections straight forward. In the second of these posters, as S.P.B. Mais enjoyed a reputation as one of the country's most popular travel writers, it was hardly surprising that the Cornish Riviera booklet (in its third and revised edition), would again feature in Alker Tripp's 1935 destination-scapes. (NRM Pictorial Collection/ Science & Society Library)

years the service had an additional Torbay portion. Separate Torquay and Penzance trains were eventually re-established but the *Cornish Riviera* was often seen hauling a fourteen-coach rake to accommodate Plymouth-based servicemen. During the war, holiday trains continued to the West Country as visitors sought respite from the toils of war. Like a generation earlier, GWR could rekindle a degree of old-time holiday spirit for visitors to its Cornish magic kingdom.

Post-war there was a gradual resumption to a degree of normality as in 1948 the service was swamped by increasing numbers of holiday travellers as they flocked to their favoured haunts. Railwaymen formed this new type of holidaymaker as nationalisation allowed them to see for themselves what Cornwall was all about. In addition, although the numbers of private cars and coaches were increasing, the vast majority of roads remained poor. It was still a long trek by road to the west of Cornwall. Throughout the 1950s, the train remained popular, aided by British Railways Western Region's promotional efforts. For a brief period in 1954, the service was officially known as the *Cornish Riviera Express* to commemorate the Jubilee of the train, but its name reverted to its original title until rebranding in 1956, when the *Cornish Riviera Express* was officially adopted.

In January 1957, the Paddington to Penzance route received another named restaurant car train, the *Royal Duchy*. With an early afternoon Paddington departure, the train was at best an intermediate service with many stops en route including a separation of carriages to form a through section to Kingswear in Devon. The end of steam on the premier morning service came in April 1958, with new motive power as sparkling Brunswick green liveried Warship diesel hydraulic locomotives ushered in a new modern era reconnecting to GWR's heritage. The new style makeover met with favourable media reaction with the train (including the *Royal Duchy* service) now made up of Mk I coach rakes painted in chocolate and cream.

The idea of reviving GWR colours had been advocated by former premier Harold Macmillan who was a director of the railway in the 1930s and 1940s. Macmillan likened the days of the private railways to the regiment system, describing it as a mistake to destroy tradition. Western Region publicity gurus lost no time in promoting the *Cornish Riviera Express's* new motive power and in creating more modern images of the county. *The Sphere* magazine ran a three page 'By Diesel to the West Country' feature, congratulating

British Railways for their contribution to developing 'travel in the most modern conditions'. Journey times to the far south west steadily decreased but headboard-carrying days of the *Cornish Riviera Express* service ended around 1962 as new Western Class diesels began life on Western Region.

During the early days of the Paddington-Penzance service, large wheeled four coupled Dean 4-4-0 locomotives were standard motive power to Plymouth, where they would change for a similar locomotive to continue the route west to Cornwall. Churchward improved boiler performance, creating a successful range of 4-4-0 Classes such as the Dukes, Bulldogs and Cities – the latter class most frequently associated with the *Cornish Riviera*. His designs gave the company the beginnings of a locomotive family identity that provided the GWR with a fleet of modern standardised locomotives to put the company at the forefront of consistently delivered performance. From 1906, more powerful 4-4-2 and prototype 4-6-0 classes took over as motive power on the long West Country runs. Post 1918, Churchward's 4-cylinder Star Class 4-6-0s had little difficulty in hauling the train. Further enhancements came when Collett's 4-6-0 Castle Class locomotives arrived on the scene in 1923. The Castles were appreciably more powerful than any of their predecessors, but a locomotive of this type was required as the *Cornish Riviera* became progressively heavier due to passenger numbers and concomitant luggage. By 1929, the train was a thirteen or fourteen coach

In 1960, C. Byfield produced a family of contemporary illustrations commissioned by Paddington. Byfield's depictions were a modern and mysterious impression of familiar GWR destinations including many old West Country visitor haunts. A sign of the times portraying an up to date image to accompany British Railways Western Region's rapid move from steam traction to new diesel-hydraulic haulage. (Travelling Art Gallery)

formation with first and third-class dining capacity at 120 covers whereas the service had just fifty dining seats in 1905.

GWR's premier West Country services provided regular work for the new heavyweight locomotives with huge interest in No 6000 *King George V*; its first working on the *Cornish Riviera Limited* recorded as being 20 July 1927. The combination of locomotive and prominent named train provided one of the high points for GWR's publicity. King Class usage had reduced the non-stop journey time providing much needed positive marketing ammunition for the company to counter inroads made by the other railway companies.

A quick change of locomotive from a King to a Castle at Devonport allowed GWR a degree of journalistic licence promoting the *Cornish Riviera* as an official non-stop service to Truro. From the mid-1920s until the end of steam, the destination image of the train was forever associated with big steam locomotives until diesel-hydraulics took over. During this period, the *Cornish Riviera Express* was frequently double-headed by two Warship diesels or a combination of diesel and steam power. From the early to mid-1960s, the *Cornish Riviera Express* was hauled by more powerful Western Class diesels which did away with the requirement to double-head the express train. By the end of the 1960s, journey time to Penzance with Western Class haulage had been reduced to five hours, thirty minutes. In the transition period to British Rail corporate blue and grey, the *Cornish Riviera Express* would be headed by a mix of Warships, Westerns and later by Class 47 until the introduction of British Rail's InterCity 125 workings in 1979. The new Great Western Railway franchise was still operating the same made-over stock in mid-2018 prior to the introduction of new trains.

The latest carriage stock was always going to be employed on the flagship *Limited*. In 1904, the GWR decided on a programme to introduce a new, spacious and luxury coach class for its prestigious Paddington-Penzance route. Prior to the new coach stock coming on stream, the new route, initially a seasonal service for the first two years of life, had to make do with new but existing carriage types. These as noted were Dean clerestories, but they were the very last of a typically Victorian coach class design. No further clerestories were built by the Great Western. The summer service that year was made up of six coaches running all the way between Paddington and Penzance and vice versa. With the 1905 season, the Paddington-Penzance train was entirely made up of the massive Dreadnought type carriages which were the largest coaches operating in Britain at the turn of the century, measuring some seventy feet in length and nine and a half feet in width. The GWR also introduced for the first time a coach reservation system and did away with the second-class classification.

Dreadnought coaches had roomy compartments and corridors incorporating new innovations such as electric lighting throughout. They had inset end doors but no outside doors to the compartments, but specifications ensuring the coach class remained within standard loading gauge. Yet Dreadnought coaches with their internal compartment doors did not go down well with the travelling public, so their life on the *Cornish Riviera* was a comparatively short-lived experiment. GWR's carriage design underwent significant change, with a universally acceptable coach design meeting established standards of other railway companies of the time, with a new carriage known as the Toplight, based on a fifty-seven feet length and a nine feet width specification. Toplights were introduced to the *Cornish Riviera* in 1907. These mainline coaches were very distinctive because of upper windows located in the area that would be an eaves panel – these were small lights or windows appearing above the main window. They were successful with the public and one of GWR's most successful ranges of coaches, becoming very characteristic of the pre-1923 organisation. Edwardian carriage design also catered for female passengers who were for the first time treated with greater respect. On the *Cornish Riviera*, a stewardess was carried to specifically look after the 'wants' of lady passengers.

In 1912, Toplight coaches began to be built with steel panels incorporating painted wood-style panelling, the perfect soporific setting for lady passengers travelling alone to drift off to sleep on long journeys. Nevertheless, women travelling with children was an issue that would not abate. Dedicated women-only carriages might have been one thing, but a crescendo in demands for 'babies only' compartments so that travellers could be freed from the 'tyranny' of 'knitted fleecy shoes' was also seen. *The Graphic* laconically poked fun at the issue:

> 'Baby has recently taken into its head to travel all over the country, and therefore it behoves the railway company to provide special and exclusive – very exclusive, if you please – accommodation for his Babyship.'

For the well-heeled lady passenger, responsibility was probably passed to nanny.

Steel-panelled Toplights became the standard GWR coach design until after railway grouping when the company realised that many other railway companies had caught up, surpassing them for design and comfort. Simply this would not do for the *Cornish Riviera's* image. The prestige train was nearly always the first port of call for GWR to showcase new carriage stock. In 1923, the *Limited* was allocated new stock to coincide with Big Four grouping whilst in 1929, the service received new steel-panelled sixty feet coaches, making the formation GWR's longest daily non-stop service. The new thirteen vehicle train included specialist through coaches for St. Ives and Falmouth and two dining cars together with a kitchen car. In 1935, new luxury coaches celebrated the company's centenary year of its Act of Incorporation as the *Cornish Riviera Limited* was provided with new built carriages known simply as Centenary stock. This newly designed rake was wide with entrances only at each end of the carriage and replaced the new coaches that had been introduced for the service in 1929. In 1930 a pair of first class saloons were added that did much to extol the luxury image of the service.

The Centenary stock consisted of two sets of thirteen coach trains with carriage recessed doors at each end but a new feature of one window per compartment, all very well received by passengers eager to take in West Country views. Due to the war, the wide-bodied Centenary (and the Super Saloons used on the Plymouth boat trains) were put into storage in 1942 as usage on other GWR routes due to their size was problematic. Post-war, Centenary stock did not reappear on the train due to its comparative age and was substituted by a mixture of the best Collett and Hawkesworth coaches; the latter introduced in the 1940s. In British Railways times, Mk I stock began to appear on the *Cornish Riviera* in the early 1950s but in true GWR practice, a mixture of Mk I, Collett and Hawkesworth coaches in British Railways Western Region blood and custard appeared. Prestige Mk I coaches were painted in brown and cream but later repainted in British Railways maroon and by the mid-1960s there was a gradual progression to the new corporate blue and grey livery. By this time, the *Cornish Riviera Express* had lost its locomotive and coach headboards due to railway modernisation requiring frequent usage of coaches over different routes. Mk II coaches with buffet cars providing refreshment later appeared until fixed InterCity 125 Mk III stock took over in the late 1970s.

West Cornwall always commanded an upscale and distinct Mediterranean feel, as seen in this British Railways Western Region poster by Harry Riley. Traditional GWR brown hues and Azur coast blue imagery combine majestically to showcase the destination as a perfect summer holiday ground for mid-1950s families. (National Railway Museum/Science & Society Picture Library)

PENZANCE
GATEWAY TO WEST CORNWALL
Illustrated Guide (6d.) from Town Clerk, Penzance

TRAVEL BY TRAIN

The *Cornish Riviera* has provided many iconic images over the years, possessing a certain panache that many other named trains simply could not live up to. Author Andrew Martin, in *Belles and Whistles* (Profile, 2014) describes the *Cornish Riviera Express* 'as the most romantic train of the most romantic railway'. British Rail Western Region perpetuated its appeal until the mid-1960s but under the hands of modernisation the name almost completely disappeared until the 1990s. But the name – the *Cornish Riviera Express* – still lives on and survives as a sub text in the new Great Western Railway franchise twenty-first century timetable.

The Atlantic Coast Express

It is a little more than ninety years since Southern Railway's *Atlantic Coast Express* (known simply as the *ACE*) first debuted at Waterloo station at 11.00 am on 19 July 1926. The West Country express became one of the nation's most instantly recognised named trains. It was bound in tourism representing a bygone era where dreamlike memories of relaxed countryside and seaside holidays were instantly recounted. As an express service it most certainly was, utilising Southern's most powerful locomotives running over the fast legs from London, Salisbury and into Devon and only slowing up as it served numerous stations north, east and west of Exeter. The inaugural run served just five destinations; stations in Devon – Plymouth, Torrington and Ilfracombe and the Cornish resorts of Bude and Padstow. Padstow was the most westerly and distant outpost of the Southern network and some 260 miles from its Waterloo headquarters. Stops at Sidmouth and Exmouth were added in 1927. By war-time suspension on 10 September 1939, the *ACE* in every sense of the word had established itself as an iconic named train rivalling the Great Western's long-established *Cornish Riviera Express*.

The *ACE* can trace its origins to late Victorian times when the LSWR probed GWR's territory to develop new routes beyond Exeter, but this country was GWR's home turf as the company considered Devon and Cornwall to be its own back yard maintaining a stranglehold of the best routes to the far south west. Although the LSWR had absorbed the Bodmin and Wadebridge line long ago in 1846, the two railways battled it out over Cornwall but LSWR's eventual penetration of north Cornwall did not come about until the end of Victorian age. In 1896, the LSWR announced in advertising 'The North Cornwall Railway is now open to Wadebridge for

Padstow, and Newquay, and Bodmin, also Tintagel, and Boscastle, via Camelford'. By 1899, the new pleasure resorts of Bude and Padstow were easily accessible to tourists. GWR had previously surveyed the rugged landscapes of north Cornwall, something S.P.B. Mais recounts as resembling Connemara's Gaeltacht with its string of small resorts, but the company strangely disregarded its tourist potential – a decision it was to bitterly regret at the height of *ACE's* popularity in the 1930s. Yet by May 1904, the LSWR set about mounting competition to GWR's Cornish Riviera brand. Whitsun excursion advertising in the illustrated weeklies prompted announcements from a variety of railway companies which included rails to the far south west with GWR and LSWR. Fast excursions to north Cornwall's holiday and health resorts were promoted by LSWR amongst a raft of destinations it served, whilst GWR featured special motor tours to Falmouth, the Lizard and Mullion. Both companies were keeping an eye on upscale tourists. Whilst the LSWR had maintained a regular 11.00 am departure from Waterloo for the West of England since the early 1890s, the company surprisingly never exercised the same degree of panache as the Great Western did with their service; the LSWR never naming any of their timetabled trains or their locomotives. The full passenger potential of the Exeter line to north Cornwall and north Devon, except for significant agricultural and fisheries freight traffic, was never really developed until after grouping a quarter of a century later.

Within a short time of starting the *ACE* provided a distinctive travelling experience as Waterloo station was vibrant with travelling passengers especially on summer Saturdays with the adventure commencing from platforms ten and eleven. The train was designed as a multi-portioned express with eight sections and separate coaches for the more easterly stations of Sidmouth, Exmouth and Exeter, the north Cornwall destinations Bude and Padstow, Plymouth and finally the north Devon section for Torrington and Ilfracombe. During the summer months, when demand was high, two trains would run daily apart from Saturdays when it ran in four parts. At times, though, there may have been as many as six separate trains to cope with the numbers of passengers heading west (calculated at some 3,800 bookings for seats) for *ACE's* destinations. Whether the express could be truly described as a luxury train has been questioned but its unique composition was something rather distinctive, giving the impression of travelling in

A couple of years into the *ACE* service, collaborative approaches were clearly evident between the destinations served by the train and the Southern Railway. This 1928 Bideford for Westward Ho! poster illustrated by F. Whatley depicts the resort and bridge over the estuary. In order to attract upscale visitors, north Cornwall and Devon had been portrayed by the LSWR since late Edwardian times as ideal locations for playing golf. Together with surfing they were to remain dominant promotional themes throughout the life of the service. (NRM Pictorial Collection/Science & Society Library)

BIDEFORD
for WESTWARD HO! GOLF LINKS
NORTHAM, APPLEDORE & CLOVELLY.
Free Guide from Publicity Office, Bideford, or Northam.
S.R."Atlantic Coast Express" from Waterloo, Salisbury and Exeter.

a parcels train made up of a number of brake composite carriages accommodating space for a guard's compartment and the masses of passenger luggage for varying holiday destinations. As the *ACE* was competing with the *Cornish Riviera Express*, Southern invested in its culinary offer with a mix of buffet, kitchen and open restaurant cars. What is without debate was the train's celebrity status, being equally well-appointed for both first and third-class travellers and quickly establishing itself as one of Southern's two flagship services but one to never carry a Pullman specification, unlike the *Golden Arrow*.

To understand this position, a look at the history of Pullman's south west of England services is necessary; there had always been a complete dearth of West Country Pullman trains. The GWR had had its *Cornish Riviera Express* since the early years of the twentieth century, which progressively became a pretty luxurious affair with new stock and widely promoted as an unique brand. The company dabbled with Pullman services for two summer seasons before launching its own ultra-luxury equivalent with the Super Saloons in 1931 designed for ocean liner services. A short-lived and largely unsuccessful *Devon Belle* Pullman service over Southern metals did not appear until after the Second World War, so over the years there was effectively a complete absence of Pullman to south west England. Moreover, before grouping, the LSWR, as a former Southern Railway constituent company, did not have a long-term track record of courting Pullman in the same way as near neighbours LBSCR and SECR had done.

LSWR had experimented with Pullman provision for several years; in 1880 the company borrowed Pullman car *Alexandra* from LBSCR for its west of England services, but by and large, eschewed a longer-term relationship, preferring to develop its own on-board catering and sleeping car arrangements. Catering contractors Spiers and Pond had run LSWR's restaurant and buffet cars for some time and this successful arrangement continued until 1919, as the company were awarded the contract for Southern's new south west division as well as for its inter-regional traffic. In the 1890s, LSWR developed plans for a new fleet of high specification stock for the growing Plymouth ocean liner market but this and new sleepers were later sold when the company withdrew from direct American boat train competition. So, no Pullman for the *ACE*. When it launched, it had to make-do with a mixture of existing pre-grouping LSWR coaches (including Ironclad carriages) and post 1923 Southern stock for a short while. The train was heavily loaded with its initial formation of largely single coach sections of composite first, third and brake. David St. John Thomas and Patrick Whitehouse in their history of the Southern Railway suggested that the new service at its outset was no marvel. Not mincing their words, they wrote, 'Riding (on the *ACE*) was rougher than on the Great Western, seating infinitely inferior to the LMS, picture windows slow to appear and woodwork rougher hewn'. But a second-rate product was not to last, as in 1928 new olive green liveried Maunsell steel-panelled bogie restaurant cars consisting of a first-class kitchen car and a third-class open saloon were introduced to the service.

In a short period, there would be no other named train quite like it, characterised by its almost unique collection of brake composites (as many as eight out of ten vehicles) for the many different end destinations. Indeed, it was recognised as the country's most multi-portioned train service and its inclusion added a distinct flavouring as its composition could change for fluctuating seasonal demand. At different times of the year, there might be between two and five trains in the busiest part of the holiday season whilst when run as a single train, it might have up to eight sections.

New stock provided first-class travellers with an exceptional level of spacious and comfortable accommodation. Large thirty-six-ton dining cars would travel as far as Exeter or when the north Devon portion ran as a separate relief train to Ilfracombe. Whilst the multi-portioned *ACE* did restrict some movement around the train (like the *Cornish Riviera Express* with its slip coach sections), it was nonetheless a fast and efficient luxury train service for premier paying passengers, who, courtesy of the train's brake composite carriage make-up, never had to worry about their holiday luggage or to think about changing coach or train to reach their desired destination. Different sections of the *ACE* also created a unique cosmopolitan flavour, coupled with a degree of camaraderie as fellow passengers conversed with each other about holiday plans, the places they would visit and things to do, the train being considered ideal for golfers when the service was launched. *The Bystander* reported:

'Some time ago the Southern Railway, in order to slake its thirst in the cup of competition, sought a new name for one of its trains, and went to the public with a money prize in its hand, asking for the best name for that protentous train of theirs which slides out of Waterloo in the mornings and goes away and hides itself somewhere on the Atlantic seaboard. However, one of its own guards did the public in the eye by winning the prize himself with the phrase "Atlantic Coast Express", an apt and a stout fellow. For you wake up eventually at a place called Padstow, which hides round behind a promontory against which Atlantic rollers hum their sinister song; and there you will find, hidden away from all the world, just across the picturesque Padstow Bay, a super golf course called "St. Enodoc".

The train was very much in vogue and handy with its combination of destination brake carriages to carry those golf clubs.

David St. John Thomas and Patrick Whitehouse said the *ACE* was simply unique:

'There was no other train like it, changing its character amazingly per time of year and week. In summer half a dozen or more trains might all claim themselves the *Atlantic Coast Express*; it could indeed run in nearly as many separate complete trains at Bank Holiday weekends as it did in 'portions' on winter weekdays.'

Standard seating accommodation of the *ACE* in its early days was 396 passengers but its increasing popularity meant several relief trains could be added. Coupled to all of this was Elliot's powerful promotional output where word of mouth discussion was recognised as a successful tourism ploy. In modern marketing parlance, the *ACE* was a tailored customer service providing passengers with a premier named train serving the many smaller cool destinations of east Devon and the Atlantic shores of north Cornwall and Devon. No other train service did this. Hardly surprising, that its distinctive customer offer cultivated a celebrity West Country smart-set following in the summer months

With John Betjeman's blossoming career as a writer and broadcaster, Elliot tapped into a rich vein of interest in rural affairs as a restless middle-class were anxious to preserve rural Britain from terminal decline by championing the countryside and the ways and lives of its inhabitants. The establishment of the National Trust in 1895 and the Royal Society for the Protection of Birds were unconscious contributors to the notion of countryside and its Englishness.

By 1936, Elliot's thoughts were to align Southern Railway's connections with the public's evolving fascination with English

ATLANTIC COAST EXPRES

The illustration on this Southern Railway poster, produced in 1935, was by Charles Shepherd depicting no. 850 *Lord Nelson* hauling the express train. The *ACE* service, by this stage, was well established assuring passengers a carnivalesque and jolly West Country travelling experience competing directly with GWR's *Cornish Riviera Express*. (NRM Pictorial Collection/Science & Society Library)

rurality and the West Country in particular. Betjeman was one of a bank of key supporters associated with travel guides to the far south west and his support was influential. In time, north Cornwall simply became known as 'Betjemanland' as he continued to make regular journeys to his home county along the Withered Arm and the Camel river to Padstow. The mood and spirit of north Cornwall was further enhanced as Southern commissioned railway poster work created by marine artist Norman Wilkinson, who had a life-long fascination with the sea.

S.P.B. Mais continued to write travel material for booklets under the theme of *Rambles to the West Country* to support the routes and destinations of Southern Railway's premier (non-Pullman) service. This poster from 1938 illustrated by Audrey Weber was typical of rural images used to encourage travellers to the countryside as an alternative to usual coastal resort rush. The *Walks in North Devon* booklet dovetailed perfectly with the ACE routes in the north of the county. (NRM Pictorial Collection/ Science & Society Library)

The sum of the whole brought about a new dimension to the company's travel marketing and formed part of a celebration of the nostalgic countryside literature which the railways played their part. Batsford's rural England guides similarly helped to stimulate interest in the beauty and ways of the countryside and the exquisiteness of the built environment. Harry Batsford and Charles Fry had already written a title called *The Cathedrals of England,* using a similar thematic approach in *The Face of Scotland* to include a chapter on Scottish buildings; a move, according to Buchan, to be celebrated 'for Scotland is far richer in the handicraft of man than is commonly believed'. Thus, before the war turned the world upside down again, a multitude of publications and colourful posters represented perfect time capsules of a long-gone Britain.

The tourist potential of England's country landscapes needed little prompting in the inter-war years as a crop of new travellers were determined to experience rural hinterlands. Elliot's promotional strategy called on the assistance of S.P.B. Mais who was commissioned to write about the *ACE* West Country route since his ardent campaigning for the preservation of the English countryside and its traditions made useful marketing tools. In 1929, Mais penned *West Country Holidays,* which set out 'to lure the family man and all that is his to the wonders and delights of East, North, and West Devon, North Cornwall, districts served by the S.R.'s luxurious flyer "The Atlantic Coast Express" from Waterloo.' *The Tatler* correspondent went on 'Certainly no more effective piece of holiday literature, from the "See Britain First" point of view, has been offered (free for the asking) than this new series from Mr Mais's clever pen.' The following year, Southern produced poster advertising in support of Mais' editions of *Southern Rambles* with a 'Hike for Health' headline. His output was prolific and equally well-read coining the phrase of the most celebrated travel writer of his day. Southern later packaged Mais' writings in a booklet produced in 1936 called *Let's Get Out Of Here*; a guide to walks from the *ACE* route and quickly followed by a second booklet published in 1937. Known simply as *ACE* this well-known book portrayed a whimsical look at the train's journey supported by many evocative drawings and illustrations by muralist and artist Anna Zinkeisen informing passengers of what could observed from each coach compartment.

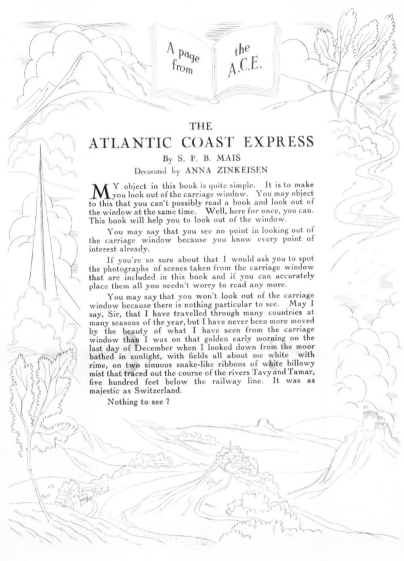

A page from the A.C.E.

THE
ATLANTIC COAST EXPRESS
By S. P. B. MAIS

Decorated by ANNA ZINKEISEN

MY object in this book is quite simple. It is to make you look out of the carriage window. You may object to this that you can't possibly read a book and look out of the window at the same time. Well, here for once, you can. This book will help you to look out of the window.

You may say that you see no point in looking out of the carriage window because you know every point of interest already.

If you're so sure about that I would ask you to spot the photographs of scenes taken from the carriage window that are included in this book and if you can accurately place them all you needn't worry to read any more.

You may say that you won't look out of the carriage window because there is nothing particular to see. May I say, Sir, that I have travelled through many countries at many seasons of the year, but I have never been more moved by the beauty of what I have seen from the carriage window than I was on that golden early morning on the last day of December when I looked down from the moor bathed in sunlight, with fields all about me white with rime, on two sinuous snake-like ribbons of white billowy mist that traced out the course of the rivers Tavy and Tamar, five hundred feet below the railway line. It was as majestic as Switzerland.

Nothing to see ?

WHAT TO SEE FROM THE WINDOWS OF THE
ATLANTIC COAST EXPRESS
ON SALE + PRICE 2'6
AT BOOKSTALLS OF THE
SOUTHERN RAILWAY

This 1937 poster designed by Doris Zinkeisen featured a booklet on what to see from the windows of an *ACE* carriage as the train heads westwards. The publication was written by S.P.B. Mais and illustrated by the poster designer's younger sister, Anna. Both Zinkeisen girls were awarded scholarships at the prestigious Royal Academy of Schools in Piccadilly and were the toast of London's clever set. Such celebrity endorsements ensured the Atlantic coast way booklet proved to be a great commercial success cementing Southern's reputation as a pioneer of integrated marketing and press communications activity. (NRM Pictorial Collection/ Science & Society Library)

Southern's recently introduced Maunsell-designed coaching stock replicated successful ideas from other railway companies – one of the key passenger-focused features used in new carriage design and construction was the adoption of wide window bays. From the railway's perspective, Mais's text importantly explored the beauty and seasonality of the route as the *ACE* became a year-round service. These developments saw a significant surge in passenger traffic by the mid-1930s, particularly with the eastern upscale resorts of Lyme Regis in west Dorset and Budleigh Salterton and Sidmouth in Devon all becoming more popular and served by direct *ACE* connections. Sidmouth had gained a reputation as a 'quiet summer retreat, where the sun shines on most (summer) days and bathing is delightful' before the Great War.

Accessible from London on LSWR metals in little more than four hours, Sidmouth was positioned as an exclusive resort by its local authority managers who were reluctant to use commercial freedoms presented under the 1921 Health and Pleasure Resorts legislation permitting resorts to spend modest amounts of money on promotional advertising. Gardiner alludes to the local authority who 'worked to keep it that way, vetoing plans for a holiday camp to be built nearby, making a supreme effort to limit day-trippers, declining to lay on any entertainment or publicise itself'. Despite Sidmouth's disdain of the modern tourist, in summer the south west division of the Southern Railway became one of the country's busiest railway routes. During the twenties and thirties, Southern and Great Western fought over the bragging rights of who provided the best West Country service but in truth, some degree of marketing collaboration took place between them and with the many resort tourism authorities working in tandem to promote the region. The south west long-distance routes were all within a less than 300-mile radius of London, leaving both companies free to mount fast-steam hauled services to Devon and Cornwall's awaiting holiday destinations.

By late 1938, the *ACE* received a makeover with Maunsell carriage sets repainted in the new light green or malachite green livery. In September 1939, the *ACE's* title immediately disappeared from timetables and a slower service with additional stops ensued. After the war years, new Bulleid coach stock began to appear from early 1946, transforming the train. These coaches were not considered to be radically different to Maunsell's designs in terms of their layout but they were longer, and they looked rather different with a body profile comprising a smooth curve from the floor to the roof line of the carriage; they certainly complemented the look of the *ACE* with its new Bulleid locomotives. Another post-war feature was the inclusion of more open saloons for third-class seating carriages, together with Bulleid's novelty Tavern Cars noted in the 1948 winter timetable. Introduced in May the following year, the Tavern Cars were designed to bring an element of jollity to an austerity and food rationed Britain, bridging a gap between food losing money and drink (especially beer) making a profit. Blood and custard liveried British Railways Mk I vehicles started to appear on the south west section from 1951 so the *ACE* could be made up of both Bulleid (malachite green) and Mk I sets (blood and custard) for the different destinations.

Following service resumption on 6 October 1947, the routes to the Withered Arm had new and powerful motive power with Merchant Navy, West Country and Battle of Britain locomotives together with, as noted, new Bulleid coaching stock. The *ACE's* reputation was not dented by the war years; Southern's locomotives had a contemporary feel, style and art-deco streamlined design that certainly caught the public's imagination. And Cornwall and north Devon offered the opportunity of an enjoyable 1947 Christmas with the mid-morning *ACE* departure ensuring a string of destinations and hotel discoveries could be reached by late afternoon.

Across the West Country, modern Pacific locomotives could be seen in almost every nook and cranny of the former LSWR metals. Modernity and heritage were strange bedfellows but Southern Railway and later British Railways Southern Region over the next fifteen years constantly sought to capitalise on these assets by developing themes and images for the *ACE*, often reflecting a subtle form of superiority over the destinations served by the *Cornish Riviera Express*. The service was further enhanced with significant acceleration of the West Country train. Despite road competition, the 1950s were an extremely busy time for the *ACE* with additional relief trains for summer weekend work brought in to complement the phased section departures. At times, British Railways Southern Region western division was hard stretched to provide adequate relief trains for *ACE* services having to cope at the same time with the popularity of Bournemouth and Weymouth holiday trains. The situation eased somewhat with the elimination of steam hauled boat trains in Kent as many light Pacifics were transferred. The Exmouth Junction (Exeter) and accompanying shed received significant locomotive numbers resulting in many original-condition lighter Spam Cans (rebuilt light Pacifics were in fact heavier) pulling services on the feeder lines of Cornwall and on the Ilfracombe line until the end of steam. Ultimately, steam traction on Southern metals retreated westwards but with rebuilt Merchant Navy and light Pacifics, the West Country was left with a super-abundance of modern, rebuilt Pacific power, revolutionizing travel to the west with three-hour *ACE* services in either direction.

Even up until 1963, the *ACE* still had strong passenger demand with five separate departures from Waterloo. Spacious Bulleid corridor carriages and new Mk I hauled sets characterised the numerous departures which now included additional stops. The 10.15 am Ilfracombe and Torrington portion would call at Templecombe, Seaton Junction and Barnstaple Junction before splitting coaches (for Torrington) and continuing all stations to Ilfracombe, the 10.35 am Padstow and Bude service would call only at Axminster and Halwill Junctions then virtually all stations to Bude and to Padstow, a 10.45 am portion would call at Lyme Regis and Seaton, the traditional 11.00 am Torrington and Ilfracombe service calling at Sidmouth Junction, Eggesford and Barnstaple Junction before all stations to Ilfracombe. Finally the 11.15 am Plymouth, Padstow and Bude departure calling at Yeovil Junction, North Tawton and Okehampton (for Plymouth) before Padstow and a connection to Bude. Even in its last year of operation, the Seaton and Lyme Regis departures were the only portions to be dropped.

By the late 1950s there was a significant increase in populist car ownership and in the growing numbers of coach companies but travelling long-distances was not quick or easy. The motorway and trunk road building programme was still in its infancy and for those who could afford it, British Railways introduced an alternative with several long-haul car carrying services later to be rebranded as Motorail. The long West Country trek was time consuming eating into holiday time requiring effort and planning. Roads were not designed for significantly increased vehicle volumes and were often in a poor state of repair, leading to a new phenomenon of the traffic jam. British Railways countered, introducing a car tourist service in 1957, operating between

29.

BUDE

ILLUSTRATED GUIDE FROM CLERK TO THE COUNCIL DEPT 'P. COUNCIL OFFICES, BUDE

SOUTHERN RAILWAY

In the immediate post-war years, British resorts and the railway companies worked hand in glove to attract well-off visitors for summer holidays who might otherwise have ventured abroad although foreign currency restrictions forced many to holiday at home initially. Bude and Boscastle had long been promoted in poster advertising by the LSWR as early as 1909. By the 1930s, north Cornwall's coves were ideal locations to be promoted for their sunshine and surfing qualities. In this 1947 illustration by Herbert Alker Tripp, the new fleet of smooth-cased locomotives would come to define a speedy *ACE* service to the West Country and the Withered Arm in the 1950s. (NRM Pictorial Collection/Science & Society Library)

Paddington and St. Austell in Cornwall with later operations transferred to work between Surbiton and Okehampton. Whilst not strictly part of the *ACE*, the car tourist service was normally made up of eight CCTs together with a couple of coaches and a restaurant car as the Surbiton service had an 8.03 am breakfast-time departure. It certainly portrayed a modern image of adventure as passengers watched their cars loaded on to CCTs and then boarding the carriages in the goods yard by way of step-ladders. The transportation of heavy motor cars required hauling by rebuilt Merchant Navy Class locomotives such as no. 35017 *Belgian Marine* allocated for car tourist duties. For affluent passengers, the West Country car carrier proved attractive as Devon and Cornwall's delights were immediately at hand, reached from London in less than four and half hours. The western car tourist service, unfortunately, was not to last, operating for just eight summers between 1957 and 1964, eventually succumbing to the car as road infrastructure and travelling times improved.

From its introduction until the end of steam, the image of the *ACE* was always associated with a variety of locomotive classes the first being a new fleet of King Arthur Class hauling West Country expresses. The *ACE*, as far as Exeter, was dominated by the Arthurs but the more powerful Lord Nelsons later took over on a regular basis and could run without stopping to Salisbury in ninety minutes, where locomotives were changed with a further non-stop run to Exeter. During the war years, both locomotive classes powered West Country trains (although journey times lengthened due to wartime restrictions) before the newer and more powerful Merchant Navy Class were drafted on duty closely followed by the slightly smaller West Country/Battle of Britain Pacifics becoming mainstream locomotive designation.

By the early 1950s, Merchant Navies were putting more than a mile a minute runs on the Waterloo-Salisbury-Exeter sections. So much so, the *ACE* and Merchant Navy reputations on the down train to Exeter had become a 'legend for speed exploits.' In 1953, Merchant Navy classes across Southern Region were temporarily withdrawn with new Britannia Classes taking over. Nevertheless, the *ACE* in British Railways era was dominated by a powerful mix of Merchant Navy, West Country and Battle of Britain Classes in rebuilt and streamlined forms until steam's passing. It was not difficult to spot the *ACE* as it operated first with a locomotive

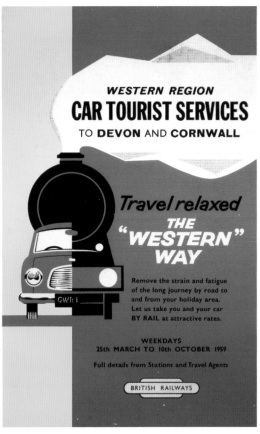

In the first 1957 poster, British Railways Western Region promoted train travel as a preferable alternative to driving to holiday destinations by accommodating cars aboard a specialist train to Cornwall. By 1959, Western Region, who had begun to wrest control of former Southern West Country routes, offered travellers who could afford it the Restaurant Car Tourist Service, a convenient and relaxed holiday and return journey to Devon and Cornwall bypassing the irritation of road congestion. (NRM Pictorial Collection/Science & Society Library)

headboard attached to the buffer beams and then later as a permanent fixture with a standard fixing across the smokebox door of the locomotive.

Times ultimately were changing though. From September 1962, Western Region took responsibility for the line west of Salisbury with full control of Cornwall's northern rural routes passing on 1 January 1963. This was the land of the Withered Arm, a popular term used to describe the railway map west of Exeter as they resembled a tree. The celebrated holiday express at its conclusion was headed by Warship diesel-hydraulic locomotives (like the

ATLANTIC COAST EXPRESS   LONDON AND THE WEST COUNTRY   From a Water Colour by RICHARD

This carriage print representation of an early British Railways period *ACE* service was created as an original water colour by landscape artist Richard Ward. Having produced artwork for Brooke Bond Tea's picture card series, Ward was an accomplished artist with many subject interests including transport. The ACE was one of a series of four former Southern Railway based illustrations he produced for the organization in 1956. (Travelling Art Gallery)

Cornish Riviera Express) but commencing and finishing journeys at Waterloo. The headboards and coach boards that so defined the post-war train also disappeared. Railway pundits suggest Western Region did their best to exact revenge by ensuring the old LSWR West Country route was relegated to secondary line status. If this was not bad enough for Southern stalwarts, the route eventually suffered the ignominy of single-track reduction for large parts of the Salisbury-Sherborne-Exeter section.

On 5 September 1964, the train that had had its heyday in the inter-war years and had carried more through sections to more destinations than any other train in the country was gone. Likewise, the motive power shed at Exmouth Junction was closed as all remaining services west of Exeter became diesel-operated. And so too, the lines to the rural idylls of the Withered Arm were unceremoniously lopped off by a Beeching cleaver swung with real vengeance; the Padstow and Bude Cornwall branches in 1966, Okehampton to Plymouth in 1968 and finally the Barnstaple to Ilfracombe line in 1970. As Devon and Cornwall morphed into mass tourism destinations served by the car and the coach, the *ACE* as a famous named train was consigned to the railway dustbin.

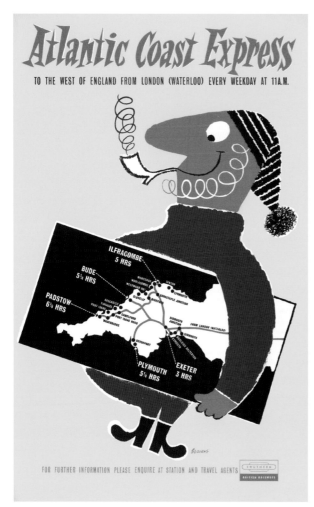

When these posters were produced by British Railways Southern Region at the end of the 1950s, the westerly arm of the Waterloo *ACE* service still served an extensive network of routes and coastal resorts. A considerable level of marketing support from Waterloo continued to be poured in to the *ACE*, particularly targeting families who preferred train travel. This ensured significant passenger numbers until its final days. Unfortunately, it was not to last under Western Region and within a decade memories of a more refined restaurant car infused journey were confined to history.

Pines, Chines and Perpetual Summers

The Bournemouth Belle and The Pines Express

The *Bournemouth Belle* was one of Britain's most prestigious Pullman services. Apart from a few instances, the *Belle* remained steam-hauled until its final demise in 1967 as the line was finally electrified. When the Pullman service started, although electrification was in full swing around Southern Railway's London commuter lines, there appeared to be little appetite for the company's western division to adopt electric traction. As large amounts of coal were used in the production of electricity, coal producers saw steam locomotives, which consumed vast quantities, as primary industrial markets. Social historian Harold Perkin reminds us that coal-owners sat on railway company boards; their influence pervasive and inescapable.

Before the mid-Victorian period, Bournemouth as a resort hardly existed. Its coastal settlement in 1830 was described as a breeding place for bustard and hen-harriers, consisting of just 695 people in 1851 and not recorded separately as a development until 1871. The second half of the Victorian era saw substantial expansion as a small community developed rapidly into a town of substance. It was planned as a high-class resort and beneficial to the needs of invalids. Bournemouth's pines 'were thought to impart to the atmosphere qualities which were particularly valuable for lung patients.' With recuperative airs, the late 1800s saw Bournemouth establishing itself as a seaside resort of standing attracting a 'very superior class of visitor' but the direct railway link to Southampton and London was relatively late in arriving. Pimlott suggests that the 'growth of Bournemouth was retarded by the delay in extending the railway from Poole until 1870.' Law takes a similar view, observing 'Bournemouth's improvement commissioners resisted the arrival of the railways for many years, allowing it to maintain its exclusivity until as late as 1888.' In 1871, the population of the embryonic town was 5,896 whilst ten years later it had grown to 16,859.

Yet by the twentieth century, Bournemouth had become the third largest fully-fledged seaside resort in the country. An editorial feature, '*The Tatler's* Hotel List', recorded five hotels in the town – the Royal Bath Hotel, Bourne Hall Hotel, Hotel Metropole, Weston Hall Hotel and Hotel Mont Dore – all meeting the high standards of the publication's exacting readership. The Mont Dore Hotel, although conveniently situated with a short drive through Meyrick Park to the nearby railway halt did not last, being used as military hospital during the Great War and then subsequently purchased by the local authority in 1921 to provide the town with its impressive municipal building.

With such elegance, Bournemouth's hotels required appropriate expresses to match traveller expectations. In the 1890s, the LSWR incorporated a couple of specialist vehicles with the legend Pullman Drawing Room Car inscribed on coach sides for its direct line to the resort. The regular running of Pullman cars on Bournemouth services was widely advertised in upmarket titles at the time.

LSWR's posters attracted affluent holidaymakers; by 1912 the town was promoted as an ideal Christmas destination. *The Bystander* regarded 'Bournemouth – "City of Pines" by

Between the Victorian and Edwardian eras, Bournemouth became one of the country's most prominent tourist destinations requiring top rank train services. The Pullman car third carriage in the rake forms part of a double-headed LSWR Bournemouth express. Headed by locomotive class T9 No 285, this must have been a heavy rake and indicative of passenger demand.

This second photograph is of a stationary Pullman car together with other LSWR stock at Bournemouth Central station. The idea of inserting a single or couple of Pullman cars on to express trains was dependent on the volume of business a supplementary service could sustain. Nevertheless, this approach was also used by LBSCR for a variety of south coast routes especially for their Newhaven boat trains. (John Scott-Morgan Collection)

the Southern Sea, two hours only from London – is one of the premier homeland winter resorts. All the essentials to health and pleasure, including an abundance of sunshine and plenty of amusement, are here.' As if acknowledging an impending conflagration and the restrictions on foreign travel this would bring, the publication in the following year extolled the benefits of holidays at home, noting the merits of short-breaks in Hampshire and Dorset. 'It is along "The Path of the Sun" that the London and South-Western Railway expresses its wish to lead us, and many will follow with pleasurable obedience. For this line has indeed a positive plethora of beauty spots' that included the resorts of 'Bournemouth, Swanage', further afield 'the glades of the New Forest' and 'the dales of Dorset and Somerset'. In Edwardian times, Bournemouth gained a reputation as amongst the most fashionable of seaside resorts. Located between the town's Central and West stations, the LSWR in 1906 constructed Meyrick Park Halt with halt signage for 'golf links, cricket ground, Talbot Woods & Winton' that did much to reinforce the upmarket residential and visitor location it served.

Before the Great War, the population grew to almost 50,000 but the town retained its central features as one of the best looking and least commercial of British resorts with several highly distinctive and swanky hotels such as the Royal Bath exemplifying its image. During the early 1920s, Bournemouth benefited from a re-found enthusiasm for holidays. In the final years of pre-grouping, LSWR introduced new Ironclad superior coaching stock (also used on Southampton boat trains) to the Bournemouth route where better off tourists would be encouraged to stay for a week or two.

By the late decade, Bournemouth had cemented its reputation as one of the country's top-drawer tourist destinations. Whilst

A typical Edwardian railway scene with well-dressed passengers standing beside a shuttle service working between Bournemouth Central, West and other local stations to Poole. Sandbanks at this time would have been a comparative wilderness. (John Scott-Morgan Collection)

This rare 1916 LSWR Bournemouth destination poster by Walter Hayward Young depicted the town as a very fashionable resort. For those who could afford it, it was an ideal location to escape the travails of the Great War in both summer and winter. The collaborative role of the municipal tourism department was noticeable, inviting readers to acquire the illustrated Bournemouth guide. The broad sweep of the beach to the west of the town draws attention to the Poole side of the Chines. As early as 1907 the *Bournemouth Graphic* newspaper was reporting on visitors happily spilling over into Branksome and Upper Parkstone courtesy of the new tramway at County Gates. Poole tried to carve its own upscale niche, despite the closeness of its big neighbour, receiving in the inter-war years two impressive Southern Railway posters commending the delights of the harbour's sun, sea and sand qualities.

there would always be a degree of jostling over who was top dog, Bournemouth was always one of the premier division's leading players, consistently investing in its core destination product. Aristocratic land holdings were sold off to many municipal authorities and thus became a prominent feature of the post-war period. In Bournemouth, Sir George Tapps-Gervis-

Meyrick rid himself of his local ground rents in 1921. The extensive town-centre gardens had been a central resort feature since Edwardian times but the addition of the splendour and elegance of the Pavilion Concert Hall and Ballroom, opened in 1929, created an entertainment complex that so defined the town in the inter-war period. Bournemouth in 1923 had been chosen by the BBC as one of a select band of provincial radio stations with a broadcast output described as rather informal and dignified but mirroring much of local life and activities at the time.

Located on the swish Westover Road, regarded by many as the equivalent of London's Bond Street, the Pavilion was later extended as a theatre in 1934, whilst the glass-clad Winter Gardens, home to the Bournemouth Municipal Orchestra, was rebuilt mid-decade. The Pavilion Theatre and the Westover Road setting with its new cinemas and upscale shops was featured in railway advertising, together with the tree-lined Chines and the vast beaches of Bournemouth Bay that made the town so appealing to holidaymakers. In the years before the war, the resort would receive some two million visitors per annum. Despite these undoubted attributes, the Southern had to be convinced of the merits of launching a Pullman train, especially considering the cold winds of depression and the fact that the local populace of the then west Hampshire town had received its own upscale and direct London train – the *Bournemouth Limited* – in July 1929.

Brighton had had a long-term association with Pullman, but Bournemouth was different as it was not a day-visitor resort and, not at the time, a place of daily commuting. Charles Fryer paints a somewhat subdued view of the town, suggesting that it 'lacked the popular attractions of Brighton or Margate'. Fryer goes on to say that Bournemouth:

'was a place for rest and recuperation and, though not a place where one could "take the waters", had some of the qualities of a spa. Many nursing and convalescent homes were sited there. Affluent people retired to spend the evenings of their lives among its pine trees. Its whole atmosphere differed from that of Brighton; its culture was that of the symphony orchestra rather than the music hall.'

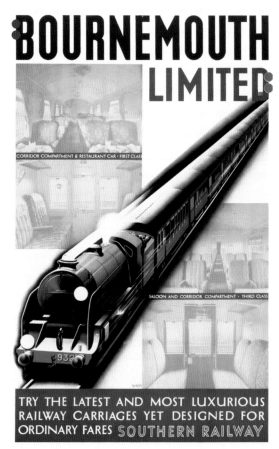

(NRM Pictorial Collection/Science & Society Library)

Bournemouth, by the late 1920s, had secured a highly prosperous resident base. The Southern Railway responded to commercial pressures by introducing a dedicated luxury service to meet the needs of the town's affluent folk heading to and from London whilst the *Bournemouth Belle* Pullman was positioned as a tourist train. The first Bournemouth Limited poster from 1929 illustrated by Patrick Cockayne Keely promoted the resort's quick and direct access being the perfect venue for winter sunshine, whilst the later 1938 poster designed by Charles Shepard highlighted new carriage stock with both open and traditional corridor seating allocated to the luxury express with its vibrant and modern malachite green livery.

Whilst some elements may be recognisable, Dr Juliet Gardiner presents us with a more upbeat assessment of what made Bournemouth such a highly attractive location for the railway visitor:

'Seaside holidays were as socially calibrated as any other activity. Some resorts attracted the middle classes whose idea of a holiday was to have a rest, stay in a "nice hotel" if they could afford it, or a boarding house if not, sit in deckchair and read, knit or doze,

BOURNEMOUTH

"BOURNEMOUTH LIMITED" NON-STOP to or from LONDON in 2 HOURS | **Illustrated Guide free** · from Town Clerk · | **CORRIDOR EXPRESS TRAINS** · · FROM ALL PARTS · ·

The *Limited* was also featured in copy as part of an outstanding 1933 Southern Railway Bournemouth destination poster. Illustrated by Henry George Gawthorn, he positioned a young couple carrying tennis rackets in the new Pavilion garden setting extolling the town's exciting upscale image. Bournemouth's out of season delights were again highlighted by Gawthorn's later 1939 'Winter in the Southern Sunshine' Westover Road poster, clearly demonstrating the company's commitment to maximizing year-round revenues.

Winter in the Southern Sunshine and Warmth of

BOURNEMOUTH

CITY GAIETY AMID RURAL SURROUNDINGS
SOUTHERN RAILWAY

stroll along the esplanade, have a knickerbocker glory in a café, listen to a band playing on the promenade bandstand, admire the municipal floral clock, maybe a game of bowls, tennis or mini-golf while the children paddled, built sandcastles, shrimped in rock pools or watched Punch and Judy on the beach.'

By the early 1930s, Bournemouth was featured extensively in heavyweight promotional activity advertised as a 'Mediterranean Watering Place' and an intrinsic part of Southern's 'Sunny South' passenger campaign. The town, uniquely situated in England's southerly latitudes, provided an enticing holiday combination of 'mild climate, villas and palm trees'.

The *Bournemouth Belle* train had a fortuitous start to life, largely driven by GWR's half-hearted Pullman engagement, resulting in Pullman cars in 1931 being returned to former LSWR metals for ocean liner specials. Periodic running of boat trains on demand provided the capacity for Pullman cars to be run as a dedicated premier-class Bournemouth train. Whilst not the ideal time to launch a brand-new luxury service, when it commenced on 5 July 1931, the *Bournemouth Belle* received considerable press coverage. *The Tatler* described Bournemouth as one of Southern Railway's 'show' resorts with a 'special and luxurious train service to be known as the *Bournemouth Belle*' but *The Illustrated Sporting And Dramatic News* took the view that the general public was still unaware of Pullman's supplementary fares. Bournemouth was still a favourite resort of *Graphic* readers viewing the new 'Special' as good news. *The Sphere*, on the other hand, must have received a personal escorted tour as they waxed lyrical about the new enterprise that must have been music to the ears of the local tourist board burghers:

'In summer and autumn, the railway journey to Bournemouth is particularly delightful, for it traverses the woodland beauty of the New Forest, through the heart of which one passes between Lyndhurst Road and Christchurch. Then there is, when one leaves the luxurious first and third-class Pullman of which the "Bournemouth Belle" entirely consists, Bournemouth itself, with its glorious bay, miles of sandy beach, striking cliffs, public parks and gardens, steamboat excursions, motor-coach tours, golf, bathing, tennis, indoor amusements of all kinds including facilities for dancing at the King's Hall and elsewhere, and last but by no means least its magnificent Pavilion with all sorts

This dazzling Southern Railway poster of the early days of the *Bournemouth Belle* hauled by one of its latest top-line locomotives. Classic umber and cream cars defined the luxury Pullman product in the inter-war years. The illustration by H Molenaar in this 1933 treatment would be later adapted in further later Southern *Bournemouth Belle* posters of the inter-war period. (NRM Pictorial Collection/Science & Society Library)

The 1930s 'Winter in Warmth at Bournemouth' posters illustrated by Langhammer was a collaborative effort between railway companies and the local tourist authority. Southern Railway's execution shown here also had an LMS version using the same poster layout but with copy changes highlighting 'Travel by the "Pines" Express'".

of attractions, and a fine Municipal Orchestra. Add to these a particularly interesting and beautiful surrounding country, which makes it so admirable a centre for holiday makers.'

The *Bournemouth Belle* was a summer-only service, running on weekdays and continuing to be so until mid-decade. The train initially comprised first-class cars from Great Western's experiment; *Evadne, Loraine, Ione, Joan, Juana, Eunice* and *Zena* as well as six twelve-wheeled cars from LNER's *Queen of Scots* train. Most of the stock was relatively new having been built between 1920 and 1925 but the initial ten car train contained four new third-class Pullman cars nos. 81-4. The Weymouth extension discontinued after the first season but in its first years of operation, a winter-time Sunday Bournemouth service also operated. From 1 January 1936, the service became a daily train available all year around. Stopping only at Southampton, the express Pullman was stylish, very popular with affluent passengers and well patronised with a rake of up to twelve Pullman cars running at the busiest of times. Southern's Sir John Elliot noted that the *Bournemouth Belle* was popular, arousing considerable interest and the affection of thousands of holiday passengers using Southern. Like most Pullman services during the Second World War, the *Bournemouth Belle* was suspended with the opening shots of hostilities in 1939. Kidner says the train 'suffered the indignity of being pushed into Tolworth goods sidings' but like the *Brighton Belle* sets, its non-use ensured long-term durability.

The Pullman recommenced duties on 7 October 1946, providing Southern's new Pacific Merchant Navy Class locomotives with the perfect opportunity to stretch their legs over a decent run. No. 21C18 *British India Line*, then just over a year old, hauled the inaugural run of the reinstated service made up of ten Pullman cars weighing over 400 tons. The service would also be used for new locomotive experimentation; diesel-electric no. 10202 locomotive was seen hauling the *Belle* in the early 1950s. Having been parked up for most of the war period, the train's reappearance was very much welcomed by the travelling public. Fryer sums up the mood impeccably:

'After wartime neglect much of the Southern Railway's ordinary coaching stock was in a poor state and to travel in a train that was not only luxurious but clean, with bookable seats and refreshments to hand, was an experience which made the modest supplement seem negligible.'

The down all-Pullman *Bournemouth Belle* express just passing Weybridge in 1947. Headed by Southern Railway Merchant Navy Pacific 4-6-2 no. 21C11 *General Steam Navigation* in glorious malachite green livery helped to spice up the drabness of the immediate post-war years. (John Scott-Morgan Collection)

Nevertheless, post-war resumption of the *Belle* was different, reflecting for the first-time the changing nature of luxury travel. Like the immediate post First World War period, a similar situation occurred a generation later as pent-up demand for continental travel was again unleashed. The lure of exciting holiday destinations abroad for those with the money to spend was always intoxicating, especially as new national short-haul airlines were ideally placed to service such needs. So, the *Belle* was run with only four first-class cars, with the remainder of the heavyweight eleven or twelve-carriage train – sometimes approaching 500 tons – catering for third-class passengers but a customer base still willing to pay the Pullman supplement.

BOURNEMOUTH
BRITAIN'S ALL-SEASON RESORT
EXPRESS TRAINS FROM WATERLOO THROUGH TRAINS FROM THE
'BOURNEMOUTH BELLE' DAILY   MIDLANDS AND NORTH
GUIDE BOOK 6d FROM INFORMATION BUREAU BOURNEMOUTH

By the early 1950s, Bournemouth's railway destination initiatives had been passed to British Railways, who positioned the town as Britain's premier all-season resort and easily accessible from all parts of the country. Using a well-tried format, Sir Herbert Alker Tripp's illustration captures the bay setting with particular emphasis on the vista towards the east of the Bournemouth and Boscombe Piers. In many ways it is a re-interpretation of Walter Hayward Young's 1916 LSWR work.

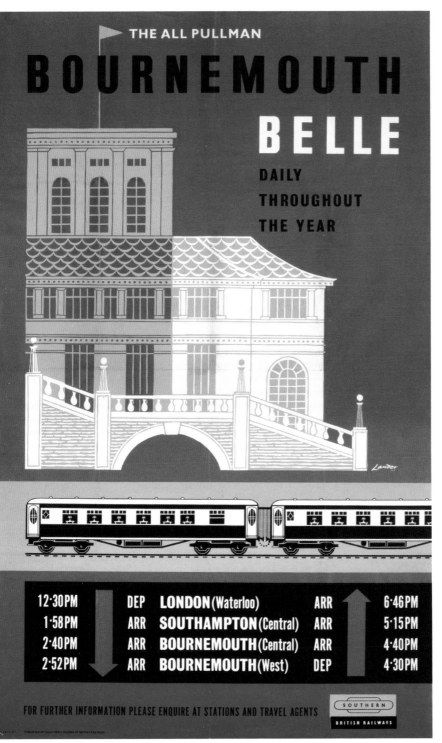

Some thirty years after its launch, the *Bournemouth Belle* could still guarantee a marketing budget for dedicated posters. Illustrated by Reginald Montague Lander, the creative approach still utilised the Pavilion building to showcase the resort. (National Railway Museum/ Science & Society Picture Library)

Bournemouth was now a broader-based destination but for the middle-classes the resort still had a pull. The *Bournemouth Belle*, according to John Baker White, a former MP (and spook) who had conducted a nationwide survey of Britain's hotel and tourist industry, was part of a trilogy of glamorous Pullman trains including the *Golden Arrow* and the *Brighton Belle* which were probably the most comfortable trains in the world, providing an unexcelled standard of personal service meeting the high expectations of overseas visitors. The *Bournemouth Belle* was popular to the end of its days running on many occasions with a steam hauled service until line electrification and the introduction of the new buffet/restaurant-car multiple-unit trains.

In 1960, the *Belle* received a batch of former east coast stock including twelve-wheeled cars, giving the train a real vintage look and feel. Its composition also changed in the later years as the train's two K Class brake coaches were removed, replaced by new standard Mk I BG full brake carriages. Certain conventions applied to premier services even in British Railways days, as ordinary passenger-carrying brake coaches would not do, as multi-coloured green, maroon, blue and grey liveried full brakes were added to the Pullman rake. A matching chocolate and cream Western Region BG was even purloined from an inter-regional train much to the annoyance of the region's management. But the kaleidoscope of colour did not deter passengers, as one former railwayman from Bournemouth shed reported delighted holiday makers still streaming off the *Belle* at Central towards the end of the service.

Southern Region, in fact, had been offered the six-car *Blue Pullman* sets as replacement stock for the *Bournemouth Belle* but had declined the offer, probably due to the reputation of the DMU train's poor riding quality. By time of *Bournemouth Belle's* final running on 9 July 1967, hauled by a Brush Type 4 diesel locomotive, the carriages were life expired, requiring urgent upgrade. Unfortunately, despite demand for British Rail's new Pullman approaches, with a focus of running Pullman services on InterCity routes, the Southampton to Bournemouth line never qualified and did not get a look in. As railway journalist Brian Haresnape noted, 'line electrification was only justified by a narrow economic margin, which was achieved by making the 'new' electric trains from rebuilt 1951-design BR standard Mk I carriages. The added cost of providing Pullman-type accommodation was prohibitive'.

Pullman had brought railway romance to the south coast, but Bournemouth would have to wait again for the best part of another

The train's Pullman cars in the last few weeks of operation were by now looking a little worn but still attract a mainline steam-hauled Waterloo presence. (Neil Davenport/ Online Transport Archive)

A grubby looking Light Pacific no. 34001 is in charge of the *Bournemouth Belle* but still looks impressive running through Clapham Junction in May 1966. Marcus Eavis/Online Transport Archive

twenty years until the *Belmond British Pullman* dining trains started running again making periodic appearances to the resort. But it was well worth waiting for, as Fryer records. 'As a passenger experience, travel on the *Bournemouth Belle* was more rewarding than on any other possible Pullman journeys in southern England.' As an international destination, Bournemouth has retained its resort image. The local tourist authority would argue even now that the towns of Poole, Bournemouth and Christchurch have maintained an oasis of middle-class values, and as one of Britain's premier destinations they have never lost that certain degree of former elegance and panache. Certainly, multi-millionaire Premiership footballers seem to agree; Sandbanks and its environs provide the perfect village refuge.

There will be those who argue that the *Pines Express* was never a luxury train. Yet the route to the north of the country from Bournemouth via Bath cemented two important tourist centres to the Midland Railway and Somerset and Dorset system. Trains travelling on this route contained substantial first-class sections, ferrying northern elites to Bath (and Bristol) and then a few years later on to Bournemouth West. Midland's Bath Green Park station was a classic statement of Victorian architecture when opened in 1870. Designed by the company's architect John Holloway Sanders, the impressive structure blended well with Bath's Georgian facades, providing the right atmosphere to attract well-off travellers to the city. By 1874, the terminus was linked to the Somerset and Dorset Railway, providing a new route between the industrial north of England and the elegant resort of Bournemouth, the New Forest and Dorset's coastal communities well and truly putting the route on the Victorian holiday map. By the turn of the twentieth century, the resort started to receive large numbers of visitors from the Midlands and the north of England as well as London based holiday traffic. The *Clifton Society* reported in June 1895, 'The tourist season is now upon us. As usual the arrangements made by the Somerset and Dorset Railway are very liberal with excursion tickets available from three to fifteen days'. The same publication reported on 1908 Easter holiday business. 'On the Somerset and Dorset Joint Line Bournemouth continues to attract a large number of people, and the bookings from Bath, on Monday, were heavy, 222'.

From October 1910, express holiday trains from the north ran into Bournemouth West station over the Somerset and Dorset route via LSWR connections at Corfe Mullen and Broadstone providing

BOURNEMOUTH
The Centre of Health & Pleasure
Guide Book free from Publicity Manager, Town Hall, Bournemouth.

TRAVEL BY L M S "PINES" EXPRESS FROM THE NORTH & MIDLANDS

This inter-war poster, illustrated by Leonard Richmond, highlights the *Pines Express* service with its direct access and ease of transport to the resort from northern England and the Midlands. The creative approach used by LMS in this poster differs slightly from the glamorous town-centre stylisation endorsed by Southern and the Great Western. The bay view is from the Boscombe end of the town noted for its village atmosphere and more populous numbers of guest houses and smaller hotels.

the direct Bournemouth link. For the first time, the joint Midland Railway and LSWR services were flavoured with an unofficial naming of the *Pines Express* and a direct response to the Great Western's Birkenhead and Bournemouth offering. Business was

This inter-war Great Western poster by G. D. Tidmarsh was clearly targeted at upscale visitors from its stations in the Midlands and the north of England. The illustration of a well-dressed woman overlooking the Bournemouth Pavilion, the beach, pier approaches and the bay was probably based on a balcony view from newly constructed art deco styled four-star Palace Court Hotel.

BOURNEMOUTH

FOR HEALTH & PLEASURE

Illustrated Guide free from Town Clerk

EXPRESS SERVICE & CHEAP FARES GWR

FROM THIS STATION

brisk for GWR as the company continued to promote its northern line access with dedicated Bournemouth posters until the beginning of the Second World War.

By the spring of 1927, LMS recognised the potential of the Bath and Bournemouth route to drive upscale tourist traffic from its Bradford, Leeds and Sheffield heartlands as well as from Bath and nearby Bristol, all linked to the company's system. The *Pines Express* had been an informal title used for some years, although it did not receive LMS's official sanction until 7 May 1928. Yet by 1927, the company were highlighting the destination in northern newspapers as 'LMS Bournemouth for Sunshine' with an advertising strapline of 'The Land of Chines and Pines' promoting through express restaurant car trains. Tourist tickets were sold daily whilst in addition, short-break weekend-tickets were issued on Fridays and Saturdays to capture potential end of season travellers. Not only had there been a long LSWR/Midland Railway association followed by the Southern/LMS relationship, the GWR had for many years taken the opportunity to promote Bournemouth as a leading destination to northern audiences.

The company positioned the town in its advertising as 'Britain's all-seasons' resort', running expresses through to the town from the north of England. Bournemouth was included on the October 1929 itinerary of the American Tourist Agents' Tour of Britain, with the party reaching the town via the Somerset and Dorset line. Whilst the Great Western did not have any direct association with this route, the company had been involved with the well-established Birkenhead and Bournemouth service as well as a long-term reputation for working well with tourism partners in America.

Inter-regional services continued to funnel into Bournemouth for much of the first half of the 1900s, which also included an LNER train linking the town directly with Newcastle and the north east. Yet it was the *Pines* named train that attracted public attention; the thousands of pine trees adorning the Chines were a long-term Bournemouth image feature. The *Pines Express* cemented the Somerset and Dorset's reputation, becoming as familiar a south coast train as its famed Pullman *Bournemouth Belle* countryman. The *Pines* and the Somerset and Dorset line for a large part of the twentieth century was one and the same; its closure, according to Michael Williams, has 'generated more melancholy, more nostalgia and a greater sense of loss than any other of the lines that Beeching closed'.

London by Sea

The Southern Belle and Brighton Belle Pullmans

LBSCR's Brighton route had seen regular Pullman working since the last quarter of Victorian times. It seems an odd location to select a route for the country's first frequent (more than one journey) truly luxury service. Yet Brighton possessed a curious mix of residents. True it had its upmarket populace, but the town had grown rapidly in Victorian times assuming the mantle of 'London by Sea' becoming both a commuter town and destination. The railway company, described as a 'snobbish outfit', did not want to be known solely for carrying third-class excursionists.

By the end of the 1870s, the town's resident population had swollen significantly to around 80,000. With the provision of a Pullman service, LBSCR could maintain a superior market position attracting prosperous customers who grew significantly in numbers during summer months. Promotional literature by the mid-1880s pronounced Brighton as a town filled with London society in the fashionable season; guide-books described the wonders of the pavilion and the pace of development of the 'great watering-place' resort. Oliver Wendell Holmes noted Brighton was a 'magnificent city built for enjoyment'. His week-long visit left a huge impression.

> 'Many watering-places look forlorn and desolate in the intervals of "the season". This was not the time of Brighton's influx of visitors, but the city was far from dull. The houses are very large, and have the grand air, as if meant for princes; the shops are well supplied; the salt breeze comes in fresh and wholesome, and the noble esplanade is lively with promenaders.'

Holmes, a medical doctor, also put the town on his 'hygienic map' observing the qualities of Brighton for the aid of bronchial problems.

LBSCR first piloted the Pullman idea in 1875, borrowing Midland's *Mars* parlour car. The carriage was purported to have stayed with LBSCR for some time, with the trial extended with three further individual Pullman cars during following years, *Alexandra*, *Albert Edward* and *Globe*. Still, it was not until 5 December 1881 that a complete all-Pullman four coach express service was developed. These stylish Pullman cars were not brand new but were built at Midland's Derby works some years before and named after royal children. *Globe* was renamed *Beatrice*, followed by *Louise*, *Maud* and *Victoria*.

The inaugural run, dubbed the *Pullman Limited Express,* offered an upper-class drawing room atmosphere where passengers could relax in restful surroundings and in more spacious compartments. The Pullman offering provided innovation in rail travel (for a price) which was over and above the so-called first-class service provided by the main railway companies. In cold weather, the Pullman car's interior was comfortably warm, thanks to an oil-fired stove heating a hot water system making foot warmers unnecessary, toilet and wash basin facilities were provided and a polite request would bring tea and freshly-prepared sandwiches from *Victoria's* pantry buffet, all delivered by uniformed staff in attendance. These elements comprised the complete package of romance, luxury and personal attention. The London and Brighton Pullman was really the first complete Pullman train in Britain and despite Midland's efforts on its Anglo-Scottish expresses was perhaps instrumental in registering in the minds of the travelling public the notion of Pullman as synonymous with a regular and superior first-class service.

Of the original four Pullman cars, *Beatrice,* is accredited as being the first railway carriage in the world to be electrically lit. On a trial trip in October 1881, Pincaffe and Lachlan, engineers of the French Fauré Accumulator Company, switched on the lights in the first tunnel and kept them on all the way back from Brighton to London. Since the train made several unadvertised stops, the Frenchmen rather feared the lights would go out before the train could arrive. This did not happen, much to the annoyance of gas engineers who were busy promoting established gas technology to the railways. Gas companies rather conveniently overlooked the fact that escaping gas invariably turned railway accidents into infernos, by setting the smashed woodwork of the carriages ablaze – something that was going to occur for some time into the twentieth century until the arrival of steel-paneled stock. For Fauré, who designed the equipment, it was a triumph and likewise for George Pullman, who naturally introduced electric lighting to his

American Pullman cars. Pullman continued to put great emphasis on developing the British market for luxury travel and on 2 June 1882 registered his British Pullman Palace Car Co. as a separate legal entity and a subsidiary of the Chicago based US company.

The fifteen-year Pullman sleeping car contract with the Midland Railway expired in February 1888 and was not renewed. Pullman had not been able to interest either LNWR or the Great Western with his wares and as Brian Haresnape noted 'he (Pullman) turned his attention to one company that did like him – the London, Brighton & South Coast Railway'. Pullman services became the norm on the line when on 11 December 1888, three new dedicated Pullman cars – *Prince* (buffet), *Princess* (ladies) and *Albert Victor* (smoking) – were added and joined by a LBSCR six-wheeled railway van painted in Pullman livery to house a dynamo providing power for lighting. Another was added in 1895, along with a further three Pullman cars – *Her Majesty*, *Duchess of York* and *Princess of Wales*. The two matching vans were known as Pullman pups, so at busier times the two pups would be placed at the end of an up to six car Pullman express formation.

These facilities were additionally provided on Newhaven continental boat trains and other LBSCR routes such as Eastbourne and Hastings where passengers similarly paid a premium fare. The Brighton Pullman service was officially known as the Pullman Limited Express and the Pullman Limited – a non-stop service. On 2 October 1898, a new Pullman service was introduced for the Brighton line known as the *Brighton Limited* although it had to wait until 1899 to appear in official timetable and accompanying marketing literature. The Sunday-only service (which ran from October to June) together with the daily unnamed Pullman service became so popular that further changes were on the horizon. Visitor interest in the town increased as further amenities were added. Pullman writer Antony Ford records developments taking place at the time which saw a 'substantial building programme, involving an extension to the promenade by a further six miles; the addition of a new outdoor swimming pool, water gardens and renovated aquarium, together with a seemingly implacable building of attractive lodges and small hotels'.

In the early 1900s, some of the fastest Brighton runs were recorded by 4-4-0 Class locomotives but the LBSCR was to turn to specially tailored tank locomotives to man its Pullman services, dispelling

From the turn of the twentieth century, the Brighton Pullman clerestory service is headed by one of a dozen class 2-2-2 locomotives built for the LBSCR between 1880 and 1881. These were a long-running locomotive class with some stock lasting up until the eve of the Great War. The second image shows the newly branded down *Southern Belle* taken at Tooting Bec. Headed by LBSCR class 2-2-2 locomotive no. 329 Stephenson, it clearly shows a mix of traditional clerestory and the more modern elliptical Pullman stock so likely to date from around the second half of the Edwardian era. The third photograph is from an earlier period where the clerestory Pullman cars were still painted in their original dark mahogany brown and gold lining livery. (John Scott-Morgan Collection)

the myth they were steam locomotive poor relatives. A series of powerful acceleration 4-6-2T and 4-6-4T Class locomotives was introduced to cope with the dense network of many lines crossing over each other and in hauling heavy, well patronized Pullman with loads of more than 280 tons. At the same time, three further cars were ordered by the company; *The Arundel*, *The Chichester* and *The Devonshire*. In 1906, the first of three new thirty-five ton, tri-axle bogie wood panelled Pullman coaches appeared on the route. These were named *Princess Ena, Princess Patricia* and *Duchess of Norfolk*. All of them were painted for the first time in the umber or white and chocolate brown livery which was to be later adopted as the standard LBSCR livery.

By this period, locomotives were painted in umber so matching the same colour scheme used on Pullman cars. These clerestory-roofed cars were the last to be sourced directly from Illinois, marking the end of the first Pullman era. In 1907 the British Pullman Palace Car Company was secretly acquired by Sir Davidson Dalziel (later Lord Dalziel of Wooler). He financed the purchase of new rolling stock through another of his companies, the Drawing Room Car Company. A new train, a new owner and a dashing Edwardian age required a new name.

Prior to this, all of Pullman's operations were concentrated on short-distance routes, although the LSWR experimented with Pullman stock to Southampton and Bournemouth. Because its business model was based on passengers paying a supplementary fee, a feature some railway companies disliked intensely, Pullman was never ever able to extend its operation universally across Britain's railway network. Changes were afoot though as the British Pullman Palace Car Company had been acquired from the trustees of George Mortimer Pullman, who had died ten years earlier and were now in the hands of Dalziel. Since his death, the Pullman business in the United States had been run by Robert Todd Lincoln, the son of the late president. Whilst not exactly ignoring their British operations and European interests, the Pullman Company was firmly entrenched in expanding its US interests. Fortuitous timing for Dalziel – a Wagon-Lits director since 1893 – who had overseen the company's rapid European development. He had the ability to transform the British business, merging the best ideas from London's finest dining establishments by transferring these initiatives to the railway carriage. This Dalziel achieved through close co-operation with a small number of railway companies

The three following photographs collectively demonstrate the majesty of the *Southern Belle*. The first shows the new rake of Pullman cars post 1908 hauled by LBSCR class B4 4-4-0 locomotive no. 46 *Prince of Wales*. The B4s worked the heaviest of express trains until withdrawn around 1912 and were considered by commentators as some of the finest locomotives of their day. The location is south of Coulsdon heading towards the coast.

through the financing of an extensive carriage building programme of newly branded Pullman dining cars designed for luxury daytime travel. Besides, the leading railway companies by this stage had well and truly got to grips with the catering side of the passenger transport business. Dalziel's initiatives were ground-breaking and built with an empathy towards the discriminating needs of Edwardian consumers. To develop an elegant and profitable travel business model, Dalziel selected a group of pre-grouping railway operators that had faith in his ideas. By doing so, the image of the British Pullman Company was changed to a progressive organisation with new initiatives such as the naming and active promotion of the flagship *Southern Belle*.

The second involves LBSCR's Atlantic no. 40 as the train approaches Brighton. The introduction of five striking H1 class locomotives between December 1905 and February 1906, numbered 37 to 41, and a further six later superheated H2 Atlantic class engines introduced between June 1911 and January 1912, did much to cement the image of the *Southern Belle* as they were reserved for prestigious workings establishing new standards of speed and reliability. Ironically, by 1910 it was estimated some thirty per cent of the company's stock was in the queue for repair accounting for a varied mix of locomotive classes recorded hauling the Pullman train.

LBSCR's luxury train was born for the Brighton route, although there is some dispute as to when the *Southern Belle* ran for the first time; 1 November 1908 now appears to be generally accepted start date. It was a sumptuous seven-car train, operating seven days per week and all year-round catering well for Brighton's image as a very well-to-do town characterized by its tea rooms, hotels, beaches and clean air all frequented by a chic clientele. Hamilton Ellis captures the period wonderfully. 'In public estimation, as well as in fact, the train *arrived*. People flocked to it. The briefly great reign of

In April 1914 the LBSCR introduced a powerful new class of 4-6-4 tank locomotives, known as Brighton Baltics, for the south coast routes. Despite their operational success, and the fact they were the last LBSCR locomotives to be built at Brighton, a group of individuals considered their use did little to promote the commercial success and image of the then world's most luxurious train. In this picture, no. 332 is seen leaving Brighton station. (John Scott-Morgan Collection)

King Edward VII was at its zenith, and far more imposing than the more recent flight of Halley's Comet!'

New Pullman stock was built in Britain for the first time by Birmingham-based Metropolitan Amalgamated Carriage and Wagon Co. Ltd. Carriage design was now distinctly British-looking, less American in appearance, mirroring coach developments found elsewhere on Britain's railways. The *Southern Belle* included car names like *Belgravia* and *Grosvenor* and was billed as 'the most luxurious train in the world' designed to encourage bands of first-class passengers to the resort. It was also the first Pullman train to be built in England with double bogie twelve-wheeled cars that had modern-looking elliptical rather than clerestory

This poster from the NRM's portfolio is from around 1920 although there is some doubt over its source; either LBSCR or Brighton Tourist Board. Produced in the *Southern Belle* era, it demonstrated the resort's year-round destination attributes. Using a creative theme of health and pleasure, the sea airs could be gently taken in on Madeira Drive's well-known sheltered walk which Brighton had become famous for. (NRM Pictorial Collection/Science & Society Library)

THE FAMOUS SHELTERED WALK, MADEIRA DRIVE.

roofs. Internally, the cars reflected three different decorative styles mimicking approaches taken on many new luxury ocean liners.

A French Renaissance style was applied to *Verona* and *Albert*. *Princess Helen*, *Grosvenor* and *Bessborough* had an Adams style finish whilst *Belgravia* and *Cleopatra* incorporated a Pergolesi finish. Pullman cars were built with internal mahogany panelling, fine soft coloured carpeting, damask silk blinds and settees in green morocco all appealing to lady passengers. Due to the comparatively short journey, catering arrangements remained minimal. Food and drink were served by attendants from a central kitchen and pantry section within the *Grosvenor* car. From 1910, the journey frequency was increased to twice daily on Monday to Friday services. Further Pullman cars were built in 1911 to support demand for the commercial success of the *Southern Belle* service.

Dalziel, wishing to maximize his investment, caused a sensation by introducing third-class Pullman cars in 1915 for a new type of customer who wanted a treat but felt out of place in first-class. With a third-class ticket, it was possible to travel on any of the many inexpensive day excursions from London to Brighton. For most people, this meant that, once installed on a Pullman service in one of the opulent third-class seats, the day-excursionist could enjoy the same impeccable service as that of first-class for a modest supplementary fare of one shilling and sixpence. Changes to the running order came with the Great War but by March 1919 the *Southern Belle* resumed as a Sunday service. Pullman services were suspended during the coal strike of spring 1921 but continued thereafter without problems. During the summer, the twice daily LBSCR *Southern Belle* service formed part of a broader and well-established 'England's Sunny South' tourism promotion.

By July 1924, the Southern had come into being and was reflected a broader and more inclusive service; first-class Sunday only and first and third-class services at all other times. Post-grouping was a time of steady expansion for Pullman; *Southern Belle* received further Pullman cars rebuilt from First World War ambulance trains; *Iolanthe*, *Viking* and *Rosamund* were the additional supplements. The *Southern Belle* remained a steam service until replaced by the new electrified *Brighton Belle*. But it was well-worn when steam traction finally finished, having carried four and a half million passengers between London and Brighton and run over one and a quarter million miles, equivalent to fifty times around the globe. So, echoing the many Royal names used on the Brighton Pullmans over

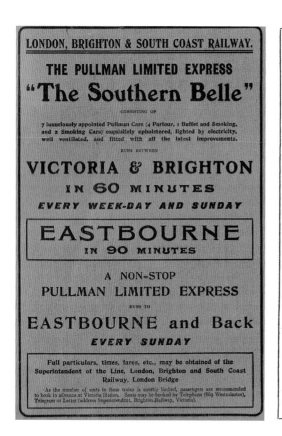

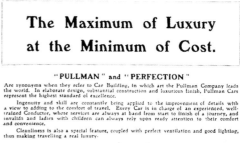

LBSCR and the Pullman Company over the years combined to produce a significant variety of marketing literature to promote the *Southern Belle*. (James S. Baldwin)

the years: 'The *Southern Belle* is dead – long live the *Brighton Belle*' might have been the Victoria station announcement as the Brighton steam-hauled Pullman ended its days in June 1934.

Almost immediately, the *Brighton Belle* became a celebrity - one of the world's best known and loved trains. Yet when it commenced service in 1934, the fifty-three-mile line between London and Brighton had had a Pullman service for the best part of fifty years. In 1929, a decision was made to electrify the line from London to Brighton with work lasting four years. The Southern Electric (drawing power from a third live conductor rail) as the system was snappily called, evolved under the direction of Sir Herbert Walker, general manager of the Southern Railway. His board's business strategy was to electrify suburban lines – a process that had been begun by the LBSCR before the Great War. They had used overhead wires but Southern adopted a third rail option as a more convenient and less expensive solution to push coastal electrification. But there was still a significant financial cost; almost £2,750,000 to take electrification to Brighton past the London suburban electrified area.

Electrification was then extended to Hove, Shoreham-by-Sea and Worthing in the west and Lewes, Seaford, Bexhill and Eastbourne to the east. By 1938, the third rail had reached Littlehampton but not everyone was happy with coastal route electrification as the Central Division line was plagued by the 'rattle, noise and lack of smooth running on the London-Brighton section.' Yet during the inter-war period, Brighton proved to be an extremely popular day visitor destination. The *Daily Herald* reported in Easter 1933 that over 150,000 passengers had been taken to the popular resort, more than the total population of the town itself.

Overall visitor numbers were on the up; the increase of £72,000 per year in gross receipts to cover new and old capital costs for electrification was recovered in the first six months, representing a twenty-two per cent increase in passengers. With this kind of volume, Brighton was never going to be deprived of its premier Pullman after over half a century of profitable service. By December 1932, the new deluxe electric Pullman units – *Southern Belle* as they were then known – were being trialled to selected media. In response to the opportunity of the electrified line, the Pullman Company ordered a complete set of new Pullman trains built by Metro-Cammell Carriage & Wagon Company of Birmingham. From the front, the third-class motor parlour brake cars looked just like the stock used elsewhere on Southern's electrified lines but

By ELECTRIC to BRIGHTON

On November 15 the Prince of Wales inspected the central control tower at Three Bridges of the new electric line to Brighton which was opened yesterday by the Lord Mayor.

The whole of the track has now become electrified, the rolling stock nearing completion, and daily trials are constantly taking place. In this connection the writer has recently had the opportunity of making a trial trip in one of these all-electric trains *de luxe*, when it was found that nothing had been spared in their construction to make the journey an ideal one for the passenger.

Space will not permit the writer to comment on all the interesting characteristics to be found on this new electrified service. It is, therefore, proposed to make reference to such points as should appeal to the general public.

There will be two distinct types of Pullman trains in operation—the "Southern Belle" unit, consisting of five coaches, and the "City Limited" unit (which will be mainly for the use of the business man), consisting of six coaches, each unit containing one Pullman car.

The company propose to run every hour two non-stop trains, two fast trains stopping at principal stations, and two trains stopping at all stations. In slack periods of the day these electric trains will be made up of six coaches, whilst twelve coaches will operate during the rush hours.

The question of fares has been given every consideration, and throughout the year there will be a service of cheap trips, including the ordinary excursions—in fact the whole section, having now become electrified (no steam trains running over the Brighton route after January 1 next), existing fares now operating will continue as before.

In taking a brief survey throughout the various compartments on these trains, which are all of the corridor type, one is impressed with the attractive panel designs which have been introduced into the coaches—beautifully varnished pictures worked in wood appear in the panels throughout the coaches in various colour designs.

The driver's cab is quite a compact arrangement, containing simple mechanism for successfully controlling the train, whilst a periscope has been fitted in the guard's compartment by which he is able to constantly view, in a comfortable seat, the whole length of the train.

An interesting development has been made in the construction of certain of the coaches by introducing a small four-seat coupé compartment, which can be reserved for parties of four passengers, and may be termed the "family compartment"—the seats, of the armchair type, can be moved to any position required.

The lighting throughout the train is certainly the "last word" in electrical schemes of train lighting. Apart from mural and central roof lights, individual seats possess an electric light which is operated by switches, so that the passenger may switch "on" or "off" as desired. In the Pullman section small electric push buttons have been fixed into the back of the seats which communicate with the attendant on the train by the flashing of a small red light, this indication being conveyed to the attendant's compartment as to the particular passenger requiring his services.

The ventilation throughout the train is certainly worthy of note. By the system introduced, a constant supply of fresh air is conveyed throughout the train, with outlets for extracting impurities. There is no need to open windows to obtain a fresh supply.

The approximate seating accommodation on the new electric trains is as follows—"Southern Belle" (five-car unit), 40 first-class passengers, 152 third-class passengers. "City Limited" (six-car unit), 92 first-class passengers, 226 third-class passengers.

To conclude, it may here be mentioned that the lighting section on the trains is a separately controlled unit which would not be affected should a breakdown occur in the train service.

THE FIVE-CAR UNIT of the "Southern Belle." Every hour two non-stop, two fast, and two "stopping at all stations" trains are to be run over the new electrified rails

AT THE RED HILL SUB-STATION : The insulators to safeguard the tremendous power carried by the cables of the new electrified line from London to Brighton

LUXURY is the keynote of the new line. The third-class compartments excel in comfort and opulence of appointment many first-class carriages

ON THE "SOUTHERN BELLE" : A first-class car designated "Type A." This particular coach is named "Iris." All the trains are made up of corridor type coaches

A SIX-CAR UNIT known as "The City Limited" which, designed for the use mainly of business men, is composed of one Pullman car and five other coaches

The Sphere cultivated a close relationship for its readers with Britain's inter-war railway companies especially in projecting a modern image. The electrification of Southern's suburban lines as well as its routes to Brighton and other coastal resorts with all new electric luxury Pullman trains and carriages were big news features at the time. (Illustrated London News Ltd/Mary Evans)

they had no through corridors. They were likewise the heaviest coaches used in Britain at the time weighing in at sixty-two tons, but they were finished in Pullman's corporate umber and chocolate brown branding and bore the Pullman badge below the driver's windows – known as the 'motorman'. The motor brakes (or parlours) contained four large electric motors each sufficient to power the heavy train (especially with a full complement of passengers) but still sufficient space to incorporate luggage compartments – passengers still travelled with heavy trunks and suitcases in the 1930s. Pullman also anticipated greater usage of the *Brighton Belle* electrified service so the motorized brake parlours and third parlour were built with slightly cramped 2+2 seating in contrast to 2+1 on other steam-hauled Pullman trains.

The *Brighton Belle* was the world's first regular Pullman all-electric service although the 'first' accolade might have gone to Europe with the *Golden Mountain Pullman Express* – a short-lived service which began in 1931 and lasted only for one season. The *Brighton Belle* immediately became the country's premier electric train service and at once the most famous electric multiple-unit (EMU) in the world. The 5-BEL (its Southern designation) EMU was officially

The *Brighton Belle* was featured in its own bespoke promotion. Speed, directness and frequency were used to support the service in this 1934 Shep poster. Destination-led themes were also close at hand with this 1935 Southern Railway poster illustrated by Chas Pears. Brighton's direct and easy access with through trains from all parts of the country were also key messages as well as the availability of local authority tourist brochures. (NRM Pictorial Collection/Science & Society Library)

renamed by Margaret Hardy, the Brighton mayor on 29 June of 1934. Indeed, it simply became known as the *Belle* (there were in fact three sets of five car units) characterized by plush decor, deep armchairs and pink lampshades and known for providing a regular and timely non-stop service from London to the south coast in style. The *Brighton Belle* was different to the original vintage Pullman carriages first introduced to its other mainline prestige competitor – the *Golden Arrow* in 1929 – but was like the Arrow's new steel-sided stock delivered in 1930. The *Brighton Belle* introduced a new lexicon for train travel. Art Deco and Jazz-Modern were adjectives used to describe the new Pullman train's surroundings. The *Brighton Belle* was also a main-line seaside special, being the ultimate party train, a train for late-risers and promoted for party outings and evenings by the sea. The *Brighton Belle* offered a slightly decadent and racy form of luxury attracting the ranks of royalty on occasions when they visited Brighton. King Boris of Bulgaria, who listed train driving amongst his hobbies, was content to talk to the motormen on a private trip to the town in 1938.

The *Brighton Belle* thus began its legendary existence destined to outlive all the other Southern and British Railway era *Belle Pullman* services. The train with its initial three-trip Monday to Saturday and two-trip Sunday schedules became the railway's crown jewels. In later years, the frequency of trips increased to six and four respectively and once the service became housed in Brighton, two additional trips were built into the timetable, making eight Monday to Saturday journeys each way. The *Brighton Belle* had become renowned for its punctuality as a sixty-minute non-stop service; it had entered folklore. The heyday of the *Brighton Belle* service was extremely popular with Brighton-based theatricals as they could rely on its timings to get them to and from work in London. In the days before celebrity culture, the *Belle* was a train to be seen on; a kind of 'autograph album on wheels'. The *Brighton Belle's* longevity in some part was due to its wartime history. With the outbreak of war in 1939, the *Brighton Belle*, in common with all other titled trains, had their title and destination roof boards removed. Unit 3052 was damaged by bombing at Victoria station on 9 October 1940 and taken out of service. After a first short withdrawal for the National Emergency, the *Brighton Belle* began running again, albeit with rationed food and customers as well as staff who had been up all night on duty in the Home Guard. Subsequent bombing made it necessary to withdraw all Pullman cars in May 1942, hiding them in unlikely places for their own protection. The *Brighton Belle* was eventually reinstated following repair to unit 3052 on 6 October 1947.

The *Brighton Belle* entered nationalized British Railways operation the following year and began a long period of almost uninterrupted service life. The wartime break and the less intensive use of the three sets of unit stock allowed one to form a Sunday only *Eastbourne Pullman* service until 1957. By the early 1960s, though, the lady was beginning to show her age. There were some attempts to modernize the *Belle's* image and by mid-decade, the appearance of the train's power unit ends were modified with changes to lining out and the imposition of an elongated Pullman crest in place of the traditional style that had adorned the vehicles since original manufacture.

In 1967, the Pullman Division had completely passed into British Rail hands with the *Belle* refurbished and repainted in the standardized British Rail blue and grey livery much to the chagrin of many. The Pullman cars lost their names and numbers and the name *Brighton Belle* was painted on the lower facia of the cars with the British Railways logo replacing the Pullman badge. This represented the last stage in the life cycle of the *Brighton Belle* as the service was gradually wound down. In 1969, the *Brighton Belle* became a cause célébre when Lord Olivier found he could no longer receive grilled kippers for breakfast – these were reinstated, following an outcry in the national press. Yet closure of the Pullman service was inevitable; protests were noisy and many but even celebrities could do nothing to postpone the eventual demise of the luxury train. As author Michael Williams ruefully commented, 'No more grilled kippers and steaming pots of coffee at breakfast on the *Brighton Belle'*.

The train was eventually withdrawn on 30 April 1972 but even a hardened British Rail organization was not prepared for the consumer backlash it faced on abandoning the service. Something of profound importance had been lost to the corporate book keepers and perhaps because it was British Rail and a nationalized industry, it probably felt it could get away with such actions. The service was promptly suspended the following day on 1 May 1972. The last runs of the *Brighton Belle* included sell out Cheese and Wine and Champagne specials but the end came with the *Belle* going out in a blaze of glory. The official reasons given by British Rail for closure was a replacement set of similar quality and provision was just too expensive to justify; it

By 1953, the *Brighton Belle* received a modern A.N. Wolstenholme image makeover emphasizing its speedy travel service and very much in the style his other work with other named train expresses. (NRM Pictorial Collection/ Science & Society Library)

THE
BRIGHTON BELLE

WEEKDAYS

LONDON (VICTORIA)	dep	11	0	am	3	0	pm	7	0	pm
BRIGHTON	arr	12	noon		4	0	pm	8	0	pm
BRIGHTON	dep	1	25	pm	5	25	pm	8	25	pm
LONDON (VICTORIA)	arr	2	25	pm	6	25	pm	9	25	pm

SUNDAYS

LONDON (VICTORIA)		dep	11	0	am	7	0	pm
BRIGHTON		arr	12	noon		8	0	pm
BRIGHTON		dep	5	25	pm	8	25	pm
LONDON (VICTORIA)		arr	6	25	pm	9	25	pm

BRITISH RAILWAYS

must be remembered this was another period of austerity as the inflation-rife years of the 1970s took hold. A Brighton Pullman route service had lasted some ninety years apart from the war duration. The *Brighton Belle* had personality, a journey aboard

exuded an air of excitement but the days of being taken to the seaside in elegance by this wonderful train had finally come to an end (at least for the time being!).

Brighton Belle's legacy does not quite end when British Rail pulled the plug. So popular was the unique electric Pullman, all fifteen cars were sold to a variety of purchasers with none actually scrapped, although one of the motor third cars, no. 90, had the misfortune to be partly destroyed in an arson attack and was subsequently vandalized beyond repair and consigned to the scrap yard in 1995, whilst motor third no. 89 survives in permanent hospitality use. Belmond owns seven former *Brighton Belle* cars, whilst a further six cars are owned by the 5-BEL Trust, a charity organization charged with the responsibility of bringing back the Pullman cars to life in mainline operating condition. The Trust, since its inception in 2009, has raised in excess of £5m, owning kitchen firsts no. 79 *Hazel* and no. 82 *Doris*. Motor thirds nos. 88 and 91 are the new power cars and trailer thirds nos. 85

A mid-1960s
Belle service in traditional livery leaving Brighton. By this time a yellow warning panel had replaced the original Pullman insignia on the front of the motorvan. (John Scott-Morgan Collection)

The Brighton *Belle* outfitted in British Rail corporate blue and grey livery in later years. The train is passing through Clapham Common. (Harry Luff/Online Transport Archive)

and 87 additional passenger capacity. The problems of restoring the Pullman cars to create an all-electric powered multiple set again with mainline ticketing have been immense, stretching the limits and the skills of expert railway engineers and technologists. The restoration of an operating *Brighton Belle* unit has created unique problems that have had to be overcome by specialist teams and only achieved by bringing everyone together under one roof. The logistics of restoration planning have been ground-breaking, requiring the skills of many craft-based organisations around the country and a management team to ensure the necessary vehicle heritage and integrity is not compromised in the quest to bring the iconic luxury train back to full operating capability. Electric traction with integrated power cars brings its own complexities. The restoration of the *Brighton Belle* to mainline standards is the largest and most intricate electric heritage railway project undertaken in the UK.

Gordon Rushton, the 5-BEL Trust's marketing director says:

> 'The logic ran that the choice offered was either a static museum exhibit or a running train. The former was rather sad; the latter was an immense challenge: the latter was chosen. This pre-supposes that *Brighton Belle* has to earn enough to maintain itself in operating condition, and to do that its full dining potential has to be realised.'

This the taxing problem the planning team was required to overcome, the need to offer a modern-day luxury dining experience in order to create a viable income-earning product that could compete with the best of country's luxury dining and excursion trains. In its heyday, the three *Brighton Belle* operating units were different, as their regular Brighton and London journeys had a restricted 'light' culinary offer. The 5-BEL Trust had a stock of four third-class motor and trailer cars with the more cramped 2+2 seating. Whilst accommodating larger numbers of passengers (forty-eighty and fifty-six respectively), the market for twenty-first century luxury dining-trains requires extra on-board room and carriage space to attract high-end excursion traffic. Customers in these cars can now expect a new 2+1 seating style plan providing the all-encompassing Pullman dining experience that would be encountered on other steam, diesel or electric hauled trains. This requirement added to strains on the restoration process as the original vehicles were not designed for the revised changes. The central alleyways of the third-class Pullman cars have had to be adapted for the specification change – something many purists could hardly object to when the cars were likely to go for scrap as they were unfit for quality dining and had ceased to be used by heritage railways. When no. 79 *Hazel* joined no. 82 *Doris* in 2012, the pairing of the two kitchen firsts was once again achieved as a two-car unit that made the first-class specification so unique and when the train becomes fully operational again it will join the ranks of Britain's top luxury trains providing a fine-dining experience. To achieve this, two specialist gas-burning kitchens have been created to

5-BEL Trust's Doug Lindsay putting the finishing touches to the first layup of Car 85, *Gravetye Manor* as it completes its internal refit. The specification is based on the unique design of the original Pullman car with reworked marquetry, new carpets with rewoven 1930s fabric, newly designed Pullman table lamps and shades and re-plated hat racks reflecting the sumptuous style of the original 1930s train. (5-BEL Trust)

provide a top-notch culinary preparation area. One has been installed in one of the saloon cars – no. 85 – whilst another has been built back into car *Doris*. The two kitchens will function alongside each other in the rake formation to provide the quality of the dining experience demanded by clientele these days.

These may be the ultimate aspirations, but the 5-BEL Trust's immediate intention is to get a set of cars operating as a single revenue earning unit. In 2016, the organization took a decision to relocate all its Pullman cars to a new restoration centre as it required a facility where four cars could be worked on simultaneously. The move from Barrow Hill to the W.H. Davis, Shirebrook facility cost six months of work, made more difficult as a result of onerous conditions imposed by the Rail Regulator for the wiring of the two motor units for main line operation. As *Railway Magazine* reported, the 5-BEL Trust is keeping its fingers crossed that, following mainline testing, excursion running will soon be achieved. Gordon Rushton sums up the job complexities:

'The only way that the train could hope to operate on today's busy third-rail railway network was a complete refit of the traction, control and brake gear, with strengthening of the fabric better to improve "crashworthiness". The delightful irony is that the trains that ousted *Brighton Belle* have been stripped and refitted under her as they went for scrap themselves. B5 and British Rail Mk VI bogies have been fitted, with equipment from 4VEP/4CIG to give 2,000 continuous horsepower for five cars. In addition, the engineering assessment team were surprised to confront *Brighton Belle's* monocoque construction, that promoted the train to Mk II status and not the old British Rail Mk I. Thus, with all the required safety gear fitted, with powerful performance, excellent braking and a high crashworthiness value, the restored *Brighton Belle* will offer sparkling performance, excellent stopping power, a comfortable ride, and an iconic restoration of Britain's only Art Deco luxury electric train.'

As a result, the train will initially enter service as a four-car formation: two motors; a kitchen saloon; and first-class car *Doris*. It is likely that a fifth car first-class *Hazel* will be added in due course. A sixth car is also available for subsequent addition. However, with four cars, the capacity will be just over 100. *Hazel* has twenty seats and Car 87 has a further forty-two seats, making the maximum capacity 174 seats, with forty of those in 1+1 format and the remainder in 2+1. It has been arranged to fit lifting shoe gear on the train which will retain its capacity to operate in push-pull mode with other Class 400 series units, Class 33s and Class 73s. It can also be loco hauled as a trailing non-powered load with a high ETS output power unit like a Class 68. Thus it will, in the future, be possible to operate off the third rail and run elsewhere in the country on mainline routes so the modern *Belle* is not restricted to operate only in the south of England. The view of the Trustees quite rightly is that getting the *Brighton Belle* to operate successfully on the third rail must be the leading priority.

Gordon Rushton admits sustaining public interest has not been easy:

> 'Such massive restoration works – notably in wiring and safety electrics has taken much longer and cost much more than one could ever have imagined. This accounts for the extended times and expense involved with this project. The support of the heritage movement is much valued, and is allowing this train to win through, so that there is hope that public operation can begin again in 2020. The *Brighton Belle* has staunch, generous sponsors and when complete, the train will be unique.
>
> 'In aiming for a profitable operation, the people who elect to patronize the train will expect the highest possible service offer. We have from the start co-operated with professional on-train caterers, who like the 5-BEL Trust, rise to a challenge. Menus are currently under wraps, but a "top-tip" is not to expect to lose weight on a trip on the *Brighton Belle*! The journey back through the lush countryside of southern England will take at least three hours quietly speeding down leafy byways, better to allow the comfortable consumption of an excellent meal.'

Bringing back the *Brighton Belle* has been an adventurous project of great dimension. Its reintroduction will recreate one of the world's great trains; a trip will never be forgotten. The 5-BEL Trust says that weekly, letters come in from people relating how they remember having seen that stripe of umber and cream singing through the Sussex countryside. And the *Brighton Belle* experience will be available again and improved beyond measure. This will be the re-entry point of a fondly remembered heritage train, now transformed for twenty-first century operation, and ready to wow everyone again with the purity of Art Deco, the delights of its food, and the sheer comfort of its Pullman interior. What better way to close the British chapter of luxury rail travel?

Notes

Introduction

1. YEOMAN, I and McMAHON-BEATTIE, 'Luxury Markets and Premium Pricing'. *Journal of Revenue and Pricing Management* 2005.
2. HOLT, D., *How Brands Become Icons – the principles of cultural branding*, HBSP, 2004.
3. YEOMAN & McMAHON-BEATTIE 2005
4. PIMLOTT, J.A.R., *The Englishman's Holiday: A Social History* Faber and Faber, 1947
5. PERKIN, H., *The Age of the Railway: A Social History of the 19th Century*, Edward Everett (2016 reprint)
6. FRYER, C., *British Pullman Trains: A Tribute to all Britain's Steam, Diesel and Electric Pullman Services*, 1992
7. SHERWOOD, J. and FALLON, I., *Orient Express: A Personal Journey*, Robson Press 2012.

Chapter 1

1. MAJOR, S., *Early Victorian Railway Excursions: The Million Go Forth*, Pen and Sword, 2015.
2. SIMMONS, J., 1984.
3. GREEN, R., *Building the Titanic*, Carlton Books, 2005.
4. BRADLEY, S., *The Railways: Nation, Network and People*, Profile, 2015.
5. KIDNER, R.W., *Pullman Trains in Britain*, Oakwood Press, 1998.
6. DE WINTER HEBRON, C., *Dining at Speed*, Silver Link Publishing 2004.

Chapter 2

1. REIGER, B., *Technology and the Culture of Modernity in Britain and Germany 1890-1945*, CUP, 2005.
2. FLETCHER, R.A., *Travelling Palaces: Luxury in Passenger Steamships*, Pitman, 1913.
3. GRAVES, R. and HODGE, A., *The Long Weekend: A Social History of Great Britain, 1918-1939*, Cardinal, 1940.

4. HENDRY, R., *British Railway Coaching Stock in Colour* Ian Allan, 2002.

5. REED, C., *Gateway to the West,* L&NWR Society, 1952.

6. WOLMAR, C., and SOLOMAN, B., *The Golden Age of European Railways*, Pen & Sword Transport, 2013.

Chapter 3

1. MULLAY, A.J., *Streamlined Steam* David & Charles, 1994.

2. GARDINER, J., *The Thirties: An Intimate History*, 2010.

3. BRYAN, T., *The Inheritance: The GWR Between the Wars* Amberley, 2013.

4. LAW, M.J, 'Charabancs and Social Class in 1930s Britain' *Journal of Transport History* 2015.

5. FURNESS, R., *Poster to Poster: Railway Journeys in Art*, JDF & Associates Ltd, 2009.

6. HARRINGTON, R., 'Beyond the Bathing Belle' *Journal of Transport History* 2004.

Chapter 6

1. PARK, K., REISINGER, Y and NOH, E., 'Luxury Shopping in Tourism' *International Journal of Tourism Research* 2010.

Appendix 1

1. JENKINSON, D., *British Railway Carriages of the 20th Century Vol 1*, Guild Publishing, 1988

2. BRAY, M., *Railway Picture Postcards*, Moorland Publishing, 1986

3. JENKINSON 1996.

4. BELL, J.J., *The Story of Scotland*, Harrap, 1932.

5. JAMES, L., 2006.

Select Bibliography

Adamson, R. and **Nettleton, C.**, *Winston Churchill and The Bulleid Pacifics*, Friends of the National Railway Museum, 2014.

Atterbury, P. and **Furness, R.**, *Speed to the West: A Nostalgic Journey*, Poster to Poster Publishing, 2016.

Barr, A. and **Levy, P.,** *The Official Foodie Handbook*, Ebury Press, 1984.

Batsford, H. and **Fry, C.,** *The Face of Scotland* Third Edition, B.T. Batsford Ltd, 1937.

Beckerson, J., 'Making leisure pay: the business of tourist marketing in Great Britain 1880 – 1950', *Journal of Business Archives, Sources and History*, 76, 1-11, Business Archives Council, 1998.

Beerbohm, M., *Yet Again*, Chapman and Hall, 1909.

Behrend, G., *History of Trains De Luxe: From the Orient Express to the HST*, Transport Publishing Company, 1977.

Behrend, G. and **Buchanan, G.**, *Night Ferry*, Jersey Artists Ltd, 1985.

Bell, J.J., *The Glory of Scotland*, George G. Harrap & Co. Ltd, 1932.

Bennett, A., *The Great Western Railway and the Celebration of Englishness*, PhD dissertation in Railway Studies, University of York, Railway Studies Institute, 2000.

Bennett, A., *Great Western Lines & Landscapes: Business and Pleasure, Heritage and History*, Runpast Publishing, 2002.

Booker, J., *Travellers' Money*, Alan Sutton Publishing, 1994.

Bradley, S., *The Railways: Nation, Network & People*, Profile Books, 2015.

Bradshaw, G., *Bradshaws's Descriptive Railway Hand-Book of Great Britain and Irela*nd 1863, reprinted Old House Books and Maps, 2010.

Bray, M.I., *Railway Picture Postcards*, Moorland Publishing, 1986.

Brendon, P., *Thomas Cook: 150 Years of Popular Tourism*, Secker & Warburg, 1991.

Bryan, T., *The Inheritance: The Great Western Railway between the Wars*, Ian Allan Publishing, 2013.

Bryan, T., *Britain's Heritage: Express Trains*, Amberley Publishing, 2017.

Bucknall, R., *Boat Trains and Channel Packets: The English Short Sea Routes*, Vincent Stuart Limited, 1957.

Cannadine, D., *The Decline and Fall of the British Aristocracy*, YUP, 1990.

Cannadine, D., *Aspects of Aristocracy: Grandeur and Decline in Modern Britain*, YUP, 1994.

Cannadine, D., *Class in Britain*, YUP, 1998.

Carle, N., Shaw. S. and Shaw, S. eds. *Edwardian Culture: Beyond the Garden Party*, Routledge, 2018.

Chevalier. M. and Mazzalovo, G., *Luxury Brand Management: A World of Privilege*, John Wiley & Sons (Asia) Pte. Ltd, 2008.

Correia, A. Kozal, K. and Reis, H., 'Luxury tourists: celebrities' perspectives, In Tourists, perceptions and assessments', *Advances in Culture, Tourism and Hospitality Research*, 8, 43-51, 2014.

Cova, B. Kozinets, R.V. and Shankar, A., *The New World of Tribalism, in Consumer Tribes*, Butterworth Heinemann 2007).

Divall, C., 'Civilising velocity: Masculinity and the marketing of Britain's passenger trains, 1921-39', *The Journal of Transport History*, 32(2), 164-191, 2011.

Duff, D., *Victoria Travels: Journeys of Queen Victoria between 1830 and 1900*, Frederick Muller Ltd, 1970.

Elliot, J., *On and Off the Rails*, George Allen & Unwin, 1982.

Engel, M., *Eleven Minutes Late: A Train Journey to the Soul of Britain*, Macmillan, 2009.

Faulkner, J.N. and Williams, R.A., *The LSWR in the Twentieth Century*, David & Charles, 1998.

Fletcher, R.A., *Travelling Palaces: Luxury in Passenger Steamships*, Sir Isaac Pitman & Sons Ltd, 1913.

Ford, A.M., *Pullman Profile No 4: The Brighton Belle and Southern Electric Pullmans*, Noodle Books, 2012.

Frank, R.H., *Luxury Fever: Money and Happiness in an Era of Excess*, Princeton University Press, 1999.

Fryer, C., *British Pullman Trains: A Tribute to all Britain's Steam, Diesel and Electric Pullman Services*, Silver Link Publishing, 1992.

Furness, R., *Poster to Poster: Railway Journeys in Art, Vol. 1 Scotland*, JDF & Associates Ltd, 2009.

Gardiner, J., *The Thirties: An Intimate History*, Harper Press, 2010.

Glym A. and Williams, A., 'Luxury Brand Marketing: the experience is *everything*', Journal of Brand Management 16(5-6), 2009.

Grant, S. and Jeffs, S., *The Brighton Belle: The Story of a Famous and Much-Loved Train*, Capital Transport Ltd, 2012.

Graves, R., and Hodge, A., *The Long Weekend: A Social History of Great Britain 1918 – 1939*, Cardinal, 1940.

Green, R., *Building the Titanic: The Creation of History's Most Famous Ocean Liner*, Carlton Books, 2005.

Haarhoff, G. and Kleyn, N., 'Open source brands and their online personality', *Journal of Brand Management*, 20(2), 14-114, 2012.

Haid, O. *'Eternally Will Austria Stand…': Imperial Tourism in Austria between Timeless Predisposition and Political Statement* in *Royal Tourism: Excursions Around Monarchy*, Long, P. and Palmer, N., eds., Channel View Publications, 2008.

Ellis, C.H., *The Trains We Loved*, Pan Books Ltd, 1947, reprint 1971.

Ellis, C.H., *The Royal Trains*, Routledge & Kegan Paul, 1975.

Hannavy, J., *The Victorian and Edwardian Tourist*, Shire Publications, 2012.

Hanley, L., *Respectable: Crossing the Class Divide*, Penguin Random House, 2016.

Harrington, R., 'Beyond the bathing belle: Images of women in inter-war railway publicity', *The Journal of Transport History* 25(1), 22-44, 2004.

Harris, M., *LNER Carriages*, originally published by David St. John Thomas Publisher, Thomas & Lochar imprint, 1994, reprint Southampton, Noodle Books, 2011.

Haresnape, B., *Pullman: Travelling in Style*, Ian Allan, 1987.

Harrison, R.E., *Admission for All: How Cinema and the Railways Shaped British Culture, 1895-1948*, PhD dissertation in Film Studies, London, University College London, 2014.

Heffer, S., *High Minds: The Victorians and the Birth of Modern Britain*, Random House, 2014.

Heffer, S., *The Age of Decadence: Britain 1880 to 1914*, Random House, 2017.

Hendry, R., *British Railway Coaching Stock in Colour: For the Modeller and Historian*, Ian Allan Publishing, 2002.

Hennigs, N. Schmidt, St. Wuestefeld, T. and Weidmann, K.P., *Brand Heritage in the Luxury Industry; creating and delivering continuous value to consumers* Paper presented at the 2012 Summer Marketing Educators' Conference, Boston, Ill, August 17-19, 2012.

Holland, J., *An A-Z of Famous Express Trains: An Illustrated Trip Down Memory Lane*, David & Charles, 2013.

Holland, J., *The Times History of Britain's Railways*, Times Books, 2015.

Holmes, O.W., *One Hundred Days in Europe, The Works of Oliver Wendell Holmes Part Ten*, Houghton, Mifflin and Company, 1887.

Holmes, O.W., **Medical Essays 1842-1882**, *The Writings of Oliver Wendell Holmes Part Nine*, The Riverside Press, 1891.

Holt, D., 'How Brands become Icons - The Principles of Cultural Branding', *Harvard Business School Press and Harvard Business Review*, 81(3), 43-49, 2004.

James, H., *Travels with Henry James*, Nation Books, 2016.

James, L., *The Middle Class: A History*, Little, Brown, 2006.

Jenkinson, D., *British Railway Carriages of the 20th Century: Volume 1: The End of an Era, 1901-22*, Guild Publishing, 1998.

Jenkinson, D., *The History of British Railway Carriages 1900-1953*, Pendragon Partnership, 1996.

Kidner, R.W., *Pullman Trains in Britain*, The Oakwood Press, 1998.

Kingston, P., *Royal Trains*, David & Charles, 1985.

Kumar, A., *Stately Progress: Royal Train Travel since 1840*, National Railway Museum, 1997.

Kynaston, D., *Family Britain 1951-57*, Bloomsbury Publishing, 2009.

Lash, S., *Critique of Information*, Sage, 2002.

Law, M.J., 'Charabancs and social class in 1930s Britain', *The Journal of Transport History*, 36(1), 41-57, 2015.

McLean, A., *The Flying Scotsman: Speed, Style, Service*, Scala Arts & Heritage Publishers, 2016.

McKibbin, R., *Classes and Cultures: England 1918-1951*, OUP, 2000.

Maggs, C., *A History of the Great Western Railway*, Amberley Publishing, 2013.

Major, S., *Early Victorian Railway Excursions: The Million Go Forth*, Pen & Sword Books, 2015.

Medcalf, A., '"We are always learning": Marketing the Great Western Railway, 1921-39, *The Journal of Transport History*, 33(2), 186-211, 2012.

Morel, J., *Pullman*, David & Charles, 1983.

Mullay, A.J., *Non-Stop! London to Scotland Steam*, Alan Sutton Publishing, 1989.

Mullay, A.J., *Streamlined Steam: Britain's 1930s Luxury Expresses*, David & Charles, 1994.

Nock, O.S., *The Limited*, George Allen & Unwin, 1979.

Okonkwo, U., 'Sustaining the luxury brand on the internet', *Journal of Brand Management* 16(5), 302-310, 2009.

Packer, P., *On the Trail of the Royal Scot*, The History Press, 2009.

Park, K.S. Reisinger, Y. and **Noh, E.H.**, Luxury shopping in tourism, *International Journal of Tourism Research*, 121, 164-178, 2010.

Peel, D., *Locomotive Headboards: The Complete Story*, The History Press, 2006.

Perkin, H.J., *The Age of the Railway: A Social History of 19th Century Britain*, 1976, reprint, Edward Everett Root, Publishers, 2016.

Perkin, H.J., *The Rise of Professional Society: England since 1880*, Routledge, 1989.

Pigott, N., *The Encyclopaedia of Titled Trains: The ultimate directory of Great Britain's named expresses*, Mortons Media Group, 2012.

Pimlott, J.A.R., *The Englishman's Holiday: A Social History*, Faber and Faber, 1947.

Pope, R., 'A consumer service in interwar Britain: The hotel trade, 1924-1938', *The Business History Review*, 74(4), 657-682, 2000.

Pope, R., 'Railway companies and resort hotels between the wars', *The Journal of Transport History*, 22(1), 62-73, 2001.

Pring, M., Beer, S. Hartwell, H. and **Bray, J.**, 'Local foods: marketing and the destination', *The Routledge handbook of sustainable food and gastronomy*, Sloan, P. Legrand, W. and Hindley, C., eds., Routledge, 2015.

Pugh, M., *We Danced All Night: A social history of Britain between the wars*, Vintage Random House, 2009.

Quinzio, J., *Food on the Rails: The Golden Era of Railroad Dining*, Rowman & Littlefield, 2014.

Ransom, P.J.G., *Iron Road: The Railway in Scotland*, Birlinn, 2013.

Rieger, B., *Technology and the Culture of Modernity in Britain and Germany 1890-1945*, CUP, 2005.

Roberts, K., *Class in Modern Britain*, Palgrave, 2001.

Robertson, K., *In the tracks of the 'Bournemouth Belle'*, Crécy Publishing Limited, 2016.

Rosen, A., *The Transformation of British Life 1950-2000: A Social History*, Manchester University Press, 2003.

St. John Thomas, D. and **Whitehouse, P.**, *SR 150 – A Century and a Half of the Southern Railway*, David & Charles Publishers, 1988.

Sandbrook, D., *White Heat: A History of Britain in the Swinging Sixties*, Abacus, 2006.

Savage, M., *Social Class in the 21st Century*, Penguin Random House, 2015.

Semmens, P.W.B., *The Heyday of GWR Train Services*, David & Charles, 1990.

Shaw, S., *Dawn of the New Age: Edwardian and Neo-Edwardian Summer* in *Edwardian Culture: Beyond the Garden Party*, Carle, Shaw and Shaw, eds., Routledge, 2018.

Sherwood, J.B., and **Fallon, I.**, *Orient Express: A Personal Journey*, The Robson Press, 2012.

Shin, H., 'The art of advertising railways: organisation and coordination in Britain's railway marketing, 1860-1910' *Business History*, 56(2), 187-213, 2014.

Simmons, J., 'Railways, hotels, and tourism in Great Britain 1839-1914', *Journal of Contemporary History*, 19, 201-222, 1984.

Simpson, E., *Hail Caledonia: The Lure of the Highlands and Islands*, Amberley, 2017.

Smith, W., *A Yorkshireman's Trip to the United States and Canada*, Longmans, Green and Co., 1892.

Tissot, L., 'How did the British conquer Switzerland: guidebooks, railways travel agents 1850-1914', *The Journal of Transport History*, 16(1), 21-54, 1995.

Tungate, M., *Luxury World: The past, present and future of luxury brands*, Kogan Page, 2009.

Tungate, M., *The Escape Industry: How iconic and innovative brands built the travel business*, Kogan Page, 2018.

Turner, D., 'Managing the "Royal Road": The London and South Western Railway 1870-1911', PhD dissertation, University of York, Institute of Railway Studies and Transport History, 2013.

Turner, D., *Victorian and Edwardian Railway Travel*, Shire Publications, 2013.

Twain, M., *The Innocents Abroad*, Penguin Books, reprinted as first edition 2002.

Alec-Tweedie, E.B., *America As I Saw It: or, America Revisited*, The McMillan Company, 1913.

Wallop, H., *Consumed: How We Buy Class in Modern Britain*, William Collins, 2014.

Walton, J.K., 'Power, speed and glamour: The naming of express steam locomotives in inter-war Britain', *The Journal of Transport History*, 26(2), 1-19, 2005.

Watts, D.C.H., 'Evaluating British railway poster advertising: The London & North Eastern Railway between the wars', *The Journal of Transport History*, 25(2), 23-56, 2004.

Williams, R., *The Midland Railway: A New History*, David & Charles Publishers, 1988.

Williams, M., *On the Slow Train – Twelve Great British Railway Journeys*, Arrow Books, 2011.

Williams, M., *On the Slow Train Again, - Twelve Great British Railway Journey*, Arrow Books, 2012.

Williams, M., *The Trains Now Departed*, Penguin Random House, 2015.

Williamson, A., *The Golden Age of Travel: The Romantic Years of Tourism in Images from the Thomas Cook Archives*, Thomas Cook Group, 1998).

Wilson, R.B., *Go Great Western: A History of GWR Publicity*, David & Charles, 1970.

Wooler, N., *Dinner in the Diner: The History of Railway Catering*, David & Charles, 1987.

Wolmar, C., *Fire & Steam: A New History of the Railways in Britain*, Atlantic Books, 2007.

Wolmar, C. and **Solomon, B.**, *The Golden Age of European Railways*, Pen & Sword Transport, 2013.

Wragg, D., *The Race to the North: Rivalry & Record-Breaking in the Golden Age of Steam*, Wharncliffe Transport, 2013.

Wuestefeld, T. Hennigs, N. Schmidt, St. and **Weidmann, K.P.**, 'The impact of brand heritage on customer perceived value', *International Journal of Marketing*, Springer, 2012.

Yeoman, I. and **McMahon-Beattie, U.**, 'Luxury markets and premium pricing', *Journal of Revenue and Pricing Management*, 4(4), 319-328, 2005.

Newspapers and Periodicals

Aberdeen Evening Express
Aberdeen Press and Journal
Belfast Newsletter
Birmingham Mail
Birmingham Post
Britannia and Eve
Bystander
Cheltenham Chronicle
Chichester Observer
Clifton Society
Cornishman
Coventry Evening Telegraph
Country Life
Daily Herald
Daily Telegraph
Derby Evening Telegraph
Dorset Life
Dundee Courier
Dundee Courier and Advertiser

Dundee Evening Telegraph
Evening Standard
Evening Telegraph
Edinburgh Evening News
Fifeshire Advertiser
Globe
Gloucester Echo
Gloucester Journal
Graphic
Greenock Telegraph and Clyde Shipping Gazette
Illustrated London News
Illustrated Sporting and Dramatic News
Leeds Mercury
Lincolnshire Echo
Liverpool Mercury
Milngavie and Bearsden Herald
Morning Post
Northern Daily Mail
Portsmouth Evening News
Railway Magazine
St. James's Gazette
Scotsman
Shields Daily Gazette and Shipping Telegraph
Sketch
Spectator
Sphere
Standard
Steam Days
Sunderland Echo and Shipping Gazette
Tatler
Tatler and Bystander
Times
Western Morning News and Daily Gazette
Wigan Observer and District Advertiser
Yorkshire Evening Post
Yorkshire Post and Leeds Mercury

Websites

Crane, S., *The Scotch Express*, 1899, https://public.wsu.
edu/~campbelld/crane/scotch.htm, accessed 24 February 2018

Mitchell, B. Chambers D. and Crafts N., 'How Good was the profitability of British Railways, 1870–1912' (No: 859, *Warwick Economic Research Papers*, Department of Economics, University of Warwick, p.12, 2009. http://www2.warwick.ac.uk/fac/soc/economics/research/workingpapers/2008/twerp_859c.pdf, accessed 21 July 2017).

Smith, J.A., Book review - Pimlott, J.R.R., *The Englishman's Holiday: A Social History* (The Spectator, p.24, http://archive.spectator.co.uk/article/27th-february-1948/24/the-history-of-holidays, accessed 28 August 2017).

Wolmar, C., Rail 711: *The Transsiberian is a must for all rail lovers*, (http://www.christianwolmar.co.uk/2012/12/rail-711-the-transsiberian-is-a-must-for-all-rail-lovers/ accessed 4 January 2018).

Index